THE MAN CALLED DENG MAJOK

The publisher wishes to acknowledge and thank Dr. Douglas H. Johnson for his invaluable help and support for Africa World Books and its mission of preserving and promoting African cultural and literary traditions and history. Dr. Johnson and fellow historians have been instrumental in ensuring that African people remain connected to their past and their identity. Africa World Books is proud to carry on this mission.

Copyright © 1986 Francis Mading Deng

ISBN (Paperback): 9780645719109

First published in 1986 by Yale University Press

No part of this publication may be reproduced, stored in a retrieval system, or transmitted, in any form, or by any means, electronic, mechanical, photocopying, recording or otherwise, without the prior permission of the publishers.

This book is sold subject to the conditions that it shall not, by way of trade or otherwise, be lent, re-sold, hired out or otherwise circulated without the publisher's prior consent in any form of binding or cover other than in which it is published and without a similar condition including the condition being imposed on the subsequent purchaser.

Cover design, typesetting and layout: Africa World Books
Unit 3, 57 Frobisher St, Osborne Park, WA 6017
P.O. Box 1106 Osborne Park, WA 6916

A portrait of Chief Deng Majok taken in the late 1950s, when he was in his late fifties.

THE MAN CALLED DENG MAJOK

A Biography of Power, Polygyny, and Change

Francis Mading Deng

To my son
Dennis Biong

Contents

List of Illustrations and Maps	ix
Updated Preface	xi
Acknowledgments	xv

Part One The World of Deng Majok

1 The Perspective of a Son	3
2 A Look at the Man	14
3 The Dinka and Their Values	21
4 Leadership at the Crossroads	40

Part Two Power

5 The Struggle for Recognition	53
6 Campaign for the Chieftainship	69
7 Success	88
8 Peacemaker, Lawgiver, and Modernizer	116

Part Three Family

9 The Curse to Love	143
10 The Empire at Home	160
11 Turmoil beneath the Calm	176
12 The Economics of Polygyny	190
13 Invasion from Within	210

Part Four Diplomacy

14 Bridging North and South	223

Part Five Tragedy

15 The End to Glory	247
16 In the Shadow of a Giant	255
17 Deng Majok in Perspective	272
Appendix on Sources and Method	283
Index	291
Afterword: Revisiting the Man Called Deng Majok	295

Illustrations

Frontispiece: A portrait of Chief Deng Majok taken in the late 1950s, when he was in his late fifties.
1. Chief Kwol Arob with some policemen near one of the earliest cars to go to Ngokland in the early 1930s. Photo by K. D. D. Henderson.
2. Chief Deng Majok (fourth from left) with Arab chiefs in an intertribal celebration in 1954.
3. Michael Tibbs, the last British district commissioner in the area, with Homr Nazirs, Babo Nimir (right), and Serrer El Haj Ajbar.
4. Initiation operation among the Agar Dinka, whose practices in this respect are similar to those of the Ngok Dinka.
5. Initiates during their recovery period, their heads covered with palm hats, a bundle of sorgham stalks in the place of spears, with a musical instrument made of gourd. Courtesy of the Sudan Government.
6. A Dinka "gentleman" with initiation marks on his forehead, decorated with beads and a feather in his hairdo. Courtesy of Sarah Errington/Alan Hutchison Library.
7. Part of a Ngok Dinka dance. Photo by Michael Tibbs.
8. Building a cattle-byre. Photo by K. D. D. Henderson.
9. Chief Kwol Arob's rest house at Abyei. Photo by K. D. D. Henderson.
10. Three British district commissioners (from left): J. W. Robertson D. C. Western Kordofan, Jim Stubbs D. C. Aweil, Jack Poole D. C. Tonj; and a senior medical inspector, Alec Guickshanck. Photo by K. D. D. Henderson, March, 1935.
11. Cattle tethered at a cattle camp. Courtesy of Sarah Errington/Alan Hutchison Library.
12. A man tethering a cow. Courtesy of the Sudan Government.

13. A gentleman singing over his personality ox.
14. Arabs riding horses. Courtesy of the Sudan Government.
15. A fishing party. Courtesy of Sarah Errington/Alan Hutchison Library.
16. An Arab woman grinding grain on a stone. Courtesy of the Sudan Government.
17. A primary school class. Courtesy of Sarah Errington/Alan Hutchison Library.
18. Prayers and sacrifice over newlywed women so that the marriages might be blessed with children.
19. Prime Minister Sadig Al Mahdi, who visited Abyei as prime minister in 1967.
20. Chief Deng Majok in August, 1969, just before he was taken to Cairo, where he died. Standing behind him (from left) are the author; Beshir Achier, Deng Majok's secretary; and Bona Malual.
21. Dr. Zachariah Bol Deng (right) with the author in Cairo during the last days of their father's illness.
22. A funeral ceremony for Agar Dinka chief Rok Rech. Courtesy of Sarah Errington/Alan Hutchison Library.
23. Chief Deng Abot making a public address during President Nimeiri's visit to Abyei in December, 1972.

Updated Preface

I have told the story of my father, Deng Majok, the late Paramount Chief of the Ngok Dinka, in a number of publications. This Preface is not so much about him as it is about the legacy of Ngok leadership, including my father and his predecessors, and the lessons that can now be drawn and applied in managing their sensitive and strategic area between North and South Sudan -now two separate states.

This third edition of The Man Called Deng Majok is appearing at a time when the Ngok Dinka of Abyei are experiencing a crisis with existential challenges to their security and stability between these two sovereign states. This crisis underscores the wisdom of their legendary leaders in the way they managed inter-communal relations at this turbulent border area. Oral history among the Ngok Dinka has it that during the 19th-century upheavals, when Sudan was torn apart by the invasions of the Black African Southern region by slave raiders from the Arab-Muslim North, and tribal wars raged between the tribes, the Ngok Dinka leaders and their Missiriya Homr Arab counterparts reached an agreement that restored peace, harmony, and cooperation between their tribes and extended protection to the Dinka tribes further south.

The Missiriya in their seasonal migration to Ngok Dinka territory in search of water and grazing for their herds, which was associated with raids for slaves and cattle, confronted fierce resistance from the Ngok Dinka. This was before the Arabs had access to guns and both sides still used spears as their weapons of war. The Dinka used light spears, tong, which could be darted from a distance. This contrasted with the heavy spear, rek, that the Arabs used and which required jabbing at close proximity. The Arab raiders however rode horses which gave them advantage both in attacking and in retreat. But the Dinka could throw their light spears at riders from a distance and inflict preventive hits on the horses and the riders. There was therefore a degree of parity in their internecine warfare.

As there was no central government authority to ensure law and order and whatever government penetration down to the local level was in any case associated with the slave raids, tribal peace settlements were the only way of ending the violence. Since Arab herders needed access to the river, peaceful coexistence became a priority for them. Dinka oral history has it that the Arab Chief, Azoza, approached his counterpart, Arob Biong, and said that he was no longer after the cattle the Dinka had captured and that all he wanted was peace, harmony, and brotherhood between their respective tribes. The two leaders are said to have then entered into a pact of kinship in which they bled themselves to ritually mix blood to become 'relatives.' That relationship was honored by generations of leaders in the two families and their kin groups. These included on the Ngok side; Kuol Arob, the son of Arob Biong, and Deng Majok Kuol, who succeeded his father; and their counterparts, Nimir Ali Julla, and his son, Babo Nimir.

That was the relationship that the British colonial administration found and reinforced. The Ngok Dinka and the neighboring Twic and Ruweng Dinka tribes were administratively annexed to Kordofan Province in the North to provide them with better protection against Arab slave traders. The other tribes later opted to return to Southern Sudan administration while the Ngok Dinka under Chief Kuol Arob chose to remain in the North as a gatekeeper and a constructive buffer between the neighboring Southern and Northern tribes. Kuol explained his choice to his fellow Dinka chiefs from the South that he was in effect safeguarding their land. If he were to separate from his Arab neighbors and join his Southern kith and kin, the Arabs would fear losing easy access to water and grazing and might even claim ownership of the land, instead of the appreciative guests they then were. That would mean war, which he wanted to avoid in favor of peaceful coexistence and cooperation. Kuol Arob became very popular among the Arabs and developed a close partnership with Nimir, his Arab counterpart. The neighboring Southern tribes also appreciated the protective role he was playing for them at that volatile border. Deng Majok, Kuol's son, in close alliance with his friend Babo, Nimir's son, who succeeded his father as the Paramount Chief of the Missiriya Arabs, consolidated the relationship through a close friendship and partnership. The relationship entailed contributing and sharing cattle in the dowries of family members.

Before departing at the end of colonial rule, the British again offered the Ngok Dinka the right to revert back to the administration of Southern Sudan. Chief Deng Majok followed his father's foots teps by opting to remain in the North to play a bridging role between the North and the South. He saw his role as that of needle and thread that stitched the two parts of the country into unity. As a result of this bridging role, he became so popular with the Arabs that Arab Chiefs elected him President of the Missiriya Rural Council in which he represented a small minority. As was the case with his father, Deng Majok was also much appreciated by the neighboring Southern tribes as their protector at the border. Deng Majok was himself very well aware that his close relationship with his Arab counterparts was the best way of ensuring protection for his people and their Southern kith and kin.

Chief Kuol Arob and his son Deng Majok, were prophetic in their vision, as what they feared is now happening. The cordial ties between the respective Ngok Dinka and the Missiriya Arab Chiefs and their communities were interrupted and severed by the two civil wars between North and South Sudan, which were triggered by the dominating policies of Arabization and Islamization of the South adopted by successive post-independent governments in Khartoum. In due course, the Ngok Dinka fully identified with their kith and kin in both wars of liberation. Ngok freedom fighters distinguished themselves for their gallantry and rose through the ranks to leadership roles in the military and political leadership of South Sudan. The two wars were fought mostly in the South and were guerrilla in nature. This meant that the civilian populations were exposed to the terror and atrocities of the government forces without the protection of their guerrilla warriors in the forest. This was particularly true of the Ngok Dinka in Abyei who were more exposed to government armed forces from the North with no significant rebel presence to counter the brutalities of the army.

The first war, (1955-1972), was ended by the 1972 Addis Ababa Agreement by granting the South autonomous regional government within national unity. It also gave the Ngok Dinka of Abyei the option of remaining under the administration of the North or reverting back to South Sudan. That provision was never honored by the regime in Khartoum and the regional government of the South refrained from risking the resumption of hostilities with the center over Abyei. Although peace prevailed between the North and the South, Abyei remained in a state of continued insecurity and repression which eventually triggered a local rebellion that spread to the South. That, together with the unilateral abrogation of the autonomy arrangement by the central government, contributed to the second war of liberation by the South in 1983.

The second war was eventually ended by the Comprehensive Peace Agreement (CPA) of 2005 which granted the South the right to self-determination through a referendum in which South Sudanese overwhelmingly chose independence, declared on 9 July, 2011. The Abyei Protocol of the CPA gave the Ngok Dinka the same right granted them by the 1972 Addis Ababa Agreement - to decide whether to remain in the North or join the South. The Abyei referendum was to be held simultaneously with the Southern Sudanese referendum. History however repeated itself in that the government in Khartoum obstructed its implementation and the independent government of South Sudan avoided risking conflict with Sudan over Abyei. Once again, Abyei found itself still engulfed in a virtual continuation of conflict when the North and the South were again at peace. An area that was supposed to be a conciliatory zone of peace has now become a crumbling bridge.

The report of Abyei Boundaries Commission whose findings were to be final and binding was rejected by the Government of Sudan. The case was taken to the Permanent Court of Arbitration, (PCA), in 2008 whose decision was to be final and binding. Although initially accepted by both countries, Sudan obstructed the demarcation of the borders. The combination of dishonored referendum agreement and disregard for internationally demarcated borders has left Abyei vulnerably poised between the two countries.

Abyei suffered two full scale invasions by the army of the Sudan, May 2008 and May 2011. The United Nations Security Council, deeply concerned by the violence, escalating tension and mass displacement of population, decided to establish the United Nations Interim Security Force in Abyei (UNISFA), on 27 June 1911. The overwhelming choice of the Ngok Dinka in their 2013 community organized referendum has not been recognized even by the government of South Sudan that had facilitated it. In view of the impasse over the status of Abyei, it is imperative that a common ground acceptable to the key parties be explored. Abyei remains threatened by persistent attacks by the Missiriya from the North. Despite the much-appreciated protection efforts of UNISFA, it has not been able to fully secure the entire area.

In February 2021, the Twic Dinka also staged an attack against the Ngok Dinka to contest the Southern borders in which they allege Ngok encroachment under the UNISFA mandate. This has resulted in sustained hostilities that have continued to the time of writing in February 2023. Tragically, this inter-communal violence is symptomatic of what has become a trend throughout South Sudan since independence. It is a manifestation of what the opponents of South Sudan had foretold, warning that the independence of South Sudan would result in tribal wars that would render the country ungovernable and endanger the peace and security of the region. The Ngok Dinka crisis is compounded by the fact that it has become international, involving two countries which have so far not been able to agree on the status of the area. Without state protection, the Ngok Dinka survival as a people with a defined territory is now severely threatened by forces from both the North and the South.

My 'Afterword' to the second edition of The Man Called Deng Majok updated the developments up to 2008 before the South became independent. The situation now calls for revisiting the history of cordial relations at this critical juncture to discern lessons that might be learned and applied to the management of inter-communal relations. In my opinion, constructing a better future requires developing an interim arrangement acceptable to the two governments of Sudan and South Sudan and to the two communities, the Ngok Dinka and the Missiriya. This should include:
- establishing self-administration for the Ngok Dinka under the shared sovereignty of the two governments of Sudan and South Sudan and granting dual citizenship status to the inhabitants of Abyei as stipulated in the Abyei Protocol;
- ensuring security over the entire Ngok territory, as defined by the PCA, in collaboration with UNISFA;
- facilitating the return of internally displaced and refugees to their areas of origin, in safety and with dignity in accordance with international human rights normative standards;
- delivering social services and development opportunities to the wider area, including the neighboring communities, on equitable bases;
- promoting peaceful coexistence and cooperation with the neighbors to the South and North, in particular, the Missiriya and the Twic Dinka; and
- negotiating the final status of Abyei that grants the residents of Ngok Dinka the right to determine their destiny and based on a common ground accept-

able to the two Sudans.

There is now a tendency among some Ngok Dinka radical elements who are opposed to the inherited leadership of the traditional Dinka system to criticize the decisions taken by successive Ngok Dinka leaders in their constructive management of the volatile North-South borders. Current developments and the worsening security situation which pose existential threats to the Ngok Dinka however underscore the wisdom of the decisions taken by the traditional leaders and elders of the Ngok Dinka in ensuring peace and security with their border communities of the North and the South. The renowned Apuk Dinka Chief, Giir Thiik, once told me that if it were not for the protective role played by the Ngok leaders at the North South border, some of the Dinka tribes to the South of the Ngok Dinka might have disappeared. That is a historical lesson of which our Southern neighbors should be very mindful.

In light of the inadequacy of the capacity of the national governments in both Sudan and South Sudan to establish law and order throughout the countries and the inability of UNISFA to effectively protect the population within the entire borders of Abyei as defined by the PCA, multiple mechanisms for ensuring the security of the area are now imperative. The first is to strengthen the defensive capacity of the local community under an autonomous state administration. The second is to mediate and promote peaceful coexistence and cooperation between and among the border communities to the North and the South. The third is to foster cordial ties between the two governments to ensure peace and cooperation among their border communities, to improve their bilateral relations and promote security cooperation and development partnership between them and to the benefit of all their border communities. Finally, the role of the international community will continue to be needed to maintain peace, security and stability in the region until the two countries can agree on determining the final status of Abyei between them.

Perhaps the most important lesson to be drawn from the wisdom of the traditional leaders of the border communities is to turn Abyei away from being a point of confrontation back to its historical bridging role as a meeting ground of constructive management of diversity toward peaceful coexistence and cooperation. Neither country is willing to cede Abyei to the other and the Missiriya fear the return of Abyei to South Sudan as endangering their traditional rights of access to water and grazing lands in Ngok Dinka territory, which they see as shared. The most viable option for the area then is to be self-governing under a shared or joint sovereignty of the two countries that should cooperate in ensuring the security, stability, and development of the area in the mutual interest of the border communities and the two governments. The ultimate decision should be left to the Ngok Dinka to determine their status. The policy objective for the two countries should be to strengthen the bridging role of the Ngok Dinka to make it attractive to the people. That is the legacy of the legendary leaders of this border area that their descendants are called upon to honor and apply in facing the challenges of the changing times.

Francis Mading Deng
Woodstock, New York
February 2023.

Acknowledgments

For a work of such an extensive nature, which involved the contributions of a wide range of people, acknowledgments are always difficult: the temptation is to cover everyone by broad generalizations. Fairness, however, dictates that a few institutions and individuals be mentioned by name. Among these, a special word of appreciation goes to the Ford Foundation, which not only generously supported the initial phase of data collection but also made it possible for me to devote my time to the completion of the project. I am also grateful to the Woodrow Wilson International Center for Scholars for facilitating my work on the project by inviting me to spend several months at the center as a guest scholar early in 1984. The final revisions and editing of the book were completed during my eighteen months' tenure as the first Distinguished Fellow of the Rockefeller Brothers' Fund in New York. Although my duties with the fund involved seminars, lectures, and other consultations, I am most grateful for the broad support, encouragement, and exceptional cooperation and friendship I received from colleagues, trustees, and Rockefeller family circles.

To my brothers and cousins who helped to conduct the interviews and to all those who responded to my questionnaires, in addition to my profound gratitude, I would like to say that I hope they find the book a worthy tribute to their invaluable contributions.

Many individuals assisted with the typing of the interview materials and the manuscript at the various stages. Among these I must mention Brenda Burke, Marianne Burkhar, Nancy Bialic, and Susan Jones. Ms. Burke also helped with the initial compilation and classification of the interview materials.

During my brief period at the Woodrow Wilson Center, I was privileged to make the acquaintance of the distinguished Africanist from the University of Wisconsin, Crawford Young, who read the manuscript and made constructive comments and suggestions that not only enriched it but also gave me valuable support and encouragement at a critical time. Robert O. Collins of the University of California, Santa Barbara, and Prosser Gifford, Deputy Director of The Woodrow Wilson Center, also read the manuscript and made helpful comments.

In my acknowledgments to *Africans of Two Worlds*, I said, "A special word of appreciation must go to Marian Ash of Yale University Press, who, by combining firm editorial objectivity with encouragement and support, gave me a challenge that proved a very constructive contribution to the value of the book." These words ring even truer when applied to Marian Ash's contribution to this book. Her inspiration, support, and editorial excellence were indispensable to the realization of the objective that it represents.

Continuing preoccupations with various research and writing projects inevitably levy a heavy toll on one's family responsibilities. By being a close partner in all my work, acting as a sounding board, discussing ideas, sharing the strains and only vicariously the pleasures, and always supporting me with her unfailing faith and encouragement, my wife, Dorothy Ann, has turned this toll into a pleasurable and constructive companionship. Even when the exuberance and vibrations of their ages sometimes dictated otherwise, our four boys, Donald Deng, Daniel Jok, David Kwol, and Dennis Biong, have all displayed remarkable tolerance, understanding, and respect for the long hours I spent at my desk. Their contribution is priceless, and so are my sentiments of appreciation, love, and affection.

While I am deeply grateful to the institutions and individuals I have mentioned here, and while this book would not be what it is without their contributions, I remain solely responsible for any errors, shortcomings, or failures that may have remained undetected or unremedied.

Part 1: The World of Deng Majok

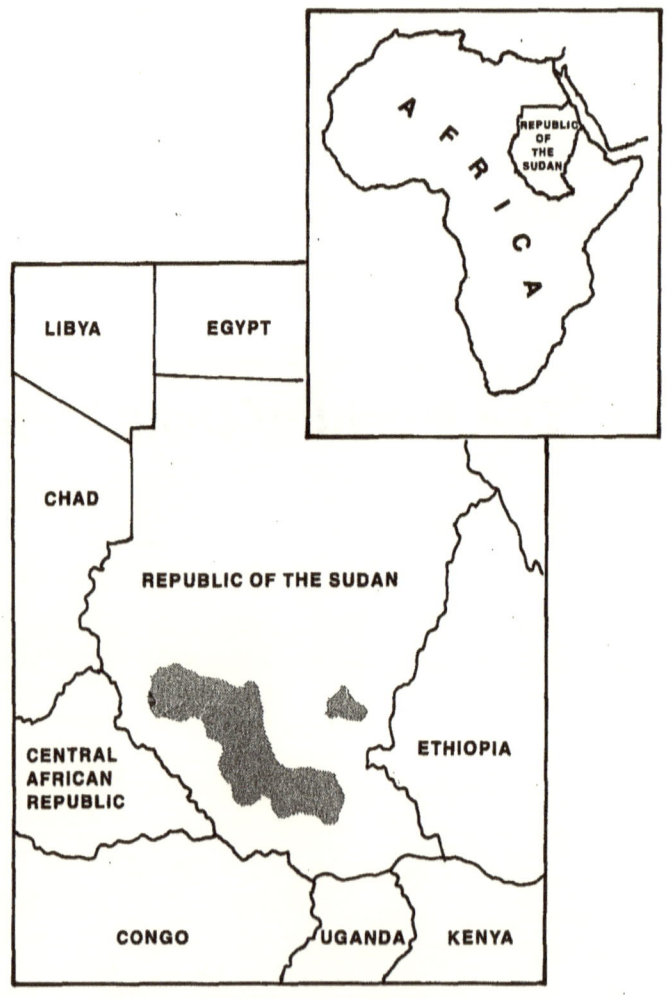

Map 1   The Dinka of the Sudan

1   The Perspective of a Son

It was one of those days when peace and tranquillity seemed to screen out the turbulent realities of our world. The year was 1969, the month July. As I sat looking out my office window on the thirtieth floor of the United Nations Building in New York, I saw sailboats gliding gracefully up and down the East River and small hydroplanes landing and taking off, seemingly without a sound. Had I recalled similar moments in my life, I might have suspected that something dreadful was about to happen. But I had no time for recollections; Al, the spirited messenger from the Caribbean, came in with a cable. My heart jumped. What could it be about? I saw that it was from England. My brother, Zackariah Bol, was there, interning in tropical medicine. But why was he cabling me? There were too many possibilities for me to focus on one. So I hurriedly tore open the yellow Western Union envelope and read the message. Our father, Deng Majok, had been brought to Khartoum, seriously ill, perhaps dying; Bol was returning to the Sudan immediately.

Bol and I were the same age, but we were not twins; we were half-brothers by different mothers. He is the fourth child—second son—of the first wife; I am the first child of the fourth wife. Of all our brothers and sisters, we were the closest, having grown up together from the beginning, attended the first elementary school opened in our area, and continued our schooling both in the South and the North, parting only after secondary school. Bol had gone to Europe to study medicine, beginning in Leipzig, finishing in Padua and Bologna, and specializing in England. I had studied law at Khartoum University, proceeded to postgraduate studies in England and the United States, and, after obtaining a doctorate at Yale University, joined the Division of Human Rights at the United Nations Headquarters in New York. In the process, Bol had been away from home for ten years and I for seven.

By coincidence, I had just been assigned to attend a human rights conference in Cairo that would take place in a few weeks. It was therefore easy to arrange leave to the Sudan before the conference. I left within a few days of receiving Bol's message. After changing flights in London, we landed at Rome to refuel. Passengers disembarked and remained in the transit lounge during the refueling time. As we were reembarking along with the new passengers, Bol and I suddenly came face to face in the doorway of the aircraft.

Within an hour of our arrival in Khartoum, we were guided to the hospital where our father was. As we entered his room and were announced, Father struggled to his feet to greet us. He seemed stooped and was obviously wobbly and unsteady on his feet. In his prime, there would have been no doubt about his erect stature and commanding personality. But we were about to see a different man, as Father rose from his bed in that large room which accommodated several other patients, surprisingly and allegedly because there was no private room available. He was wearing a gown that was light enough to reveal how reduced to skin and bones he was; he looked as though he were rising from his grave. We hurried our pace to save him any further steps. Father embraced us, at first one at a time, then both together, one under each arm, repeating his greetings and hugging us over and over again as though he needed to feel us to believe that we were real.

One of our brothers who was taking care of him asked, "Father, is there any need to send the letter?" It was handed to us in an open envelope addressed to Jaafar Mohamed Nimeri, the young officer who had successfully led a coup only two months before. Since the communists were Nimeri's most influential allies, the political atmosphere was charged with leftist slogans. Native administration in general, and tribal chiefs in particular, were among the avowed enemies of the Revolution. In the Arab North, chiefs had been dismissed and chieftainship abolished. The situation in the less sophisticated South was allowed to linger on, but the handwriting was on the wall, especially in the anomalous case of our father, poised as he was between North and South.

Father's immediate concern, however, at least the one articulated in the letter just handed over to us, was touchingly different. He wrote of how he had served the Sudan from the time he was in his early twenties, assisting his own father, through his full assumption of responsibility in his thirties, to his present old age of nearly seventy. The only favor he was asking of the revolutionary government was to bring back his two sons who were abroad so that he could see them before he died. Obviously, now there was no need to deliver the letter.

We quickly arranged for Father's transfer to the private clinic of Dr. Abdel Wahab Zein El Abdeen, who was popular with the southern Sudanese, partly because he was reputed to be half-southern. But his diagnosis was discouraging. Although Dr. Abdel Wahab continued to give him reassuring attention, he spoke to us quite candidly: Father was suffering from terminal cancer. It was too advanced to be halted. The end could come any time.

But there was no way we could just fold our hands and wait for the end. First, we tried through the National Health Commission to authorize his transfer to London or Cairo, but we were told that the government could not spend money on a terminal patient. We still felt that it was important for us to do something in the hope that we might save our father's life, or at least demonstrate that we were doing our best to do so.

Father himself realized the gravity of his condition, but his zest for life remained overwhelming. We learned that Dinka elders, who were experienced in such matters, had intimated to him that he was dying and should return to settle the affairs of the tribe and designate a successor, but Father's reaction had been to dismiss them as having self-serving motives.

Accompanied by his secretary, Achier, an Arabized Dinka whose Muslim name was Beshir, we took Father to Cairo where he was admitted to the Maadi Military Hospital. The specialists confirmed Abdel Wahab's opinion. But they, too, could not say when the end would come. It was obvious, however, that Father was deteriorating rapidly. One day Bol and I went to see him and found him lying on his back, speechless and almost motionless; but his eyes, though sunk deep into the sockets, still glowed with piercing intelligence and awareness. We had been in Cairo about a week. After the visit to the hospital, we went back to the hotel and lay awake far into the night, pondering how long his death might take and what its practical implications would be. We had finally fallen asleep when the telephone rang. A glance at my wristwatch told me that it was about four o'clock in the morning. Bol took it. He did not need to say anything. Father was dead.

It was impossible for us to conceive of that reality. Father could not be dead; the world simply could not function without him. Only he could manage the family, the tribe, and our difficult borders between the Arab North and the African South. And only he could adequately protect his people against the unscrupulousness of the security forces in the South-North civil war that had crept into our area. But there was no room for doubt or speculation. Father had died and left us as his senior sons. The day of reckoning had come. We must rise to the occasion and step into his shoes in accordance with tradition. Nor was there time for reflection, since there were practical problems to be solved.

The most urgent issue that confronted us as soon as we arrived in Khartoum was how to transport the body home. Abyei, our home town and the administrative headquarters of our tribe, is some six hundred miles from Khartoum and totally cut off for the six months of the rainy season, from June to December. There was a small airstrip, but no plane had ever landed there during the rainy season. The only hope seemed to be to go by train to El

Obeid, the headquarters of Kordofan, and then proceed by the large Mercedes Benz military trucks that stood a chance of breaking through the mud, although at a slow speed. But that would take too long for the body and might even be against health regulations.

And yet, the only dying declaration Father had made to us was that he must be taken back to be buried in the tribe. "My sons," he had said, "I do not know whether this illness will allow me to live or whether I shall die. Should I die, knowing your people, the Dinka, they may say that it is impossible to take my body home during the rainy season and that I should be buried here. I am not a man to be buried wherever I happen to die. I am a man who, whatever the difficulties, should be taken and buried at home in my tribe." Father had spoken so immodestly that we burst out laughing once we were out of his sight. "I will go even further and say that I am a man known to the South and the North, a man on whose grave a tomb (or a monument) should stand."

We were now in the situation he had predicted. Father had imposed an impossible task upon us as a sacred duty. We had to do something. Our host, Bona Malual, a dynamic young Dinka politician with whom Father had shared mutual admiration, took us to Joseph Garang, the communist minister in charge of southern affairs. Joseph immediately started a chain of contacts that went to the top. Nimeri himself gave orders that all possible efforts be made to fly the body to Abyei. A military plane stood ready the next morning. But radio contacts with Abyei revealed that it was impossible for the plane to land there. The response from all nearby towns of Kordofan was the same. Even El Obeid, which offered the best prospect, had had too much rain and the airport was closed. Just as all hope seemed to be vanishing as the day slipped by, an unexpected message came from Abyei: it had actually not rained for some time and, after the airstrip was inspected, it was found to be quite dry. With some leveling, it could land the plane. Because of ominous weather conditions that afternoon, the flight had to be scheduled for the following morning, and an especially skilled and experienced pilot was charged with the mission.

Since the evening of our return to Khartoum word of Father's death had already circulated. The Ngok Dinka community, considerable in numbers, had mobilized, and from the morning of the second day the traditional funeral singing and dancing with which the Dinka mourn their chiefs were in full progress in several areas of the three principal towns.

On the morning of our departure for Abyei, a large crowd of Dinka men went to the hospital and carried the body all the way to the airport, booming traditional hymns and mourning songs. The cabinet ministers who turned up at the airport to pay their respects waded through the crowds with considerable difficulty.

We landed and refueled in El Obeid, where we were met by the governor and the provincial authorities, who wanted to pay their last respects to a man of whom they were truly proud. A crowd of Dinka mourners appeared at the airport, singing hymns and funeral songs, and had to be held back from the plane. Then we took off, meandered through the high hills of the Nuba mountains, and flew over the lush, green, swampy plains farther south. After losing his way and overshooting Abyei by a considerable distance, the pilot anxiously retraced his route over that vast, unfamiliar landscape. When he eventually spotted Abyei, he expressed his relief by performing acrobatic feats that at first gave us a dramatic false alarm but quickly brought us to the ground. As soon as the plane landed, a shower started. According to Dinka belief, this was an expected blessing for the chief, but as far as the pilot was concerned, there was no time to be spent on amenities; he took off immediately. As soon as he was off the ground, it began to rain heavily. And for the next month it continued to rain so hard that it was impossible for a plane to land in Abyei. The miracle of Father's return had been confirmed.

After the years we had spent in the Western world, even Khartoum seemed to Bol and me no more than an oversized village, so Abyei appeared to be on a different planet—slushy, muddy, and miserable. It took some days before the beauty of the nature we had known came back into focus. Otherwise, our overwhelming impression was that of the misery on the faces of the people. During Father's short absence, they had suffered torture, harassment, and even death at the hands of the security forces, who seemed to be everywhere, displaying the tools of occupation. The Dinka had obviously longed for the return of the only man they felt could protect them. When they first heard of the plane bringing Deng Majok, they assumed that he had recovered and was coming back to resume control. Instead, he was brought back a corpse in a sealed casket. Their hopes for survival seemed to fade into a nightmare of helplessness.

But it was not only the Ngok Dinka who suffered the loss. Sentiments of mourning the death of Deng Majok pervade the interviews quoted in this book from beginning to end; there is no need to stress them here. Suffice it to quote from an Arab who knew him well, Ibrahim Mohamed Zein, an educator from Kordofan. After an extensive analysis of the implications of Deng Majok's death, Ibrahim concluded:

> Deng Majok is a loss to the family, he is a loss to the area of Abyei, he is a loss to the whole area of Dar Mirsiriya, he is a loss to Kordofan Province, and he is a loss to the Sudan. He was the guarantor of stability in the area; he was the hope for a stabilizing leadership. Once he was gone, the situation began to shake and shake until it fell apart.

As the problems in Abyei became progressively worse and assumed national dimensions, that sentiment was to be echoed over and over again, not only at all levels within the Sudan, but also elsewhere in the Middle East.[1]

1. During the crises of early 1983, when violence erupted in the South and threatened a

There is, however, a dimension to Deng Majok's story other than the political. And again I quote from Ibrahim Mohamed Zein.

> For a very long time I have wondered why social researchers or scholars who write books do not write about the personality of Deng Majok. I think he offered a tremendous opportunity for study. For a man to be able to marry hundreds of wives and be capable of producing hundreds of children, a number of which, if you multiply on the average of even a few children per wife, could approximate a thousand boys and girls—that is extraordinary. And then you add to that the children of his children and their children!
>
> For a man to provide livelihoods for such large numbers of wives, to administer them so efficiently, and to have children who, wherever you find them, are among the best in their conduct, in their dress, and in their general appearance, both boys and girls, never giving any indication that numbers had any negative effect on quality—for a man to do all that was a rare strength. I personally think that Deng Majok was a most extraordinary character.

This book is a biography of that extraordinary man. I have relied heavily on the evidence gathered from interviews, not only because of the scarcity of documentary sources, but also as a matter of principle. The main motivation in most of my work on the Dinka has been to counter the denigration of oral literature and the overemphasis on written, mostly published, sources for understanding the culture of a predominantly preliterate society. This is, of course, only one aspect of the general disregard for traditional people as a source of knowledge. As one elder explained it:

> The educated youth have pushed us aside, saying that there is nothing we know. Even if an elder talks of the important things of the country, they say, "There is nothing you know." How can there be nothing we know when we are their fathers? Did we not bear them ourselves? When we put them in school, we thought they would learn new things to add to what we, their elders, would pass on to them. We hoped they would listen to our words and then add to them the new words of learning. But now it is said that there is nothing we know. This has really saddened our hearts very much.[2]

South-North civil war, it was alleged by regional and national security authorities that it had been initiated by a dissident Ngok Dinka group led by the sons of the late Deng Majok, who favored separating from the administration of Kordofan in the North and joining one of the provinces of the South. Many of the alleged leaders, including several of Deng Majok's sons, were arrested and placed under detention. The Arabic press, including the London based *El Ahdath*, lamented the loss of Deng Majok as the man who had made the difference on the South-North borders and that his sons had deviated from his bridging policies.

2. Chol Adija, in Deng, *Dinka Cosmology* (London: Ithaca Press, 1980), 286-87. Also quoted in Deng, *Africans of Two Worlds* (New Haven and London: Yale University Press, 1978), 26, and *Recollections of Babo Nimir* (London: Ithaca Press, 1982), 6.

Traditional education largely consists of information transmitted orally from generation to generation. Bulabek Malith, then a middle-aged traditional Dinka, explained the process in these words:

> Your grandfather gives you his words, the words of the land. And if you are a man who has lived among elders and you have listened to them and you are a man who holds words in his heart, and you keep words in your heart well, those are the ways of learning among our people. Knowledge of the words is what a man tells his children, a child who stays with elders. Elders will talk about the affairs of the past and a child who listens will hear them and when he one day has children, he will tell them the same things.[3]

In an interview for this study, Chol Piok, then an elder in his seventies, observed:

> How does one know the words of the country? Even those of us who are sitting here, were we not children once? We were children, and the words that were said, we heard elders like me tell to younger people. If a child has an alert heart, then he will come and sit near an elder and ask him for the words of the past. The elder will tell the child, hoping that the child will hold these words in his head and tell others later on. But if he is a child with a reckless heart, then he will walk carelessly, concerning himself only with the affairs of girls or the cattle-camps.

"That is how God created man," concluded yet another elder.[4]

For reasons of its cultural, moral, and spiritual significance, the passing of knowledge down to successive generations is more than an objective transmission of facts. As is obvious from the above quotations, transmission of the actual words implies an educational process that is both informative and normative.

Because of its lineage and kinship orientation, knowledge of oral tradition is internally based within the group most directly concerned and weakens with distance from the inner circles of that group. As Monyluak Row expressed it in an interview for this book, "When it comes to the things that have occurred, one does not know the affairs of another person's family." However, because of their public nature, the historical traditions of the leading lineages tend to be more widely known than those of ordinary families.

Since oral tradition and the manner of its transmission aim at serving the cultural, moral, and spiritual objectives of the lineage and the society at large, the concept of the truth involved is a fluid and dynamic one that melds

---

3. Deng, *Cosmology*, 253, quoted in Deng, *Africans of Two Worlds*, 31.
4. Chief Pagwot Deng, in Deng, *Cosmology*, 251; quoted in Deng, *Africans of Two Worlds*, 30.

facts with fantasy and myth in a storylike fashion founded on deep moral assumptions and judgments. It is a creative, more-or-less approach to the truth, molded and adapted with the benefit of experience and hindsight. Usually, it is an explanation of the way things are, how they came to be, and how they should be ideally, rather than a recounting of frozen facts, as would be the case in written records.

Oral knowledge, therefore, represents a living approach to the truth, whose functional purpose is primarily aimed at serving the narrator's objectives in a particular factual situation. Written history, of course, is also an interpretation, a processing and recasting of the truth, usually to serve some contemporary purpose; to that extent, there is an inherent policy consideration in the selection and formulation of allegedly objective facts, but less room for maneuvering. Dinka oral tradition, on the other hand, is a model of how pragmatic, dynamic, and policy-oriented man's perception and utilization of history can be.

This should not be understood to mean that the Dinka have no concept of objective truth. Quite the contrary, they often claim to tell nothing but the truth. In the interviews for this study, for instance, informants often stressed that they would report only what they had "seen" and "heard." Chol Piok declared:

> The words of Deng Majok, which I heard, and all the things in Deng Majok's life, which I saw, are the things I will talk about. If there is anything I know about Kwol Arob, I will also say it . . . the words of Kwol Arob were said in my presence. My tongue was there, my ear was there, and my eye was there. There will be things which were not told me by someone else: things which I saw, things which I heard and things on which I spoke. Those are the things relating to Kwol Arob. And I need not mention Deng Majok because we grew up to maturity together.

In another context, Chol Piok stated emphatically, "What one has not seen with one's own eyes or heard with one's own ears, one does not state as a fact." Monyluak Row prefaced his account with an expression of modesty about his age in relation to the history he was about to cover: "Mading, as we sit here, both you and I are children [relative to the generation of Deng Majok and his father], even though each one of us has his own particular dates for his age." Throughout the interview, Monyluak was careful not to comment on issues where he felt the credibility of his knowledge might be doubtful. Questioned on one of the early courtship adventures of Deng Majok and a fight that had allegedly ensued between him and a competitor over a girl, Monyluak responded: "I think you should ask other people to give you information on these cases. I did hear of the fight in the dance, but I did not understand it very well. I heard of his spearing a man from your clan in a dance, but I am not sure whether the conflict arose over a girl. I have never learned the truth. Some elders may be in a better position to explain that point."

Chief Madut Ring, in reporting how he and Chief Lang Juk, both of the Twich Dinka, had sacrificed bulls on the grave of Deng Majok, thereby acknowledging him as their chief, added, "When one says something, it should be found to be true when investigated in the future." And Deng Abot, the rival half-brother of Deng Majok, after making a comment unflattering to his deceased brother, remarked, "My brother Deng is dead, but we will meet again in the next world. . . . One must speak a truth that will be heard by God there above and the powers here on earth."

Even more positively, a number of those interviewed categorically asserted that their commitment to telling the truth was not compromised by the fact that they were talking to the sons of Deng Majok. Chol Piok, Deng Majok's distant nephew, expressed a widely shared sentiment when he said, "Let me tell you, son of my brother, there is nothing to be hidden. . . . Even if your father had stolen something or whatever wrong he might have done, I would tell you so that you know that I tell the truth." Juac Dau began his account by saying that he had relationships with Deng Majok's children, and then added, "but that is not important; the real issue is the truth and the interest of our area."

Notwithstanding this commitment to telling the truth irrespective of the relationships involved, I always opened my interviews by urging the informants not to consider my identity as the son of Deng Majok a reason to tell me only what they thought I wanted to hear about my father. For instance, in my interview with Chol Piok, I said:

> What is important is that we talk freely so that one says anything one wants, whether it is a good thing or a bad thing. I do not want you to think that because you are talking with the son of Deng Majok you must say only good things. Say everything. You were one of the people closest to Deng Majok. And if there is something good or something bad, even if it were so bad that you might feel embarrassed to say it, please say it and I will think it over and decide what to do about it.

I achieved the best results by arguing convincingly that I have a vested interest in knowing both the positive and the negative aspects of the truth about my father. Sometimes, when I felt this approach was called for, I had to stress that if the book merely glorified my father without revealing his dark side, it would not be considered credible and therefore could not serve a positive purpose for the name of my father. This, for example, is how I explained it to Chief Babo Nimir:

> Let me say this: when one writes a book, one wants to be honest with one's self and produce a work of intellectual integrity. Of course, it is understandable to avoid certain things, but if one wants to write

about a person, one must say the facts as one sees them. If the book turns out to be all praise for my father, it will not be of much value. It can only be of value if I maintain an objective enough position to be able to include criticisms that are well placed.

I also encouraged my brothers, who conducted some of the interviews, to press for the truth. Charles Biong, who attended my interview with Ibrahim El Hussein, for instance, interjected these words, "Uncle Ibrahim, the saying goes, 'Full virtue is only with God.' No man is so good that he has no shortcomings. When Deng Majok was alive, if you had been approached and asked, 'Ibrahim, tell the truth to Deng Majok; tell him his shortcomings which, if remedied, would make him perfect,' what would you have said those shortcomings were?"

Even though Ibrahim did not mention any shortcomings, his answer had a convincing ring of sincerity: "My sons, by God, by God: is God not our Creator? If I knew of any negatives about Deng, I would have told you, 'These were his negatives.' I know of no negatives."

It should not be thought that the dynamics of my relationship to my informants were always negatively constraining; they might instead elicit information that would otherwise be withheld from a stranger. For instance, some confidential communications might more appropriately be revealed to a relative, such as a grandson or a son. That was the essence of Ibrahim El Hussein's point when he spoke of what he termed Deng Majok's "secret" practices, which involved using the services of the local Muslim Arab "holy men" and drinking water containing the ink with which Koranic verses had been written on a plate and then washed into blessing or healing water. Since Deng Majok was not known to be a Muslim and was indeed a Dinka spiritual leader by traditional criteria, this was indeed "a secret." Ajuong Deng, addressing himself to the reasons Deng Majok gave for his numerous marriages, offered a variety of candid arguments and ended with the words: "This was what you meant when you asked me to tell you even things that he and I talked about in confidence. When your father used to travel and something major occurred, however far away I might be and however late in the night it might be, he would insist that I be fetched. So, I must tell you the truth of what transpired between us."

Over and above the precautions I have taken to guard against distortion while maximizing the benefits of the insider's standpoint, I believe that my previous works on the Dinka add to the buffer zone between my father as the subject and me as the observer.[5] Indeed, some of the cultural themes around

---

5. These include: *Tradition and Modernization* (New Haven and London: Yale University Press, 1971); *The Dinka of the Sudan*, (New York: Holt, Rinehart and Winston, 1972); *The Dinka and Their Songs* (Oxford: The Clarendon Press, 1973); *Dinka Folktales* (New York and London: Africana Publishing Company, 1974); *Dynamics of Identification: A Basis of National Integration in the Sudan* (Khartoum: Khartoum University Press, 1974); *Africans of

which the story of Deng Majok is told are substantiated in those earlier works. But while I have made use of my previous works in structuring a conceptual framework, I have tried to allow the interview material to speak for itself, intervening only for the purpose of maintaining the analytic themes of the book.

One last point: as in my previous works with Dinka oral material, my objective has been not to provide quantitative analysis of statistical evidence, but rather to present a qualitative selection of representative samples to illustrate the themes. I am keen to let my informants come through as individuals with knowledge to share expressed in their own manner of speech, rather than as numbers in support of my own formulation of the truth told by proxy. I have taken their statements at face value, neither attempting to verify their validity nor assuming their accuracy. What counts is the overall theme of the truth; how the factual details are formulated is the prerogative of the teller, who could be a historian, a philosopher, or a poet.

Two Worlds (New Haven and London: Yale University Press, 1978); *Dinka Cosmology* (London: Ithaca Press, 1980); and *Recollections of Babo Nimir* (London: Ithaca Press, 1982). One chapter in the *Recollections* is on Deng Majok.

2   *A Look at the Man*

Deng Majok was about six feet three inches tall, slender and fine-featured, with a nose that was proportionate to his elongated face and a stern yet gentle expression. His eyes were deep and penetrating, glowing with intelligence, vitality, and courage, all of which generated an unmistakable aura of power. Accentuating the charisma of his face was a scar on his upper lip, the result of a wound inflicted by a lion's claw while he was heroically fighting the beast to save his younger brother, Arob. He was always meticulously dressed in the full attire of Arab chiefs, nazirs, or 'sultans': a long white robe with a carefully folded long scarf thrown across the shoulders and a white turban neatly wound around the head. He seems to have been very particular about his appearance and the impression he made on people. Even as a young man in his twenties, he radiated a commanding personality, and it was obvious that he had great dreams for his own future.

In many ways, Deng Majok's life was a dramatic fusion of glory and tragedy. To his people he was legendary—as a person, a family man, a tribal chief. His power and the aura of his influence extended far beyond his tribal domain. He brought peace, harmony, and positive cooperation to the formidable borders between the Arab North and the African South, where warlike pastoral tribes had been wont to clash in a violent struggle over pastures and water, aggravated by racial tension and animosity. Both politically and culturally, he transcended the barriers that divided the Africans of the South from the Arabs of the North. While building up a cross-cultural image and enhancing his position by adopting what he considered best in the ways of the Arabs, he stood among them with head held high, exceedingly proud of his identity as a Dinka. Indeed, his being the only "southerner" among his northern colleagues, with whom he shared the administrative jurisdiction of Kordofan Province in the Arab North, gave him a uniqueness that spotlighted his identity and stature. He strongly identified himself with the North, protected the interests of the Arabs in his area, and in fact sometimes appeared to favor the Arabs over his own people. And yet, by so doing, he won the admiration, the acceptance, and the support of the Arabs for himself as a Dinka among Arabs and as a leader of a friendly minority that deserved a special place. Having disarmed the Arabs by thus identifying himself with the North, Deng Majok felt secure enough to confront them and count on the support of crucial elements among them whenever his vital interests or those of his people were threatened by any Arab, whether a leader of a neighboring tribe or a central government official.

But there was a tragic side to what was otherwise a success story. From the early days of his childhood and throughout his life, Deng Majok suffered a deep sense of insecurity on account of the disapproving attitude of his father, Kwol Arob, or what he saw as lack of paternal love. The problem had its roots in the marriage of his mother, Nyanaghar, to his father. Nyanaghar was the first woman to be engaged to Kwol Arob. But when she rejected him and eloped with another man, Kwol married Abiong. Afflicted with a disease that was diagnosed as a curse for rejecting the chief, Nyanaghar later repented and accepted the marriage. She was given to Kwol after Abiong had already been installed as first wife but had not yet borne a child. Nyanaghar begot Deng Majok as her firstborn, while Abiong first begot a daughter, Agorot, followed by a son, Deng Abot (also known as Deng Makuei). The Deng brothers grew up together, with Deng Majok being recognized as senior on account of age; while the younger Deng, as the son of the first wife, was considered to be entitled to religious and spiritual seniority in the family. But because of the anomalies of the situation, this lopsided seniority was never comforting or fully acceptable to Deng Majok.

Opinions are divided about Kwol's feelings toward Deng Majok. There are people who believe that Kwol loved Deng Majok very much, perhaps even more than he did Deng Abot. Certainly, the consensus of opinion is that Kwol recognized Deng Majok's abilities very early and used them effectively, once he was old enough to assist his father in the administration of the tribe. But this only made Deng Majok feel more valued for his abilities and services than loved as a son. Deng Majok was convinced that Deng Abot was more loved by their father, and the evidence for that was his preference for Deng Abot as heir to the throne, even though he was younger and admittedly less capable.

Besides, the story of his parents' marriage left Deng Majok with a stigma that his father often threw up to him insultingly. And indeed, even after they had been reconciled and married, Nyanaghar is said to have continued to be tough-minded and hot-tempered. She and Kwol got into frequent and terrifying fights throughout their married life. On the other hand, Nyanaghar is sometimes admired and praised for having been outspoken and self-assertive. People go even further to say that Deng Majok did indeed inherit his mother's strong personality, that it is a brave woman who bears a brave son, and that it is a brave man who makes a good leader. These are all valid propositions. In fact, they genuinely reflect the ambivalence or contradictions the Dinka feel on the issue. But they also represent ways of flattering Nyanaghar's descendants, and especially her son, Deng Majok, whose life unquestionably proved the validity of the argument. Chief Kwol himself criticized his son's behavior as a reflection of his mother's character. For a son to be insulted in this way in the man's world of the Dinka was a severe reproach that must have deeply injured the strong pride of Deng Majok.

The story of Deng Majok's life can be seen in two main themes or phases. The first reveals Deng's self-assertiveness and his objections to what he considered inequitable in his father's treatment of him and his mother's side of the family, combined with a constant struggle to win his father's approval and favor. The second shows an acceptance of the reality that he was not loved, at least not to the degree he expected or hoped for, as a result of which he seemed to have resolved to fend for himself and fight whoever stood in the way of what he felt to be his due, using whatever means available to him, some of which conformed with tradition and some involving change and modernity. Unfortunately, his main foes were to be his father and his half-brother.

Deng Majok's victory over them was to be achieved at immense cost. He had to carry on and never cease to meet the highest standards of leadership to prove his own worth despite his father, striving to excel in every way and beyond any doubt. Nothing would be good enough that did not make him truly legendary, the kind of man who had never existed before and would never exist again. To prove that his standards were above those of everyone else, the periods before and after him had to be worse. And of course, that became a tragedy for so many!

Deng Majok himself was not modest about his place in the history of his people and country. Dinka values normally give prominence to the forebears as the prototypes of virtue, and their achievements are always exalted far beyond those of their descendants. The Dinka never claim to have done better than their fathers. But Deng Majok was an exception, for he always boasted about his achievements as compared to those of his father's reign. He obviously saw himself as having excelled his forebears in his deeds.

Deng Majok never believed in making wills or dying declarations, perhaps because he had been instrumental in the gross violation of his father's last wishes. He is reported to have said on several occasions: "Once you are dead, why should you care what happens! That problem is for the living." Paradoxically, however, he was concerned about the future of his chieftainship after his death. He even sought my legal opinion in his last days: "Since you have studied law and looked into the books, do you think it is possible for Deng Abot to reclaim the chieftainship when I am gone?" I assured him that even if Deng Abot did, he would not stand a chance of success. He was relieved. And yet, despite his apprehensions, Deng Majok never prepared any of his sons to succeed him, nor did he consolidate the position of his heirs as the leaders. Up to the very end of his life, he made no move to designate a successor. It was as though he was concerned about his chieftainship for himself, even after his death. As I said earlier, the only dying wish he expressed was to have his body taken back home. Although a modest brick structure is all that now marks his grave, there is little doubt that he will one day have the tomb or monument he felt he deserved.

Deng Majok used to say that a child loved by his father is not the same as a child loved by God. What he meant was that by doing what is right, you win God's favor and that is more important than being loved by your father simply because you are his favorite son. He obviously felt that he met God's standards and approval. Another story has it that Deng Majok classified men into three categories: sons of women, sons of men, and sons of God. Sons of women are too pampered by their mothers and are therefore docile and unadventuresome. Sons of men are too obstreperous and aggressive. Sons of God are blessed with sound reasoning, wise judgment, and prudence of action. It is obvious whose son he felt he was.

A notable feature of Deng Majok's story is that he was able to accomplish so much in the modern context of the Dinka without formal education. Indeed, he was illiterate. Although he learned a few words of English, he never spoke the language. He was fluent in Arabic but had a poor accent.

Deng Majok's only education or training for the responsibilities of chieftainship was through the dynamics of his situation as a chief's son who was known from the beginning as a contender for the throne. Dinka society has a remarkable way of combining a distinction between the class of *kic*, appropriately translated as "commoners," and that of *bany*, the chiefs, with an egalitarianism that does not permit social barriers between the classes. It is true that the chiefly classes are likely to be the largest and the chiefs themselves the wealthiest in terms of livestock and agricultural produce. Their huts and cattle-byres (enlarged huts in which animals are kept) are likely to be the most numerous and the best built. Nevertheless, Dinka children, whether from the chiefly clans or commoners, grow up together more or less eating the same food, playing the same games, attending the same dances, sleeping in the same huts and cattle-byres, herding together, flirting together, and, all in all, learning and training together. As children begin to mature, activities previously manifest in games and informal ways of preparing them for initiation into adult roles start to become more institutionalized and formal. And as was argued earlier, passing on knowledge is a function of communication within the family, and both the form and the content of such information are directly related to the status of the family and the position of the individual in that context.

Despite this egalitarianism, the Dinka have a profound recognition of and respect for the status of chieftainship, and being the son of a chief carries with it certain expectations of responsibilities and privileges, depending on one's position in the chiefly hierarchy. For instance, it is the son of a chief who is normally expected to be the first to receive initiation marks. And it is the son of the chief who should have the final say in any discussion or talk with other groups or within the group. These roles require special, though informal, in-house instruction or training from appropriate circles. This means that while there is no formal education or training for children of the chief, there is no doubt that the very context of chieftainship prepares them for the requirements of their status in a practical way. Although there is no set form for addressing the children of the chief, "Son of the Chief" and even "Chief" is popularly used from an early age and carries with it certain qualitative connotations of character and behavior patterns. And while this is true of sons and daughters of the chief in general, it is particularly true of the senior sons, and especially the one expected to succeed his father. The attitudes of the people toward him, the way he is made aware of the social expectations and requirements of leadership, and the way his own performance is viewed in terms of those expectations and requirements can be very significant in fostering and developing, or in frustrating the development of, a leadership personality. It is, of course, much easier when there is a consensus on the heir to the throne, which was the case with Deng Majok's father, Kwol Arob. It is more difficult when the situation is uncertain and controversial, as was the case with Deng Majok, and also with his sons.

It is in such cases of controversy and competitiveness that certain circles with a vested interest in the leadership prospects of a particular son can become crucial in reinforcing the informal education and training of a chief's son to foster his qualifications and prospects for leadership. And here, maternal relatives are generally acknowledged by the Dinka to be among the most reliable allies of a chief's son, even though there must be support within the agnatic group for the maternal relatives to be effective.

Told in retrospect, the story of Deng Majok reveals a chief's son who demonstrated leadership qualities from an early age and was encouraged, reinforced, and supported by significant circles within his agnatic kinship and by most of his loving and wealthy maternal relatives. In all the phases of his growth, from early childhood through adolescence and into adulthood, Deng Majok is presented as having stood apart from his peers in revealing the attributes of leadership. Foremost of these were the qualities of hospitality and generosity, the ability to articulate and soothe with words, and the power to persuade and reconcile people. Among the characteristics for which he was also known from childhood were good judgment, physical and moral courage, dignity of bearing and outlook, and a general nobility of character. Recognizing and praising him for these attributes was also a way of fostering them in him. It was in many ways both a descriptive and a prescriptive process, as much an acknowledgment of existing qualities as an educational and training facility in preparation for leadership—in other words, a self-fulfilling prophecy.

As might be expected, this egalitarian picture of Dinka society has begun to change as opportunities for education and employment have introduced new criteria for self-advancement and social and economic stratification. As an innovator who favored education in particular and social and economic development in general, Deng Majok contributed significantly to this change even at the risk of becoming outmoded by the process of change himself.

One major aspect of Deng Majok's life remains a mystery that the Dinka ascribe to a curse inflicted upon him by a maternal uncle, and that is his attitude toward women. As one reads the story, some questions come to mind that may help to clarify certain aspects of his personality and attitude in this respect. Given his close identification with his mother, whom he obviously adored (so much so that he would tell his wives to observe her ways and follow her example even though she had long been dead), and given the association the Dinka make between a mother's personality and that of her child, did Deng Majok feel hurt by his mother's having initially rejected his father and eloped with another man? Or did he perhaps feel sympathetic toward his mother, especially in view of the fact that his father relegated both him and his mother to the second position, though they both felt more than qualified for the first one? Perhaps he felt both but could not admit it to himself, far less to others, without defeating his own ends; for neither condemning nor condoning his mother's conduct would have promoted a sense of dignity in the Dinka context. One can surmise that it would be more convenient subconsciously to project such ambivalence away from his mother and onto women in general.

Throughout his life, Deng Majok was never put off by women rejecting his marriage proposals and eloping with other men before he eventually married them. On the contrary, he seemed to relish facing the challenge of pursuing them and eventually defeating his rivals. Some of those women even became his favorite wives. And yet, he had a deep-rooted suspicion and mistrust of women. He considered their loyalty and fidelity questionable. He once said to me about a favorite son of a favorite wife: "Mading, why don't you advise your brother? You can never trust the heart of a woman. With his way of behavior, who knows where his mother brought him from!" Deng Majok's wives and daughters had to be closely guarded and watched. Flirtation with his daughters was out of the question. A man had to marry to become close. To smile at a young wife of his was a step in the wrong direction. Deng Majok was a very jealous man.

Deng Majok loved and revered women, both as partners and as mothers, but in an ambivalent way; he looked down on them as weak specimens that had to be protected but dominated. Perhaps he found polygyny the perfect medium for a gratifying superiority and dominance. Indeed, marriage was one way in which he not only broadened his base and scope of power and influence but also proved his manhood and his ability to achieve his goals even without his father's cooperation. He not only won most of his wives from other men, but also married many of them against his father's will.

And indeed, what could be more valid proof of his unique power and virility than marrying into virtually all the Dinka tribes in the region and amassing a company of wives whose estimates vary between what was probably the real figure of two hundred to the exaggerated figure of four hundred, most of whom bore children, though in varying numbers, and were almost totally devoted to him?

What is more, although he himself was an intensely jealous man, Deng Majok could not tolerate jealousy on the part of his wives. He even had the sophistication to call it a disease of which women had to be cured.

I should not give the impression that Deng Majok's wives were miserable objects of his lust or oppression. Quite the contrary, in the social and cultural context of their time, they were viewed, and viewed themselves, as a select, privileged group. They were the best-dressed of all Dinka women, physically the most comfortable, and probably the most indulged in terms of material goods. Although he could be extremely rude, aggressive, and terrifying, especially to women, Deng Majok could turn into the most charming, compassionate person, with a gentle and concentrated smile on his face, when he talked with a woman to his sensuous liking. It is not so much the former propensity but the latter qualities for which his wives remember him. Their accounts reflect feelings of genuine devotion.

It is nearly always a matter of preference or degree whether any particular case is to be considered unique or an example of a more pervasive norm. While there is a great deal to learn from the story of Deng Majok, the weight of evidence indicates that he was a unique individual, not necessarily because he was created so, but largely because he adopted and integrated into his Dinka value system elements of Arab Islamic culture and the British colonial administrative code of conduct, creating a dynamic fusion of tradition and change in a way that distinguished him, at least in degree, from his forebears and contemporaries.

Whatever the formative factors behind his personality and his drive for power and achievement, Deng Majok was and has remained long after his death a figure who towers over everyone else, which was what a former governor of Kordofan had in mind when he likened him to "a pyramid." I have still to meet a man who leaves no question whatsoever about his superiority, even among his administrative superiors, as my father did. This is admittedly so in the eyes of a son, but it is abundantly supported by a consensus of opinion from others. He ran his family and the tribe almost by his mere existence.

3 The Dinka and Their Values

Although Deng Majok's life was admittedly exceptional and in many respects unique, he was the product of his society and was nourished, inspired, and sustained by its value system. Sometimes he stepped out of his traditional context to adopt ideas from his Arab neighbors and his British administrative superiors, but it was the traditional values that provided him with the foundation, the motivation, and the springboard for his actions. Besides, although the foreign element was a vital catalyst to his innovations, traditional mores constituted the yardstick for measuring his achievements, especially in the eyes of his own people, even when that sometimes entailed a contrast with the past.[1]

The Dinka are the largest ethnic group in the Sudan, numbering over two million in a country of only twenty million people and several hundred tribes. Though they engage in agriculture and grow a wide variety of crops (sorghum, millet, maize, sesame, beans, groundnuts, pumpkins, okra, tobacco, and others), their culture is dominated by cattle (and to a lesser extent by sheep and goats), to which they attach a social and moral significance far beyond their economic value. Their land, a flat configuration of thick forests and open plains, lacks stone, iron, or any material resource of significant durability. This is perhaps why Dinka culture is poor in visual arts but strikingly rich in verbal skills. Poetic abilities and the powers of articulation and persuasiveness are inculcated and encouraged in a child from the earliest years and continue to be highly prized as determinants of intelligence, character, influence, and social stature. And yet the Dinka are

---

1. For details of the Dinka cultural and moral values summarized in this chapter, see the works referred to in chap. 1, n. 5, above.

excellent builders, constructing huts and cattle-byres that have circular mud walls reinforced with wattles and conical roofs with rafters of remarkably smooth thatching. Dinka houses can last for over ten years, which in a land infested with timber pests is no mean feat. Their houses, indeed, have been described as among the best native dwellings on the African continent.[2]

The world of the Dinka is a combination of environmental attractions and hardships. During the dry season, which lasts for six months from November to April, the blazing tropical sun bakes the land, killing virtually all vegetation and turning the area into a thirsty arid zone, with shimmering mirages of pools and lakes separated by a cracking pavement of dark clay soil. With the coming of the rainy season, which lasts for the remaining six months from May to October, the land is miraculously transformed: first, with the early rains, deep green grass carpets the plains; lush natural vegetation follows, and the world suddenly becomes alive with the hustle and bustle of birds[3] and insects of all shapes and colors, the flashing of plentiful fish in the rivers, the concerted tunes of frogs and crickets, not to mention the

---

2. Major Court Treatt, who traveled throughout Africa during the first quarter of the twentieth century, reaching Abyei in 1929, wrote: "As we drew nearer and obtained a clearer view of the village standing on rising ground, it seemed that we had stumbled on the master-builders of the tribes; instead of the usual undersized, vermin-infested native huts we beheld large, clean-looking dwellings about twenty-five feet in diameter, decorated with twisted grass-work and magnificently thatched." *Out of the Beaten Track* (New York: E. P. Dutton & Co., 1931), 60. In another context, Major Treatt described the inside of a Dinka dwelling:

> My first impression of roominess and excellent workmanship was pleasantly buttressed by the realisation that the floor was dry and the hut itself warm, and I subsequently found that this temporary home of mine measured 25 feet in diameter beneath a domed roof 20 feet high. Excluding the center pole at a height of seven feet off the ground was a wooden platform covered with clean grassmats, and beneath this platform was a small open fire, the smoke from whose hearth of lumps of based ant-hill earth protected the sleepers from mosquitoes." [p. 79]

Major Treatt concludes his account of Dinka dwellings: "Their huts, whose thatching is beyond all praise, are the most efficiently built native dwellings I have seen. And even the remnants of former huts . . . bear testimony to the excellence of their architecture" (p. 124).

In a private letter dated February 24, 1932, one of the letters to relatives and friends which he kindly passed on to me, K. D. D. Henderson sketches pictures of a dwelling hut and a cattle-byre and observes that the latter holds about fifty head of cattle a night. Since every animal is tied to a peg with sufficient space left between the animals to avoid entanglement, this evidently means that the byre is very spacious.

3. Among the varieties which Henderson mentioned in a letter dated March 3, 1932, were: "Teal, whistlers, pintail duck, comb duck, Egyptian geese, sacred ibis, wood ibis, maribou storks, saddle storks, greater and lesser egrets, golden crested crane, cormorants, herons, pelicans, fish eagles," all of which he describes as "almost as common hereabouts as sparrows." Major Treatt also observed, "small water-holes speckled with myriads of water birds. . . . Duck and geese grubbed in the lush water grass of these pools while numerous species of storks promenaded the banks with the dignity of their kind; from time to time teal would swoop down in shining curves and once or twice we saw the rare pygmy goose sliding with its deceptive apparent slowness above the surface of the pools" (pp. 59–60).

bellowing of cows and bleating of goats and sheep. But even the blessings of the rainy season exact a price: ferocious wild beasts and the creeping world of snakes and scorpions becomes a greater menace to humans; the Nile and the network of other rivers and lagoons that permeate the area frequently overflow and flood the land, bringing crocodiles and hippos into the villages. Despite the hardships of the extreme climatic conditions, the Dinka have a burning love for their land, and until the late 1950s, when the allurements of modernity began to pull them toward urban centers, to leave Dinkaland was considered a depraved action that was almost certain to provoke a slanderous song.

Dinka settlements are spread over a vast territory covering about one-tenth of the nearly million square miles that make the Sudan the largest country in Africa. There are usually several miles between clusters of huts and cattle-byres in settlements or villages, each accommodating only a few families whose homesteads are also well separated. Large in numbers, widespread in settlement, and segmented by the topography of their land, the Dinka are a conglomerate of some twenty-five independent groups that are also segmented by autonomous subgroups, all of which share a striking pride in their race and culture. All this makes for a paradoxical combination of individualism and exclusiveness of interests with an equal emphasis on communalism and a collective sense of purpose.

For a variety of reasons, not least their geographical location and historical background,[4] the Ngok Dinka, as David Cole and Richard Huntington have observed, "are the most hierarchical of all Nilotic peoples, a situation that seems rooted in Ngok traditions, deepened through Arab contacts and exacerbated by the colonial state."[5] Ngok society is divided into nine subtribes: Abyor (the subtribe of the Pajok lineage, which provides the paramount chief), Achak, Achweng, Alei, Anyiel, Bongo, Diil, Mannyuar (the

---

4. Discussed in chapter 4, below.

5. "African Rural Development: Some Lessons from Abyei," unpublished manuscript, Cambridge, Mass., Harvard Institute for International Development, October 1985, chap. 5, p. 37. In another context, Cole and Huntington also observe: "The central institution of Ngok society is the chieftaincy which represents the entire tribe. The Ngok are unique among all the Dinka tribes in that they have developed centralized institutions. In most Dinka tribes leadership is diffusely shared among religious leaders known as 'masters of the spear.' . . . The origins of these Ngok political traditions are complex. . . . Perhaps [the Ngok] share tradition with the Shilluk, the only other Nilotic people with a centralized polity.

"Southall [Aiden, in his article "Nuer and Dinka Are People: Ecology, Ethnicity and Logical Possibility," *Man*, n.s. 11 (1976): 463–91] has suggested an ecological argument. Ngokland is the only part of the Dinka area where the ridges are dry enough to allow a great deal of contiguous settlement. In this they resemble the Shilluk, who are settled in a long chain of villages on the high West bank of the Nile. Additionally, the Shilluk and the Ngok are both vulnerable to pressure and attack from the Arab North. Finally, the Ngok, uniquely among Nilotic people come under an Arab system of administration." *African Rural Development*, 6. For details of the anomalous administrative status of the Ngok, see "Leadership at the Cross-Roads."

subtribe of the Dhiendior lineage, which occupies the second position), and Mareng. The paramount chief, known by the Arabic title of *nazir*, and his two deputies, *wakil(s)*, have jurisdiction over the whole tribe. But to a significant extent, each of the subtribes is autonomous under its own chief, known as *omda*. The subtribe is further divided into two or more sections, each of which is headed by a *sheikh*.[6] It is within the section that descent counts and the lineage becomes a political entity under a clan-head known as *nom-gol*. Otherwise, the clan or the lineage is an amorphous group that may be widely spread throughout the tribe, although they trace their origin to a founding father from whom the name of their clan is usually derived.[7] Dinka clans are divided into those from whom Divine Chiefs of the Sacred Spears descend (collectively known as *bany*, chiefs) and the ordinary ones known as *kic*, which may be translated as "commoners." But the distinction in Dinka society is a functional one which, as we saw earlier, entails no class barriers of the kind familiar to the West.

A vital institution that reinforces territorial identification among the Dinka is the age-set, which every Dinka joins on coming of age, usually in his mid-teens, after undergoing an initiation ceremony, a painful ordeal which, in most tribes, involves scarring across the forehead deep lines varying in number from seven upward, according to the height of the forehead and the bragging courage of the young man. The Ngok Dinka, unlike some other tribes, exempt women from this ordeal, although they are organized into age-sets that correspond to those of their male counterparts.

The custom of scarring the forehead was not uniformly practiced by all the Ngok subtribes. Some, including Abyor, the subtribe of Deng Majok, used other formalities for age-setting, including instructions in responsible social behavior, military training, and rituals of symbolic promotion into adulthood. Indeed, Deng Majok's age-set, Ajingjing (the Giant Biting Ants), was the first in Abyor to adopt the custom of scarring the forehead, and he himself, though unusually young for the operation, led the group and was the first to undergo the ordeal, adding significantly to his reputation for physical and moral courage. After having led Ajingjing, Deng Majok subsequently decided to join his age-mates in the junior age-set, Turuk (The Turks), another novel action previously unknown. It is alleged that he insisted on having his scars retraced in another initiation ordeal to qualify him a

---

6. This is an Arabic term sometimes used to describe a status of political or religious leadership or pedagogic authority.

7. As Lienhardt noted, "The agnatic genealogical structure of his whole clan . . . is not known to a Dinka; he knows that there are likely to be many sub-clans of his clan, all descended from wives or sons of the clan founder, whose name and existence have been forgotten long ago by members of his own sub-clan." "The Western Dinka," in *Tribes without Rulers*, ed. Middleton and Tait (Oxford, 1959), 105–06; see also Howell, "Notes on the Ngok Dinka," 32, *Sudan Notes and Records* (1951), 256.

second time, an absurdity which has the flavor more of myth than of reality but is said to have indeed happened.

Painful as initiation is, the aesthetic and social dignity associated with it is a source of great joy and gratification for every Dinka. It allows a young man to graduate from the status of a boy, *dhol*, to that of *adheng*, a word with the positive connotation of "gentleman." To see a Dinka before and after initiation is to witness the remarkable power of symbolism and ritual, as the dignity of bearing, the responsible conduct, and the overall poise of a gentleman take over the carefree, servile status of boyhood.

Age-setting is essentially a system of military regimentation aimed at developing courage and fighting abilities in young warriors. That is why age-sets are functional institutions of the subtribes as the warring units. Within the subtribe, fights may break out between the sections or the lineages, but only clubs, not spears, are used. In the more serious fights between the subtribes and the tribes, spears and shields are used.

On graduation from initiation, members of the preceding age-set compose and perform insulting songs against the newly initiated set, provoking them into an institutionalized fight called *biok*, which is in part a game but can result in serious injuries. The young men are of course expected to fight back, but they are always forced to retreat—partly in defeat, inexperienced as they are, but also as a courtesy to their seniors. What counts the most is the show of courage. And here, too, the stories about Deng Majok's courage are striking. It is said that the senior age-set, Ajingjing, once defeated his adopted age-set, Turuk, in a *biok*, forcing them to stampede away. Deng Majok stood his ground defiantly, bragging that he would rather die than run. His age-set was forced to come back and defend their front with a commendable courage that their seniors had to acknowledge in a tie. The point is always made with dogmatic assertion that Deng Majok never showed his feet to his adversaries, whether in a *biok* or in any other fight.

Biok is not only training for warfare, it is also a manifestation of rivalry between age-sets both for the position of military dominance and for the attention of the girls. As a rising generation of young, robust, and eligible men, the newly initiated warriors are seen by their seniors as a threatening group that must be humiliated, if only playfully, to keep them in their place.[8]

8. According to Paul Howell, "The initiative does not have to come from the junior age-set but usually does and usually in the form of rude songs which cast reflections on the waning popularity among the girls of the age-set senior to them" (252). To my knowledge, the initiative is always taken by the older age-set in the form of scandalous songs in which they impliedly challenge the qualification of the younger generation to rise to the level of warriors and eligible partners of the corresponding female age-set. The theme of their songs is to identify the members of the younger age-set with their mothers as children still and to insult their mothers by association, even if they had sibling brothers in the senior age-set. For the younger age-set to insult their seniors, even in retaliation, would be totally inappropriate and unacceptable.

While the functions of the generations change with age and status, the age-set system confers a lifelong corporate identity, comradeship, and mutual dependency on its members. They grow from warriors to family men and gradually age to be tribal elders with an authoritative voice in public affairs.

Although territorial organization and the age-set system are the pillars of Dinka political order, the central unit that injects the blood of life into all the organs of Dinka social structure, whether based on territory, descent, or age, is the family. To the Dinka, the family is the backbone of society and the foundation of its value system. The main objective of the Dinka family is procreation and the continuity of the male line. The overriding goal of every Dinka is to marry and produce children, especially sons, "to keep the head upright," *koc nom*, after death. Dinka religion does not promise a heaven to come, and although the Dinka believe in some form of existence that conceptually projects this worldly life into a hereafter, death for them is an end from which the only salvation is continuity through posterity.

As Godfrey Lienhardt put it, "Dinka fear to die without male issue, in whom the survival of their names—the only kind of immortality they know—will be assured."[9] A man who dies without issue to carry on his name is said to perish, *riar*, and become truly mortal. But, even then, members of his family are under a moral obligation to marry a woman for him, to live with a relative and beget children to his name. Equally, a man who dies leaving behind a widow of childbearing age devolves a moral obligation on his kinsmen to have one of them cohabit with her to continue bearing children to his name. Deng Majok's desire for as many children as possible was therefore only an exaggeration of what is otherwise a fundamental theme in the Dinka social and religious outlook.

This worldly orientation of religion has the effect of making the Dinka intensely religious, with high standards of moral values that Ngok leadership, and especially Deng Majok, effectively utilized to consolidate peace, justice, and the rule of law. The consequences of good and evil for the Dinka are not deferred; they are here and now. And every illness or misfortune is believed to have some moral cause in the actions of the victim, a close relative, or an evil-doer. Charles and Brenda Seligman observed, "The Dinka, and their kindred the Nuer, are intensely religious, in our experience by far the most religious peoples in the Sudan."[10] Major Titherington, whose encounter with the Dinka goes back to the early days of colonial rule, wrote

---

9. *Divinity and Experience: The Religion of the Dinka* (Oxford: The Clarendon Press, 1961), p. 26.

10. *The Pagan Tribes of the Nilotic Sudan* (London: G. Routledge and Sons, 1932), 178. David Cole and Richard Huntington observed, in their *African Rural Development*, "If it is possible to rank peoples according to their religiosity, then the Dinka must be counted among some of the most religious peoples of the world. They are intensely respectful of Divinity in all of its many manifestations" (7).

of "the higher moral sense of the Dinka. Deliberate murder—as distinct from killing in a fair fight—is extremely rare. Pure theft— as opposed to the lifting of cattle by force or stealth after a dispute about their rightful ownership—is unknown; a man's word is his bond, and on the rare occasions when a man is asked to swear, his oath is accepted as a matter of course."[11]

In the words of Godfrey Lienhardt:

> God is held ultimately to reveal the truth and falsehood, and in doing so to provide a sanction for justice between men. Cruelty, lying, cheating and all other forms of injustice are hated by God, and the Dinka suppose that, in some way, if concealed by men, they will be revealed by him . . . God is made the final judge of right and wrong, when men feel sure that they are in the right. God is, then, the guardian of faith—and sometimes signifies to man what really is the case, behind or beyond their errors of falsehood.[12]

Morally and ethically, the Dinka divide the spiritual world in two under the overall command of the One God.[13] The clan spirits, *yieth* (singular *yath*), and the ancestors are virtuous and will harm a person only as a punishment for wrongdoing. Ancestral spirits are usually symbolized by totems of animate or inanimate existence and are treated as relatives to whom cattle are dedicated and sometimes slaughtered as a sacrifice. *Jak* (singular *jok*, pronounced differently from the founder of Pajok clan, Jok) are spirits that are essentially not related to specific clans but can be acquired from those already possessing them or may fall on individuals of their own choice. Of course, God and other all-embracing deities may also choose to fall on a person and possess him, but that freedom of choice, a prerogative of the Almighty and his close associates, is different from the whimsical and sometimes menacing self-imposition of the *jak*. Although they can be adopted, tamed, and used for good, *jak* are essentially evil and destructive. They are generally the cause of illness, misfortune, and death. The Dinka, indeed, refer to a serious illness or disease as *jok*. When God and the clan spirits are angered by wrongdoing, they will recruit *jak* to inflict harm, even death, as a punishment. *Jak* can also be summoned by an evil person to

---

11. "The Raik of Bahr el Ghazal Province," *Sudan Notes and Records*, 10 (1927): 159, 169.

12. *Divinity and Experience*, 46–47.

13. Dinka religion can be described as monotheistic in that they believe there is only one God, *Nhialic*, a word with the connotation of "above" or "in the Sky." As Lienhardt observed, the Dinka "assert with a uniformity that makes the assertion almost a dogma that 'Divinity (God) is one.' They cannot conceive of Divinity as a plurality and, did they know what it meant, would deeply resent being described as polytheistic" (156). But they also believe in a complex set of spirits, some of whom have godly attributes and are sometimes described as gods.

inflict unwarranted harm on an innocent one. And even if a person is not entirely innocent, the use of such methods as opposed to depending on God and the ancestral spirits for judgment is considered an evil deed that will sooner or later prove counterproductive and bring harm on the user. Such other practices as the use of witchcraft, the evil eye, oracles, or fetishes are particularly loathed as mean, immoral, and non-Dinka in origin.

The hierarchy of spiritual authority in this world is headed by the father as the representative of God and the ancestors. God is believed to create every person in the mother's womb, using man's "urine of birth," and although this means that both parents are partners in creation, the values of ancestral continuity give the father seniority over the mother. But dominant as men are in Dinka society, women occupy a paradoxically pivotal role, not only because they are the main source of wealth through marriage, but especially because society depends on them to rear children and inculcate in them the values on which the lineage system is founded. Because the relationship between the mother and the child is so intimate during the formative years of infancy and childhood, her influence is critical. A Dinka mother will nurse for two to three years, during which period she must devote her full attention to the child and avoid any sexual relationship with her husband. To violate this taboo is believed to cause a spiritual contamination that may bring illness and perhaps death, not only to the child, but also to other babies in the neighborhood.

On reaching the age of weaning, a child, whether male or female, especially a firstborn, is sent to the mother's relatives, where the maternal connection is reinforced. The relationship between a child and the maternal relatives, especially the grandfather and the uncle, is regarded as very special. Though the case of Deng Majok might be exceptional in degree, maternal relatives are generally believed to spoil their daughter's children, especially firstborns—and particularly sons. This is why the maternal grandfather and uncle are believed to be uniquely effective in their power to bless or curse, for they give a great deal that must affect the child's conscience, in which is rooted the efficacy of the curse.

And yet, while they develop in the child a special regard for his maternal side, the influence is not directed toward turning him against his paternal kin. On the contrary, the maternal relatives realize that his position in society is dependent on his role in his father's family and how well he manages to promote the interests of his clan. It is by succeeding among his paternal kin that a child can best project the image of his maternal relatives. So, as was the case with Deng Majok, the latter give him all the moral and material support they can in order to reinforce his position in his father's family.

Of course, the Dinka, including the women, recognize as a fundamental premise the continuity of the male line and the way it subordinates women to men, but mothers, both directly and through their male relatives, exert such a dominating influence on their children that society must guard against their potential threat to the male-oriented ancestral values.[14] The Dinka resolve this paradox by recognizing two modes of filial love and affection and ways of expressing them. Love for the mother is understood to be a function of the heart, which everyone knows a child feels but which society dictates should not be too conspicuously expressed or displayed. On the contrary, a child is expected to be very discreet about showing love and affection toward the mother, avoid calling her "Mother," and address her by her name. From an early age, a child is required to resist his mother's influence, especially if it detracts from the ancestral ideals of family unity and solidarity.

On the other hand, since love for the father is considered a function of the mind, it is expected to be cultivated and developed in a child and should be more visibly displayed, to make up for any deficiency in the natural sentiments of love. The importance of this function increases with the size of the family. (It was exceptionally great in the case of Deng Majok's family, but the principles involved apply to every Dinka father.) One must always refer to him as "Father," never by his name, must obey and revere him, and should take him as the model of what to be and do in the service of ancestral ideals. As the symbol of unity and solidarity around which family sentiments revolve, it is with and toward him that all should identify and demonstrate unreserved loyalty, even if that should entail an open disavowal of the sentiments for the mother and the maternal connection. By and large, the mother and her kin-group will understand that this show in no way detracts from their closer bond with the child.

The delicate balance between the collective interest of the family and the exclusive interest of the individual member is obvious in the manner in which marriages are celebrated.[15] Generally, the Dinka recognize two par-

---

14. The manner in which the clans divide into segments, resulting in a parochialism of loyalties at the expense of the wider unity of the clan, is sometimes attributed to the effect of women and maternal kin. For the story of how women allegedly caused the original break into clans, see Nebel, *Dinka Grammar* (1948), 129. For another story that demonstrates the tensions and conflicts between paternal and maternal loyalties, see *Dinka Grammar*, 134.

15. Godfrey Lienhardt explained Dinka ambivalence in this respect in the following words: "The Dinka positively value the unity of their tribes, and of their descent groups, while also valuing that autonomy of their component segments which can lead to fragmentations. The basis of this occasional contradiction lies in each Dinka ambition. . . . A man . . . wishes to belong to a large descent group because the greater the number of his agnatic kin who have still not formally segmented into separate agnatic groups, the wider the range of people from whom he can hope for help . . . in quarrels either within the tribe or outside it. On the other hand, each man wants to found his own descent group, a formal segment of the sub-clan which will for long be remembered by his name, and wants to withdraw from his more distant agnatic kin in order not to be required to help. . . . These values of personal autonomy and of cooperation, of the inclusiveness and unity of any wider political or genealogical segments and the exclusiveness and autonomy of its several subsegments are from time to time in conflict." "Western Dinka," in *Tribes without Rulers*, ed. Middleton and Tait (London, Routledge and Kegan Paul, 1958), 117–18.

allel procedures in the performance of marriage. Legal, social, and material formalities are left to be arranged or negotiated by the elders, while courtship aimed at winning the love, or at least the consent, of the girl is left to the man and his friends or members of his age-set. Theoretically, these two sets of roles should complement one another, but in fact, as the stories of Deng Majok's marriages so abundantly demonstrate, they do not always go together; indeed, they often come into conflict. When they do, the position of the elders theoretically should prevail; but to disregard the wishes of young men or women is not without its risks. Quite often, to counter the position of their elders or otherwise assert themselves, young people will resort to such alternatives as pregnancy, elopement, abduction, and, occasionally, especially for women, suicide. Dinka social attitudes allow a considerable measure of freedom for young men and women to meet and socialize, so there is always opportunity for a couple to plan and do whatever they wish.

The most important aspect of marriage among the Dinka is the exchange of cattle. Conversely, one of the most significant values of cattle among the Dinka is that they are directly responsible for the continuation of the lineage and the race, since it is with cattle that men procure wives to beget children to perpetuate the line. When a man is killed, whether intentionally or accidentally, his relatives are compensated with cattle, which must be used to find a wife who will live with one of them to beget children on behalf of the dead man. Because they are so important to the attainment of their overriding social and spiritual goals, the Dinka regard cattle as sacred, approximating human beings in value. They are indeed regarded as God's special gift to his chosen people, the Dinka, and therefore the most noble form of wealth.

Dinka mythology has it that God once gave the Black Man, by which they mean the Dinka, a choice between the cow and a secret gift called "What." When the man reached for the cow, God warned him to consider carefully, for there were great things in the secret of "What," but the Dinka kept eyeing the cow. God then said, "If you insist on having the cow, then I advise you to taste her milk before you decide." The Dinka tasted the milk and declared, "Let us have the cow and never see the secret of 'What.'" That secret was later given to the other races and became a source of their inquisitive minds, which eventually led them to scientific and technological inventiveness. The Dinka, on the other hand, has continued in his obsession with cattle.

And yet, except for the sacred bulls, which are consecrated to the ancestral spirits and are kept in the possession of the family head as studs, the most important animals from the viewpoint of aesthetic cultural preoccupation are oxen, which have the least economic value but with which young men identify themselves and are identified by the society. This is why they are known as "personality oxen." Ownership of personality oxen is determined by their colors. The Dinka distribute all conceivable color patterns to the male members of the family according to their mother's seniority of marriage and their own order of birth. The issue of color distribution was critical in the power struggle between Deng Majok and his half-brother Deng Abot. Any bull born into the herd or accruing through marriage automatically goes to the person whose color pattern it is. Once initiated, a man is then formally recognized as the owner of the ox or oxen with his color pattern, or is otherwise presented with one; and from then on the ox becomes a symbol of the young man's personality, individuality, and social status. Both in terms of courtesy and intimacy, he becomes known by a metaphoric name derived from the color pattern of his ox and otherwise fully assimilates himself into a world of poetic imagery and fantasy associated with his ox in any way, color, or shape.

While young men view personality oxen as symbols of virility, power, and defiance, a personality ox is a bull castrated from early calf-hood and therefore also symbolizes docility and submissiveness to the will of the "father," a term the Dinka apply to the relationship between the owner and the personality ox. The castrated bull-calf is raised by an owner who may ultimately not be the one to derive aesthetic pleasure from the full-grown bull. Once the ox has reached maturity, it may be kept by a member of the family or bartered for a cow. Usually, the prime mover is not the owner of the ox but the man interested in acquiring a personality ox, for which he is willing to give the more materially valuable cow-calf. Bartering for a bull is itself an important event celebrated by song, dance, and—ironically—a festive slaughtering of other animals for meat. It is significant that Deng Abot, who was assumed to have been undoubtedly loved by his father, gave as an example to the contrary the fact that his father bartered for Deng Majok's brother, Biong, and not for him, Deng Abot.

The Dinka love for cattle entails a great deal of labor. Every morning, as soon as the cattle are released to graze, the byre must be cleaned, the dung removed, the urine dried, and the place kept as neat and odorless as possible. Even the outside area in the home compound, where the cattle are tethered for a part of the morning or the evening and sometimes for the night, must be kept clean and dry. Cow-dung is taken every day and either spread on the farmland behind the homes for fertilizer or dried to be used as fuel. Boys and young men sleep in the ashes around the large conical heaps of smoldering dried cow-dung that provides the warmth and generates the smoke to discourage flies and mosquitoes. When not grazing around the village or farther afield, every animal is bound by a rope knotted around its neck and tied to a peg. A Dinka learns from childhood to recognize each rope and each peg for every animal, however large the herd.

The economic activities of the Dinka, which rotate around herding and farming, fall into four seasons.[16] *Ker*, the season beginning from May to early July, and *Ruel*, from July to October, make up the rainy season. *Rut*, extending from November to February, and *Mai*, from February to May, are

---

16. See Howell, "The Ngok Dinka," 243–45.

the dry season. During *Ker* the early rains fall, the fields which had been cleared earlier are planted, and the cattle gradually return to camp near the villages. Some cows are kept at home to provide milk for the villages. By the end of *Ker* and the beginning of *Ruel* in July, mosquitoes proliferate and it becomes necessary to bring the cattle home for protection in the cattle-byres at night. *Ruel* is the period of heavy rains and permanent residence in the villages. Most of the agricultural work, including harvest, falls in this season. The second crop, *anguol*, which sprouts from the cut stems of the old crop, is harvested in the middle of *Rut*. The cattle, which have been taken away to far-off camps to protect the farms, are brought back to the villages during the harvesting of the second crop. This is a period when the farms have to be properly protected from the cattle, as they crave the flavor of the second crop. Conflicts often occur between cattle-owners and the farmers because of crop destruction. *Rut* is the coldest season, as the north winds come in November. As the pasture is exhausted, the cattle are driven out in small herds to graze farther away along the upper reaches of the watercourses. During *Mai*, the distant camps begin to grow in size, as there is little grass left near the permanent villages. This is the hottest time of the year: water supplies are scanty and wells are dug near the permanent settlements. This is the season of disease, and the Dinka eagerly await the blessings of the early rains of *Ker*.

Despite its environmental hardships and the labor involved, cattle camping is an experience of great joy and aesthetic gratification for the Dinka. In far-off areas, many families or sections herd together, forming large camps that may stretch over miles in diameter. Since it brings together young men and women who are not necessarily related by blood, cattle camping provides an excellent opportunity for flirtation and courting. For the same reason, it is also an occasion for heightened preoccupation with the aesthetics of self-decoration, the singing display of personality oxen, and the exhilarating pleasures of song and dance.[17]

Dinka values and practices relating to cattle generally reflect the politi-

---

17. Major Treatt observed this aspect of Dinka life: "During the rainy season, the cattle are grazed during the day and brought into their special houses at night; but as the rainy season ceases, and the receding water leaves behind a tangled mass of nourishing grass, there comes to the Dinkas the most blissful period of their lives when they trek with their beloved beasts to the cattle camps on the edges of the swamps where, setting up striped posts to guard beasts from evil, they settle down to a picnic life in which every day is to them a high day and holiday" (124–25).

Major Treatt apparently shared their sentiments, though, of course, only from a romantic standpoint: "Writing in prosaic London, with its cold-faced buildings and smell-less streets alive with energy, with fire and food and light obtainable, so to speak, at the mere pressing of a button, I find myself longing for the lazy beauty of one of their cattle-camps or I picture the ash-covered Dinkas singing and dancing around their drowsy animals while the smoke rising in sleepy spirals from the dung piles is silhouetted against the glow of the setting sun. You can keep all your electricity and inventions, all your so-called luxury and hygiene, but give me the warm light of Africa and the smell of the manure-smoke fires of the Dinkas" (125).

cal, economic, social, and cultural themes of their life in general. It is significant that the first real conflict between Deng Majok and Deng Abot occurred over the issue of which of the brothers had the authority to decide when and where the cattle should move while camping far away from home.

And, indeed, most of the tensions and disputes within and among groups in Dinka society are in one way or another connected with cattle. As Deng Majok's dramatic appropriation of his father's cattle shows, competition over cattle can be crucial in the relations between brothers and between fathers and sons. Urging relations to contribute to a marriage, claiming a share in the bride-price, demanding compensation for sexual or physical offenses, and seeking to enforce all kinds of kinship rights and obligations connected with the distribution of cattle are among the many reasons for the notorious litigiousness of the Dinka. Competition for pastures or sources of water and the defense of herds against cattle raids or seizure in self-execution of debts are among the factors that account for the warlike reputation of the Dinka.

The main dance among the Ngok Dinka, *Lor*, is essentially a war dance and includes all the acrobatic skills of warfare, displayed to the tune of drums and songs of battles actually fought or slanderous words leveled against past and future enemies. Each subtribe enters the dance scene in a stampede heightened by the emotions of their own songs, with which they then dominate the dance. The other subtribes, especially past or potential enemies, withdraw to regroup and return again, booming their own songs. As men move, or leap or run, parrying spears in throwing positions or acting as though they have hit the enemy, girls curve and fold their arms in a symbolic retreat from the otherwise bullish, though sensually subtle, approaches of the dancing warriors. With the introduction of hostile war songs and the presence of the girls, the dance may become emotionally charged; tensions can mount to the point where the chief has to intervene, ending the dance or otherwise ensuring that no violence erupts. Nevertheless, the provocation of the dance may result in a declaration of war. It was under such circumstances that Deng Majok distinguished himself as a peacemaker and the leader most capable of ending the violence of tribal warfare, thereby outwitting his father and rival brother.

Despite the warlike profile of the Dinka, their moral values emphasize the ideals of peace, unity, harmony, persuasiveness, and mutual cooperation. Ironically, it was through these traditional values, built upon in a modernizing framework, that Deng Majok won his popularity and influence as an ideal leader by both traditional and modern criteria. These values are highly institutionalized and expressed in a concept known as *cieng*, which is fundamental to Dinka moral and civic order. Godfrey Lienhardt writes of *cieng*: "The Dinka . . . have notions . . . of what their society ought, ideally, to be like. They have a word, *cieng baai*, which used as a verb has the sense of 'to look after' or 'to order,' and in its noun form means 'the custom' or 'the rule.' "[18] Father Nebel translates *morals* as "good *cieng*" and *benefactor* as a man who knows and acts in accordance with *cieng*. He also translates *cieng* to mean "behavior," "habit," "nature of," or "custom."[19]

At the core of *cieng* are such "human" values as dignity and integrity, honor and respect, loyalty and piety, and the power of persuasiveness. *Cieng* does not merely advocate unity and harmony through attuning individual interests to the interests of others; it requires assisting one's fellowmen. Good *cieng* is opposed to coercion and violence, for solidarity, harmony, and mutual cooperation are more fittingly achieved voluntarily and by persuasion.

Cieng has the sanctity of a moral order not only inherited from the ancestors, who had in turn received it from God, but also fortified and policed by them. Failure to adhere to its principles is not only disapproved of as an antisocial act warranting punishment, but, more importantly, as a violation of the moral code that may invite a spiritual curse—illness or death, according to the gravity of the violation. Conversely, a distinguished adherence to the ideals of *cieng* receives temporal and spiritual rewards. Although *cieng* is a concept with roots in the heritage of the ancestors who still sanction adherence to its principles as an ideal order, it is largely an aspiration that is only partially adhered to and, indeed, often negated. Hence, it can be improved upon even through innovation. Deng Majok's achievements in this respect were viewed as much as a fulfillment of traditional ideals as an innovation.

The contradiction between the requirements of *cieng* and the violent reputation of the Dinka can be explained in terms of the gap between the ideal and the real, institutionally manifest in the differences between generational roles. While elders strive to live by the ideals, the young warriors find self-fulfillment, social recognition, and dignity in their valor, fighting ability, and defensive solidarity. Consequently, they tend to overindulge in militancy, often provoking wars that must be fought by all. Nevertheless, frequent and pervasive as it is, warfare reflects a negation of the ideals, an alternative that should only be resorted to when peaceful methods have failed. This is why Deng Majok's successful abolition of tribal warfare was so highly appreciated by the Dinka as a fulfillment of what they had always aspired to but had tragically always violated for lack of effective control over the aggressiveness of the warrior age-sets on the part of the leaders.

One of the ways in which Dinka culture sustains a level of conformity and continuity is by providing alternative access to dignity that accommodates and institutionalizes even elements of what would otherwise be a violation of the norms. Age is a form of social recognition that gives every Dinka a deep sense of worth and dignity almost in itself. As I have already mentioned, an

---

18. Lienhardt, "Western Dinka," 106–07.
19. Nebel, *Dinka Dictionary* (1954), 315.

initiated man is *adheng*, a "gentleman"; his virtue is *dheeng* (dignity). But initiation is only a key or a point of entry to the complex values of *dheeng* and their varied avenues to individual and social dignity. *Dheeng* is a word of multiple meanings—all positive. As a noun, it means nobility, beauty, handsomeness, elegance, charm, grace, gentleness, hospitality, generosity, good manners, discretion, and kindness. Except in prayer or on certain religious occasions, singing and dancing are *dheeng*. Personal decoration, initiation ceremonies, celebrations or marriages, the display of "personality oxen"— indeed, any demonstrations of aesthetic value, are considered *dheeng*. The social background of a man, his physical appearance, the way he walks, talks, eats, or dresses, and the way he behaves toward his fellowmen are all factors in determining his *dheeng*.

From its various meanings, one can discern at least three kinds of *dheeng* or dignity. The first is the status people acquire through material resources and social responsiveness, which is measured not only in terms of generosity and hospitality but also by personal integrity and responsible conduct. The second derives from birth or marriage into a family with already established status. The third is more sensual in nature and stems from physical attractiveness and various forms of aesthetic display.

To the Dinka, power and wealth must serve moral and social ends or else they do not confer *dheeng* on the holder. The word for chief, *bany*, also means "rich" or "wealthy"; but a man of wealth who is stingy or frugal is *ayur*, the opposite of *adheng*. Conversely, a man of modest means who is generous and hospitable is praised as *adheng*, and even as *bany*. On the other hand, a man who is exaggeratedly generous or hospitable far beyond his means is considered vain and a show-off; although he is not despised in the way a stingy person with means would be, his performance falls short of *dheeng*. The ideal behavior is for a person to have the means and to display a social consciousness commensurate with them. That is *adheng* in the classic sense. It is therefore not surprising that Deng Majok's exceptional generosity and hospitality and the abundance of his sources of wealth are often correlated.

Since the dependent members of the family, women and children, do not control the material means to *dheeng* except with the consent of their elders, they have to preoccupy themselves with the second and third avenues to the dignity of *dheeng*. Women pride themselves on being wives and mothers; youths, especially males, take pride in being the descendants of a particular line. Women and children brag a great deal, especially in songs, about being the wives or progeny of a particular person or family line. A Dinka wife will refer to her husband interchangeably as "he" or "I," thereby identifying herself with him and vicariously enjoying his status and dignity. A father or mother is designated by the name of the firstborn, male or female, as Father or Mother of so and so. In the case of a polygynous father, this must be the firstborn of his first wife. This title carries with it both respect and intimacy, an honor which Deng Majok felt deprived of when his father assumed the name of Deng Abot's elder sister and became known as Wun-Agorot, Father of Agorot, even though he, Deng Majok, was his oldest son.

So important is family affiliation that to be a divorced woman or a widow or an orphan (a status the Dinka extend to adults) is to be deprived and degraded. The death of a mother, acknowledged to be exceptionally close to the child as she is, afflicts the orphan, especially of a young age, with a severe social disadvantage. Such a child should be given much attention and love, not only by the father, but also by the stepmother; these, however, are attempts to compensate for a loss that cannot be remedied. Although his mother died after having had six children, Deng Majok and his brothers and sisters are generally considered to have been "orphaned" by their mother, and although they were well treated by their father and stepmother, they nevertheless suffered the indignity of inequitable treatment as a result of their mother's death.

Although the family identification is important to *dheeng*, it is self-adornment and the aesthetic which most preoccupy youths and women as a way of enhancing their status and dignity. These comprise a whole range of concerns and activities. Natural beauty or handsomeness is a great blessing. To be physically complete in the sense that one is without an obvious defect is so essential that to be lame, blind, deaf, or in any way disabled or deformed is to be plunged into an indignity for which only the most unusual persons can adequately compensate; but when they do, they win remarkable recognition for dignity. Otherwise, social consciousness dictates that handicapped persons be shown courtesy and given due care, though this merely underlines the disadvantages they suffer.

Among the Dinka, too, physical attractiveness can be other than a gift of God. There is much every Dinka can and does do to enhance an already existing beauty or handsomeness or to create attraction where there might otherwise be none. Beautification with beads and bangles, making up with colored ashes and oil, and bleaching the hair reddish or blond are examples of the preliminaries to full-blown aesthetic display. Chief Babo's memory of Deng Majok, when he first met him in 1923, as "a striking young man, decorated with Dinka ornaments—ivory bangles and a set of metal coils on his arms," shows both the place of these objects in Dinka aesthetics and Deng Majok's early preoccupation with his appearance. It is noteworthy that Babo added: "But of course, he was clothed," which revealed the other side of Deng Majok—innovativeness. Chol Piok's description of ambushed Nainai as he lay dying also illustrates the importance the Dinka attach to ornamental beautification: "He was a striking gentleman, wearing four ivory bangles on his upper arms and large copper coils on both his lower arms, the kinds of coils our people used to wear. And in addition, he had a large string of blue beads wound around his waistline."

The most institutionalized forms of this aesthetic display are singing and dancing. How the Dinka gratify their inner pride through song and dance is easily apparent in the way in which they bear themselves in the process. While singing or dancing, a Dinka puts himself into a trancelike state that is easier felt than described. Here, too, the image of Deng Majok looms high in the memory of the Dinka. Witness these lines from his dancing chant:

> Oh Kon, Kon, son of Dau,
> I am a gentleman who dances without fearing his bones
> A gentleman as graceful as something delicious.

But singing and dancing are mere gestures in an overall association of aesthetic beauty with artistic movement. A Dinka is aware that the way he bears himself in any activity of a physical nature is as important as the substantive meaning of the activity. An extension of these aesthetic concerns is manners—not only the etiquette governing one's behavior toward others, but also standards of a personal nature. These are prescribed for all, but are more vigorous for men beyond the age of initiation but short of old age. The concept of a "gentleman," *adheng,* is very pronounced in Dinka society. A gentleman should be composed, should not wander about in a way that elicits invitations; and when issued an invitation should not readily accept. Saying no to invitations is practiced to the point of hypocrisy. But the opposite, being the host, calls for a determined and insistent self-assertiveness that cannot be refused. The way Deng Majok walked with his head poised high above his long neck and the way he is said to have restricted the circles from which he would accept invitations, not to mention his notorious reputation for exaggerated generosity and hospitality, show how he fared in respect to these aesthetic values.

A final set of concepts crucial to the values of leadership and according to which Deng Majok proved himself beyond doubt are *dom,* establishing control over a group, *muk,* maintaining and sustaining the group, and *guier,* improving the lot of the group. Each of these concepts connotes the observance of the principles of *cieng* and *dheeng.* A chief establishes control and "holds" the land or the group, not only by the mere fact of wielding power and authority, but also by using his position wisely to ensure peace, security, and prosperity. The continuity or stability of that state of affairs is maintained through *muk,* which literally means "keeping," a word also applied to child-rearing, including handling, feeding, looking after, protecting, and raising. *Guier* goes a step further to imply improvement of the existing situation, whether through reconstruction or reform. These values are mutually reinforcing and cyclic in nature. When a chief has taken over the reins of power (*dom*), has stabilized his benevolent control over the situation (*muk*), and has introduced reforms to ensure a constructive and stable leadership (*guier*), he is described as having held (*dom*) the land. There can be no doubt that Deng Majok during his lifetime did all three.

Traditionally, a Dinka chief is not a ruler in the Western sense but a spiritual leader whose power rests on divine enlightenment and wisdom.[20] In his installation ceremonies, people raise his right hand toward the sky, symbolizing the will of his people and acceptance by the divine powers above. In the case of aggression against his tribe, when force is necessary to stop force, the chief should pray for victory far away from the battlefield. In a war between his own factions, he should not take sides, but rather should pray for victory, draw a symbolic line, and place his sacred spear upon it, while willing that the group that crosses it to attack will suffer heavy casualties. In order to reconcile his people, the chief should be a model of virtue, righteousness, and, in Dinka terms, "a man with a cool heart," who must depend on persuasion and consensus rather than on coercion and dictation. The word for "court" or "trial," *luk*, also means "to persuade." Godfrey Lienhardt wrote on this aspect of the Dinka:

> I suppose anyone would agree that one of the most decisive marks of a society we should call in a spiritual sense "civilized" is a highly developed sense and practice of justice, and here, the Nilotics, with their intense respect for the personal independence and dignity of themselves and of others, may be superior to societies more civilized in the material sense. . . . The Dinka and Nuer are a warlike people, and have never been slow to assert their rights as they see them by physical force. Yet, if one sees Dinka trying to resolve a dispute, according to their own customary law, there is often a reasonableness and a gentleness in their demeanor, a courtesy and a quietness in the speech of those elder men superior in status and wisdom, an attempt to get at the whole truth of the situation before them.[21]

Paul Howell has observed that the chief among the Dinka

> cannot impose his authority without the consent of the people. In this sense, he represents the "voice of the people" and articulates their wishes. He is invited to arbitrate and by patient persuasion leads the disputants to reach a compromise. [He] has, of course, ritual powers which strengthen and emphasize his function in society as a peacemaker. He articulates moral values inherent in the social system. He has the power to curse but is not expected to use his powers to his own ends and certainly does not impose his authority by threat or curse, unless, in so doing, he is in fact representing the opinion of the more level-headed elements.[22]

Despite the ideals of Dinka concepts of power, a conspicuous factor in

---

20. Cole and Huntington have noted: "At the center of Dinka religion are The Masters of the Spear, among the Ngok it is the great chief, *bany dit*, who is holder of the Sacred Spears" (chap. 5, p. 7).

21. "Man in Society," in *The Listener* (London: B.B.C. 1963), 828. See also Lienhardt, *Divinity and Experience,* 248.

22. "The Ngok Dinka," 262–63. See also Deng, *Tradition and Modernization,* 149–50.

resistance of the warrior Nilotic tribes, the South was never penetrated by the Arabs, even though it remained a hunting ground for slaves and big game.

The division between South and North has been formalized and reinforced by more recent political developments. The Turko-Egyptian rule of the Ottoman Empire, which began in 1821 and continued until 1885, was Islamic; and although it could not extend effective control over the South, except for a flourishing trade in slaves and a succession of terrorizing expeditions, its policies reinforced the Arab Islamic identity of the North and therefore the South-North dichotomy.[4] However, being corrupt, oppressive, and alien, the Turko-Egyptian administration was resented and resisted as a government of infidels.

The situation exploded in 1882 when the nationalist leader, Mohamed Ahmed, who soon became known as the Mahdi (the Savior), mobilized the Sudanese people against the Turks, meeting with spontaneous, nationwide support that cut across the South-North dividing line. Initially armed with only spears and swords, the Mahdists won battle after battle, growing increasingly zealous and confident in the process, until they succeeded in miraculously overthrowing the Turkish regime in 1885. The final showdown ended the life of General Gordon, the British hero of the China war who had been commissioned jointly by Britain and Egypt to evacuate Khartoum but had overstretched his mandate in the hope of defeating the Mahdists; Khartoum fell and Sudan became independent. The Mahdi died shortly afterward, but his successor, Khalifa Abdullahi, ran a theocratic state with an iron hand that was to devastate the country for thirteen years. Although the Mahdists, like the Turks before them, never succeeded in controlling the South, the whole period of the nineteenth century is remembered by the Dinka as "the time when the world was spoiled," a total destruction of the world as they knew it.

The Anglo-Egyptian reconquest of 1898 ironically restored the Sudan to colonial status but brought relief to the peoples of both the North and the South. While introducing social and economic development to the North, the British recognized and respected the Arab Islamic identity and even characterized the government as Muslim. On the other hand, they viewed the South as pagan and primitive, requiring protection and tutelage but little, if any, development.[5] Although Christian missionaries were excluded from the

---

4. Robert Collins has noted, "It was not until the Egyptian Government opened the Bahr el Ghazal and Equatoria provinces and brought relative security and unity to the Sudan, that the trade assumed gigantic proportions." *The Southern Sudan,* 14.

5. See Collins, *Shadows in the Grass: Britain in the Southern Sudan, 1918-1956* (New Haven and London: Yale University Press, 1983), 14-15. For details of the separate policies adopted toward the South and North in the religious, educational, and economic fields, see also Beshir Mohamed Said, *Cross-Roads of Africa* (London: Bodley Head, 1965); Deng, *Dynamics of Identification,* especially chapters 2 and 3; Mohamed Omer Beshir, *The Southern Sudan: Background to Conflict* (London: Hurst, 1968).

North, in the South they were licensed and encouraged to play a "civilizing" role in "spheres of influence," which was defined as helping to avoid denominational rivalry and conflict. By law, the southern region was regarded as "Closed Districts," and contact between the South and the North was regulated and severely restricted.

In both the North and the South, the British adopted indirect rule, leaving the administration of the tribes to their chiefs with only occasional visits by the British District Commissioner. And yet, through their remote control, the British established peace, security, justice, and a system of civic order that contrasted sharply with what had previously prevailed.[6] Of course, the British were resented and resisted as foreign rulers, and a nationalist movement, spearheaded by Egypt and the North, eventually mobilized the whole nation into a movement for independence. But so wide was the gap between North and South, that when Sudanization came in 1955, of the eight hundred posts that had been occupied by the colonial powers, only four junior positions went to the South. In August 1955, southern fear of Arab domination triggered a mutiny that began with a battalion but soon spread throughout the South. It was eventually contained only because of the intervention of the British governor-general, who, though at the tail end of his rule, promised justice for the rebels and was still trusted.

The southern Sudanese were able to agree with the northern Sudanese on the declaration of independence on January 1, 1956, with the understanding that the southern call for a federal relationship with the North would be given full consideration. That consideration was never given. The reaction of the South began to develop into a civil war that was to continue for seventeen years until it was ended by the Addis Ababa Accord of 1972, which was promptly enacted into law as the Southern Sudan Provinces Regional Self-Government Act (1972), and gave the South regional autonomy within national unity.

The stability the Nimeri regime subsequently enjoyed was in no small measure due to this agreement, which dramatically changed southern attitudes from separatism to a desire for unity. Undoubtedly the most significant achievement of Nimeri's regime, the solution gave the Sudan a tremendous political, economic, and strategic boost in international relations. Problems later surfaced in the South surrounding the extent to which the Addis Ababa agreement was being implemented or violated, and Sudan is now back in a state of civil war.

While the line of demarcation between the North and the South has been neatly drawn and observed in the history of modern Sudan, the Ngok Dinka present somewhat of an anomaly on the South-North borders. Their land,

---

6. Sir James Robertson, the civil secretary of the crucial years leading to independence, wrote in his *Transition in Africa* (London: C. Hurst and Company, 1974), 8–9: "Our duty in our districts was to keep the peace, to see that fair dealing was meted out to the people, and that the Sudanese were not sacrificed to foreign enterprise or foreign development."

being ideally suited for both agriculture and animal husbandry, is a seasonal meeting point between the pastoral tribes of both the North and the South, who go there in search of pastures and water. Although ethnically and culturally a southern people, the Ngok have been administered in Kordofan, one of the provinces of the North, since the days of colonial intervention. For these economic and administrative reasons, the Ngok area has become a crossroads between the North and the South.

This unique position has been fostered and reinforced by the bridging role that Ngok leaders have consistently played on the South-North border for a number of generations. Ngok legends of leadership begin with Jok, the founding father of the leading lineage, Pajok. Dinka myths of creation have their Adam and Eve, Garang and Abuk (with their son Deng); and, with some effort, Pajok lineage can be traced several generations beyond Jok.[7] But mythology has it that Jok was the one who opened the Byre of Creation and enabled his people, the Dinka, to exit into freedom. This is how he acquired his praise name, Athurkok, "The One Who Broke Through."[8]

Jok emerged from the Byre of Creation with two large "Sacred Spears," one leaflike and one lancelike, symbolizing his spiritual powers to bless and curse. To this day, these spears have remained the insignia of chieftainship among the Ngok Dinka. Otherwise, the power of Pajok's lineage is said to be derived from their clan spirit, Ring, "The Flesh," so-called because divine power is believed to be inherent in their being.

Having opened the Byre of Creation, Jok subsequently overcame a series of challenges. On his way, he was confronted by a large river which he could not cross because of the hostility of the powers in the waters. Sometimes described as spiritual beings and sometimes as people, these powers are said to have been "truly white."[9] Jok tried to negotiate his way by offering

---

7. In the version given Godfrey Lienhardt by Chief Giir Kiro (otherwise known as Giir Thiik), Jok is referred to as one of the descendants of Agothyithiik of Paghol, the dominant lineage of the Apuk Rek Dinka. "Jok became big and took the land" and "Mathiangdit (a praise name for some un-named person), the son of Jok, became important and seized the country." Lienhardt also notes that "the sub-tribes in which Pajok lineage has primacy are large and flourishing." In Giirdit's version, the eldest son of Agothyithiik is said to be Anau, and in Pajok's nomenclature Jok is said to be the son of Man-Angau (The Mother of Angau) which sounds close to Man-Anau (Anau's mother). Giirdit's eldest son, Mou, in the interview with his father, concluded with his father's affirmation, "Actually, the name of the clan Paghol (their clan) includes Pajok." See Deng, *Cosmology*, 39, and *Africans of Two Worlds*, 37–40.

8. The Dinka obviously do not seriously believe that life began with Jok. Dating the origin of the Pajok to the time of creation is merely a metaphor that revitalizes Dinka belief that God has a hand in the creation of every individual. The values associated with God's involvement become particularly pronounced in the case of divine leaders, especially during challenging historical moments. The first to be created means being inspired to provide spiritual leadership as God's chosen son in a given community, at a given moment of time, and under a particular set of critical circumstances.

9. Some of the versions of the myth mention the powers in the river as men, and sometimes there is also a mention of a man in a saddle, which presumably refers to early contact with

them cattle and other material goods, but the powers remained hostile and unmoved. In the face of strong protest by the tribe, Jok decided to surrender to the river powers his only daughter, Achai, in order to save his people. Having first decked her out in ivory bangles, beads, shells, and other ornaments of beautification, Jok held Achai's hand and walked with her into the river, singing the hymns of his lineage and holding the Sacred Spears pointed backward to indicate the peacefulness of his intentions. As soon as the water was deep enough to reach Achai's head, she was seized by the powers of the river, which then caused the waters to recede, allowing the people to cross on dry land.[10]

Jok later competed for leadership with Longar, the founder of Dhiendior clan. The legend of Longar as the spiritual hero of the Dinka is widely spread among all the Dinka tribes.[11] But among the Ngok, spiritual leadership is attributed to Jok, perhaps because of the recognition, support, and reinforcement that his lineage has received from their Arab neighbors to the north and the successive administrations on the national level. With the flexibility and adaptability for which oral history is known, mythology has been reinterpreted and molded to explain and justify existing realities.

Longar is now presented in the oral history of the Ngok as a rival leader, half-brother, or relative who claimed to be spiritually more powerful than Jok and therefore the leader. Longar issued a challenge to Jok that they let their sacred bulls, after being invoked, fight to determine whose prayers would bring victory to his bull.[12] Jok's animal, Mijok, was a peaceful and gentle bull who kept his distance from the herd and generally behaved like a chief. Longar's bull, Mangar, on the other hand, was aggressive; with his long, sharpened horns, he had terrorized the bulls and killed many. Jok was at first reluctant, but, pushed by Longar, he accepted the challenge. Nevertheless, the attack came almost as a surprise. Longar's bull approached the

---

foreigners who might have been horse-riders. Dinka reference to these people as "truly white" might be an exaggeration of what must then have been still an unfamiliar skin color of the Europeans or the Arabs.

10. According to Titherington ("The Raik Dinka," in *Sudan Notes and Records* [1927], 21), the Dinka did not "take to the vile, but common practice of selling their fellow tribesmen into slavery." If it is assumed that Jok was forced to surrender his daughter to slave traders so as to permit his people to cross the river, it is obvious from the moral attitude described by Titherington what a tragedy it must have been. This is presumably why tradition has conceptualized and preserved it as an act of human sacrifice to the spiritual powers of the river rather than a surrender into slavery.

11. For the various versions of the myth of Longar collected by Lienhardt from the Western Dinka, see *Divinity and Experience*.

12. While men identify with castrated bulls as personality-oxen used primarily for aesthetic display, the Head of the Family usually possesses a full bull—a stud—dedicated to ancestral sacred spirits and regarded as sacred, to be kept in the herd and eventually killed in sacrifice to the clan deities when it reaches an advanced age. The power of the bull is supposed to symbolize the spiritual power of the Head of the Family as the worldly representative of God and other deities, including ancestral spirits.

it is camouflaged as "play," they obeyed my orders with a will. Endless lines of yelling natives rushed hither and thither with our boxes, sweat and falling rain streaking their covering of gray wood ash so that they resembled a crowd of striped and ghostly shapes. But amongst them all one tall Dinka, standing naked in the centre of the turmoil and urging on the flying figures with shrewd and mighty blows from a massive club, caught my eye. Suddenly, I realised that this was no less a personage than Kwol himself, Kwol who had discarded his "uniform" at the first sign of rain and carefully rolled it in a cow-skin. Where trouble was at hand, the excellent fellow had "come off his perch" and in that downpour he stood as human and as naked as the humblest of his followers.[23]

K. D. D. Henderson, having been District Commissioner in the area between 1930 and 1936, was unequivocal in his admiration of Kwol Arob. In a letter dated February 24, 1932, during his first visit to the area while inaugurating the opening of the first "road" to Abyei, he wrote, "The Chief, Kwol Arob, is a most impressive figure, though a bare six foot six inches and so shorter than most of his people." Some days later, in a letter dated March 3, he added, "There can be no doubt that Kwol is an extraordinarily fine Chief and settles all their disputes justly and finally." In his response to the questionnaire of this study, Henderson's admiration of Kwol Arob continued undiminished by the passage of time. He wrote, "I regarded Kwol as a most outstanding ruler and his people as a completely *adult* race."

Later on, the British reduced Kwol's dominion by splitting tribes off one by one and giving them their independence under the administration of the southern provinces. Eventually, they offered Kwol himself the option of disaffiliating his tribe from Kordofan and joining his people in the South, but Kwol preferred to remain in the North to continue the bridging role his father had begun—primarily to provide protection for his people, but ostensibly to promote South-North cooperation on the borders.

Chief Giir Thiik, who witnessed the discussions in which the British and the southern leaders tried to persuade Kwol Arob to join the southern administration, had this to say about the event: "We talked—your grandfather was brought by the government—your grandfather, the great Kwol son of Arob; and he said, 'You, Kwol, you are like an Arab—but you are a Dinka. I would like you to unite with the other Dinka and become the district of

---

23. *Out of the Beaten Track*, 50–51. Sir James Robertson, who served as District Commissioner in the area between 1934 and 1936, notes in *Transition in Africa:* "Chief Kwol Arob of the Ngok Dinka [who] lived in a buffer area between the Arabs and the great mass of the Dinka to the South . . . had the diplomatic habit of changing his dress to suit his company. When he came North to Muglad he would don the flowing white robes and turbans of an Arab sheikh; going South, he wore the topee, shirt, tie and trousers of a Southern Chief; but in his own country, he appeared in the usual Dinka dress—nothing more than a few beads" (50–51).

Gogrial.' Your grandfather refused." After refusing to join the South, Kwol pulled Giirdit aside.

> We went and stood a distance away. Then he said to me, "Son of my father, what you tell me, it is not that I do not know it. . . . If I were to pull away from the Arab, he would destroy my things. If I were to turn my back on him, he would spoil my things. So please leave me. And if my people increase one day and they know the way things are done and know that they are one people with you, they will come. No one forgets where he belongs. I will come to you. But if I were to come to you now and speak toward Wau, the Arab would spoil the things behind my back. . . . Even of this land of mine he might say, 'It's my land.'"

Under Deng Majok, Ngok area even more than ever before became a meeting ground for the neighboring pastoral peoples of both the North and the South. Arabs would come down in search of water and grass during the dry season, while southern tribes would move up during the rainy season to escape the floods. Because of its administrative position and its significance as an intertribal and interracial grazing ground, Ngok area became a national crossroads and a microcosm of the Sudan, in much the same way that the Sudan is a microcosm of Africa.[24]

---

24. K. D. D. Henderson, after explaining that "if the South, while remaining essentially Southern, could yet become an integral part of an independent Sudan it could help to bridge the inevitable gulf between Muslim and non-Muslim, Asian and African, white or brown and black, in the African future," goes on to say, "The Ngok Dinka, on the Bahr el Arab, had joined Kordofan Province at the reoccupation and had played precisely such a role as intermediaries between the Homr Baggara and the Dinka of the Bahr al Ghazal." *Sudan Republic* (London: Ernest Benn Limited, 1965), 164n.

Part 2: Power

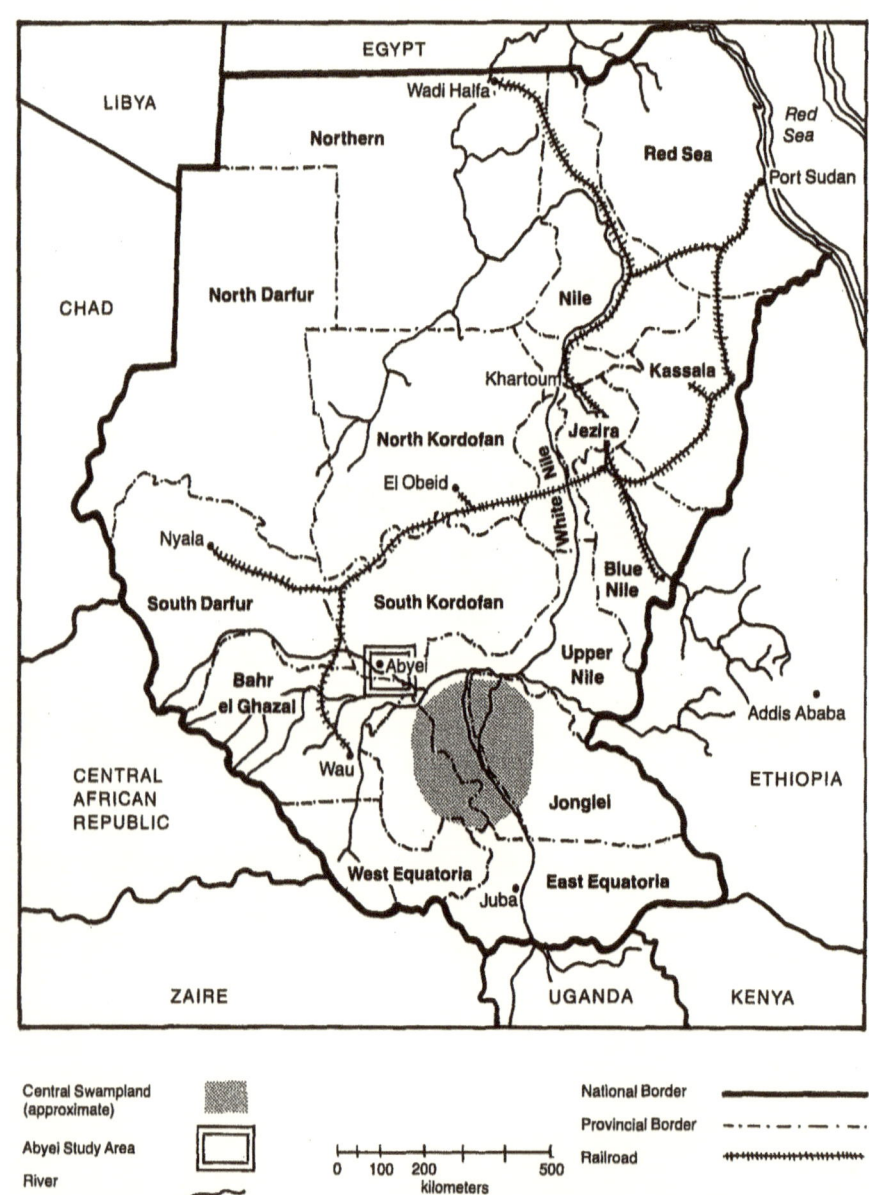

Map 2   The Map of the Sudan

5   *The Struggle for Recognition*

When Deng Majok was still in his twenties, he paid a visit to his great uncle, an elder by the name of Bulabek Biong, as he lay dying. Achwil Bulabek, one of the dying man's sons, was there. He gave this account of what transpired between his father and Deng Majok.

> Deng Majok came to my father and said: "Grandfather [Great Uncle] I have come because I have heard that you are dying. Our people have their own traditions. It is said that the people of our clan do not contest for chieftainship; that if chieftainship is contested, it will cause death. That is why I came to ask you. Here we are both under our father. Our father is of course still strong. The spirit of death does not distinguish between children and elders. If it chooses to kill a child, that child will die. If it chooses to kill one's father and the father dies, then a son is expected to step into the position of his father. What I want is the truth. What should I do if the question of succession arises in the future?"
>
> My father then said, "You, Deng, I am going to tell you the truth. I am not going to live any longer. And I am not going to leave you with a word that might lead you to the curse of death. I have nothing more to gain from trying to win your friendship. You will no longer buy me any clothing so that people can say Bulabek has become a friend of Deng. Let me tell you that it was to the wedding of your mother, Nyanaghar, that we, the sons of Biong, all went; we did not go to Kwol's second marriage, the wedding of Abiong, the mother of Deng Abot. That was performed by your grandfather, Arob, alone. But all the four of us (half-brothers of Arob) went to your mother's wedding. When our marriage to your mother was rejected, our ancestral spirits followed her until she was brought back to us. That was something

the sons of one man did together. So, with respect to chieftainship, if the people of the tribe should oppose your becoming chief, leave it; do not push for it. But if the tribe should want you to be chief, then accept it willingly. You will not be accursed with even a headache if seniority is the qualification. Your mother is the senior wife. So, no illness will befall you on account of seniority. And now, give me your hand." Deng extended his right hand. My father held it. Then he raised it up: he raised it up three times. Bol, the son of my mother was there; and Miyan, the son of my father was there. They were witnesses. Deng cried. He cried over his dying Uncle.

The story of how Deng Majok succeeded his father, Kwol Arob, is a drama with deep roots in the background of Kwol's marriage to Deng's mother, Nyanaghar, whose great-great-grandmother, Awut, was a captive princess from the Beigo. It is not clear whether the Beigo were Arab, African, or a mixture. They are sometimes described by the Dinka as "Arab" and sometimes identified with Shatt. Though the Ngok use the term *Arab* rather loosely, the Beigo were in all probability not Arab.[1] They inhabited part of the land the Ngok now occupy, stretching northward. The Ngok and the Beigo used to fight and seize captives who were taken as slaves. The Dinka practice, however, was quickly to adopt and assimilate such captives as family members to the point where their outside origin soon became obscured. If they were girls, they were considered "daughters" or "sisters" by their "masters," who would then marry them off with cattle as they would any female relatives. Awut had been the daughter of a Beigo chief and was honored as such even in her captivity.

Patal Biliw gave this account of Awut and the roots of her impressive destiny:

Awut was a girl from the Beigo—the people called the Beigo who inhabited this area before the Ngok. She was the daughter of the Beigo chief. She was captured by my ancestor, Pajook. That is how she became known as Awut Pajook.[2] Awut was then married to Bagat, the chief from the Dhiendior lineage. Bagat paid a bride-price of a hundred cows. He made a fence and filled it with a hundred cows. Bagat came and begot Ajuong. Ajuong came and begot Deng. Deng came and begot Abuk. Abuk came and begot Nyanaghar, the mother of Deng.

My ancestor Pajook had blessed Awut and said, "Awut, my daughter, your descendants will one day inherit the central position in the leadership of this land."[3]

---

1. For a discussion of the Shatt and Beigo, among others, see Henderson, "Migration of the Messiria," 54–56.

2. Pronounced differently from Pajok. The word *Pajook* is derived from *Jok*, spirit, and connotes "of the spirits."

3. Henderson notes that, "the Beigo seem to have formed a superior caste. The Fur Sultan, Mohamed Fadl, was born of a Beigo princess. A Beigo ruled the Shatt in Muglad and led the

Most accounts of Deng Majok's maternal background place emphasis on the genealogy of his mother's mother, Abuk, rather than his mother's father, Kir Bar, perhaps because of the leadership status of his grandmother's line. But Dan Agok spoke of Nyanaghar's paternal line and how her mother, Abuk, married her father, Bar:

> Deng Majok's mother was Nyanaghar, daughter of Kir, son of Bar, in the Diil subtribe of the Ngok. Bar had eight sons, including Kir. Their lineage was called Pabukjaak. When the war with the Nuer had scattered our people, Pabukjaak went and settled in Ruweng. There, they found themselves in confrontation with the Nuer. Pajok lineage had moved and settled on the highlands of Lot. Because of the danger to which Pabukjaak were exposed, people went to fetch the sons of Bar. They were brought and settled at Lot on the spot known as the Small Lot. To this day, it is still known as Lot of Bar.
>
> Then Bar wanted to marry for his son Kir. In the past, marriage was arranged according to the choice of families. Elders would say, "This son of ours should marry a girl from that family." When Bar decided to marry for his son Kir, he chose a girl called Abuk, the daughter of Deng, son of Ajuong from Anyiel section. Abuk came and gave birth to Nyanaghar.

> When Nyanaghar became of age [reported Chol Piok], Arob Biong, your great-grandfather, released cattle for her marriage to your grandfather, Kwol Arob. As you know, we have our Dinka customs, according to which a family marries a wife for a relative who has died before marrying. Nyanaghar was betrothed to be the wife of Arob's son who had died before he married. Kwol Arob was to marry her and beget children for his dead brother. But Nyanaghar strongly rejected the marriage on the grounds that she would not be wife to a dead man. The matter was discussed at great length. But she would not be persuaded.
>
> Nyanaghar was then being courted by a man called Malual Adol from Mannyuar, the father of Makuach Adol. Your grandmother rejected Kwol and eloped with Malual Adol though your grandfather's cattle had already been paid. Kwol withdrew his cattle. Only one black cow-calf remained. The mother of Deng Makuei [Deng Abot] was subsequently married. She consented to be the wife of Kwol's dead brother. Then the spirits went and afflicted Nyanaghar with a disease that made her body swell in the family of Malual Adol. Her body swelled so much that she could not even get through the doorway. That is when she was returned and brought back. Dhiendior, the lineage of Ajuong, Nyanaghar's maternal kin, went and

---

Nyingulgulek rebels south of Dar Fartit, where his descendants still rule them. The beauty of the Beigo women is singled out for especial mention by Sheikh Mohamed El Tunisi (A.D. 1800) and the Kordofan Dagu, who are not Beigo, call themselves by that name" (54–55).

took her back, saying, "Will the daughter of our sister die for a reason that is so obvious? Malual Adol, what will you do if she should die? Are you going to compensate for her death?" They went and brought her back. And then they took her to Arob Biong, Kwol's father.

"She was carried in a bed," said Achai-Chol, one of the senior daughters of Deng Majok. "When they arrived at the house of Kwol Arob, they explained that the illness had been divined to be the curse of the chief's ancestral spirit, Ring, the Flesh, and that if she were not brought to be healed by the chief and given to him in marriage, she would never recover. They asked him to forgive the past and heal her, and to accept her for a wife."

Nyanluak, one of the middle daughters of Deng Majok, elaborated on Arob's reaction:

> Our great-grandfather, Arob Biong, then said, "If you people have now persuaded your daughter to accept my son's marriage, then there is no problem; I wanted her for my son with all my heart. If our Spirit, Ring, has now gone after her, it is because of what was in our heart. Ring follows our heart's desire."
> Nyanaghar was then asked, "And what do you say now, Nyanaghar?"
> She said: "What more can I say? Am I not crippled now? What more value is there to me? And what else can I do?"
> Her hands were taken and she was given to our grandfather. As soon as she came, animals were slaughtered in sacrifice to heal her. She immediately recovered. Her body went down to normal.

Deng Abot, who was to be Deng Majok's rival half-brother by Kwol's other wife, stressed to me his father's initial reluctance to have Nyanaghar back:

> When your grandmother eloped with another man, people gave up, leaving her to the home she had chosen. But in those days, the spirits were much closer to man than they are today. Our clan spirits followed Nyanaghar. She was later brought, after my mother had been married and brought home. She had been crippled by our clan spirit, Ring. So, she was brought home to Father with a cow of atonement. People then worked on my father, persuading him to accept her. But Father refused, saying, "This is a woman for whom I was bewitched in my youth, singing over my ox in the cattle camp.[4] Although another girl had already been designated for me [Deng Abot meant his own mother], I wanted to marry her [Nyanaghar] all the same and have both women as my wives. But since she rejected me and went off with another man, I no longer want her."

---

4. To have been rejected by a girl is conceived as bewitching because it implies that there was something seriously objectionable about him when there was nothing. Whenever one feels wronged by another, whether in word or deed, one is likely to complain, "*Cit e wiel*"—"This is bewitchment."

But in those days, words used to meet and harmonize. Father's uncles all assembled and persuaded him to accept her. He had both women as his wives.

Deng Abot's claim that his mother was the first to be betrothed to Kwol Arob is corroborated by the account of his half-brother, Allor-Jok: "Kwol first saw Abiong [Deng Abot's mother] as a little girl. And then he went and found Nyanaghar, a more grownup girl. Kwol Arob took a cow and betrothed Abiong. He then went and married Nyanaghar."

"Then Anyiel came," said Chol Piok:

> The whole tribe came to bless the two wives. Anyiel came, bringing with them a lancelike spear, a leaflike spear, and a billy goat. Those things were brought to bless the two wives. Both women were now in the house of Arobdit, Kwol's father. They were asked by Anyiel to come out. The blessing rites were then performed. The lancelike spear [which symbolizes a son] was placed on the right shoulder of Deng Majok's mother and the leaflike spear [which symbolizes a girl] was made to rest on the shoulders of Deng Abot's mother. Then they were sprinkled with the sacred ashes.
>
> Arobdit asked, "Why are you doing that? Is this not the senior wife?"
>
> They said, "No! Our blessing is the way it is."
>
> Deng Majok was then born to Nyanaghar and the girl, Agorot, was born to Abiong; she was later followed by Deng Makuei. Deng Majok was born a boy in fulfillment of the lancelike spear which his mother had been made to support. People said, "Nyanaghar should be the first to have a son. And Abiong should first have a daughter."

Patal is even more explicit about the intentions of the elders in their ritual blessing:

> Abiong came and stayed without conceiving a child; then Nyanaghar was brought and she too remained without a child. After remaining childless, Kwol Arob sent word to his maternal relatives, the Anyiel tribe: "Please come and bless my wives; they are without children."
>
> When they were blessed, a sleeping skin was laid on the ground. And the mother of Deng Majok was first seated on Kwol Arob's left side; the mother of Deng Makuei was seated on his right side. Anyiel then came, singing their hymns and bringing with them their sacrificial goat. They changed the seating of the women. They placed Abiong on the left and Nyanaghar on the right. Then they grounded in front of Abiong the leaflike spear that symbolizes a girl. And they grounded in front of Nyanaghar the lancelike fishing spear that symbolizes a boy. Arob Biong said, "Why are you doing it that way?"
>
> They said, "That is the woman who will bear the chief; Nyanaghar is the one who will bear the chief."

The issue was debated until their word was accepted and the goat was slaughtered in sacrifice.

When the women gave birth, Abiong gave birth to Agorot and Nyanaghar gave birth to Deng Majok.

But as Monyluak Row points out, "Kwol then began to say that the girl he married after Nyanaghar had rejected him was his first wife." Deng Makuei, who was born to Abiong after Agorot, was allotted the pied color pattern, Mijok (a design of black on the front and hindquarters with a white body), due the first son of the first wife, and was also allotted the sacred cows of the First House. Deng Majok was allotted the second color pattern, Marial (a different design of black and white). In due course, the metaphoric names derived from the color Marial, for which Deng Majok was to become known, acquired such wide recognition and prominence that it became a case of the man giving the name and the color pattern a status of seniority rather than the other way around. Among his ox-names were Arialbek, "The Saddle Bill Stork," Awet, "The Crested Crane," Athokyom, "The Brown with a White Spot on the head" (another color pattern of the second class), or simply Marial. It was as though Marial and not Mijok was the color pattern of the firstborn. But this fact would evolve with Deng's stature; initially, he saw it only as a relegation to the second position.

Chol Piok observed that what really embittered Kwol Arob against Deng Majok was his mother's initial rejection of him:

> That was what continued to hurt in the heart of Kwol Arob. He would later say, "The child whose mother rejected me with bitter hostility, how could he succeed to my throne?" That was, of course, very painful to Deng Majok. And how could it not pain him? Kwol used to say it to him all the time. He would insult him on that account. He would say, "Is it the strength of your mother's eyes when she rejected me that has given you such a strong head?" He would insult him that way. That would pain your father's heart very much.

And yet Chol Piok maintains that "there was nothing [negative] at all" in the relationship of Nyanaghar with Kwol. "He became her true husband. Abiong had her other husband—the dead man—while Nyanaghar had Kwol as her true husband and not a relationship of procreating in the name of the dead. She was then ritually treated in accordance with our Pajok rites and she remained Kwol's wife."

The fact is that Kwol Arob's relations with Nyanaghar were ambivalent, reciprocal in conjugal love and affection but also turbulent and subject to fights, for it must not be forgotten that there was a consensus on Nyanaghar's hard-headedness to the end.

"The relationship of our grandfather and our grandmother was far from ideal," said Nyanjur, one of Deng Majok's middle daughters. "It is said that our grandmother's head was very strong. She was a tough-minded woman."

The cowives seem to have been quite cordial and harmonious in their relationship with one another. Deng Abot offers this insight:

> From the time we were born, your grandmother's hut and my mother's hut were always next to one another. The distance between them was like where we were sitting before and where we are now sitting. My mother's hut would be here and your grandmother's hut would be there. Until she died, Nyanaghar was never separated from my mother for a distance as far as outside this house. But Nyanaghar was a brave fighter. She and my father got into a great deal of terrifying fights. . . . And when Deng Majok also became a fighter, jumping here and there, my father saw him as having acquired his mother's ways.

There is very little information about Deng Majok's childhood prior to his weaning among his maternal relatives. This is not surprising, given the fact that weaning usually takes place at the age of two or three, when children are still too small to have a recognizable or memorable personality. Besides, given the health hazards of traditional society and the high rate of infant mortality, the Dinka deliberately discourage any significant recognition of a child as a person until the age when its survival can reliably be counted upon. To do otherwise is believed to be a bad omen that might attract the evil eye. This is why the Dinka tend to refer to children in nonhuman terms as "things," sometimes even calling them "dogs"—though in a nonpejorative sense—to play down their worth and hopefully deflect the eye of the envious evil-doer and increase their prospects of survival.

Even the information available on Deng Majok from the weaning period tends to focus on the love and affection he received from his maternal kin and on his initial tough-mindedness, which is later contrasted with his subsequent emphasis on the peaceful resolution of conflicts and resort to justice through the government and the role of law. Otherwise, there appears to be a consensus that Deng Majok revealed at an early age all the attributes and virtues of leadership that both facilitated and justified his succession to chieftainship. Beyond these facets of Deng Majok's childhood, it is his relationship to people, and particularly to his father and half-brother, Deng Abot, which is given considerable attention as it lays the foundation for their subsequent rivalry over power.

The story of Deng Majok's childhood during the weaning period is told by his maternal cousin, Ajuong Deng Tiel, the chief of Anyiel section:

> When Deng was weaned, he was not taken to his mother's parents' family, the family of Kir Bar. When it was time to wean him, my grandfather Tiel said, "The son of Nyanaghar, the daughter of my sister Abuk, is not to be weaned by her grandmother Abuk while I am alive. He will be weaned with me. He is the son of my sister's daughter." So your father was taken and weaned there.
> Your father grew up there during his weaning years. He was a

child whom no one dared to touch. He feared no man and feared no child. And if an elder committed any wrong against him, he would never let the matter go. It is said that he had this attitude from the time he was still a small child. And even when he himself was the one who provoked people, my grandfather Tiel would say: "He is not to be touched. He is the one who has inherited my grandfather's character. He is in the image of my grandfather, Ajuong. And he is in the image of my father, Deng Ajuong. My father was a man without ears; he never listened to anybody. He only spoke to himself; only the word of his own head was the word he cared about. Deng Majok will be like my father one day."

Your clan, Pajok, used to deny your father by saying, "This head of his is not our kind. It is the head of Deng Ajuong." Until your father died, that was the case. And even you, Mading, your own determined heart, that is the way it is being viewed today. People say, "He is the breed of the lineage of Deng Ajuong. They are formidable. Their feud never ends."

Chol Piok explains how Deng cleverly reversed what was a nickname to the ox-name of the most senior color—Mijok [Ngok] or Majok [Others].

As Deng Majok grew, he became known as Deng Majoh—Deng the Doggish. This was not because there was anything bad about him. He had acquired a small puppy dog while he was a small boy. And he was so fond of the dog that he used to eat together with the dog. The same dishes out of which human beings ate were the same ones from which he ate with his dog. The dog had no separate dish. So Arobdit, his grandfather, said, "Well, since he is so attached to the dog, he should be called Deng the Doggish." And that is how that name came about and continued. It was later twisted by the Twich and the Rek into Majok, which is a bull praise-name that Deng preferred and adopted as part of his official name.

But even the nickname itself eventually lost its comic origin and acquired a dignity that reflected the personality of Deng Majok.

"When his weaning period was over," resumed Ajuong, my grandfather Tiel said, 'The cows that he used during his weaning should go with him.' Those cows were taken with your father. My grandfather then said to Kwol Arob, 'Please see to it that nobody takes these cows. And you, Chief, please do not dispose of these cows! Spare them so that they may multiply and be the beginning of Deng's wealth.'"

After giving birth to three boys (Deng Majok, Biong Mading, and Arob) and three girls (Ayan, Awor, and Abul), Nyanaghar died when her children were still quite small. Abiong took care of all the children, hers and Nyanaghar's, with great love and affection, hardly distinguishing among them. Deng Majok and Deng Makuei grew up as brothers, friends, and close companions.

"Deng Majok and Uncle Deng Abot had excellent relations," said Achai-Chol.

> They were like full brothers, children of one mother and one father. And so were their brothers, Biong Mading and Allor Maker. That was how they interchanged their relationships as brothers. Each one of them was closer to his half-brother than he was to his full brother. When we were born at Noong, only a stream separated the houses of our father, Deng Majok, and our uncle, Deng Abot. Deng Abot built on this side of Noong and our father built on the other side of Noong. And they lived together as though they were not half-brothers but full siblings.

Ibrahim El Hussein, an Arab friend of the family, also stressed the close relationship between the Deng brothers: "They would never part from one another; they were as close as twins." "It was such a wonderful relationship," confirmed Abdalla Hamadein, another Arab friend of the family: "If you saw Deng Makuei and Deng Majok then, you would take them for twins. You could hardly differentiate between them. They walked together and slept together in one bed." Deng Abot himself had this to say about his relationship with his half-brother, Deng Majok:

> Deng and I were close in age. And Nyanaghar died while we were barely teenagers—both of us. We all remained with my mother. Abul, the youngest child of Nyanaghar, used to sleep on my mother's back while Awor, the second youngest, slept in front of my mother. As for me and the son of my father, Deng, we never fought, never! The simple children's fight we never fought.

And in the words of their half-brother, Allor-Jok:

> All the younger sons of Kwol had excellent relations with Deng Majok before the issue of chieftainship arose. In fact, Manyuol, the brother of Deng Makuei, lived with Deng Majok. And even I, although I had my own cattle, whenever I went to him and asked for anything, he would always give it to me. When I became of age, he had truly wonderful spears made for me.

According to Matet, Deng Majok was wise enough not to leave his father and join his maternal kin after his mother's death:

> Had Deng gone to his maternal relatives after his mother's death, he would not have succeeded to the chieftainship. His father would have built a home for him there and he would have lived there. If he had returned later, he would have found the other Deng more acquainted with his father and with the tribe. That is what Deng Majok realized and rejected. He stayed with his father and his maternal uncles would only visit.
>
> One maternal uncle even came and settled near him. This was an old man called Bar Kir. He built his cattle-byre near Deng Majok. His purpose was to oversee the children of his sister.

Deng Majok is said to have been exceptionally brave. Initiated at a strikingly young age, he faced with remarkable courage the most painful operation that upgrades a person from the status of a boy to the highly respected status of a gentleman. As the oldest son of the chief, it was thought appropriate that he should lead his age-set and be the first to undergo the operation, even though he was technically still too young to be initiated.

"Your father grew up that way but became *The Deng* after he was initiated," observed Chol Piok. "And he was initiated while still a small boy. Kwol said, 'Even though my son is this small, he will be the first to lie down and receive the initiation marks. It is better that he be initiated even if he should die at the scene of initiation.' When Deng Majok lay down, people were afraid that he might cry."

It is said that to celebrate his initiation, Deng slaughtered lavishly for the festivity. In the words of Malith Mawien, "He slaughtered eight of his own cows just for initiation. They were cows of prestige. We heard of it here [in Twichland]."

Then followed the customary mock-fights between the age-sets, *biok*, an institutionalized competition for dominance between the outgoing senior age-set and the emerging, self-assertive junior warriors.[5]

"Deng Majok was first a member of Ajingjing age-set," said Chol Adija:

> But when his real age-mates were later initiated, he left the senior age-set, Ajingjing, and joined his age-mates in the junior age-set, Turuk. When Ajingjing began to fight with Turuk, people like Agong Deng and Ajang d'Anhiany would nearly kill him, but he would never succumb. He was beaten and beaten and beaten until he would nearly die. But he would never give in. Kwol Arob would get very angry with those who beat him.
>
> When the battle of Aguet-tor was fought, he was still very young and Kwol Arob prevented him from going into battle. Kwol totally refused to let him go. Deng cried and cried because he was not allowed to go to battle. But Kwol said to the people who were holding him back, "If you let him go and he gets killed, I do not know how you people will escape from me." So he was physically restrained from going to battle.

According to Monyluak Row, Deng Majok was also resented by some people because of his air of dignity and pride, which placed him above the activities of his age-mates:

> In those days, people used to fish. After catching fish, young men would go to fetch firewood in order to roast the fish on an open fire. Large quantities of firewood would be gathered. One person would work on cleaning the fish in preparation for roasting. Another person

---

5. For Howell's argument of *biok* as a cause for the breakup and segmentation of the Ngok into sections and subtribes, see "The Ngok Dinka," 252–53.

would be charged with the responsibility of roasting the fish. And yet another person would cut it up. And then the people would eat. It is said that Deng Majok would not participate in such activities. Whenever his age-set went to fetch a bull for meat for the marriage of an age-mate according to the custom called *biol*, he would not go. If people went to hunt, he would not go.

Despite his tough-mindedness, Deng Majok is said to have had "great respect for his father," to use the words of Chol Adija. According to Chol Piok,

> He would quarrel with his father to the point where everyone would know that they had quarreled and that Kwol was angry with his son. Then, at night, he would come with a cow and say, "Father, I appease you with this cow."[6] His maternal relatives were a family of great wealth. Whenever he wanted anything from them, it was given to him the same day. So he would appease his father and their quarrel would end. That is the way they lived and lived. And he would quarrel with his father because his father had a tendency to suppress the rights of his mother's side of the family. That is what he would not accept.

Deng's attitude toward his father was part of a more general pattern, for he is said to have combined his physical courage and tough-mindedness with reason and a disposition toward resolution of conflict and reconciliation: "When he was still a child, your father was very hot-tempered," began Pagwot Deng.

> He was very easily provoked. But he was a man who reasoned well with words. His was the hot temper of a man who could also speak well! He would not overlook anything that touched him. He would pursue the matter to the end. And yet he was for good relations. Among his companions, even if he fought with another child, he would insist that they sit and eat together.[7] He did not believe in nursing grievances into a continuing bitterness. He believed that people should fight but then sit and eat together, leaving aside the conflict. That was the way he behaved.

Perhaps the theme most emphasized in the stories about Deng Majok is that he was exceptionally generous and hospitable. From his childhood, these qualities in him were not only striking but almost compulsive. "He would attend his father's court, which would be filled with people," said Chol Piok.

> He would stand and watch. And as he stood, he would see a person who looked hungry and would nudge him to follow him. Sometimes

---

6. Material gifts, especially of cattle, are made as a token of apology and appeasement.

7. Eating together is a gesture of reconciliation in much the same way as abstaining from sharing food is a gesture or symbol of conflict or serious disagreement.

he would go and sit apart, then send someone to fetch the person who looked hungry. That person would come and be provided with food.

As the court of your grandfather, Kwol Arob, progressed into the evening, Deng Majok would be there. He was still just a little boy not yet initiated. And as the people began to disperse, he would be standing by, watching the condition of every person. If he saw a person looking weak and seemingly unfit to travel, he would stop him and sit him down. He would give him accommodation and feed him. And the next morning, he would again give him food, and only then would he permit him to travel. That is the way he did things and did things.

"If Deng Majok saw a man passing by, he would meet him and invite him into his place," said Patal Biliw. "If the traveler refused and said, 'No, I do not want to stop,' Deng would insist so much that he would quarrel with the traveler." As he matured, these attributes continued to develop and became more strategically focused. "Your father began to assert himself when he became of age," said Ajuong Deng.

When he began to outwit the people, there was no other way through which he did it but one. When he saw that his relations with his father were rather strained and realized that his father's preference seemed to be for his other son, Deng Abot, he withdrew. But your father had a great deal of initiative.

He developed an attitude whereby, whenever he saw an Arab, even if he were passing some distance away, he would invite him in and entertain him well. Whenever he saw a Dinka traveler, even if he were passing a distance away, he would invite him in and entertain him. Food was always in abundance. Milk was always available. He himself was never inclined to eat.[8] He would call a person in and offer him what he had. During the lean period before the harvest, he would be particularly concerned about hungry people.

Then he realized that tobacco was in great demand. He would buy tobacco even though he never smoked. Whenever he saw a person craving tobacco, he would go and fetch tobacco and offer it to him.

"He would fill his pockets with tobacco," confirmed Patal. "He would then wait until the afternoon when the shade of the tree [under which his father held court] would be filled with visitors; he would then take the tobacco from his pockets and distribute it to the people. He, of course, never smoked. So he kept the tobacco only for the guests. He would also have a lot of food prepared and keep it until the court-tree was full of people. Then he would ask for all the food to be brought." "That was how your father became so familiar to the public," continued Ajuong Deng.

---

8. Which for the Dinka is a quality of dignity and pride.

Every visitor would leave chanting, "Deng Majok, Deng Majok, Deng Majok, Deng Majok." People would say, "This son, even though he is without a mother, is the leader." Even before he married, he was nearly always the host for the food that came from the house of Deng Abot's mother. People would say, "We ate in the house of Deng Majok." And Deng Abot would be there all the same. That was what endeared your father to the Arabs and the Dinka. He went on that way until he married. Then came the disaster for his enemies.

"The criticism of his fellow Dinkas and brothers was that Deng Majok was reckless with his wealth," said Mithiang Aguek. "Let him destroy his wealth in that wasteful manner," they would say, "he will learn one day." His generosity had become well known. Whenever Arabs arrived at Noong, they would ask specifically for the home of Deng Majok. He would extend to them a very warm welcome and accord them maximum hospitality. He consistently maintained this line, building a strong image and character.

Tigani Mohamed Zein, an Arab educator who was later to know Deng Majok well, told of their first encounter:

> My circumstances let me come in contact with Chief Deng Majok when I was fifteen years old, to be precise, in 1935. I was on a trip to Bahr el Arab and we put up in Deng Majok's village as his guests for the first time. It was at a place called Naam [Noong]. That was the first time I saw him. He was then a young man in his prime. My view of him was that he was an excellent young man with a future. He was witty and very generous. I recall that he slaughtered a lamb for us. This was a well-bred lamb, fat and delicious. The taste of its meat left an impression on me; I still remember it to this day. Since that time and over the years, I have enjoyed hospitality in the home of Deng Majok on numerous occasions. I came to the conclusion that the animals Deng Majok slaughtered for his guests were exceptional.

At first, while favoring the eventual succession of Deng Makuei as the son of the senior wife, Kwol Arob raised the brothers as political equals and even appointed them his assistants with equal status. But with time he became increasingly ambivalent toward Deng Majok. Accounts of their relationship are conflicting. Deng Majok himself was convinced that his father did not love him. He would portray his role in the father-son relationship as one of constant attempts on his part to please his father, which met with constant rebuffs. All in all, he saw himself as a son disfavored by his father.

On the other hand, it is said that Kwol Arob saw a great deal of administrative and diplomatic competence in Deng Majok, which he made use of. This was especially the case in his dealings with chiefs of other tribes and with the government. Whenever central authorities came to make their administrative rounds or Kwol Arob went on state visits outside the tribe, he took Deng Majok with him. Nyanbol Amor, Deng Majok's second wife, explains the ambivalence of the relationship between Kwol and Deng:

Kwol Arob used to get angry with Deng Majok because Deng used to voice his claims with his characteristic toughness of mind. But when issues between the Dinka and the Arabs arose, he would turn to Deng. He felt that Deng handled those situations well. Whenever issues involving other tribes arose, it was always Deng who took the initiative and managed the situation.

Kwei, the third wife, who had known Deng Majok from their childhood days, went further: "Kwol Arob was very fond of his son, Deng Majok; he loved him dearly until the day he died . . . Kwol spoke of Deng highly as the son of a great lady—Nyanaghar." Some people indeed argue that despite his apparent attitude to the contrary, Kwol Arob loved Deng Majok even more than he did Deng Abot; but that viewpoint is hard to defend. It is quite obvious from the exaggerated nature of such arguments that they reflect an effort to rationalize an apparently negative attitude which must have been difficult to explain or justify.

Achai-Chol is one of those who portrayed the relationship of her father and grandfather by such a rationalization:

> Superficially, their relationship appeared to indicate that Kwol Arob did not love his son, Deng Majok. When they all sat face to face in public, Kwol would side with Deng Makuei. But he would then call Deng Majok in at night and talk to him privately, advising him how he should conduct himself. He used to do it tactfully so that he would not be suspected of favoring Deng Majok.

Nyanluak rationalized to an even greater degree the contradiction in the behavior of their grandfather: "Kwol's preference for Deng Makuei appeared to be a ploy. He would speak positively to Deng Majok in private, encouraging him to work on promoting himself for chieftainship. But in public he continued to favor Deng Makuei; he would say to his clan, 'Deng Makuei is to be the chief.'"

Achai-Jur probably came closer to the truth:

> Kwol Arob praised Deng Majok in his heart. He realized that he was the one most likely to benefit his people, the Ngok, as a whole. But why he used to pull back was because he was guarding his own power: he was afraid that Deng Majok might prematurely succeed to chieftainship. That was why he appeared to dislike Father. But in fact he did not dislike him. On the contrary, he used to praise him a great deal. He used to say that Deng Majok was the one who would serve the good of his people.

Deng Makuei himself denied that his father loved him more than he did Deng Majok, citing their father's role in enabling Deng Majok and his sibling brothers to barter cow-calves for bulls, a means of acquiring "personality oxen" which the Dinka associate with aesthetics and social dignity. But Deng Makuei does concede that the relations between their father and Deng Majok were less than ideal, to say the least, for they quarreled very often: "What caused conflicts between Father and Deng Majok was that Deng flirted with daughters of our relatives; he flirted with girls who were related to us. Deng Majok also wanted to seize other people's things here and there. And that is never liked by a chief. My father disliked it." Deng Makuei admits that he was close to his father, but as a result of his own initiatives, not because of spontaneous favoritism on the part of his father. "Deng Majok, on the other hand," according to Deng Makuei:

> provoked hostility and then claimed to have been ill-treated. As for me, whenever I thought of something, I would go to my father even if I were far away in the cattle camp and I would ask my father in a polite way. I would talk to him with a son's respect for his father. That is why you hear people say that Deng Abot was close to his father. It was not my father who would call me: No, son of my brother, I swear to you as I speak to you now in Arabland, it was not my father but myself who took the initiative.

Ironically, some people argue that Deng Makuei's complacency with his father ultimately worked against him, while Deng Majok's militancy and self-assertiveness against his father developed in him an independent personality and an image that eventually worked in his favor. "Deng Makuei was almost unwittingly kept in the background or pulled back by Kwol Arob because he listened to his father," said Mithiang Aguek. "Deng Majok pulled out of his father's tracks much earlier. That was how Deng Majok started and continued to overtake Deng Abot, who continued to listen to his father."

A theme that emerges in the complex relationship between Kwol Arob and Deng Majok at this stage is that Kwol recognized Deng's qualities, especially in the modern administrative context, but still felt that Deng Abot was the senior son for leadership in accordance with tradition, for he never wavered on the status of Abiong as his first wife and therefore the mother of the heir. This view is widely shared among the Dinka. According to Chol Piok, "Why Kwol was rather negative about Deng Majok was because he thought that Deng Majok would overwhelm Deng Makuei and deprive him of his rights. He realized that Deng Makuei's heart was not the same as that of Deng Majok. Deng Makuei would despair angrily. But Deng Majok would never despair. Those were the things Kwol used to say."

Achwil Bulabek agreed:

> What his father feared was that Deng Majok would capture the chieftainship. That was why he tried to trim him down. Abiong was, of course, the surviving wife. It was she who had a wife-husband relationship with Kwol. Those were the small issues that caused problems between them. Whenever Deng noticed mistreatment by his father or his father violated any right that was his, he would not overlook it; he would quarrel with him and people would then say,

> "Deng and his father had a quarrel." But Deng never committed a wrong against his father. It was only that he insisted on representing the position of his dead mother.... Kwol feared that Deng was going to capture his chieftainship.

Despite Kwol's determination to discourage Deng Majok from aspiring to the chieftainship, it seemed obvious that he was fighting a lost cause, for the destiny of Deng Majok had long been set and he himself was working effectively and successfully to facilitate the realization of that destiny. Achwil, a close witness to it all, testifies: "To whomever saw Deng Majok, it was obvious from his behavior that he was *the* son of the chief. And people got to like him very much. Even the elders of his section, people like Deng de Mathii, loved him very much." Dan Agok, a nephew of Deng de Mathii, confirmed that his uncle, who had the ox praise-name of Deng Jok-Ngol,

> used to leave at night and visit Deng Majok at Noong. He would say, "You, Deng Majok, even though you have been assigned the Marial color pattern and the Mijok color pattern is given to Deng Makuei, you are the son of the first wife. You will still become the chief, if people like me, Deng de Mathii, are not dead. When the cattle were withdrawn from your mother's marriage, one black cow-calf and a bull, Malual, were left in the marriage." Deng de Mathii and Deng Majok frequently exchanged visits with one another. Deng Majok would leave Noong to spend the night with Deng de Mathii and then leave the following morning. When the chieftainship was later contested, Deng Majok had already listened to the words of Deng de Mathii.

"So, your father's leadership was something the Creator gave him from the beginning," concluded Achwil. "His was a gift founded in his being from the time the tribe blessed his mother to beget a son to be the chief, a position which my father [Bulabek Biong] later reaffirmed as he lay dying."

1. Chief Kwol Arob with some policemen near one of the earliest cars to go to Ngokland in the early 1930s. Photo by K. D. D. Henderson.

2. Chief Deng Majok (fourth from left) with Arab chiefs in an intertribal celebration in 1954.

3. Michael Tibbs, the last British district commissioner in the area, with Homr Nazirs, Babo Nimir (right), and Serrer El Haj Ajbar.

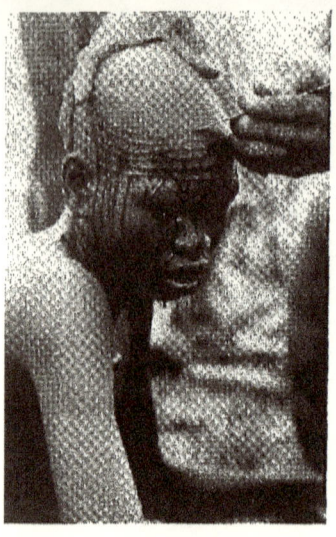

4. Initiation operation among the Agar Dinka, whose practices in this respect are similar to those of the Ngok Dinka.

5. Initiates during their recovery period, their heads covered with palm hats, a bundle of sorgham stalks in the place of spears, with a musical instrument made of gourd. Courtesy of the Sudan Government.

6. A Dinka "gentleman" with initiation marks on his forehead, decorated with beads and a feather in his hairdo. Courtesy of Sarah Errington/Alan Hutchison Library.

7. Part of a Ngok Dinka dance. Photo by Michael Tibbs.

8. Building a cattle-byre. Photo by K. D. D. Henderson.

9. Chief Kwol Arob's rest house at Abyei. Photo by K. D. D. Henderson.

10. Three British district commissioners (from left): J. W. Robertson D. C. Western Kordofan, Jim Stubbs D. C. Aweil, Jack Poole D. C. Tonj, and a senior medical inspector, Alec Guickshanck. Photo by K. D. D. Henderson, March, 1935.

11. Cattle tethered at a cattle camp. Courtesy of Sarah Errington/Alan Hutchison Library.

12. A man tethering a cow. Courtesy of the Sudan Government.

13. A gentleman singing over his personality ox.

14. Arabs riding horses. Courtesy of the Sudan Government.

15. A fishing party. Courtesy of Sarah Errington/Alan Hutchison Library.

16. An Arab woman grinding grain on a stone. Courtesy of the Sudan Government.

17. A primary school class. Courtesy of Sarah Errington/Alan Hutchison Library.

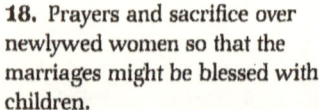

18. Prayers and sacrifice over newlywed women so that the marriages might be blessed with children.

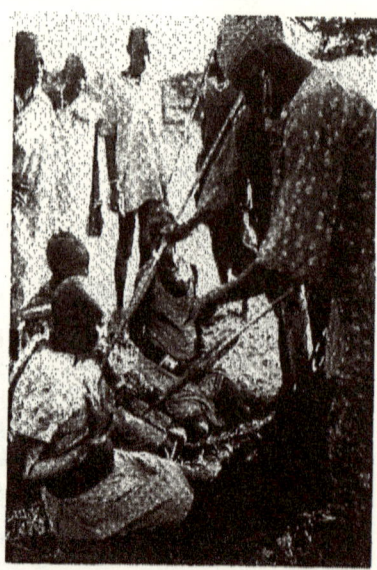

19. Prime Minister Sadig Al Mahdi, who visited Abyei as prime minister in 1967.

20. Chief Deng Majok in August, 1969, just before he was taken to Cairo, where he died. Standing behind him (from left) are the author; Beshir Achier, Deng Majok's secretary, and Bona Malual.

21. Dr. Zachariah Bol Deng (right) with the author in Cairo during the last days of their father's illness.

22. A funeral ceremony for Agar Dinka chief Rok Rech. Courtesy of Sarah Errington/Alan Hutchison Library.

23. Chief Deng Abot making a public address during President Nimeiri's visit to Abyei in December, 1972.

6 Campaign for the Chieftainship

As competition for leadership began to crystallize, Deng Majok started to consolidate the qualities he had revealed from early childhood and to use them consciously to promote his political image and gain popular support. But the more he won over the public, the more concerned his father became, and the more his preference for and support of Deng Abot became manifest.

Initially, according to Allor-Jok, Deng Majok's use of the family resources for hospitality attracted attention: "As Deng Makuei was still small, Deng Majok was the one in charge of everything. Whenever guests arrived, it was Deng Majok who offered them his hospitality as the son of the chief. That was how he became known to everyone, including the Arabs and the southern tribes."

Apparently, there came a time when Chief Kwol Arob grew concerned about the popularity of Deng Majok's hospitality and sought to encourage Deng Abot to become more self-assertive as a host. As Matet Ayom observed, "Whenever guests arrived, their father, Kwol Arob, would want Deng Makuei to be the one to receive and entertain them. But Deng Majok would always be the first to appear." In doing so, he sometimes depended on Abiong, Deng Makuei's mother who, in the words of Dan Agok, "was a truly chiefly lady. She treated Deng Majok so nobly that she would refuse to cook for the guests of her own son but honor the guests of Deng Majok. That was the beginning of Deng's reputation. He and his stepmother, Abiong, had a very good relationship."

"As he was growing up," observed Chol Piok, "Deng Majok never had any complaints against his stepmother, Abiong, the mother of Deng Makuei. His relations with her were so good that he never seemed to miss his own mother. And Deng would always bring so many things from his maternal relatives and place them in the house of Abiong; they were never placed in the hands of any other woman. His cattle were milked and butter was made in the house of Abiong."

Abiong's loving attitude toward Deng Majok was not without stepmother qualifications, however. As Matet Ayom observed, "She became a mother to both of them, but a woman never places the child of her cowife to the forefront. She may feed him well, but she would not want him to take the lead over her own child." Dinka culture requires that an orphan, and especially a motherless child, be shown special love and affection by all, and in particular by the surviving parent. But the Dinka also recognize that whatever other relatives can do, no one can effectively replace the mother. In situations of polygyny, rivalries between the surviving wife and the children of the dead wife do arise in which the surviving wife is likely to have an advantage over the motherless children. "A man often adopts the voice of his wife," commented Matet. "Deng Majok had no support, while Deng Makuei's support was his living mother." In Achai-Jur's words, "The interests of a person whose mother is dead are never as well protected as those of a person whose mother is living. The mother of Deng Makuei was the one who cooked for all the people. So she had control over the affairs of the family."

Apparently, Abiong's control was quite formidable. Though Nyanaghar was well known for her unusually hot temper and hard-headedness, Abiong, too, had a reputation as a domineering woman, and, according to Monyluak Row, was "very spoiled by Kwol Arob."

The more Deng realized his father's prejudice against him, the more determined he seemed to be to demonstrate those qualities which he felt necessary for leadership. He became particularly noted for mediating opposed positions and creating channels for communication and reconciliation with the leaders of the neighboring Dinka and Arab tribes.

"Whenever tribes came into conflict in the grazing area of the *toc*," observed Matet Ayom, "it would be Deng Majok who would initiate moves for peace. He would approach the Twich and he would approach the Rek, and he would make peace between them. If there was a conflict between Bongo and Abyor, he would rise and make peace between them. If Anyiel and Bongo were in conflict, indeed, if any tribal groups were in conflict, he would rise, call for peace, and hold meetings. He did all this before he was the chief. His were only the words of a son of the chief." Matet goes on to give an account of an incident in which Deng Majok distinguished himself as a peacemaker:

> One time, the Abyor section went to raid the Twich for cattle.[1] That was when the Twich first recognized Deng Majok as the future

[1]. The British had not yet fully succeeded in establishing law and order on the South-North border. After describing Baggara Arab raids under Ali El Gulla of the Missiriya,

chief. Deng got up and went to the camp of the Twich. There he found an elder by the name of Rian Gorkwei, the chief of the Twich. Deng went with some people on horseback. The horses entered the cattle-camp in a display of riding skills. That was the traditional Arab way of honoring their hosts and announcing their arrival. Our people adopted it from the Arabs. The best riders raced their horses to the home of the hosts, who would then get up to hold and unsaddle the horses. On this particular occasion, Bol Bulabek, one of the companions, raced his horse into the herd, knocking down cattle as he went.

The elder called Rian Gorkwei got up and said, "O people of Arob Biong, is this an intimidation or a raid?"

Deng Majok responded: "Uncle, it is only that the horse got out of control; no offense was intended. It is neither raid nor intimidation. Please cool down and welcome us as visitors. I have come accompanied by these people to see you. I shall tell you what I have come for when we are seated."

Rian Gorkwei turned to his people, who had grabbed their spears and were about to fight. He said: "O Twich, stop! The wrong is shifting to your side. Deng Majok has reversed the situation. He has passed the responsibility over to you. Should you harm anyone after this, the wrong will be on your side."

The spears were then laid down and the visitors were led into the camp. The horses were unsaddled. After they were seated, Deng Majok said: "The reason I came was to tell you to graze without fear of any attack by our people. The Abyor tribe will move this way. And here you are camping in this area. We should graze our cattle in peace. Even if the cattle should mix while grazing in the daytime and a man from Abyor offends a man from Twich, I would like you, Uncle Rian, to call me and we shall settle the matter together. I myself will come in front of you because you are my elder. We shall discuss the matter and make peace for our people to graze together in peace."

Rian Gorkwei said, "My son, they say you are Deng, the son of the second wife of Kwol, but that you were the first to be born. Whatever people may say about the seniority of your mothers, you will be a leader of men in accordance with the words you have just spoken." Rian said these words as an agreement of peace was concluded between them. Then Deng left. His father, Kwol, was informed, "Deng Majok has made peace between the Ngok and the Twich, so the two tribes are now grazing amicably together."

Kwol's only comment was, "I see."

Henderson observes: "The Dinkas were their own worst enemies, for the Twij and Malwal resistance to the Government, which lasted into the nineteen twenties, cut them off from any chance of redress. A particularly flagrant raid in 1915 was heavily punished, however, and the reoccupation of Darfur curtailed the area of irrepressibility ('Migration of the Missiria Tribe,'" 71). This uncertain state of affairs underscored the role of the chief as a peacemaker, and Kwol Arob had established in his area a more advanced state of civic order. See Henderson, "Migration of the Missiria," 71.

Achwil Bulabek tells of another occasion involving another tribe, the Rek, in which Deng adopted a different strategy for peace, also before he had become chief:

> We had captured the herds of the Rek. The Rek rose up in arms to attack us. Kwol Arob and the government came to prevent the fight. They went and spent the night near our cattle-camp. Kwol gathered the cattle and returned them to the Rek. We then proceeded to the *Toc*. The Rek went and grouped their camps together to prepare for an attack. Deng Majok and Deng Makuei had their horses saddled and went to the Rek, accompanied by the government police led by an Arab sergeant-major called Mekki. The Rek were under the leadership of Lual, the brother of Chief Yor Maker. Deng spoke to the son of Lual, also called Deng, and said, "Deng, son of Lual, here you have come with your tribe, Ajuong. You are now camping at Baarngop and we at Nyiel. We have the river between us. You, the Rek accuse us of moving at will. We have now settled that matter. If I should hear of any provocation from your side, then your head and mine will remain here in the *Toc*. I will not do anything to offend you, but should you think to yourselves, 'The Ngok once raided our cattle so we, Ajuong, should avenge,' then know that you and I will face one another in single combat while Ajuong and Abyor face each other in battle."

Apparently, that threat was effective in ensuring peace between the Ngok and the Rek in the grazing lands of the *Toc*.

Babo Nimir, the paramount chief of the neighboring Missiriya Arabs to the north, reports an incident involving the Dinka and the Arabs in which Deng Majok intervened for the cause of peace while Kwol Arob was still the chief.

> I remember when his father was still the chief, some people among the Abyor and the Kalamna Arabs fought toward the area of Fadhalla. I was not there. Deng came to the scene. When he came, he said, "You, Kalamna, here you are holding the leadership, and you also want to show your manhood by fighting. Do you want to keep them both, leadership and manhood?[2] No! Either you hold onto your manhood and surrender your leadership, or you keep your leadership and surrender your manhood." They were pleased by his words. They said, "It will be according to your words. We shall abandon manhood; leadership is enough for us."

Notwithstanding Deng Majok's remarkable contribution to the cause of peace among the herding tribes of both the South and the North, and the fact

---

2. Manhood here symbolizes the show of force considered to be repugnant to the role of a chief, which should principally be one of peacemaker.

that he was already becoming recognized as the effective leader in the cattle-camp, Deng Abot, backed by their father, regarded himself as the leader and therefore the one entitled to make decisions on matters relating to cattle herding. Rivalry on this matter was to come to a climax on a small issue concerning when and where the herds should move. Monyluak Row tells the story:

> The herds had moved to Yar cattle-camp. After some time at Yar, Deng Majok said, "Brothers, the cattle are starving. I think we should move from here. We shall move to Lot camp." But the others refused; Biong refused and Deng Makuei refused.
>
> The following day, Deng Majok said, "If you have refused, let me tell you that I made that decision because I believe I am your senior brother and that herding and camping are my responsibility. Now that you have refused, I shall move alone and leave you with the cattle. We are not going to contest the cattle by the force of the arm. But I will take my personality oxen."[3] Then he took his oxen and moved them to Lot, where a large section of Abyor was camping.
>
> A man who had been at Yar went to Abyei and said to Chief Kwol, "Your son has moved his oxen from the cattle-camp." Kwol heard this and got up with members of his age-set, Koryom. They traveled and arrived at Lot early in the morning. Deng Majok got up, took seats to the edge of the camp, and seated the guests. He then had milk brought to them. When the milk was offered to the guests, Kwol Arob said, "I am not going to drink this milk." His age-mates also said, "We are not drinking either." But Kwol told them, "You should drink the milk; knowing my son Deng, you will only aggravate the situation if you do not drink it."
>
> Deng remained silent. Koryom gave in and drank the milk. Discussions then began. Kwol spoke and said, "Deng, I would like you to take your oxen from here. You are the eldest of my sons. The oxen must be taken back into the herd at Yar camp." Deng said, "So you really want me to move back to Yar?" Kwol said, "Yes!"
>
> After a moment of reflective silence, Deng said, "Father, I must tell you that I will never go back to Yar. This year, even when the rains fall and the cattle of the Ngok return home, I will pass through Tolmach and go on to Lopong. I shall see Yar only next year on my return to the *Toc*. If I see Yar this year, then may I be struck dead by the power of our clan spirit, Cholwich."

"The cattle-camp had to be divided," noted Achwil Bulabek.

> Deng swore, "I will never follow a way that was decided upon by

---

3. A personality-ox among the Dinka does not only symbolize the man who owns it but also his cattle-wealth. When a man wants to terminate an engagement or even a completed marriage, all he has to do is take back any personality ox or oxen which he might have paid and that symbolizes the withdrawal of his bride-wealth cattle.

my younger brothers; as long as I am the eldest who should be in charge of the cattle-camp, I will never go! May I die the day I follow the children!" Kwol remarked, "Knowing my son Deng, he will never accept any word I say now. Leave them to go their separate ways." Deng said, "Father, we will go our separate ways, but one way will in the end be forced to join the other way."

It was a major conflict. They were only reconciled much later in the rainy season when the cattle had returned to the villages.

Deng Majok's other grievance had to do with Kwol Arob's inequitable allocation of cattle to the brothers. "Whenever a girl was married and the cattle were brought and divided, Kwol would give Abiong [Deng Abot's mother] more cows than he would give the House of Nyanaghar [Deng Majok's deceased mother]," recalled Dan Agok.

Among our people, the Dinka, a son starts his conflicts with his father over cattle. What caused conflict between them was that Deng Makuei's cattle were always more than Deng Majok's cattle. That was the case until they married.

Deng talked to his father in front of uncles like Mijak Kwol. He said, "Father, why is it that I do not have a good share of cattle from our herd?" People like Mijak turned to Kwol Arob and said, "The boy is right. Why is it that he does not have a fair share in the herd?" Kwol said, "Mijak, how could you people speak with the voice of Deng Majok? What you have just spoken are not your own words; that is the voice of Deng Majok." Mijak said, "No, it is not the voice of Deng Majok; it is my own voice. How can you treat your son so unfairly? Why should he not possess a good share to be seen as the herd of the son of the chief?"

Apart from the cattle he distributed, Kwol Arob still maintained a large herd as the collective property of the family. According to Chol Piok, "The cattle of Kwol were so numerous that women milked indiscriminately. His cattle wealth was so large that only the small calves were tethered. The calves which had been weaned were left to run loose."

Deng Majok made dramatic moves to rectify the inequities of cattle distribution between him and Deng Abot. The story sounds unbelievable, but it is told by the Dinka with surprising consistency.

"It is said that your grandfather made two cattle-byres, one for Nyanaghar and one for Abiong," recounted Monyluak Row.

He made one byre small and the other byre spacious. It was the cattle-byre of Abiong that he made large, while the small one was the byre of the sons of Nyanaghar. The herds were tethered outside around the hearths, but nobody bothered about which cattle were going into which byre. When the cattle were about to be taken into the byre, Deng Majok thought of a plan. He said to his brother Biong: "Enter the byre and remain there. I will take the cows and hand them over to you." He had fetched twigs and firewood to make a fire to light the byre so that pegs could be visible.

Deng Makuei slowly released his cattle into his byre, confident that his large byre would accommodate the bulk of the herd and that Deng Majok's byre could accommodate only a few cows. Biong went into their byre and received the cattle Deng Majok handed over to him. Deng would release a cow and hand it over to Biong. He released cows and released cows and released cows, stuffing that small byre with cows. The byre became so full of cattle that the animals began to fight for space. Then Biong shouted, "Deng, the cattle are killing themselves; the byre is full!" Deng rushed to the cattle-byre and shouted back at Biong, "Don't be a fool. Tie two cows to each peg and use the support-poles of the byre as pegs to tether more cows." Then he went back to bring more cows into the byre. He kept on releasing cows and releasing cows and releasing cows. The cows inside the byre continued to fight, roaring and roaring as they struggled for space. Some cows went into the hearth and others mingled with the calves. The cattle-byre was completely stuffed with cows.

Meanwhile, the cattle-byre of Deng Makuei, which was larger and supposed to accommodate more cattle, did not get enough cows to fill the space. The cows that went inside were few and many pegs were left unused. When all the cattle had been taken into the byres so that no more were left outside, Deng Majok went into his byre and said to Biong, "Let us take the firewood and build a fire outside the byre." They did. Then he said, "Now, let us take the cattle out of the byre. We will find accommodation for them in other people's byres tomorrow morning. But from tonight on, they have become our own." The following morning, when Kwol Arob came, he found the cattle of Deng Makuei still inside the byre. He gazed at the cattle and felt confused. He was so confused that at first he remained silent. After a while, he asked, "What happened?" The sons of Abiong did not know what to say to their father. And Kwol did not know what to say to Deng Majok about how so many cattle had shifted to his byre.

After noting the injustice Deng Majok experienced because of his mother's death, Achai-Jur remarked, "But Father had his own strength of personality to make up for that inequity." She goes on to explain that her father and Deng Abot had different interpretations of their father's intentions when he made the cattle-byres. "Abiong's sons thought that their father merely wanted them to take the cattle into the byres, but Father interpreted their father's instructions as an indirect way of asking them to divide the cattle between them." According to Achai, Deng Majok and his brother Biong stuffed the byre without tethering the cattle. "Deng Abot and his brothers, on the other hand, took in one cow at a time and made sure that the cow was properly tethered before taking in the next. That way, they wasted time, while Father took most of the cattle into the byre without wasting time pegging them. Cleverness was one of the ways in which Father defeated his half-brother,

Deng Abot." "That way, Deng Majok completely outwitted his half-brother, Deng Makuei," concluded Atem Moter.

"The following day," said Mithiang Aguek, "when the cattle were taken out of the byres, Kwol wondered what had happened. Biong Mading told his father what had happened and how they had tied five cows to each peg. When he heard that, Kwol remarked that Deng Makuei had no one else but himself to blame for having been outwitted by Deng Majok."

Chol Piok reports that Deng Majok made the cattle-byre and appropriated the cattle on his own initiative and without his father's express consent: "Food stuffs of all kinds were brought from his maternal relatives and he used them for building the byre. . . . After he built the byre, he made pegs and made pegs and made pegs—so many pegs. He hammered the pegs inside the byre and in the courtyard in front of the byres." He then moved to fill his byre with cattle in the manner described by other versions of the story. "Many of the cows he took were with young calves. He was now disaffiliating himself from the joint ownership of Kwol's family. That was how he acquired his original wealth."

After Deng Majok broke away and established his own separate herd, he apparently began to acquire considerable wealth on his own through their wide circle of relatives. According to Chol Adija, "His source of cattle wealth was from the marriages of Kwol Arob's sisters. When he had broken away from his father, he would leave and visit his paternal aunts. From whichever aunt he visited, he would not return empty-handed."

Although Chief Kwol Arob was publicly known to be biased in favor of the eventual succession of Deng Abot to the position of paramount chief, he decided, for one reason or another, to appoint both sons as his deputies in government. As Matet Ayom expressed it:

> When the government appeared and Chief Kwol would come to the North to meet the authorities, he would call them both, Deng and Deng, to accompany him. He bought horses for them. They then used to travel with their father. One acted as his father's deputy and the other acted as his father's deputy. He had now withdrawn them from the cattle-camp so that they would be with him in his court and accompany him on his official tours. They were under him as equals.

Allor-Jok, however, reveals their father's preference for Deng Makuei, despite the seeming equality of their status:

> At first, father decided to have them both under him as his deputies. They traveled with him together. But although he kept them both as his deputies, Father leaned more toward Deng Makuei as his senior son who would eventually succeed to his position as the paramount chief. On the other hand, Deng Majok was a man of exceptional charisma. He became better known to the people, and es-

pecially to the government and the Arabs. He and Babo Nimir[4] became very close friends.

K. D. D. Henderson, who was the British District Commissioner in the area, apparently witnessed the dynamics of the situation. Henderson first met the Deng brothers as their father's deputies. In his letter dated February 24, 1932, in which he referred to Chief Kwol Arob as "a most impressive figure," he wrote of the brothers, "His two sons are fine figures of men as well." Kwol Arob must have presented Deng Abot to Henderson as his eldest, by which he meant senior son and therefore the heir, but which Henderson understood to mean that he was older in age. In a letter dated March 3, while at Naam (Noong), Henderson wrote, "Naam is the headquarters of Deng, the younger one of Kwol's sons." But Henderson's own impression of the brothers seemed to favor Deng Majok; in his response to my questionnaire on Deng Majok, he wrote:

> I met Deng Majok for the first time when, as his father's deputy, he welcomed me on my first arrival at Abyei in 1932. He was still a very young man and had a half-brother, also called Deng, who was supposed to have a claim to the succession. Deng Majok fell out with his father in later years—something to do with a girl I fancy[5]—and for a while I was told that the other brother was likely to succeed. I remember the other brother as being a little taller and less intelligent.

"People then stayed and stayed and stayed," said Chol Piok.

> Then something occurred which angered Deng Majok's heart very much. That is when he fully realized that his father regarded Deng Makuei as the heir to the throne. There was an intertribal assembly at Thaarngop. As people prepared for Thaarngop, the whole tribe was of the opinion that Deng Majok should go to represent the Ngok. But Kwol refused and said, "It is Deng Makuei who will go!" That is how Deng Makuei went. Kwol remained. And Deng Majok remained. Deng Majok said, "O people, now that it is Deng Makuei who is going, the Twich will not remain ours and the Ruweng will not remain ours. Deng Makuei will not be able to stop them from leaving." And how true! Did Deng Makuei manage to keep them with us? Ruweng was taken away and affiliated to the Nuer. And the Twich of

---

4. The Paramount Chief of the Missiriya (Baggara) Arab tribes. As will be elaborated upon later, Babo succeeded his father at the very young age of thirteen and was assisted by a regent until the age of seventeen. As Kwol Arob had been a close friend of his father and had been instrumental in his election, Babo also depended on his guidance, and they became quite close. But with time, Deng Majok, being closer in age, though older, gradually assumed the friendship and became much closer to Babo. Both Deng Abot and Allor-Jok stressed that Deng Majok usurped Babo's friendship from their father.

5. For Deng Majok's conflict with his father over the marriage of his middle wife, Nyanawai, see chapter 9.

Ayuang was taken and affiliated to the Twich of Lang. When Deng Makuei returned, what more was to be said? We only wept.

That is when Deng Majok realized the truth. Our land had no leader to hold it. They remained that way with their father. Deng Majok remained coiling his belly with aches. The matter of succession remained unresolved, but whenever Kwol Arob wanted to send a representative on important matters, he would say, "It is Deng Makuei who will go!" That displeased Deng Majok a great deal.

That is when Deng Majok began to work consciously and deliberately to secure the chieftainship, preferably even in his father's lifetime. "He had already started his campaign through his generosity," continued Chol Piok. "It was through generosity that your father proved too formidable for his opponents. It is the person who gives that people like."

Deng Majok's second wife, Nyanbol Amor, who is generally acknowledged as having contributed considerably to his hospitality, recalled:

> He was always lavish in his entertainment of his Arab guests, and I am not even mentioning the special relationship between him and Babo Nimir. And even before we came, when we were still girls in the cattle-camps, we had already heard that his place was where crowds of visitors from the Rek, the Twich, and other peoples would gather and his sisters would work continuously to prepare food for guests. Then, after his sisters were married and gone, we came and Deng's home continued to be the place where everybody went, Arabs, southern Dinkas, and the people of the Ngok tribe. And all this was before he became chief. He would bring good things from the market and tell us to do this or that for guests. I was the one who took care of all his guests; all the Arabs who visited, I took care of. Nothing was lacking. I was provided with all I needed to entertain our guests. Everything was placed in my hands. All the good things from outside were placed in my care. Then Amel came with Nyanawai. He then said to me, "Nyanbol, you should now divide the things among the younger women."

Amel deserves special mention because she introduced a modern Sudanese way of life into the family and enhanced the quality of Deng Majok's entertainment and hospitality to meet the more sophisticated northern urban standards. When she was born, her family had migrated to a northern town. She spoke Dinka and was also fluent in Arabic. In her style of dress, cooking, and housekeeping, Amel was a sophisticated, Arabized woman. Although she never had any children, Deng Majok depended on her, and she became perhaps the closest wife to him. In this respect, he again demonstrated his innovative distinctiveness. Dinka law permits divorce on the ground of barrenness, but Deng Majok's priorities were no longer typical. One may, of course, argue cynically that he had many alternatives for procreation, but his feelings for Amel were profound, though also pragmatic. He provided her with china, cutlery, aluminum cooking pots and utensils, pewter and glass jars, silver or aluminum trays, and other pieces of more modern household equipment that were considered luxury items in that environment. Above all, Amel became an educator for the rest of the family. Within a short time she turned many of the family into modern homemakers and educators.

It is generally believed among the Ngok Dinka, and Deng Majok often expressed the sentiment, that Amel had a great deal to do with his becoming paramount chief because of the high quality she brought to his lavish hospitality and entertaining. "Hospitality was Deng Majok's big thing," said Amel.

> Even if a guest arrived in the middle of the night, people worked through the night. Guests who came during the day or during the night were of great concern to him. And it did not matter from which tribe they came, whether they were Dinka or non-Dinka, northerners or southerners; Deng loved them all. We used to stay up all night, cooking; we would never sleep. It was his hospitality and goodness of heart that placed him on top.

"Deng Abot was never interested in conversation with the Arabs," said Chol Piok. "But Deng Majok was. When he saw Arabs settled on the River Nyamora, he would go to visit them. And as he conversed with them, he would not eat in that Arab camp, never. He would drink only water; in those days, there was no tea. Among the Arabs, Deng started eating in the family of Aziz, who are friends of our lineage and who call themselves the Pajok of the Arabs."

Deng's attitude in this regard is part of a general characteristic that was also noted about him. Though he offered lavish hospitality himself, the circles from which he welcomed invitations to eat were very few. "Even in his large tribe of Abyor, he did not used to eat," said Chol Piok. "He confined his source of food to the clan Pajok. And even there, the circles from which he accepted food were very restricted." This is an element of Dinka aesthetics about food which, as in most cases, Deng Majok carried to an exaggerated degree. It was generally acknowledged that even in his own house he hardly ate, and when he did, it was late at night, very lightly, and only after making sure that all others had been fed. When Deng Majok chewed, he twisted or contorted his lips as though he despised food or was being compelled to eat and would have preferred to do without. This mannerism was clearly the antithesis of greed. One Arab, Ibrahim El Hussein from the family of Aziz, who observed Deng Majok closely over the years, noted:

> It was as though Deng Majok never ate at home. All his things went to others in generosity and hospitality. Where he ate I could never tell. Sometimes he would eat with us. And his ties with the Arabs were very special. The Arabs truly loved him. He was loved by all Arabs to the last man: he was loved by the family of Omran, the

Mazaghni, the Fadhliya, the Faiyrin, and the family of Kamil. All those people turned to Deng, your father. What I tell you, by God, and I repeat God, is totally free of any lie or exaggeration. He might be a little older than I, but we were about the same age. And I knew him well. Nothing escaped me. We grew up together. And his ties with the Arabs were special. Nothing ever happened to pull us apart.

According to Abdalla Hamadein, another Arab from the same family background:

> To tell the truth, Deng Majok was a blessing that filled our eyes. Deng Majok never dismissed a man calling him a thief; and Deng Majok never discriminated between people as good and bad. Deng Majok never held some people close to him and others far from him. Deng Majok was a father to all and a mother of orphans. . . . Deng Majok always saw the good side in people and overlooked the bad side. Deng Majok's generosity and hospitality made his own belly cheap to him. At his home, food would be lavishly served and Deng would direct its distribution, saying, "Give this to those people; and give that to these people; and take this here and this there!" He would distribute all the food that was served in abundance, beginning with the most distant guests and coming closer and closer until his closest circle of companions were served last. Nobody whosoever would leave his company hungry. As for him, he hardly ate anything, for, I repeat, he never valued his own belly. Deng never liked to feel food in his stomach. That was the way Deng managed this land; he led the people through their bellies.

"You know, Mading," commented Chol Piok, "the thing called food, this food that is eaten, in all its various forms, once it attracts a chief to be interested in food above other things, that is a reason for people to dislike that chief. Our people are difficult. They can dislike a chief simply because he likes food. The converse is also true. No matter what a chief does wrong, if he is hospitable and generous, he is most likely to be loved."

"The two most important things are the tongue and the belly," said Malith Mawien. "Those are the two most important things. If you say something nice to a person or if you fill a person's belly with food, you become friends." In his judgment, Deng Majok won the favor of his people on both grounds:

> That is how he won the chieftaincy. Chieftainship is what you have said well and the generosity you have shown to people. Those are the qualities which make a chief. Nobody becomes a chief for nothing. If you are to be a chief, guests should eat and get satisfaction from you. Your people should eat and get satisfaction from you. You should be able to articulate the interests of your people well. Who did not submit to Deng Majok? People from Mannyuar, Achak, Mareng, Diil, Achueng, Bongo, Alei, Anyiel, and Abyor—all the tribes of the

Ngok submitted to Deng Majok. Was it not because Deng Majok was good with his tongue? . . . And was it not because he was generous to their bellies?

Although Deng Majok won popularity on account of his generosity and hospitality, some people continued to criticize him for his recklessness with wealth; they feared that he would eventually deplete it and impoverish himself. Some called him "imprudent" and "unwise." Chol Adija observed, "A man called Monytoc once said: 'Now that Deng is so lavish with his wealth, will he one day not end up without cattle like the Dhar-Cheb tribe?[6] He will be reduced to poverty.' Deng heard it and said laughingly, 'No, I will not be like the Dhar-Cheb; I will not be reduced to poverty.'" Even his father, Chief Kwol Arob, who himself was known for hospitality and generosity, became critical of his son. According to Patal: "Kwol Arob is said to have said, 'My son, you tether the herd alongside the road so that you can feed travelers while leaving members of your family hungry! What shall I do with Deng? A son who risks the hunger of his own brothers and sisters by giving everything away to anyone that comes traveling along the road!'"

Although Deng Majok's generosity and hospitality are always linked with his success in winning the chieftainship from his father and half-brother, some people argue that they were natural virtues which Deng never used in a consciously calculating way to win the chieftainship, even though they did in fact serve that end. Chol Adija remarked on this issue: "I was one of the people who kept very close company with Deng Majok. I was with him until he died. His generosity and hospitality were never calculated for chieftainship."

As the struggle for power between Kwol Arob and his son intensified, Deng Majok became increasingly self-assertive to the point of encroaching on his father's authority, sometimes clearly overstepping his bounds. And yet it all seems to have remained strictly within the realm of family cordiality. As Patal explains: "His father would say something to the government, but Deng would intervene and say, 'Father, stop here!' Then he would add his own words and what he would say was what the government would accept. He would say the truth, which the government would readily see and accept." K. D. D. Henderson observed in Deng Majok a self-assertiveness that tended to indicate that he must indeed have been critical of his father at times in front of the British administrators. "As far as I remember, my impression of the half-brothers was that Deng Majok was quick-tempered and his brother more likely to sulk," Henderson wrote in response to my questionnaire.

Tensions between Deng Majok and his father began to mount. The better

---

6. Dar Umm Sheba, the branch of the Missiriya Baggara Arabs to whom Chief Arob Biong gave asylum from the Mahdists in the swamps of Baralil, and who were said to have been then lacking livestock and utterly poor.

known Deng Majok became, the more people felt that he should be the first deputy. But Kwol would not entertain the thought: "'No!'" he said, according to Matet Ayom, "'Deng Majok will not be the first deputy. Deng Makuei is the first deputy and Deng Majok will function as the second deputy.' Even when people wanted to compromise and have the two continue on equal terms as deputies, Kwol objected: 'I cannot let matters drift or else Deng Majok may become too used to the idea of their equality and grow ambitious. Deng Makuei is the man who should be in the lead.'"

Kwol Arob's open support for Deng Abot was very offensive to Deng Majok. He decided to remove himself from the company of both his father and his half-brother, and he established his own court tree. "That was the beginning of the rift between Deng Majok and Deng Makuei," commented Mithiang Aguek. "Apart from sometimes sitting in his father's court, Deng Majok established his own court and managed to attract large audiences. That naturally displeased Kwol Arob."

Matet Ayom recounts how an elder called Guem de Palek, from the Achueng tribe, was punished by Chief Kwol Arob because he frequented Deng Majok's court:

> Kwol had forbidden anyone from the tribe to go to the court tree of Deng Majok, since he had disaffiliated himself from the joint court with Deng Makuei. When Guem continued to attend Deng Majok's court tree, Kwol Arob had him arrested and imprisoned. He said, "This is because you went to the court tree of Deng Majok." Deng Majok took his cattle and went and paid a fine to redeem Guem from prison; he paid the fine and rescued Guem. That incident upset Deng Majok a great deal and made him join his words with Babo. Deng would visit Babo and Babo would visit Deng.

And so, Deng Majok used his friendship with Babo Nimir, the paramount chief of the Missiriya Baggara Arabs, whose influence on the British administrators had become pronounced, not only to promote his own rise, but to force his father out of power. Babo was to recall many years later the history of their friendship and how Deng Majok pursued his political ambitions. I reproduce Babo's account in some detail because it reveals quite a remarkable close relationship between leaders whose peoples were otherwise quite distant. In a way, it also shows how exceptional Deng Majok was as an individual almost out of step with his people. They first met when:

> Deng Majok was a young man in the cattle-camp with his half-brother, Deng Abot, and his brothers Biong and Arob. There were also the sisters Ayan and Abul and Awor. I knew them all.
> In 1923, Deng came to visit us at Leu. That was the first time I actually saw him. He wanted to marry, and there was an understanding between our Father,[7] Kwol Arob, and my father about his

---

7. A term of deference. In his response to the questionnaire on Deng Majok, K. D. D. Henderson observed that "Babo treated Kwol Arob as a father."

marriage. My father had said to Kwol, "Deng is my son. When he comes to marry, let me know so that I can contribute cattle to his marriage. And when his wife produces children, my sons will have a share in the wealth his daughters will bring when they are married." All this had transpired long before my time. I heard of it only later. When I saw him in 1923, he was coming to collect the cattle from our dry-season camp at Leu. He came on a horse, and with him were four or five young men carrying spears. People said: "That is Deng. That is Deng Majok, the son of Kwol; that is Deng Majok, the son of Kwol."

When he arrived, people rose to receive him. His horse was taken and unsaddled. A bed-seat was brought for him and placed next to my father's. Deng sat and conversed with my father. From the beginning he knew Arabic, but his Arabic was not much. He listened more than he spoke.[8] In the afternoon, he and my father went for a walk to see our cattle, which were grazing near the lagoon at Leu. They went and my father selected a number of cows for them. Whether they were five or six, I do not know exactly. The cattle were taken and driven away by the young men.

From being an unnoticed child, Babo succeeded his father at the very young age of thirteen and quickly rose to the position of an influential chief, whom Deng Majok befriended and won to his side against his own father:

It was after my father's death that I became close to Deng Majok, after my father had died and I became the head of the tribe. Deng was, of course, older than I, but we became very, very close friends. He would come to see me in our dry-season settlements, whether it be at Leu or Ngol or at Nugara. He would come and we would sit and chat. He would come with his followers. We would stay together for three or four or five days. And then he would return. At that time, the nazir was Kwol; Deng was not yet the nazir.

His name began to rise: "Deng Majok! Deng Majok! He is a man who shows great respect for people. He loves all his people and all the people of the tribe love him."

He drew far ahead of Deng Abot in his popularity, even though, according to the traditions of divine leadership among the Dinka, Deng Abot was said to be the one entitled to succeed his father.

Our Father Kwol Arob and our Father Mijak said that Deng Abot

---

8. Although Deng Majok was fluent in Arabic, his accent remained rather poor throughout his life. According to Babo Nimir's testimony to the author, and in the view of several Dinka elders interviewed, Kwol Arob spoke better Arabic, in addition to Nuer, than Deng Majok. Gawain Bell, who first met Deng Majok in 1947 as District Commissioner, observed: "We had a language problem, if I am not mistaken. I can't remember how fluent his Arabic was. By that time I am bound to say that I was a very fluent Arabic speaker. I had served a great deal in the Middle East and I had made a point of studying Arabic throughout my service, trying to perfect it, and so my impression is, at that time, although we could exchange pleasantries and pass the time of day, we probably did not get to know each other particularly well."

was the one entitled to succeed because his mother was the first wife. But because of our love for Deng Majok and because of his own merits, we sought to find justification for his succession in order to avoid imposing him on the tribe without a sound basis.

When we heard this [the contention that Deng Majok's mother was indeed the first wife], we called Jipur [the deputy paramount chief from the Dhiendior lineage] and asked him. Jipur confirmed this fact to me and to Rahma el Ferie [Rahma Nyok, the interpreter who was ethnically and culturally a Dinka-Arab].

Then we met the British Commissioner and explained to him that Deng Majok was the true leader and that he would be the one to inherit the Sacred Spears, the symbols of authority. His mother had been the first to be married, and although the cattle had been returned, that one cow which had remained had maintained the marriage bond.

Between Deng and me there was also an oath of brotherhood . . . we swore to be brothers. Of course, we were like brothers! In addition to that, he knew the circulating rumors kept saying, "Deng Abot, Deng Abot." He wanted to win me over to his side. So we concluded the pact of brotherhood.

He and I would sit and converse with the people. Then we would have dinner, and people would disperse, and he and I would sit conversing alone, sometimes until twelve o'clock at midnight. . . . He would be with me for three days, or four days, and then he would leave.

Whenever I visited Abyei, the same thing would happen. He would come from the cattle-camp to visit me in Abyei. We would be together for five days and six days, sitting and talking.

The conversations, as Babo intimated, were in effect occasions for plotting the overthrow of Kwol Arob:

> Most of our conversations were about leadership. We agreed that Nazir Kwol had become a very old man; that he was no longer able to execute government instructions one hundred percent. Of course, we were in favor of Deng Majok taking over. Our plans for Deng were what you people here in Khartoum mean when you say, "So-and-so is being groomed; So-and-so is being groomed to be this or that." We were grooming Deng for the day when we wanted him to assume the role of leadership.
>
> Mijak and Nazir Kwol would sometimes come to me and say, "Babo, what's this about Deng Majok? This leadership is not his; it is Deng Abot's. Son, you better stop pushing for Deng! Stop it! It is not his, it is Deng Abot's."
>
> I would say to Kwol, "Father, Deng Majok, too, is your son. Whether the chieftainship goes to Deng Abot or to Deng Majok, you will not have lost anything. In any case, nothing has happened that you should be concerned about."
>
> Whenever Deng Majok's name was mentioned, Kwol would say,

"Don't mention him. He is only a chief for the Arabs, a chief popular because of his generosity with food."

Deng was very hospitable. Whenever Arabs came to his home, he would slaughter animals for them and show them a great deal of lavish hospitality. Deng Abot, on the other hand, did not want the Arabs at all.

The advantage of Deng Majok's associating with Babo lay in the latter's closeness to the British, not only as a leader of a majority group of tribes, but also as an Arab who occupied a higher status than the Dinka in the racial and cultural hierarchy then existing in the Sudan. Babo's account continues:

Kwol saw that Deng Majok had become intimately associated with us and had become just like one of us. Whenever the District Commissioners came, he would join us and we would sit together with the District Commissioners, while Deng Abot stood some distance away.

They began to fear that should Kwol not be there, this man, Deng Majok, would probably assume the throne of leadership. They never uttered an ugly word. But Mijak and the nazir himself, our Father Kwol, would come to me and say: "What is this? This thing is not Deng Majok's; it is Deng Abot's. How can you go about trying to do otherwise? Yours is the Arab position. This is something that should be done according to our tradition. If we disregard our tradition, disaster will befall our tribe. If you ignore our tradition and promote Deng Majok for leadership, destruction will surely fall on the tribe." That is what they said.

They feared that, as I was a friend of Deng Majok and as the British District Commissioners always appreciated my views, I would probably influence the situation and enable Deng Majok to seize control of the chieftainship.

Commenting on Deng Majok's friendship with Babo, Achwil Bulabek said:

The genuine friendship that can exist between two sons of chiefs I saw for the first time between your father and Babo Nimir. Their relations were excellent. Babo would say to the government, "This is the man; Deng Majok is the person who will bring unity to our people." So one cannot swear that Babo never helped Deng Majok to become the chief. Of course, Deng was strong in his own right and had his own supporters among his people, supporters to whom he was the chief. For instance, when we finally discussed succession, was Babo present? Yet, there was a connection among all these things.

Chol Adija emphasized that the choice of Deng Majok as chief was a Dinka decision even though Arab support agreed with Dinka choice: "When chieftainship was discussed, the Arabs were not there to say anything in support of Deng Majok. It is only that the Arabs used to say that Deng Majok would be the chief. Their choice coincided with the will of the Dinka." Babo himself concluded his account with the remark that when the issue of succession eventually came up for discussion, "We then moved away from the scene."

Deng Majok's support outside his own tribe came not only from Babo and his people; he was also very popular among the Ngok's neighbors to the south. As Chief Madut Ring of the Kwach Anganya in Twichland put it:

> Kwol wanted Deng Makuei to be his successor, and at first Deng Makuei had the support of the Ngok. But Deng Majok had the support of all the neighboring tribes. Deng Makuei did not recognize the other tribes. But Deng Majok recognized them. Ngok also changed their minds about Deng Makuei. They admitted that Deng Majok was more qualified to be the chief. A person does not become a chief for nothing. It is the person who cares about people and worries about their welfare who becomes the chief.

Lang Juk, Paramount Chief of the Kwar and the Kwach tribes of the Twich, elaborated on Deng Majok's popularity among the neighboring tribes, and their influence on the British:

> As they worked together, Chief Kwol Arob preferred Deng Abot to succeed him in the future, but the neighboring areas such as the Arabs, the Twich, the Rek, and the Nuer liked Deng Majok's style better. When people gathered at intertribal assemblies and the British administrators attended, they were told by the leaders of the neighboring tribes that Deng Majok was a good leader; that whenever a person brought a case before him, he settled it justly; that he did not favor his own people over the people of other tribes; that he never ruled in favor of anybody because he was from his own area; that he gave everybody his right; that everybody left his court satisfied after the settlement of a case; that he never accepted anything that was not genuine or legitimate; that he liked the truth and everything he did was based on the truth. We would all tell the British administrators that we liked Deng Majok for all those reasons.

These testimonials from neighboring communities as to Deng Majok's chiefly qualities show the widened national context the British established to reinforce the civil order of the state. Although the role of the chief had always extended to neighboring areas through a form of tribal diplomacy, earlier successions had presumably depended solely on internal Ngok criteria for legitimacy.

It is generally agreed that although Deng Majok demonstrated the qualities of leadership and was favored by both the Arabs and southern Dinka, not only was his father against his becoming paramount chief, but most people among the Ngok seemed to share Kwol's bias against him. Monyluak Row argues that:

Deng Majok was at first very much disliked. People feared that, with his temper, he would use the power of the government to intimidate and oppress the people. Besides, your father revealed a noble character from the early days of his childhood. There is such a thing as jealousy. The Dinka hate one another simply because of the noble character one person projects and the jealousy others feel about that. To say that so-and-so is a noble person can be to provoke hostility. And then, if you honor yourself by stating your opinion with confidence, that too can provoke others. Such small factors played their part in the case of your father.

When the story of Deng Majok is now told, people wonder how a person could have been hated for his virtues. A virtue should not be a reason for resenting a person. Yet that is what happened with your father.

Monyluak's analysis falls just a little short of the dynamics of the situation, for Deng was not resented by his father, relatives, and fellow tribesmen merely because of jealousy of his virtues; it was his ambition for the chieftainship and the way he consciously or unconsciously built on his virtues to achieve his ambition which they feared and resented. But Deng Majok had gone too far and had become too formidable for them to contain.

7 Success

Kwol Arob's failure to stop tribal wars and Deng Majok's demonstrated administrative competence were to tilt the balance in favor of the latter's assumption of power from his father.

Traditionally, a Dinka chief is a divine leader who must not use force but persuasion. He may ultimately resort to supernatural sanctions by inflicting a curse on an uncooperative or disobedient subject. Divine prerogative is particularly opposed to spilling blood. A Dinka chief should not even see blood. Nor is he supposed to appear on the battlefield. He is expected to remain at home praying for victory if the war is with an enemy or for peace if the war is between factions of his own tribe. He may draw a line on the ground, place his Sacred Spears on the line, and pray that those who are pursuing aggression in disobedience to him suffer defeat. Modern administration, on the other hand, requires more than the charisma or awe of divine power. The chief has to resort to a more effective use of the state power, physically applying himself to the task and, if need be, employing the police or the security forces of the secular state power.

When tribal wars broke out in 1941, Kwol Arob acted in the traditional fashion, which did not at all impress the British colonial administrators. Deng Majok, on the other hand, got physically involved, riding to the battlefront and whipping the warriors as he struggled to disperse the front line. Although he could not stop the raging fight, the British were impressed by his actions, and he thus gained an advantage over his father that was to prove a deadly blow to the old man.

The story is told by those who witnessed the events: "Our tribe exploded," in the words of Chol Piok, who was intimately involved.

Wars began. Our people were fighting among themselves. The Bongo clashed with the Achueng at Maker. They fought and people were killed.

When the fight started, Kwol sent me: "Chol, you go to the Bongo. You are the one most acceptable to the warring factions. The Koich[1] are your people. No one will kill you. And the Bongo are your maternal kin. No one will kill you. You go and see how the situation is, where the warriors will be this evening, and where they will sleep."

So, I ran all night. I slept in Bongo. And early in the morning, when the first cock crowed, what you would call six o'clock, I crossed the River Nyamora. I scouted all the battlefronts of the Bongo at Maker, away from the river. Then I left. When I reached the pool at Kol Amer, I met Kwol Arob himself. With him was Mijak Kwol. Mijak was driving a black bull, Michar, which was to be sacrificed to stop the people from fighting.

Kwol then asked me, "Chol, where are the Bongo?"

I said, "The Bongo are very near here at the edge of the woods."

He said, "Do the Bongo know that they ambushed a person last night?"[2]

I said, "No, they do not. Who is he?"

Then he said, "They ambushed Nainai last night. He is now lying inside a hut with only remnants of breath. See him and then return to the Bongo."

I went and saw Nainai lying there. He was a huge brown man. I saw him and returned.

Kwol said, "Tell the Bongo to go away. Let them not wait for the Koich."

That is how I went. I went and met the Yom, a section of Pagwot. They held the right flank. I said to them, "O people of my mother, you ambushed a person last night, let alone the people you killed in battle yesterday."

They said, "Who?"

I said, "Nainai. So, let me tell you! Kwol Arob says that you should leave and proceed as far as Wachanguam."

The Bongo rose and took their cattle across to the other side. They did not go to Wachanguam. They went and camped at Wunlou.

Kwol Arob spoke to Deng Makuei and said, "You, Deng Makuei, run and confront the Bongo! Drive them away from Wunlou where I understand they have camped. Drive them as far as Wachanguam."

When Deng Makuei went, he found it impossible to manage the

---

1. Six of the subtribes who were the first to settle in the area, including Abyor, Achweng, Anyal, Diil, Mannyuar, and Mareng, as opposed to Paan-Cien, the three later arrivals, including Achak, Alei, and Bongo.

2. According to Dinka war ethics, ambush is extremely loathed and considered most provocative.

Bongo. They would simply boom out a war song and continue to tether their cattle in the camp.

Deng Majok got up and saddled his gray horse. And he followed. He found that the Bongo had completely subdued Deng Makuei, who was about to leave. Deng Majok jumped down from his horse and proceeded to untie the cattle of Deng Nyach's family without saying a word. All he said was, "If anyone dares, let him spear me in the back!" He kept on untying the herds.

Deng Nyach then spoke and said, "You Awet, my people, what else can you say?" And he proceeded to drive his herds away.

Each person from the Bongo saw that and drove his own cattle away. Deng Majok followed them until they reached Wachanguam in the middle of the night. And then he returned the same night.

That battle was eventually stopped. That was the battle of Maker. It ended.

Then came the battle of Dokura. That was the battle in which people like Kwol Deng, the father of Atem-Chol, and people like Mathii were killed. In that battle, many, many people were killed.

A year after Maker, "Word came that Dur Ayik, who had killed Nainai in the war of Maker, had been hanged," said Pagwot Deng, chief of Bongo. "He was taken away by the government and was eventually hanged. When the word of his death came, his tribe, the Bongo, rose up to attack the Achweng.[3] Abyor was allied to Achweng. They intercepted the Bongo at Dokura. People struggled and struggled to prevent that fight; but all in vain. It broke off the first day. The following day the war cries rose again. And the battle of Dokura was fought."

Again, Chol Piok was closely involved in that fight:

Mannyuar, Alei, and Bongo mobilized at Dungop. Kwol asked me to go to them, again arguing that I belonged to both sides and would be safe. So I ran on foot in a blazing sun. I ran and ran and ran. I passed through Dokura and Miyan Kor. Then I got to Dungop. There I met Jipur Allor (Kwol's deputy from Mannyuar). He was leading a large section of Alei (Mannyuar's ally) booming war songs. So I lowered my spears and said, "O people, stop and listen to me, I have something to tell you!"

Jipur Allor said, "Don't you see, it is Chol; have you not recognized him? He has something to tell you!"

So the singing stopped and the whole crowd stopped. Then I said, "Kwol Arob says, 'Tell the family of Allor that I have managed to control and disperse my people, the Koich.'" And it was true, he had

---

3. That was the first time capital punishment was introduced to the Dinka, and its impact was tremendous. The idea of a person being killed in cold blood was totally repugnant to their moral values even as it was seen as a deterrent which, though effective, had to be faced with the courage and valor of warriors. Reacting to the news by attacking signified both a retaliation for the cold-blooded killing and a defiance of the government's laws.

dispersed the Koich. Even when the people were eventually killed, it was old men who were killed and not warriors. A young man from Allei called Yak Bayak pointed his spear at me saying, "Don't you see, he wants to disperse our battlefront!" Right that moment, they resumed their war songs and went on their way. And I went on.

I had only gone a short distance when I met Bagat Allor at the head of Malual age-set of Mannyuar singing their war songs. I lowered my spears. And the Malual, too, suddenly stopped. I told them my message: Bagat simply dismissed me by saying: "Son of Piok, go your way. These matters will be discussed later when people return from battle."

So I went on until I met Deng Akonon. He was leading the warriors of Mithiang age-set singing their war songs. Then he said to me, "Son of my maternal uncle, have you not met with Jipur?"

I said, "Yes, I have met with him."

Again he said, "And have you not met with Bagat?"

I said, "Yes, I have met with him."

Then he said, "Those are the people leading the war. So, there is nothing I can do to prevent it."

Then I went to the Bongo. Again, I gave them the message. But as I talked, young warriors rampaged past me in the opposite direction. They came and found Abyor empty. Turuk age-set of Abyor had left for the cattle-camps. The warring age-set of their allied tribes had also gone. Mijok age-set of Anyiel had gone. Dhierget age-set of Mareng had left. And the Gol age-set of Achueng had also left. All our young warriors had gone away to the cattle-camps. That was the war that crept in on old people in Dokura and killed the elders; it killed the elders in a dreadful way.

If Deng Majok had gone instead of me, no one would have died.

One year passed. And when another year [1943] came, the Abyor planned an attack. They left. Kwol Arob also left with Mijak Kwol. The Abyor went to the home of Dheel, which was well out in the forest land. It was an area which no members of another tribe could reach. There they planned the war. That season continued without incidents. But just about the time new crops were to be reaped, the Abyor attacked the Bongo in the middle of the night. It was near those trees known as the Trees of Chan. That was the war of Nainai. In that open area near the Trees of Chan is where my cattle-byre was, the area where the *tebeldi* tree now stands. That was how far the war front extended.

That was the war that was fought. It was fought and fought and fought, with so many people killed. That was when the two Marials were killed, Marial, son of Mijak, and Marial, son of Allor. The Bongo overwhelmed the Abyor with strength. They chased the Abyor in a manner you have never heard of. They chased the Abyor until the Anyiel came. It was the Anyiel who held the front.

Deng Majok came and found the battle raging. Nevertheless, he was the one who struggled to stop the fighting. He would go to one side, and when people responded to him and drew apart, the other front would clash. He struggled alone until he was exhausted. He struggled and struggled on his horse while the battle was raging. Whenever he saw a small opening in the battlefront, he would ride into it. And when the battle closed in, he would take the horse out of that place.

Then, when he saw the situation becoming intolerable, with many people falling dead and dying, he would again step into the battle and make another attempt to separate the people. It was a war that Deng Majok worked extremely hard to prevent.

Had Deng Majok arrived before the battle started, he would certainly have stopped it. But he found the battle already raging and people already killed. Dead people lay in front of my cattle-byre. They had been killed and their bodies had been jabbed and jabbed with spears. The battle broke late in the afternoon. And it had started early in the morning. It stopped at that late hour.

"When the fight first started," said Pagwot Deng:

it was the Abyor who first planned the attack. They even told your father at Noong. But your father refused. He said, "Let it not even be known to have been contemplated! Let it not even be heard that the Abyor thought of attacking. Let it end within our own circle." And so the Abyor stopped. When Deng went and related the matter to his father, Kwol did not call the Abyor. He remained silent.

Word then leaked out among the Abyor and reached the Bongo. Even the fact that Deng had related the matter to his father and his father had remained silent without calling the Abyor to reprimand them was also known to the Abyor and Bongo. Kwol did not ask the Abyor, "What do you have against the Bongo? Why did you plan to attack the Bongo?" He never asked them. That was that.

Then the Abyor planned another attack and even mobilized at Maker and then moved as far as Mitbaai. It was there that your father stopped them. He had heard of their moves while he was at Noong. So he ran after them until he caught up with them. He made the Abyor return to their homes. He then left for Abyei. Again, he explained everything to his father. His father once again failed to call the Abyor and ask them what they had against the Bongo. He had now failed twice to check the Abyor.

We overlooked that and remained silent. Then came the following year. Later that year, the Bongo made a drum at Minyang-Loor and organized a major dance. The Abyor came to the dance of the Bongo but refused to dance. Instead, they took their spears and surrounded the dance for no reason at all. They were moving to attack without provocation.

When your father came, he gathered the Abyor together and went and met with them at a distance away from the dance area. He said to them, "Are you here to dance or to fight? You know my position; I have made it clear to you. If you have a different plan with my father, then that is different. I have told my father all that I told you on former occasions, but he has done nothing about the situation. He has remained silent. And now you come to surround a tribe that has made its drum and has brought it out for a dance and you say you want to fight them. Are you going to spear dancers, including their dancing women and girls? That cannot be. If you do not wish to join the dance, then you'd better leave now and go back to your homes. If you do not want to leave and return home, then at least stand far away from the dance. You can watch from far away and disperse once the dance ends. That is my word to you. But what you are about to do is something that has never occurred. From the time man was created, I have never heard of a tribe attacking another tribe and spearing them while they are dancing to their drum. I know of no example of this sort. So, never think of it ever again."

The Abyor then rose up determined to attack. They ignored your father's word and attacked, passing by the Achwil's village. When they emerged from the woods leading to the open area on the borders of Bongo, the people of Bongo began to emerge from their huts to face the attack. The battle began. The Abyor advanced until they were halted at Dhunydhuol, the area of the Tebeldi Tree. They were then pushed back up to the creek at Achwil's village. They were pushed across the creek. Then both sides held their front on each side of the creek and they continued to fight with the creek between them.

Deng Majok went, but it was not a fight he could stop anymore. The battle had already gotten out of hand. It was impossible for your father to stop it. People like Deng Mathii were leading the attack. But people like Mijang Kwol and Allor and Mahdi knew of the plan. They knew how it started. It was their war. And could they all have known about it and Kwol remained ignorant while they all sat in the same place?

"The following winter, the British District Commissioner came," said Chol Piok.

He convened the Assembly and said, "You, Kwol Arob, how could people be killed in such large numbers near your home? The distance between Nyinkuach, where the fighting took place, and your own home, are they not within seeing distance? Where had you gone?"

Kwol said, "I was sleeping. And when I got there, I found the battle too advanced and people had already been killed."

He said, "O Kwol! And how could Deng Majok have run all the way from Noong, which is so much farther away, and managed to reach the battle and struggled to stop the fight? Even if you had been crawling on your knees, would you not have reached it before Deng Majok?"

According to Pagwot Deng:

The District Commissioner had already begun to question the

leaders of the tribe discreetly and was told: "Had Deng been the chief, this war would not have been fought. The Abyor at first mobilized themselves, but he stopped them and said, 'Let nothing be heard about this!' And he went and informed his father. But his father never questioned the Abyor. The Abyor did it again and he once more stopped them and told his father. But his father never questioned the Abyor. So the Abyor kept this last plan secret from Deng. Is he therefore not a person who can save lives? Kwol Arob has the virtues of a true chief, but he has been misguided by his brothers. So, if Deng has proved himself so able, it would be worth giving him the chance to try the leadership of the tribe while his father is still alive."

That winter [elaborated Chol Piok], about the time the stalks of the second crop were open to cattle, Kwol was fetched to go to the North. He was called by the government. He was taken to the District headquarters at Nahud. He was then told, "You, Kwol, you have failed to stop wars. The people who have died in your hands are many. And you did nothing to save their lives. In the war of Maker many people died. And in the war of Dokura many people died. The war of Nainai again killed large numbers of people. You will have to retire and sit. Your children have matured enough to assume the responsibility. So show us which one of your two sons you want to take over."

The Englishman introduced the matter of succession in that discreet manner. He said, "Show me the one you believe will govern the tribe as well as you used to govern it."

Kwol said, "It is Deng Makuei."

The Commissioner then said, "If Deng Makuei is the one you have chosen, then you will not return home as yet. We will first go to the area without you and ask the people. All your people who are called the people of your father, Arob Biong, we shall ask. If they want Deng Makuei, then we shall accept their word. If they want Deng Majok, we shall accept their choice. Had you said to us, 'You, government, it is for you to see the one you think will be able to govern the area,' we would have talked: we would have given you our opinion. But now we shall not reveal to you all our thoughts as yet."

Kwol Arob was stunned. He did not know what to do. When he realized there was nothing he could do, he said: "I surrender. If it is the name of Deng Makuei which will detain me here and prevent me from going to my area, then I give in. And you, government, you will go and talk to my people in my presence. But although I shall be there, I will not do anything to interfere with the plan. Whatever the people say will be. If the people say, 'It is Deng Makuei,' I will have nothing to say; and if the people say, 'It is Deng Majok,' I will also have nothing to say." That is how Kwol was released and allowed to return home.

When I heard that Kwol had nearly been arrested but had been released and had just returned, I rose early in the morning and went to him. He had just come back from Nahud the day before in the late afternoon. I rose before dawn and arrived early in the morning. His age-mates had not yet gathered. I found him under the tree with Mijak Kwol and Deng Patoc. I rested my spears against the tree. Then I said, "Father of Agorot, there is something I want to talk to you about."

He immediately understood that I was going to ask him about his detention at Nahud. We went inside a small room that had just been built for him; it was a very tiny room. That is where he took his tea in the morning. I asked him about those matters. We spoke.

Then I said to him. "The people who reported you to the government are these: there was Deng Patoc (who is with you now), and Deng Nyac, and Bagat Allor. Those were the people who reported you. The day they discussed you, I was lying down under the tree. They came and sat down. And there were no other people. And then they talked. They said to the District Commissioner that they would like to talk with him without you present or any other persons present. Then they talked against you while I lay there listening. They thought I was not interested in such matters. They spoke in Dinka and Rahma interpreted into Arabic. With those enemies around you, why are you intensifying the battle with your own son? What is the matter with you? Is Deng Majok not your son? Was he begotten by someone else? Even his mother, did she beget children with someone else before you married her? This issue of Deng Majok is really a fault on your side."

Then he said, "Chol, son of my father, I do not hate him. It is just that I fear Deng Majok will outwit my people. He will not take care of the children well."

I said, "And how do you know that? What about his good treatment of people in general, will he not do the same to your children?"

Then Kwol said, "I have given in. Will I bring it up again when it was a major problem for which I was almost detained and prevented from begetting children in my family? I have surrendered. They are both my children."

Then I left. I took my spears and left. I went beyond the creek near Deng Makuei's house. There, Deng Majok, who had been sitting under the tree outside, caught up with me. He said, "You, there, wait for me!" Then he said, "What were you talking to your cousin about?" I explained to him. He laughed. He accompanied me until we reached Nyinkuac. Then he turned back at the stream in Nyinkuac. We talked and laughed.

The District Commissioner came and the assembly was convened under the court tree. People then spoke. And when people talked, all our people of the area, including elders and court members, were assembled. The old men of the tribe were included too. People like Amor Miorik were included, even though they did not hold any public position. Another elder from Mannyuar tribe who was called Kur Alak, a crippled man, was also brought in, carried on a bed.

The issue was then raised. The Commissioner said, "You people, what we have said with Kwol is this and this. And what brought the matter here is for you to choose the person you want to be chief, whether it will be Deng Makuei or Deng Majok."

An old man called Katdit got up, an elder called Katdit from our Anyiel tribe. He said, "Deng Makuei is not a chief. Deng Majok is the chief. He is our chief who will sustain us. It is he who will keep our tribe in order. As for Deng Makuei, he is not a chief. Deng Makuei is a brave man, but a brave man who never will reason. As for the man called Deng Majok, he is brave, but he combines his bravery with an ability to talk. Deng Makuei's courage knows no words. He does not talk."

People all joined in that opinion. Then the Commissioner turned to Kwol and said, "Chief, now say your word."

Kwol said, "I have nothing to say. If this is what the tribe says is their wish, how can I have a separate word? It will be as the people have spoken. So, you, Deng Makuei, you leave the matter. Let Deng Majok take my place."

Deng Makuei got up and left. Deng Majok was then installed by the tribe as the chief. He became the chief.

As soon as he was installed as paramount chief, the District Commissioner asked Deng to conduct the war trials with him. I was there. The District Commissioner said, "Where is the clan-head called Chol Piok?"

People said, "Here he is!"

And he said, "Tell us all about the fighting! We understand that you were the person sent when the people refused to obey. Tell us what happened."

I told them all as I have told you. I said, "The people who started the fight were Jipur Allor and Bagat. These are the things they said. You, Bagat, were not these the words you said?"

Bagat got angry and said, "Chol Piok, why are you after me? Am I the young men who went to war?"

I said, "You were their chief." And I went on to mention the rest of the people. I said, "There is Minyiel and there is Yak of Bayak. Those were the people." They were arrested and seated apart. Bagat Allor was questioned. But he strongly disclaimed responsibility: he passionately denied it, saying, "I was only following the warriors."

The Commissioner then said, "And why does Chol say you were ahead of the warriors on a horse? And Jipur, too, is said to have been ahead of the warriors on a horse? How could a chief be overwhelmed by his warriors while he is leading them? A chief is only overwhelmed when his people disperse and run. You are at fault. And you will be fined like all the rest."

They were fined. Deng Majok then said, "Commissioner, the person called Minyiel and the person called Yak should be both fined and flogged."

The Commissioner said, "Chief, your opinion is right."

So they were made to lie down. And that was the beginning of flogging in our area. Each one received twenty lashes.

"Deng Majok imposed punishment on his own section, the Abyor, and left the Bongo free," said Matet Ayom.

He said, "The Abyor were the first to attack the Bongo. And if wrongs are not punished according to the degree of guilt, wrong-doing will never cease in this land." So the Abyor were severely punished while the Bongo got off scot-free. That was the case that deterred the people of our land from making war.

When the case was decided [added Monyluak Row], Deng said, "It is because of the Abyor that all these people lost their lives. . . . Although the Bongo killed more people from Abyor than the Abyor killed from the Bongo, they were defending themselves against attack. I believe the Abyor should be made to pay a heavy fine of cattle. And they should be made to pay compensation for the people they killed among the Bongo. Bongo should only pay compensation for the people of Abyor whom they killed, but they should not be made to pay the fine." That is how Deng ended the case and that is how the tribe settled in peace and order. It was because of your father.

"Deng Majok then moved to settle other disputes with our neighbors to the south," continued Chol Piok. "That is how Deng Majok took over and became established as the chief. He then reorganized everything. He reconciled Bongo and Abyor. There were no more conflicts between them. That is how internal warfare ended in our area. And that is how our warring with the Twich ended. We then stayed in peace."

A year after Deng Majok took over the leadership, he went to the North to receive his insignia of office, a red robe of honor. The Arab elder Ibrahim El Hussein describes the scene of his return:

I and Mahdi and many men from the lineage of Kamil were on our horses to escort him back home. We escorted him on horseback. When we reached Akwong, the Dinka came to meet him. Crowds came, booming with songs and blowing their horns. Animals were slaughtered. Cries of joy filled the air. We stopped at Deng's village at Naam [Noong]. Your father was wearing the red robe of chieftainship. He slaughtered more cattle for us. His wives prepared plenty of food. We spent the night there at Naam.

The following day we escorted him again up to Abyei. His home was on this side of Abyei, where you buried him. Kwol Arob was in his home on the other side of Abyei. Kwol used to spend the day under the huge tree in front of his home. We went over in a crowd that filled the shade of the tree. As we approached, we greeted them: "Peace be upon you!"

Kwol refused to reply to our greeting. He was angry over the issue of chieftainship.

"Greetings," we said again, but he did not respond.

An old man of his age who was in our group said to him, "Kwol, here we are bringing your son to you, how can you not respond to our greeting?"

Then he responded and greeted us rather coldly.[4]

We went back to the cluster of trees near the area where the police station is now located. Deng Majok slaughtered a large number of animals for the festivities. It was a festivity that had no limits. Hospitality was one of his outstanding virtues.

Kwol Arob continued to be concerned about the future of his family, and in particular his two sons. He confided his concern to Achwil Bulabek, who recounted their conversation:

He called me by sending me Maleng Kwol and said, "Let Achwil come early in the morning."

I left very early in the morning—so early that it must have been about five o'clock. I went to Abyei. I found he was still sleeping in his elevated hut. Then he came and found me waiting outside. He used to rise early. He said to me, "Did you sleep here?" I said, "No, I came this morning. It was you who sent for me. Is all well?"

"Yes, all is well," he said.

One of his wives then went and brought him some water. He washed his face. Tea was then made and brought. We drank tea. People had begun to gather. There was Mabeng de Kwol and Mijak and Yowe and Malual Adhar—four—and then he and I, we were six altogether.

Then we left and went to the police center where the police station is now located. At that time, it was built of small huts.

He said, "Why I sent for you is I have been searching in my mind a great deal. You and I began to come into conflict from the time you were not yet initiated into adulthood. When the appointments of junior chiefs were discussed, you always took your independent line on anything I said. Whatever I said, you would stand against me and push your own line until you would end up winning your argument. That made me dislike you, which is why we often came into conflict. But recently I have been searching my mind as I lie down to sleep. I have thought a great deal and I have found you to have been consistently correct in the positions you have taken. What you used to tell me I find today to have been the truth, all of it."

He began to trace the issues from the time he and I had first come into conflict and said I had been right on all those issues. "Son of my father, I have come to realize fully that you have a good head. Why I am calling you today is for the sake of my children. I do not think it good for a man to wait and then make his will and wishes known as he is dying. Here are my two sons, the Deng brothers. One Deng is a

---

4. The incident is reported by the then District Commissioner in a report quoted extensively by Howell in "The Ngok Dinka," 239–93.

poor speaker. But Deng Majok is clever. Should I die and they quarrel, unless you step between them, they will never live in peace. Even the public will not reconcile them. Even your brother Bol would not be much help because he is hot-tempered. He will give his opinion against the person he believes to be in the wrong, and if his word is not heeded, he will get impatient, lose his temper, and give up. But you, you will persuade a person to see his wrong, and even if a person disagrees with you, he will think it over at night until he realizes that what you had said was the truth. So there are my children!"

While it would seem that the struggle for power was over, the truth was that, in the minds of the Dinka, once a chief always a chief. Not only did Chief Kwol Arob remain influential as the head of his tribe, but apparently the issue of who would eventually succeed him in the event of his death remained alive in the minds and hearts of his people. They did not have long to wait. Kwol was dying.

A year after Deng Majok had gone to the North and had been given his robe of chieftainship, Kwol Arob fell ill. That same year, according to Achwil Bulabek:

> There was to be an intertribal assembly in Tongliet. Deng was then the man in charge of the tribe. The Sacred Spears were still in the possession of your grandfather. When we went to Tongliet, Deng Majok said to the government that leadership and the Sacred Spears were never separated in Dinka tradition. He called Jipur Allor and the matter was explained to the British District Commissioner.
>
> Mr. Owen was then the Commissioner. He called the people to assemble. There was Jipur and Deng Majok and Deng Abot and Chol Dut, and Miyan Arob and myself, Achwil Bulabek. The chairs were then taken to a spot near a bridge. The matter was then raised. The government said that the spears should be given to Deng but that they would welcome comments from the elders present at the meeting.
>
> I said, "If it were my judgment, I would say that Kwol should be allowed to keep his spears until he dies."
>
> He said, "And what about after his death?"
>
> I said, "The spears should then go to Deng Majok. That is the day they will cease to be Kwol's and become Deng's. But if we take the spears from him now, it will be as though he were already dead. It will even hasten his death."
>
> He said, "The case will end in accordance with the opinion of Achwil. I shall leave tomorrow morning, but the Assistant Commissioner will remain. And you, Achwil, will come with me. You will tell Kwol yourself. Is he not your brother?"
>
> I said, "Yes, he is my brother."
>
> The next morning we got a ride in his car. I said, "I would like Chol Dut to accompany me. He will be my witness." So we left in the morning while the assembly was still in session. They had met for three days, but there was yet another day to go. We drove until we

reached Abyei. The day we arrived at Abyei, we found that Kwol's illness had become critical. As soon as I got out of the car, I was told of the situation.

That same evening, Kwol worsened so much that people ran to alert the tribe and gather the cattle for funeral sacrifices and rituals. The Deng brothers were still at the Assembly in Tongliet. People had been sent to them, but our paths had crossed.

Some people maintain that Deng Majok was deliberately kept out of the picture. According to Nyanbol Amor: "Word was secretly passed on to Deng Abot and kept from Deng Majok. Deng Abot rushed back home. He ran all night and arrived early in the morning." Achai-Jur elaborates on the same point:

> The person who was sent to deliver the news was told to go and sit discreetly by Deng Makuei's side and tell him that his father's condition had worsened. He was to report back immediately. Deng Makuei was informed. He in turn did not say anything to Father. He did not even say goodbye to the assembled members. He simply got up and left. Then Father heard the news from someone else. As soon as he received the news, he looked for a car and hurried back to the scene of his father's death.

Chol Piok, who was with the brothers in Tongliet, narrates the developments there:

> We were fetched by horse. Kwol had been ill for some time, but he had begun to improve. And after the people had gone to Tongliet, he suddenly got worse at night. The person who was sent said, "The Chief will not survive the night!" Deng Makuei decided to run all night. But Deng Majok remained. The next morning, he bade farewell to the chiefs and said: "I must leave. I cannot stay to the end of the Assembly. My father is dying."
> The following morning, Deng went by the Commissioner's car and we traveled on horses. At about the time cattle were unpegged to graze, we came to Mitrok. Deng also arrived at the same time by car. He jumped down from the car and entered the hut where his father lay. He approached his father and said, "Father, are you dying?" And his father said, "Is it you, Majoh?" His voice was no longer audible. He caught Deng Majok's head and placed Deng's ear close to his mouth. What he actually said to Deng, I did not hear. And Deng has never told to this day. As soon as Deng raised his head from his father, his father passed away. He died.

Achwil Bulabek recalls that as the brothers arrived:

> they rushed to their father's bedside and before he died, he uttered to them his dying will. But he had already made his will known to others before they came. In it he bequeathed to them two sets of shoes

symbolic of succession in Dinka tradition. He gave Deng Majok modern shoes, which symbolized succession to government power, while he gave Deng Makuei traditional Dinka shoes to symbolize succession to traditional spiritual authority. He said to Deng Makuei, "This is your path, the path of our ancient traditions, including the Sacred Spears, and Deng Majok's path is that of the government."

Traditionally, a Dinka chief was not allowed just to die, as that would weaken the divine power of the Spirit in the Flesh—Ring—leaving nothing to be passed on to his successor. Instead, when a chief was believed to be close to death, he would be urged to make his dying will, settle his affairs, and then surrender himself to be placed in his grave. His successor would be lifted up as the body of his predecessor was being lowered into the grave.[5] Kwol Arob was apparently saved from this ordeal by fear of the government's reactions and the presence of medical staff near his bedside.

Achwil Bulabek was to become a central figure in the developments, being a close relative and the sectional chief of the Abyor subtribe:

> The grave was then marked. People began to dig. They dug and dug and dug. Then he was placed in the grave. You know the Dinka way; as the dead chief is placed in the grave, the new chief must be installed at the same time. No moment is allowed to lapse without a chief. Abyor had already agreed on a secret plan unknown to the other tribes. Even as the grave was being dug, people were conspiring that Deng Makuei would be the heir to chieftainship. But whenever I joined any meeting, people fell silent. And when I moved to another gathering, those people too became silent. That was the plot made by Abyor.
>
> The whole of Abyor had gathered, including women. As the body was being lowered into the grave, people stampeded toward Deng Makuei. They caught hold of Deng Makuei and installed him. They brushed Deng Majok aside as though he were no longer the chief. Deng Makuei was then the chief. Deng Majok sat at a distance with his brother Arob and myself.

Monyluak Row added a third man to the lonely company of Deng Majok: "The only people of Abyor I heard stood with Deng Majok were a man called Jibir Tong and Achwil Bulabek and Deng's younger brother, Arob. Biong Mading, Deng's other brother, nearly joined Abyor."

According to Mithiang Aguek, one man daringly, if only symbolically, upheld Deng Majok as the chief: "Only one man, Kur, nicknamed 'Kur-Chuet,' 'The Meat Craver,' from Bongo tribe, got up and went to Deng

---

5. It is controversial whether the custom was, in fact, ever practiced or was a myth that served a purpose without ever being applied. On the other hand, the belief in the custom is widely spread among the Dinka. See Seligman, *Pagan Tribes of the Nilotic Sudan*, 196–98. Major Treatt describes the custom in *Out of the Beaten Track*, 125–26.

Majok. He lifted Deng's right hand and said: 'Oh, Chief, I will not be to blame; we shall be victims together. May God reward me in the end.' At that moment, Biong Mading, Deng Majok's brother, broke down in tears. The Abyor left with Deng Makuei, reciting their hymns."

"Abyor rejected our father and began to throw mud at him," said Achai-Jur. "The mud that had been dug from our grandfather's grave is what they were throwing at him."

"Abyor was jubilant in a most distasteful manner," added Nyanbol Amor.

> You know, during the burial of a chief, people dance as though no disaster has occurred, but Abyor was worse. People were jumping around jubilantly and arrogantly. Those who were identified with Deng Majok were being mocked. Deng and his brothers, Arob and Biong, had their feet nearly trampled. People looked at them scornfully. When the burial was completed, Deng called his brothers and people like Achwil and said, "Come, let us go."

According to Nyanbol Arob: "People were bragging, 'Now that we have chosen Deng Abot as the chief, what else can Deng Majok do?'"

"Then all the people left to bathe in the river [according to tradition]," said Achwil Bulabek. "We bathed separately from the rest of the people."

"Deng did not want confrontation," observed Nyanbol Amor. "He realized that he would eventually win. As we were returning home, we met the British District Commissioner, who had just arrived. He started addressing Deng as nazir, the chief. . . . They sat and discussed the situation and planned their moves."

Ajuong Deng, chief of Anyiel, the section which had initially blessed Deng Majok's mother to beget a son, recalled:

> For two days, your father sat very alone. My father sent word to Deng Majok, "Do not despair; we are coming." People would pass by and say, "You children of Nyanaghar, are you not going to be dogs, now that Kwol Arob is dead and Deng Abot has taken over!"
>
> When Anyiel arrived, they boomed their spiritual songs, stampeding into the home of Deng Majok. They took a bull and a cow and sharpened their horns as sharp as thorns and slaughtered them.[6] They lifted Deng up toward the sky and declared, "You are the chief! And that is the way it will be."
>
> Anyiel had done something similar in the history of Ngok leadership. It was Anyiel who installed Chief Biong Allor. I believe Akwei or someone had first been installed as chief. That other person was the half-brother of Biong. But Anyiel came and made Biong the chief and that was eventually the choice that prevailed. Anyiel was there-

---

6. That way, they symbolically armed themselves for the political battle.

fore known as the people who select the paramount chief to be accepted by all the sections.

"The District Commissioner had arrived and had set the following day for the discussion of succession," resumed Achwil Bulabek.

The following morning, I left my home at Nainai and headed for Abyei. The Abyor had scattered back into their homes. But in the morning a group formed and came after me. They caught up with me on the way in that area near Pagwot's home and said, "Achwil, will you not be forced to accept the way of Abyor now that people have decided to bring their case to the government?"

I stopped and stood facing the people who were following me. I said, "You, this entire tribe of Abyor, is there anyone among you who is braver than I?"

They said, "No! There is no one."

I said, "And even with spoken words, is there anyone among you, the entire Abyor, who is a better speaker than I? And is there anyone among you who is a better speaker than Deng Majok? Today, Deng will hold one flank and I shall hold the other flank and the Commissioner will be in the center of the battlefield."

When the Assembly was convened, Abyor all gathered, including women. They filled the shade of the court-tree and extended as far as the river. The whole of Abyor was there. The Commissioner then asked, "What do you, Abyor, say? Who should be the chief?"

They said, "We are opposed to Deng Majok's succession!"

He then lined the people up and asked them one by one. When he had questioned some thirty persons, he said, "That will be enough." The overwhelming number of Abyor wanted Deng Makuei to be the chief. Then he turned to Jipur Allor (of the Dhiendior lineage) and said, "Now that Abyor has obviously rejected Deng Majok, what do you say?"

Jipur said, "I am confounded!"

Then he turned to me. I was sitting all alone, separate from Abyor, who were lined up. He said, "You are the chief of Abyor and therefore their leader. What is your opinion?"

I stretched out my hands in opposite directions and said, "You see how far apart my hands are? That is how far my position is from the position of Abyor."

He said, "In what way?"

I said, "You too you are like Abyor! You yourself are like Abyor!"

He said, "Why? Why do you think I am like Abyor?"

I said, "When Kwol died, Kwol the man to whose grave you went, was he still the chief when he died?"

He said, "No!"

I said, "And who was therefore the chief?"

He said, "Deng Majok was."

I said, "And did Deng kill a person last night? Did he kill a person so that the government has at last discovered his disqualification for the chieftainship? How could Deng be honored with the robe of chieftainship this year and during the same year you come to question people about the same Deng? And it was you, the government, who placed him there. Is a chief not deposed because he has committed an offense? Chieftainship is contested when a chief dies, leaving the position vacant. Had Kwol died still holding his position as the chief, the matter would then be discussed and the one wanted by the people would succeed. But Deng Majok assumed the chieftainship while Kwol was still alive. How can you now come and question us again about the same thing?"

"But let me tell you! You hear it said that Deng Makuei is the senior son. He is not. Deng Majok is the senior son. When my father died, Deng Majok asked his opinion. When he obtained his opinion, my brothers, Bol and Miyan, were there. Only Biong, who is our older brother, was absent. My father took Deng's right hand and raised it and said, 'Chieftainship will not give you even a headache.' So, ask Bol and leave aside all these people who have been talking. They know nothing. I know more than these elders you were questioning.

"These spears were not bought with grain cultivated by anybody's mother. These spears came with our original ancestor. They are always handed down to the person who assumes the chieftainship. So ask Bol, 'Did your father say so or did he not?' My father and Kwol's father are sons of the same father. Arob, the father of Kwol, is the son of Biong and my father, Bulabek, is also the son of Biong."

He listened and then turned to Bol and said, "Bol, did you hear what Achwil has just said?"

Bol remained silent.

"Bol, it is you I am asking!"

He remained silent.

"Bol!"

Then I said, "Sir, he will never deny it. That is why he will not answer. If he answers you and denies it, let him swear on our Sacred Spears."

Then he said, "It is now clear that you, Abyor, are in the wrong. So you, Jipur, sentence them."

Jipur said, "They should be fined four hundred cows."

The Commissioner wrote that down. He finalized the decision.

I got up and said, "Sir, who are the offenders, is it the cattle or people? Abyor is a tribe with a great deal of wealth. The cattle you are now demanding in fine will be provided by noble women whose husbands are dead. Men will call on these women and say to each one of them, 'Woman, this is the reason for your membership in this tribe. A challenge has emerged.'"

Then he said, "And what would you do?"

I said, "Although you have written down your judgment, I do not agree with it; cattle have nothing to do with this. Arrest the people responsible and forget the cattle."

He said, "And who are the people?"

I said, "There is my brother, Bol. If you really want the matter to end, there is Bol, the son of my mother. And there is [Mijak] Mijangdit. These are the people carrying Abyor on their heads."

I then added other names: people like Biong Mijak and Malual Chol and his father and Matiok Malek. All those people, including people like Miyan Arob and Bulabek Deng Awak. That was why they were all arrested and taken away to jail in the North.

Deng Majok said to me, "Achwil, I am going to beg you on behalf of two or three people. And please do not insist. First, leave Mijak out; Mijak is second to our father in seniority. Now that my father is dead, even if Mijak has come to dislike me as he now dislikes me, I cannot extend my hand against him. Release him with his son, Biong. Perhaps you can save Biong with a payment of fine. Please, son of my grandfather, release them." I almost got angry with him, but he pleaded with me.

Apparently, when Abyor felt defeated over the issue of chieftainship, they tried to deny Deng Majok the Sacred Spears on the ground that they embodied a source of power separate from the authority of the government. According to Allor-Jok, "Deng Majok argued that he could not understand how his father could bequeath leadership to him without the Sacred Spears. He said that without the spears, the tribe would not fear and respect him. People said to him, 'Deng, your government power is not less frightening than the power of the spears. Honor what your father has given you and let your brother take what his father has bequeathed to him.' But Deng insisted on taking both."

Initially, according to Allor-Jok, all nine sections of the Ngok were behind Deng Makuei because it was in accordance with the will of an elder. "When an elder dies and says his word, it must be honored. Besides, Deng Makuei was acknowledged as Kwol's senior son who would inherit his divine powers. Deng Majok had already taken over the government chieftainship while Father was still alive. But the tribe upheld Deng Makuei because of the leadership of the Sacred Spears which Father had passed on to him. It was not a rejection of Deng Majok's government leadership."

The evidence of most elders seems to suggest that Abyor's position on the matter was not supported by the rest of the tribe, or else public opinion was quickly swayed by the support the British District Commissioner obviously showed for Deng Majok. According to Ajuong Deng:

> Abyor had said, "Even if Deng Majok should be made the chief, we will never leave the Sacred Spears to him." They came booming their war songs and gathered at the area between the home of Abo and the rest house. That is where they gathered carrying their spears and shields. Anyiel was on this side, and with them were some of the

Mannyuar. They all stood, ready to grab their spears and fight. The District Commissioner asked the people, "And what about the spears? I understand that they are with Deng Abot and that the chieftainship of Deng Majok is separate from the chieftainship of the spears?"

My father, Deng Tiel, said, "That is a lie! Let them mention one example in which the chieftainship of Pajok was ever split between two men, one with the Sacred Spears and the other with government authority."

"We said to the District Commissioner," added Matet Ayom:

> "Deng Majok is the chief we have chosen and it is always the chief who should hold the Sacred Spears; should there be a dispute, it is the chief who administers the oath of the spears. When our tribe goes to war with another tribe, it is the chief to whom the tribe entrusts these Sacred Spears, and he carries them leading his people and points them at the enemy. The control of the chief through his political authority and his divine control through the Sacred Spears are inseparable." When the Commissioner ordered the spears to be fetched, Abyor said, "The spears will not be fetched; if they are fetched, we shall kill the Commissioner."

According to Chol Piok, the District Commissioner became very angry and said: "'Let the spears be brought at once. Right this minute they must be fetched.' When people tried to be evasive, he called for the police and said, 'If I go myself to fetch the spears, that village where they are and even that part of Abyei close to it will not look good afterward. I will have it all destroyed by guns.'"

Matet reports that the District Commissioner then turned to Achwil and said, "Achwil, who will fetch the spears?" Achwil said, "You'd better fetch them yourself." The Commissioner mounted his horse. Biong-Cham then said: "Achwil, it is better that the Commissioner does not go. If he goes himself, that will destroy our country. Let us fetch the spears ourselves."

"Mahdi got up and made his famous statement," resumed Chol Piok:

> "My Roaring Leopard Bull! Our country has been captured. Deng Thokloi, son of my father, we cannot allow the government to fetch our Sacred Spears. Let us fetch them and give them to the government ourselves. We will then see what he will do with them."

They went and brought the spears. The spears were then placed in front of the District Commissioner. The sacred skin on which they are supposed to rest was laid down in front of the Commissioner and the spears were placed on it. The Commissioner then said, "All of you present, is there anyone who still wants Deng Makuei to be the chief?" He would pick one person from the group and ask him; and pick another person and ask him; and pick yet another person and ask him. All denied in fear.

The District Commissioner then asked Achwil, according to Matet, to take the Sacred Spears and hand them over to Deng Majok. "Achwil took the spears and handed them to Deng Majok. When Deng was about to receive them with his left hand, Achwil said, 'Hold them with your right hand. You have no curse to be afraid of.' Deng received the spears with his right hand. Hymns were then introduced. The spears were taken into Deng's house. A sacrificial bull was killed, and a lamb was sacrificed."

"The government then took Deng Makuei away and banished him to Nahud," resumed Chol Piok.

> Deng Makuei spent the dry and the rainy seasons there. He spent a whole year. He was detained in the big prison but kept in a separate area from the rest of the prisoners. No people were permitted to see him. Only the one wife that had been taken with him was allowed to stay with him.
>
> Then the government permitted him to return after warning him very strongly. The District Commissioner said to him, "Let me not hear a single word from you about chieftainship anymore. Even the position of the deputy chief that you held you have now lost."
>
> Deng Makuei surrendered. He was returned and seated in his house. He became an ordinary man.
>
> Two years passed. And when a successor to Deng Makuei was being sought, people said it should be Nyok, Deng Makuei's educated brother, but Deng Majok refused. He said "Nyok has got his job as a teacher. Let him continue in that position. Let us return Deng Makuei to his position."
>
> The Commissioner said, "But if we put him back in that position, will he not do the same thing he did before?" Deng Majok said, "No, he will not. Let us at least give him a chance. If we now deny him any position, his heart will break. So, let us place him under me."

"Your father insisted," explained Ajuong Deng. "Let him remain in his position. If he should continue to prick me, let him prick me. Our people will see how I treat him and how he behaves toward me. Should we deny him any public position because of our conflict, that conflict will continue in the minds of the people. And he will continue to feel that he has been victimized."[7]

Deng Makuei was later to give this version of the contest for power:

> Deng Majok had started the problem with our father's illness. People kept coming to my father to report, "This is what Deng Majok

---

7. While Deng Majok's position is consistent with the conciliatory orientation of conflict resolution among the Dinka, there is reason to believe that it was also a shrewd way of guarding against the possibility that Nyok, being educated, might prove a more formidable adversary, especially as he would share the bitterness over his brother's plight. Being a Deputy Paramount Chief would place him in a strategic position to undermine Deng Majok, while Deng Makuei had been too discredited to be dangerous.

is saying with Babo; and this is what Deng is saying with Rahma." That was when my father said to me: "You, Deng Makuei, as we hear it rumored, the spears might be taken from you by force. If they are taken by force, do not contest the chieftainship in court. If you do, you would be the son of a woman." That much my father told me; I cannot hide it from you, son of my brother. He said: "If you should go to court for chieftainship, you would be the son of a woman. Let the spears go; one day, they will fall down by themselves. If our chieftainship is not an ancestral heritage but a personal achievement of Deng, son of Nyanaghar, leave them to fall on their own." Deng and I did not confront one another in front of the public. Deng had already established his case with the District Commissioner.

When the District Commissioner said to me, "Deng [Makuei], you go and bring the spears," I said, "I will never hold them with this hand of my father. If you want to take them by force, then do so. I will never ask you why!" The District Commissioner saddled his horse and rode for the spears. That is when Mahdi Arob ran and caught up with him in the area which is now the airstrip. Mahdi said to him, "Go back; I will fetch them myself." So it was Mahdi who fetched them from the hut and brought them into court. Your father then got hold of the spears. I sat there only watching. Is it not over now? The issue of the spears was always discussed even when your father was alive, but I never said any more about it; I never commented on it again. Even when your father's family sacrifices bulls for the spears, I never attend the ceremony. I remember my father's words and try to protect myself. I keep my distance for self-protection from my father's word.

It might interest the reader to compare the oral evidence given by the Dinka and the official version of these events as recorded in the government files. Paul Howell, a scholar and administrator who had served as District Commissioner in the area, wrote on the succession case:[8]

> [Kwol Arob's] death was followed by a dispute over the rights of succession, for he had two sons, Deng Majok and Deng Abot. In his latter days Kwal Aruop had fallen foul of the government. In the words of a contemporary District Commissioner, "His long period of power had corrupted his integrity and he had become a tyrannous old magician, grossly favoring his own Abyor section to the detriment of the tribe as a whole. He was allowed to spend the rest of his days in his own land provided he did not interfere in tribal affairs." There is no doubt that despite his official retirement, Kwal Aruop continued to be a great influence throughout the tribe. In the meantime he had conceived an entirely unreasonable dislike for his son Deng Majok and clearly hoped to establish the succession of his son Deng Abot

---

8. "The Ngok Dinka," 263–64.

instead, an appointment which was not in accordance with government policy, since Deng Abot had proved himself the less able of the two brothers. On Kwal's death an attempt was made by a large faction of the Abyor to thrust the sacred spears into the hands of Deng Abot, which was considered by the administration to be tantamount to proclaiming him President of the Court. The events are described by the then District Commissioner, as follows:

"On his return from Kordofan in December '44 after the conferring on him of a robe of honour, Deng Majok was given a great welcome by his people. There was much singing and dancing and slaughtering of bulls. Old Kwal Aruop refused to congratulate his son or join in the celebrations. Deng Majok eventually called on his father, who refused to speak to him, gave him two fingers, and then turned away. The snub was observed with satisfaction by the old man's household.

"At the end of January '45 Kwal fell dangerously ill with stricture complications. On 7th February I reached Abyei and visited him in his hut, which was closely surrounded by a large concourse of his own Abyor section to the exclusion of light and air. A brace of medical dressers were in attendance, and their combined efforts had brought some relief. I had the crowd driven away and the old man got a night's sleep, which rallied his strength, and when I left on the 10th there appeared every chance that he might partially recover.

"In the meanwhile, I sensed an atmosphere of suppressed excitement. Deng Abot was unable to conceal it. So, before leaving, I summoned a meeting of the elders. They unanimously agreed that the magic spears were the insignia of kingship and could not be separated from the office of chief, that when the tribe had accepted the leadership of Deng Majok three years before it was understood that the spears would come to him on the death of Kwal, and that if they were handed to Deng Abot the tribe would be hopelessly divided. The elders undertook to endeavour to persuade Kwal and his close relations, who were known to support him in his hopes to impose Deng Abot on the tribe, to see reason. They also expressed themselves willing to have it out with Deng Abot. Subsequent events have shown that their efforts were extremely feeble. Old Kwal was held in such awe that none of them dared to tackle him. He was also so well protected by a junta of his close relations that they could not get near him. Before I left Abyei I made it clear that the spear business was to be settled once and for all after the Alal Dinka Meeting early in March.

"I returned to the Abyei area on 1st March for the annual Dinka Meeting to be held this year on the Alal about 20 miles south of the Bahr el Arab. Kwal was still very sick, but there appeared to be no immediate danger that he would die. A fresh meeting with the elders was held and they confirmed their earlier opinion. It was decided that a deputation should go to have it out with Kwal Aruop. At the same time Deng Abot was categorically warned that he could not succeed to the magic spears, that it was bad luck on him, but that in the interest of the tribe as a whole there was no other solution.

"That very night news was brought by a runner that Kwal was dying. Deng Abot woke me [from my siesta] to tell me at 5 P.M. I agreed to send the two brothers off at dawn in my lorry. Deng Abot did not wait, but mounting a horse went for all he was worth back to Abyei. Deng Majok went by lorry at dawn.

"About 2 P.M. on the 4th March Kwal died in the presence of the two brothers and most of the Abyor section. He was buried with all the ceremonial of a Ngok chief, though fortunately not alive, like his grandfather Biong. The Abyor were the only section present and when they had filled in the grave they began the ritual dances. The two brothers sat side by side on the ground. After a while a party with Kwal's close relations at their head came and lifted Deng Abot, who at first made a faint show of resistance, twice into the air and then placed him on an *angarib*.[9] They then heaped on him all the insignia of Kwal's office, bracelets of iron, a crown of cowrie shells, necklaces of blue beads and whatnot, and the magic spears were given to him.

"Meanwhile Deng Majok sat in his place forgotten in the general excitement. By and by braver spirits began to taunt him and when he got up to go to the river to wash he was mocked with running away.

"My lorry as usual breaking down, I did not get to Abyei until the morning of the 5th March. I visited Kwal's grave and found about three hundred of the Abyor section assembled there but no one else. I told them nothing except that I would hold a tribal meeting on the morrow. On returning to Abyei Post I spent the rest of the day finding out the true state of affairs and making a plan of action.

"I soon became convinced that the whole plot was a manoeuvre by Kwal's brothers and other near relations to secure the succession of Deng Abot who would serve their interests as Kwal had done. For since the succession of Deng Majok, the Abyor had not had it all their own way and this they bitterly resented. The *coup d'etat* had been rushed through because it was known that if the matter was referred to the whole tribe they would not get away with it. They hoped that by presenting a *fait accompli*, the tribe would abide by it through fear and that the Government would not interfere in a matter of tribal custom.

"They were unable satisfactorily to explain why they had rushed the business through. They excused themselves by saying that other sections of the tribe had not turned up, so they had proceeded on their own.

"At 11 A.M. a meeting was held of all Ngok sectional leaders, the two Dengs not at first being present. Eight spokesmen from the Abyor section came to present their case. The meeting was extremely or-

---

9. A bed made of woven rope used for sleeping and sitting.

derly, typical of such Nilotic proceedings. It was clear from the outset that public opinion was wholeheartedly against the Abyor section.

Briefly the points made by the elders were:

(1) At the 1942 meeting when Kwal was allowed to retire and Deng Majok chosen to succeed him, it had been clearly understood that Kwal could only keep his spears during his lifetime as an act of grace, and that they must be handed to Deng Majok, at his death.

(2) The spears had been inseparable from Ngok Chieftainship and there was now no reason to tamper with this accepted tribal custom.

(3) They were very satisfied with Deng Majok and to go back on the 1942 agreement would hopelessly divide the tribe.

(4) They pointed out that other sections of the tribe had not turned up at Kwal's funeral to perform the customary rites because he was no longer Chief. The Abyor spokesmen were clearly hard put to make a defense and lamely averred that they would not go back on what they had done as it would bring death and calamity on the tribe.

By 4:30 P.M. a point in the discussion had been reached at which the elders demanded that representatives from the Abyor section should go and get the sacred spears and hand them over to Deng Majok, and that in two days time the tribe would assemble and perform the full rites. The Abyor spokesmen refused to go and get them, fearing terrible consequences, if they should go back on their previous action.

I then stepped in with a short summary of the main facts and stated that it was quite clearly the wish of the tribe as a whole that the spears should go to Deng Majok. I gave the Abyor section a short interlude in which to decide whether they would fetch the magic spears voluntarily, but if they refused to deliver them, that I would get them myself. As I had clearly guessed, this called their bluff, and Mahdi Aruop, one of Kwal's brothers, volunteered to fetch them. An hour later he returned with them and they were handed over to Deng Majok.

Since the Dinka would ordinarily revere the will of a chief, and particularly of a divine leader such as Kwol Arob, there is a tendency to interpret the situation in such a way that both sides derive legitimacy from what he is supposed to have said. It is generally accepted that Kwol Arob meant to divide the leadership into two parts: secular chieftainship, with the power of government behind it, and divine leadership, with the authority of the Sacred Spears as its sanction. Those who favored Deng Majok's succession claimed that Kwol meant Deng Abot to hold the spears as a mere religious or spiritual functionary without any authority to govern the tribe but that Abyor misinterpreted his wish and sought to install Deng Abot as the chief in the combined manner of Kwol Arob. They had hoped that their action would automatically divest Deng Majok of the authority which the government had placed in him some years earlier.

Building on the dichotomy that Kwol tried to ensure in his will of the secular authority of the state and the divine prerogative or spiritual leadership, some members of Deng Majok's family concede that while he was correct in successfully fighting Deng Abot's succession as paramount chief, he clearly violated his father's will by seizing the spears through government power. "Our father later took the Sacred Spears through the power of the government," said Nyanjur. "Those spears were not bequeathed to him; they were bequeathed to our uncle. That was the way our grandfather Kwol had willed it." After persuasively restating her father's arguments for inheriting the Sacred Spears, Nyanjur concluded: "But while father was alive, the effectiveness of his spiritual power was not at all like that of Deng Makuei. Deng Makuei was far more powerful spiritually than our father, because that was what his father had bequeathed to him and the other person, our father, had been bequeathed something else. But the government went ahead and gave the spears to our father."

"It is the issue of the Sacred Spears which Deng Makuei regarded as paramount in his conflict with father," said Ali.

> And he was the one who cared the most about the religious affairs of the clan spirits. Deng Makuei gave the spirits a great deal of attention. Father, too, cared about the religious affairs of the clan spirits, but he was more preoccupied with the public affairs of the tribe and the relations of the Dinka with the Arabs. In the face of all those responsibilities and some enlightenment, he regarded the religious affairs of the clan spirits as being of somewhat secondary importance. Deng Makuei, on the other hand, never wavered on religious matters.

Alei Chol was even more forthright about the issue of the spears: "The only mistake Deng committed was taking the spears from Deng Abot. If our area should now be destroyed, it would be because of the spears. But on the issue of his taking over the chieftainship he made no mistake; he was right."

The fact that people on both sides of the succession case try so hard to reconcile their position with the alleged will of Chief Kwol Arob indicates the high moral and spiritual esteem in which the Dinka hold him as a leader. Although the British discredited him toward the end of his reign, Chief Kwol Arob's image was and remains a towering one to his people and to the neighboring leaders to the north and south. As I was growing up, the songs about him used to move me deeply as evidence of how loved by his people he must have been:

> Adau, daughter of Ken cried in dismay,
> "Black Stork, what will hurt you in this land
> A land ordered by Kwol?"
> Kwol will hear the case without bias:
> The word of the market goes to Kwol

And the case of a cow goes to Kwol;
O Kwol, keep the people of your father
And lead them to the people of the world.

My Pied Bull, the Ground Horn-Bill
I love the Black Shade of Mijok, the Ox of my
Father
I love it as I love our chief
I love it as I love our chief who is holding our
land.
My Pied One, if no disaster befalls our land
People will point at our camp because of you.
I will never leave you.
Whatever people may say about you,
Because of those horns, I love you,
I love you as I love our chief,
I love you as I love our chief who is holding our
land.

"Kwol's charisma was due to the word of God behind his leadership," said Monyluak Row. "He had the authority of God behind him. He was a man created with a cool heart; a man of gentle personality. Kwol was a chief by the authority of God. He succeeded to the chieftainship which had descended down the lineage of Arob Biong."

"Kwol's charisma was such as you have never heard of," added Chol Piok, "a charisma which, if he were seen approaching and singing his hymns, even when a battleline was drawn up and ready to rage, it would pull apart and people would leave. The battle would end."

K. D. D. Henderson, who was District Commissioner in the early 1930s, observed: "It always seemed to me that Kwol as a leader of men and a diplomat was a head and shoulder above [other chiefs]. In Bahr el Ghazal, only Gir Kiro merited comparison with Kwol. In Western Kordofan, only Ali Abu Dukka at El Odeya was comparable."

"The way Kwol Arob performed made the whole area happy with him," said Chief Lang Juk of the Twich Dinka. "He was a good person in every respect. He was a God-fearing man, and he was very generous. He helped any needy person. He loved everybody. He loved the Twich, the Rek, the Ruweng, the Nuer, and all the other tribes, even the distant Agar. He was a great leader, heard of all over; he was a great man."

Commenting on the Arab attitude toward both Deng Majok and his father, Kwol Arob, Babo Nimir, the paramount chief of the Missiriya, observed, "With respect to the Homr tribes, there was nothing we could hold against either of them. Kwol Arob himself was a great friend of the Arabs." Ibrahim El Hussein, another Arab elder, commenting on Kwol's continuation of his father's policy of friendly relations with the Arabs, said: "Our father, Kwol, became chief in this whole area. He established peace in the area and would attend meetings with the chiefs of the other tribes. Father Kwol was very good to the Arabs. He never wronged the Arabs. And his rule was very good. It was a sweet period in the history of our people."

Deng Majok's success in outwitting his father and forcing him into retirement should therefore be viewed as evidence of his extraordinary ambition, strength of character, and administrative excellence as judged by the new criteria of leadership demanded by the modern world rather than as a reflection of Kwol Arob's shortcomings as a leader of his people.

To emphasize Kwol Arob's stature as a leader of great merit is also to underscore the unique attributes of his son who found himself at the crossroads of tradition and modernization. Although the legality or legitimacy of Deng Majok's succession to chieftainship according to tradition has continued to be debated, there is virtual consensus that he was most qualified for the position, irrespective of his mother's seniority. "Deng Abot's mother was senior," conceded Nyanbol Amor, "but Deng Majok took the chieftainship because of his own personal strengths and his excellent relations with everybody."

In the words of Babo Nimir: "From the time he was a young man in the cattle-camp, he was different from the rest of the Dinka, especially with respect to his generosity and hospitality and his regard for people. He was a most outstanding personality. It is his personality which won us to his side. And God gave him leadership."

"Deng Majok had all the attributes of a leader," observed Pagwot:

> Even when they were still young boys, it was he the tribe saw as the heir apparent to the throne. When Kwol tried to push him aside, Deng had already associated himself with the public. And he was discovered by the public to be most worthy of leadership long before the issue arose. So, even if the mother of Deng Abot had clearly been the first wife and there had been no such complications as there were, what counts in the world of today is speaking ability and a good attitude toward people. Those are the things that make a chief. Even if Deng Abot had been unquestionably senior, he was rather slow in action. He could not have managed the tribe. It is the people who know best the man who will benefit them. That is why Deng Majok was chosen to be the chief.

There were clearly two conflicting sets of principles involved in the arguments of those who took up opposing positions behind the brothers. Whatever the background considerations that might have played a role in Kwol Arob's position, he was adhering to the spirit and letter of the rules of primogeniture, according to which Deng Abot was the first son of the senior wife. Those who backed him were either honoring the same custom or merely following their chief. Those who favored Deng Majok saw him as the more able of the two brothers. Their interpretation of custom or the facts surrounding its application in that particular situation was largely a rationalization or justification of a predetermined position. It can be argued that both sides were right according to the logic of their premises.

8 Peacemaker, Lawgiver, and Modernizer

"Once Deng Majok took charge of the tribe," said Pagwot Deng, "it became obvious that the people had been right in choosing him as the chief." Ajuong Deng observed that the people who had opposed him soon changed their view of him. "They saw how Deng Majok acted whenever his people were faced with difficulty. They saw Deng Majok's attitude toward the people who assembled around him. They saw how Deng Majok managed the marriages of his daughters. They observed Deng Majok in every way and concluded that he was the most able person to lead them. Some people began to admit, 'What harm we almost did to ourselves!'"

Most of Deng Majok's work had to do with the administration of justice and the maintenance of law and order. In addition to his own court, which had both appellate and original jurisdiction, his two deputies could also sit as court presidents of subsidiary courts, and the omdas and sheikhs discharged quasi judicial functions in their respective areas. Of course, they also sat with him and his deputies as members in those courts whose jurisdiction covered the whole tribe.

As Patal explained: "Deng began to bring those who had been against him close to him and turned them into his people. Most of the people who were court-members under him were people who had rejected him. The people whom he saw to be opposed to him were the people he brought into his inner circle."

Matet Ayom also stressed Deng Majok's lack of grudge against his enemies in the dispute over succession: "Deng Majok did not turn against those who had opposed him. Anyone with a cause Deng would give his rights without prejudice. And even with those who had supported him, if one had no cause, Deng would say, 'Let go of this, it is not yours.'"

Ali offers some insight into the way his father discharged his burdensome duties as paramount chief:

> Father would wake up early in the morning. He never slept to seven or eight o'clock; he was always up by six. And once he emerged to go to his sitting place, the special courthouse at home, he would find that elders had already gathered in his place. We too would have come to wait for him there. Tea would be brought and served in our presence. At that point, the elders would merely converse with our father. They would refuse to hear cases that early and would just chat and amuse themselves.
>
> At about 9:00 A.M. he would begin to hear cases at home until 11:00 A.M., when he would transfer his court to the big gathering under the Court-Tree. He would go to court after a late breakfast. But once he went to court, he would remain there all day. He would sit listening to cases and not moving at all.
>
> When he returned in the afternoon, he would be followed by a large crowd of not less than a hundred and perhaps even two hundred people. They all followed him back to the house.
>
> All the food from the different wives or sections of the family would be collected and brought in front of the crowd. All people would share in the food that his family provided. If he wanted to have a brief rest, then he would return a little earlier; but quite often, he would come as late as 5:00 P.M. and continue in company for the rest of the evening.
>
> After returning from court, he would prefer light conversation to more litigation. But toward the evening he might allow urgent cases to be heard and settled right there. Otherwise, they would just converse lightly, reminiscing at times about their younger days or talking about their ancestral ways and how people used to live. That was perhaps the only period of rest or relaxation that Father would have. He would then retire to bed around eleven or midnight.
>
> I really admired father's industriousness. He was never idle. As he sat for tea with elders, first thing in the morning, he would be informed about everything that was going on throughout the tribe. I do not know whether he had given directives to his informants or whether the people themselves realized what time was best for informing him. But in that brief morning meeting he would hear what was happening in Diil; he would hear what was happening in Mareng; he would hear what was happening everywhere.
>
> If one were to seek comparisons with our father's work, it would be identical to the work of the investigation section of the Police Department. Why? He was the center to which all information was passed. And he was loved by the Ngok. If any of his adversaries—like Matet or Chol Jipur or any other hostile person—did anything at night, my father would learn about it very early the following morning. If two sections of the tribe were planning an attack on one another, he would immediately hear of it. Even at night while he was

asleep people would come and he would be awakened and informed. Father was following everything all the time. His work was not confined to his court work.

But the court was the institution through which he exercised most of his administrative functions. According to Allor-Jok, "Deng Majok never spent three days away from his work in court. If he stayed away for three days, then he had to be in bed, sick."

As though to follow the logic that had brought him into power, Deng Majok was perhaps best known for his consolidation of peace and unity, adherence to the rule of law, and fostering of respect for authority, not only through efficient administration of justice, but also through fear of government sanctions against any violation. As Chol Piok explained, he was especially determined to bring an end to tribal warfare, using methods that were more efficient and less dependent on the not-so-effective divine authority of traditional leadership:

> The generation of Kwol Arob did not unify the words of the tribe and place them in the hands of Kwol Arob. Each tribe had its own way and any other tribe had its own way. Kwol managed them all only with his good tongue. If he did something which satisfied them all, it was because of the wisdom that was created with him. But Kwol Arob would not rise in a hurry if he heard that the people were in conflict, that the tribes were about to fight. He would only get there when things had already gone too far and harm had been done. With Deng Majok, even if an ordinary man turned up and said, "Deng Majok, this and that tribe are going to fight; this or that is going to make them fight," even if he were an ordinary commoner, Deng would jump up and go there. He would not wait until they had actually fought. He would intervene to prevent the fight and resolve the matter amicably. If there was a tribe at fault, he would show them their mistake until they recognized their wrong. He would deter them from any similar conduct in the future and impose fines on the few who were directly responsible and had led the way for the tribe to join.

According to Matet Ayom: "It was Deng Majok who brought peace and unity to the people so that they stopped tribal wars and laid down their spears and their shields. He would call a nobleman from that tribe and call another nobleman from another tribe and call yet another nobleman from a third tribe and gather them together near him to become his companions. It is because of Deng that our people have now mixed and united to become one people."

Achwil Bulabek confirmed:

> In every tribal section of the Ngok, he appointed people into his court. That was how Deng established effective control throughout the tribe. He, of course, recognized his relatives, the people of his

own family, the family of Biong Allor, but he also recognized the nobles of the land at large. He would always place them on an equal par; he treated them equally. If he found his relative mistreating an outsider, he would take the side of the outsider.

Since Deng Majok assumed the chieftainship, no more wars have been fought among our people. Let me tell you that where Deng Majok far excelled Kwol Arob is in the fact that none of our people died anymore on the tip of the spears of war. Our wars ended with the war of Nainai between us, Abyor, and Bongo. When Deng imposed severe punishment on those responsible, people were deterred and stopped provoking wars. Where Deng Majok excelled your grandfather is on the issue of the sons of Adam living without fearing death from war!

"What he used to do was visit the section," commented Juac Dau.

It is only today that the chiefs' touring of the tribes does not happen anymore. In the past, Deng used to travel up to Kolnyang, up to Diil, Rum-Amer, Mareng, Mannyuar, and other areas all over the tribe. He used to go and talk to people, elders, in every section, and explain to them how he wanted his people to live. Afterward, the elders talked to their people and relayed what Deng had said.

In the days of our grandparents, there was something called *kot*, the shield, which was used for protection during fights. It was Deng Majok who removed the shield from this area. He removed it through his policies. He removed it through his good words. In our area, there used to be a helmet that was worn to protect the head during fighting with clubs. It was Deng Majok who removed it from our heads to prevent his people from killing one another. In our area, people used to arm themselves with big clubs and spears, and sectional fights would break out and people would get killed. All these Deng Majok stopped.

Since the time of Deng Majok, the Ngok have followed a straight path, been well-behaved, law-abiding, and fearful. Deng brought the government to the people. This is why the police are here. During Kwol Arob's time, there was no government presence here; there was no government. But when Deng came, that is when the district offices were first erected here. He wanted the people to fear authority.

Ajuong goes so far as to argue that the proper integration of the Ngok power structure as one hierarchy, in which the Dhiendior lineage of Mannyuar became subordinated to Pajok, occurred under Deng Majok.

Your grandfather's relations with Allor Ajing [of the Dhiendior lineage] did not reflect a hierarchy of authority but seemed to be a relationship of equals, so that whenever there was a conflict between their sections, it appeared as though chiefs of equal status were in conflict. It would seem as though the sections were in conflict as representatives of the two chiefs. If one chief felt that the conflict should be avoided and worked for peace, it would seem as though he and his section were afraid. But when it came to your father, he said, "This cannot be! A chief who embraces all the people of the tribe should not be identified with one section."

When he found competitiveness in the clan of Allor, for instance with his uncle Jipur Allor, he was able to trim him down. Jipur fell into line in a hierarchy headed by Deng Majok. And that was the result of his policy.

His approach was that, whichever section attacked another, he reacted as the leader of all; he was the leader of all sections. He integrated them so much that the heart of the man of Abyor and that of the man of Mannyuar became one. The members of the other sections and those of Abyor equally united their hearts into one. If he found that a man of Abyor had wronged someone from another tribe, he would punish him as a wrongdoer. If he found that someone from another tribe had done wrong against a man from Abyor, he also punished him according to the truth. And he permitted everybody to become associated with him. He made them all noblemen.

He also made them share food together. He would invite this group and give them the best and then invite the other group the next day and give them the best. He treated them all equally.

"Deng Majok never favored anyone," said Chol Piok. "Even if a case concerned Biong, the son of his mother, he would pass judgment against him and even put him in jail, if he were in the wrong. He had frightened his own brothers so much that none of them could brag that they were born of the same mother, Nyanaghar, and were therefore exempt from his authority."

"It was Deng Majok who made the Pajok equal to the rest of the tribe," said Matet Ayom. "If he found a man from Pajok clan holding somebody else's right, he would take it from him and give it to the person entitled. If he found anyone holding somebody else's right, he would take it from that person and give it to the one in the right."

Allor-Jok articulated a view often voiced about Deng Majok's justice when he said, "Deng Majok equated all the people of the tribe. Deng Majok never discriminated between people. As a leader, Deng did not have a brother, he did not have a father, and he did not have a mother. All the people were the same in his eyes." Deng Majok literally lived up to the traditional wisdom that the best way to unite people and protect one's own interests and those of one's close relatives is to safeguard the interests of the stranger and more distant persons first, in order to win them over to your side.

In many other respects, since tradition as represented by his father and family elders had not favored him, Deng Majok did not have much feeling for it; and yet he could not disregard it either. It was clear that he was an innovator from the start, but he also had to justify his position and his authority through tradition. The Sacred Spears were honored from time to time, but without much of the ritual traditionally associated with possessing them. In many ways, Deng Majok was neither a traditional Dinka believer nor a Muslim, and of course not a Christian—and yet he was a bit of all those things.

"Deng would appear to have abandoned his clan spirits, but he honored them still," said Atem Moter. And according to Chol Piok, "He [and Deng Abot] would slaughter cattle in sacrifice on the shrine of their father. Even of late, Deng Majok continued to sacrifice to both his father and his grandfather. If ancestral spirits could be satisfied by sacrifices, Deng Majok would not have died."

Some of his attributes endeared him particularly to the Arabs because they were in conformity with Islamic values and very striking in a person who did not profess Islam. In traditional Dinka society, almost everyone, including children, drank the local beer, which was low in alcoholic content and was made available only on special, festive seasonal occasions: solicitation of collective labor on farms, marriages, entertainment of special guests, or offerings made to God and ancestral spirits. Deng Majok never drank; he argued that it compromised one's dignity and sense of judgment. Nearly every adult Dinka, man and woman, also smoked a pipe or chewed tobacco, but not Deng Majok; his reason was that craving sometimes forced smokers to beg for tobacco, thereby also compromising their dignity and integrity. Deng Majok would not eat the meat of any animal not slaughtered according to Muslim requirements, and he always kept a Muslim, usually an Arab, in his house to slaughter according to the Islamic rites; his argument was that he did not want his guests to have any doubts about the food they were served in his home. But Deng Majok went even further than that: he always had religious men, both Arab and Dinka, around to offer spiritual protection, and would even drink the water used to wash off Koranic verses written on a plate as a blessing. Furthermore, though performing Dinka rituals and observing the requirements of traditional religion, he also celebrated Islamic occasions, especially from the perspective of social festivity.

These attributes were of course noticed and appreciated by the Arabs. Ibrahim El Hussein made this observation: "Deng had a secret quality. He practiced what the Arabs do, sought the spiritual protection offered by Muslim Holy men. He made use of them. He had a large number of Koranic verses wrapped up. I once saw him give five cows to a Muslim Holy man to perform protective rituals. I saw him with my own eyes."

"Deng Majok did not eat bad things," said another Arab, Abdalla Hamadein. "He never smoked. He never drank alcohol of any kind. And he never told a lie."

And according to Ibrahim Mohamed Zein, yet another Muslim: "Among the things I heard about him was that he did not observe some of the Dinka customs. Some Dinkas eat animals not slaughtered in the Muslim way. They say Deng Majok never did that. It is known that he always had a Muslim in his home to slaughter his animals for meat."

One of the significant innovations of Deng Majok in his tribe was the introduction of modern education. Kwei, Deng's third wife, explains how he responded positively to the suggestion of the British that Kwol and his two sons, Deng Majok and Deng Abot, should send their sons to school in the North. Kwol's son Nyok was Deng Abot's younger brother. Both Deng Majok and Deng Abot had two sons who were known by the same name of Arob.

"Nyok was the older of the three," said Kwei, the mother of Deng Majok's Arob.

> Arob, the son of Deng Makuei [Deng Abot], was next in age, a little older than our Arob. It was then said that the boys were to be sent to school in Arabland. The British [Commissioner] said to Deng Majok, "If you and your father have children, give them to me to take to school in the North." Deng conveyed that message to his father, Kwol. The British [Commissioner] also spoke to Chief Kwol saying, "I am taking your children to the North. I am taking Arob, the son of Deng Majok, and Arob, the son of Deng Makuei, and Nyok, your own son; I am taking them away to school."
>
> Kwol said, "No! The children should remain at home to take care of the cattle."
>
> When Deng Majok saw his father's attitude toward the British, he intervened and accepted the idea of sending the children to school. Kwol said that he did not want his son Nyok to go to school, but Deng Majok insisted that all the three boys should go to school. Deng eventually succeeded in extricating Nyok from his father, Kwol, and had him go to school. In fact, Nyok was the first to go to school because he was older. The two Arobs followed later. At first, Deng Makuei and his father almost prevented Arob, the son of Deng Makuei, from going to school. So the British District Commissioner said to Deng Majok, "I will take your son Arob, even though he is still so young, and I will raise him and educate him myself." Deng Majok accepted and even persuaded Deng Makuei to have the other Arob go to school as well.

And so, through the influence of the British administrators and with Deng Majok's progressive cooperation, a number of children from the leading Ngok families were sent to far-off schools. Nyok, the son of Chief Kwol, and a maternal relative of Deng Majok by the name of Wor Abyei were sent to Catholic missionary schools in the South and became converted to Christianity. Nyok became Luis and Wor became Lino. Both were later transferred to the North to learn Arabic.

The two Arobs, the sons of Deng Majok and Deng Makuei, together with Allor Jipur, the son of the deputy paramount chief, Jipur Allor of Mannyuar, were sent to Arab schools in the North and were converted to Islam. Arob, son of Deng Majok, became Ahmed, and Arob, son of Deng Makuei, became Hassan.

Within the Ngok area itself, no missionary or government schools were established and, indeed, the Ngok remained largely uninterested in education. Gradually, the benefits of education became visible. Luis Nyok, for instance, began to help his father with registering taxpayers and issuing receipts. He even won himself verses of praise in a song:

> Nyok, the son of Kwol, the Pied One
> The Gentleman has held the country with the pen
> He writes four lines on paper
> And ends with a zigzagging road [signature]
> Making the taxes come down like a falling tree.

The manner in which Ahmed and Hassan, the two Arobs, would return on vacations dressed in their white jallibiyas with town favors to distribute to their younger brothers and sisters, not to mention their impressive display of literacy and knowledge of Arabic and English, soon won them a place of respect within the chiefly circles.

Deng Majok was not only attracted to education by its obvious merits; he also saw his support of education for the Dinka as a progressive stance that won him favor in the eyes of his British superiors and Arab neighbors. As soon as he became chief, even before his father's death, Deng persuaded the government to open an elementary school in Abyei. Lino Wor was appointed headmaster, and Luis Nyok became his assistant.

The first batch of students were mostly sons of Deng Majok and his junior chiefs, including the deputy paramount chief, Jipur Allor, and some of the omdas and sheikhs. Indeed, I do not recall any of Deng Abot's children attending the first classes, even though he had children of the right age and Luis Nyok, his sibling brother, was the assistant headmaster. Virtually all the pupils were accommodated in Deng Majok's house and his wives prepared their meals, for there was no boardinghouse then.

The overwhelming majority of the Ngok were not only still opposed to education but were highly critical of Deng Majok for sending all his sons away to school, leaving none to take care of his cattle, which were entrusted to distant relatives or client herdsmen. To the Dinka, going to school meant acquiring the ways of townspeople, abandoning the traditional values of the Dinka, and turning a child into a heartless loner who cared only for his own selfish interests and disregarded kinship obligations. Since Abyei elementary school was under the southern educational system and fell within the Catholic sphere of influence, the pupils were also presumed to be converted to Christianity, which implied monogamy, an unthinkable institution for sons of chiefs in traditional society.

Backed by the vigorous efforts of Lino Wor and Luis Nyok, Deng Majok intensified the campaign for the recruitment of pupils for the school and even imposed on his chiefs a form of compulsory contribution of children from their sections. A considerable portion of school activities, including tours around the tribe, were geared toward demonstrating the advantages of education to the chiefs and elders. Plays were staged in which education was presented not only as facilitating communications through letters, but also as leading to scientific knowledge of cause and effect, freeing the illiterate Dinka from superstitious dependency on native priests, magicians, and medicine men and introducing them to the advantages of modern medicine.

Gradually, the miracles of education began to manifest themselves. A group of illiterate tribesmen would ask a schoolboy to write the names of some strangers in the sand, while the literate children were sent away, well out of sight and supervised to ensure that they could not see what was being written. When those boys returned and could read the names on the ground of people who were totally unknown to them, it all seemed like a divine manifestation in the eyes of the Dinka. Literate sons of chiefs began to help their fathers with letters for litigants pursuing cases under the jurisdiction of other chiefs. In intra-Ngok affairs, this usually entailed correspondence between the chiefs of the subtribes, which in the case of the central court of Deng Majok himself meant correspondence with the head chiefs of other tribes. Although there was an official clerk to the court of Deng Majok, a non-Dinka from the South, Deng's sons began to play an increasing role in the clerical work of the court and in keeping the records of tax collection. But it was the leadership role played by the educated senior sons of the tribe, especially Lino Wor and Luis Nyok, the growing association of education with leadership, and the employment opportunities and attendant improvements in living conditions that became visible as the natural outcomes of schooling which began to win popular support for education among the Ngok Dinka. In due course, the demands for entry into school exceeded the available positions open, and admission committees were established under the chairmanship of Deng Majok to select the best qualified candidates.

After graduating from Abyei elementary school, children were sent to other schools outside the tribe to pursue higher education. The British persuaded Deng Majok to send some of his sons to the South to balance those he sent to the North, so that he would be in touch with both parts of the country. This strategy also applied to other children from the Ngok tribe. Many first went to schools in the South and then pursued their education in the North. Those who went to the South became Christians, while those who went to the North became Muslims.

Once children entered school, and considering the fact that education throughout the Sudan was largely free, with the government offering financial assistance for pocket money to those in need, the competition for the limited available rungs on the educational ladder—elementary, intermediate, secondary, and ultimately university—was open to all, poor and rich, rural and urban. Given the competitiveness of the traditional society, the record of the rural pupils, even compared to the more sophisticated urban population, was very good. Although it was inherent in the system that most people dropped out as they ascended the steps of the ladder, Dinka children from a preliterate background found their way to the top of the educational system and therefore to the highest prospects in opportunities for employment, especially within the government. In view of their numbers, their high level of motivation, and their father's support for education, Deng Majok's sons fared exceptionally well. In due course, they showed impressive numbers from one single family at all levels of the educational system, including university, at home and abroad. And as the number of Deng Majok's children enrolled in schools continued to increase with time, so has their representation at the various levels of the educational hierarchy.

David Cole and Richard Huntington noted, on the education of Deng Majok's children:

> The Ngok leadership balanced their weakness in provincial politics with a strength in national (and to a certain degree, international) politics. Chief Deng Majok had introduced modern education to the Ngok. Although he tried to encourage (even force) all parents to send their children to school, most Ngok were reluctant. His own children were sent to the schools because he believed in the value of education for his children and as an example to encourage other Ngok parents to make the sacrifice. His sons and [much later] daughters filled the new local primary schools and went on to secondary schools in the south at Rumbek and in the north at El Nahud. They continued to the University of Khartoum and then for advanced degrees in medicine and law in England and America. Not many of Deng Majok's hundreds of children have advanced degrees from overseas, but most of them are educated to the maximum level of their abilities and opportunities. A disproportionately large percentage of all educated Dinka are from Abyei, and among these, most are the children of Deng Majok.[1]

To appreciate the magnitude of Deng Majok's achievement in promoting education within the tribe, one has to remember the adverse conditions under which he introduced what was a most unpopular idea among his people.

Lino Wor later recorded some of their early efforts to establish Abyei Elementary School and the role Deng Majok played:

> There had been some association between me and the late Chief Deng Majok Kwol, who was very highly interested in educating his children as well as the children of others in the area.

---

1. *African Rural Development*, chap. 5, 17–18.

First only a *Rakuba*[2] was erected where the Senior Guest House is at present. Later on, it was moved to where the girls' Primary School is presently located. It was then built in the form of a *Kurnok*.[3] Later, in 1948, it was finally built with red bricks.

Among the obstacles Lino Wor listed were:

(a) Lack of textbooks to the degree that from twenty copies of the Oxford Reader and Dinka Editions, only three were left in hand after six years. We had to write the lessons on the blackboards to be copied by the pupils in their exercise books. (b) Lack of chalk. Children were encouraged to collect the white droppings of the bird called *dhel*[4] and of the hyena for writing on the blackboard. They also used charcoal to write with on paper in the place of lead pencils. (c) All the furniture and equipment and even the blackboards were made of mud. (d) No proper accommodation or feeding existed; I used to supply food for the boarders, and sometimes there was nothing at all. (e) Much of the work was done through what we call the self-help system, and those in charge of this were Chief Deng Majok himself, assisted by his omdas (sectional chiefs) and nomgols (clan-heads). I and my staff also joined in the self-help efforts.

With respect to his students, Lino Wor observed that, because of the hard conditions under which they labored, "They were fond of escaping from school. Attendance used to be very poor, but the chief brought in all his children and the children of his brothers and close relations."

On the general issue of the public attitude toward education, Lino wrote:

There had been a completely wrong idea about education to a very large extent. The Dinka were fond of saying that an educated person had been made to drink a fluid contaminated with the heart of the vulture *[aci guup pion e gon]*. This was a common belief among the Dinka. What it means is that they would abandon Dinka values and stop being concerned with the welfare of the members of their community. In other words, they were equipped to become selfish and not to be helpful to their fellow members of the tribe or family. Their hearts were supposed to turn out to be like the hearts of the vulture.

Through great efforts on our part, I and my late brother, Chief Deng Majok, worked to change this attitude. Deng Majok was full of wisdom, vigor, and intelligence. It was through him that my work became a success.

Among the factors accounting for this success, Lino Wor stressed the

---

2. A square or rectangular room made of durra stalks.
3. A better structure of wood and mud walls and thatched roof.
4. Goitered stork.

element of "full determination in planning," which he modestly qualified as "not scientific," and the adoption of

> a comprehensive system of cooperation between the staff of my school and the whole community in the area. This resulted in frequent visits to the countryside in the form of campaigns aimed at recruiting more children into the school. In all that we had the close collaboration of Chief Deng Majok.
>
> I was also very much encouraged by the ambitions of my pupils. There was high competition among them. This subsequently resulted in their attaining very good standards wherever they went. Some patiently endured the hardships and never ran away. And some even used to discuss their prospects for the future.

Lino Wor concluded his recollections with the remark, "It gives me some pride to express that my efforts have produced good fruits, and in particular to see my students climbing to higher standards of education, both at home and abroad."

It should be noted that although Deng Majok strongly favored and fostered the education of boys, he remained opposed to the education of girls. In this, he was outstripped by Dinka chiefs in other tribes and even by members of his own tribe. Later, he began to relent by sending some of his middle daughters to school, but changed his mind and withdrew them before they could complete their elementary school education. The daughters of Deng Majok who received education of any significance are those who attended school much later in his life and continued most of their education after his death.

The reason for this conservative approach to the education of his daughters had to do with Deng Majok's general attitude toward women and, especially, with the moral degeneration most Dinka associated with town life, which in turn was associated with education. It also had to do with the fact that whereas Deng Majok expected his educated sons to play leadership roles in the tribe and country and increase their employment opportunities, he saw the value of his daughters in the traditional terms of attracting cattle through marriage. Since no uneducated Dinka would think of marrying an educated girl, not to mention the girls refusing to marry uneducated men, the choice was obvious to Deng Majok. What he did not seem to have foreseen was that the educated boys among the Dinka might prefer to marry educated girls. In this he was probably misled by the initial impression that even educated men would not trust the moral character of educated women as desirable marriage partners. While it was true that education tended to limit the circles into which an educated girl, of whatever level, might marry, there soon emerged a great demand for educated girls, which was only intensified by the limitation of their numbers. Many educated Dinka were forced to marry outside their tribe into those other tribes, mostly non-Dinka, where the education of women had been given due priority.

The outcome of this discrepancy between boys and girls was eventually to be the development of a wide social gap between children of the same father and mother. Deng Majok's sons emerged as among the best educated, not only in the tribe but also in the country, while his daughters remained imprisoned in the illiteracy of tradition. His sons enjoyed employment opportunities at all levels of the economic, social, and political hierarchies of the Sudan, while the daughters remained in the subordinated status of women in traditional society, mostly married to illiterate men and on the whole living a life-style that sharply contrasted with that enjoyed by their educated brothers. This is perhaps one of the most glaring shortcomings of Deng Majok's reforms among his people.

Nyanluak, who belonged to the generation of middle daughters whom Deng Majok first sent to school but subsequently withdrew, laments the loss of educational opportunities but radiates ambivalence rather than hostility over what her father did:

> After we went to school, Father thought and said, "I don't want you girls to continue with education." When he took us out of school, we asked him why he was terminating our education. He said, "I have changed my mind; I do not consider girls suited for education. If there is any value in education, I will find it from my sons. As for you girls, I do not want you to remain in school and risk getting yourselves corrupted by the immoralities of town life. I do not want that to happen to you." That was how we left school. We then remained at home. But we did not really hold that against our father; we did not feel that he had treated us badly. In those days, education had not yet been sufficiently appreciated by our people; it was not regarded as valuable to people's hearts as it is today. If it had been today, when people's minds have been opened to the value of education, we would have argued with Father and said, "Father, you are holding us back." But as we saw it then, we felt that he was doing what he saw as the way things should be. We felt sure that he was probably doing the right thing. That was why we accepted his word and left school and remained at home the way we did.
>
> We had already invested a great deal in our education. One had suffered considerable lashings in school; and one had been denied the pleasure of living with her mother at an age when a child should be close to the mother. You lived in one place and your mother lived in another place. You could only move on foot between where your mother lived and where you went to school. If it had been today, one would not have agreed to leave school after having endured so much on account of education.
>
> Father himself invested much in our education. Whatever we wanted, he provided. We started wearing clothes from an early age. And when we went to school, he would bring rolls of material and have dresses made for us without any discrimination. We would each have three headdresses and frocks and shoes. All that is in a

milk or meat; and he would give cash to those who needed money to purchase other needs.

Even when father was in his bedroom, needy members of the tribe would come and cry in front of his hut as though there were a death in the family. And these people would be in desperate need of relief from famine or other disasters. People would come running blindly for help. There was always plenty of milk in his house. If individuals came suffering from hunger, they would be offered milk and given relief. If they came pleading the cause of the families they had left behind, Father would gather whatever there was and give it to them to run back and bring relief to their families.

And in the words of Charles Biong:

Father's character as chief overwhelmed all other aspects of his personality, whether as a person or as a family man. It was truly overwhelming. To take only one example, whenever there was famine in the area, his preoccupation was for his entire tribe and not his family. Naturally, since famines affected the entire tribe, his family too would be affected, not because he could not provide for them, but because most of the people in the area looked to him for survival. Father always paid greater attention to giving food to the needy members of the tribe than he did to his own family.[5] That also covers cases of sickness. Even if a person was in the remotest part of the area, he would see to it that a vehicle was provided to have the man brought for medical care, or he would send someone—a medical person—to attend to him.

He would always prefer to attend to a person from another area first, and then come to his people—the Ngok. He would then come to the more distant relatives, and eventually down to close relatives.

"Your father's character will never be born again," declared Chol Adija. "He was a person with wide-reaching hands. Of all the people in this land, there is not a single person who was not maintained by Deng Majok—not a single person throughout this entire tribe."

"Truly," confirmed Matet, focusing his attention on Deng Majok's hospitality, "the food that used to be prepared for the public in Deng Majok's household, no other chief has ever provided. Now that Deng Majok is no longer here, the tribe has felt some deprivation in that respect."

Emphasizing Deng Majok's deferential treatment of all people, Chol Piok observed:

---

5. This is obviously an exaggeration, but one shared by a consensus and in fact a basis for criticism of Deng Majok by his father, as quoted earlier. Dau Agok also mentions it as an example of Kwol Arob excelling over Deng Majok: "Kwol Arob excelled over your father in his treatment of his own family . . . Deng Majok always showed great generosity toward strangers but did not do as much for his children." However, it was by winning the more distant people that Deng Majok effectively broadened the base of his power. Generosity shown to the more distant and the most needy is the most noble.

Another thing, your father, Deng Majok, from the time he was a child to the time he grew up, and throughout his life, never showed disrespect even to a single elder. Until he grew up and married, he never slighted anybody, whether the person was from another tribe, or from his Abyor section of the tribe, or whatever his background. . . . But if you wronged him, never forget your wrong! Never think that he had surrendered or had feared you. Never forget! He would one day get you through the government.

It was this last aspect of Deng Majok's personality on which Monyluak Row focused: "Your father was a man whose quarrels were dreaded," he observed.

Why quarreling with him was considered dreadful was because his quarrels were as bitter and lasting as our feuds with the Baggara Arabs. . . . What your father did in carrying out his feuds with people was to connect one issue with another to get at his enemy. Whenever he saw a man determined to fight for his rights, he would put the disputed issue aside and not even use the language by which he intimidated people but would instead turn to others and say calmly, "Is there no one with a case against this person?" Then people would say, "Yes, so and so has a case against him." Then the person said to have a case against the other would receive word. Should anyone raise a case, he was almost sure to secure cattle from that man. That was how Deng frightened the Ngok. One had nowhere else to take his appeal.

Monyluak then proceeded to illustrate his point with a case involving Deng Majok's desire to marry his daughter against Monyluak's will: "The family of Wun-Kon of Diil section who are related to your family (I believe they are from your Pajok lineage), betrothed my daughter. Your father got up and said, 'I would like to marry the daughter of Monyluak.'" Monyluak refused, using the argument that the people who had first engaged his daughter were also from a chiefly clan and could inflict a curse upon anyone denying them a girl to whom they had a prior claim. Besides, he, Monyluak, being an age-mate of Deng's sons, could not entertain the thought of being his father-in-law. But Deng Majok persisted. Using various pressures against Monyluak, he eventually forced his competitors to withdraw and surrender the girl to him. Monyluak himself eventually succumbed, but only after extreme trials, as he recounts:

When we quarreled, your father handled the situation badly. He pursued it to the end. He wrote letters on behalf of people who had claims against me and sent them to the leaders of Anyanya, the rebel army in the forest. He said to them, "Monyluak has a case against him by so and so and a case by so and so and another case by so and so. Let these cases be seen and if his cattle are found, let them be seized." When I went into court with those people, I scattered them all away.

Although Monyluak won his case in the court of Anyanya, he continued to be apprehensive about what Deng Majok would do once he returned home. But he was adamant about denying Deng Majok his daughter in marriage.

> I did not succumb to his will. I gave the girl to the clan of Wun-Kon. The girl went and had a child in the family of Wun-Kon.
>
> The situation remained calm for some time. Then he called the clan of Wun-Kon and accused them of association with the southern rebel army, Anyanya. He said, "You, Kwol and your father, why do you hear of the whereabouts of Anyanya and do not report them?" They were arrested and put in jail.
>
> People would go to the family of Wun-Kon and say, "This is all connected with your feud over the girl. If you had withdrawn your cattle from the marriage and let go of the girl, you would have been safe." Deng Majok never raised the issue of the girl directly. But he would talk indirectly and say: "This relationship between us and the family of Wun-Kon, if our Spirit Ring wills that it should spoil, then we shall sever ties. Our blood ties will sever themselves. But I shall say nothing more."
>
> This began to work on the minds of the family of Wun-Kon. In the end, they called me into court and said, "Monyluak Row, we have withdrawn our claim to the girl. The girl is the wife of our brother, Deng Majok."

But Deng Majok's decisions were not just backed by coercion; tact, diplomacy, and the art of persuasion were also among his main tools. As his wife Nyanthon put it: "There was no power greater than the power of his tongue. It was with his tongue that he managed this tribe. The power of his tongue has never been seen and will probably never be seen again. Even you, his children, none of you can approach the ability of his tongue. Even you, Mading, now sitting in front of me, you cannot compensate for your father's tongue."

"When a case was too formidable for Deng Majok," remarked Matet Ayom, "he would use diplomacy and the art of persuasion, patiently explaining the roots of the problem and avoiding premature expressions of opinion until he got fully to the roots of the issue. Then he would make his statement." But, according to Mithiang Aguek, "Whenever Deng said a word, he never changed it."

And yet he would not leave the victims of his judgments without convincing them of his reasons. According to Achai-Jur:

> Why the people of the area liked Father was because whenever he ruled against a person and that person felt disfavored by him, he would send for him some time later and would talk to him at length to explain why he had decided against him and advise him about how people should relate to one another. He would talk to the person that way until the person fully appreciated his position.

Even if a person turned against him and gossiped to the public, Father would remain calm and work to win him over. Eventually, that same person would turn to Father and become the one to speak to the public in his favor.

That, indeed, was often the case in his relations with Matet Ayom, which were most ambivalent, to say the least. Matet reported:

> When I quarreled with him the cause of my conflict was the marriage of my brother, Lal, who used to elope with the daughter of Deng Majok's father. I said that Lal was not to marry the daughter of the chief. I refused. He would tell me, "In that case, stop your brother from being involved with the girl." That was what brought conflict between us. When he came to Fulah and we were reconciled, Abiem Bagat said to him, "Deng Majok, now that you are again bringing Matet close to you, you will quarrel again. When you do, know that we are not going to involve ourselves again." Then he said, "Abiem, my plan is not to push Matet away from me. I keep him close to me because he will one day be of great service to me. And what I am now claiming from him is not the same as what he will one day do for me."

Although initially known for physical courage and violent defense of his dignity and integrity, Deng Majok became strongly committed to the due process of law. Even at the most dramatic moment, when he was stabbed with a knife in an assassination attempt, Deng Majok remained very dedicated to the rule of law and the prevention of vengeance. Chol Piok relates the incident:

> When Kwol Chol attacked him with a knife and people then all piled on Kwol, who had been thrown down and was being beaten by the public, your father said, "O my people, I am not dead; spare his life, do not kill him! Do not kill Kwol Chol."
>
> Kwol Chol had married a girl. He had no cattle, but he eloped with the girl. The relatives of the girl then went and took her from Kwol Chol and said that they wanted to give her to Deng Majok instead. But Deng Majok had never expressed interest in the girl.
>
> The relatives of the girl brought her into court. And they brought Kwol Chol into court. Kwol had a knife in his pocket, unbeknownst to the people. Deng Majok was investigating the case. A man has his own intuitions about a situation involving a woman he loves. Kwol Chol believed that Deng Majok had accepted the offer of the girl's relatives. He approached step by step closer to Deng Majok as he talked, gesturing with his hands. And when his uncle, Deng Yach, was about to speak on the case, he surreptitiously pulled out the knife. Only Deng Majok had noticed the knife, but he would not give any indication that might reflect fear or apprehension. Yet, had he not noticed the knife, he would probably have been killed. As Kwol leapt forward with the knife to stab him, Deng grabbed him by the waist before the knife could reach him. So the knife was deflected and

only cut the flesh on his ribs under his shoulders. As he was pinned over Deng Majok's shoulder, Kwol continued to stab at Deng's back until he was overpowered.

Kwol Chol narrowly escaped being killed by the spontaneous reaction of the people gathered in court: "Leaders struggled and struggled and struggled to save Kwol, until the police came. And the following morning, Abyor ran to attack Bongo [the tribe of Kwol Chol]. Deng said to all those who were there, including our age-group of elders and the assembly members who were present, 'You go and stop Abyor. Is a man avenged when he is still alive and talking?' That is how Deng Majok saved the situation."

Deng Majok's authority over his tribe was enhanced, according to Mithiang Aguek, by the fact that he was the only point of contact and communication between his people and the central government:

> Deng Majok, talking to the government representatives about what he deemed to be the best way of ruling his area said, "In my area, people used to fight to the death in the past, particularly the tribes of Abyor and Mannyuar; but my main concern now is to see to it that no further fights take place, and should this be realized, there will prevail a better atmosphere for security, education, and progress. And to achieve this, the official contact or communication between the authorities and the people should be solely through me; I should be the only link between the government and my people. If there is a direct communication with individuals, anarchists will take advantage of that and the whole area will be in chaos. Whatever message the government wants to convey to the public should first come to me and I will transmit it to the people through the omdas, sheikhs, and the clan heads, until it reaches the individual. I can assure you that this system will work the best." Deng Majok, through this policy, managed to be the only person in the entire area to whom the authorities talked and listened. And when the government representatives left the area after their short visits, he would for his part summon his chiefs to pass on whatever he deemed fit to communicate to them.

British sources confirm that, as far as they were concerned, Deng Majok ran his tribe to their satisfaction. Bell, who was in the area from 1947 to the end of 1949, only two years after Deng Majok had assumed control of the tribe, explains the remoteness of the central authority that implied government dependency on the local leaders:

> As District Commissioner, I naturally visited the Ngok Dinka from time to time: but the distances were great—it was a very big district. . . . I think I went down there three times, and met Chief Deng Majok on those occasions. My opinion of him as a leader was certainly that he was accepted and respected by his people. And as he was re-

spected by his people, he was respected by me in his position as their chief. As far as I can remember, he kept very good order among the Ngok. I can't remember that we ever had any serious crime in that part of the District. Among the Baggara of Missiriya, there were frequent tribal quarrels and fights and disturbances. There was a good deal of serious crime: murders and so forth; and the same applies to the Hamar in the North. But I seem to remember that the Ngok Dinka were a particularly law-abiding people. Deng Majok, so far as I can recollect, kept his people happy and content, looked after their affairs, saw that justice was administered, and I cannot recollect that either within the tribe or as between his tribe and the Baggara, they ever had any serious trouble when I was down there.

Paul Howell, whose period overlapped with Bell in the capacity of Assistant District Commissioner, Baggara, 1946–48, and therefore had closer contact with the situation, wrote: "When I met him [Deng Majok], I judged him an outstanding figure among his peers in other areas. He was obviously an outstanding leader of his own people in rather unusual circumstances—i.e., relationships with Baggara Missiriya and as a sort of 'buffer state' position. I could put Deng Majok among those with the strongest personalities I had known in the Nilotic area."

It should be noted that these British administrators observed Deng Majok early in his chieftainship, when he was still growing into the office. Michael Tibbs, the last British District Commissioner in the area, on learning about this biography wrote to me: "Needless to say, I am delighted that you are writing a book about your father. He was unique and I greatly valued my friendship with him." Mohammed Abbas, who saw him in the 1960s, was even more complimentary:

> I came to know the late Deng Majok in 1966 when I was transferred from Upper Nile to Kordofan as Provincial Commissioner [governor]. I had already heard of the pacifying role he had played following the Arab-Dinka conflict, which had resulted from the rumors following the Sunday incidents in Khartoum during the October Government in 1964.[6]
>
> As a person, Nazir Deng was kind to his people; he had a great sense of humor, patience, and imagination. He was always compromising, but for the better. As a leader, he enjoyed a strong personality, was just, fair, and firm. He could get what he wanted by diplomacy and tact. If he had had education, I am sure he would have emerged as a high-ranking African leader.

Paul Howell elaborated on the extent to which Deng Majok's power was the culmination of a process which, at least according to him, had considerably affected the traditional egalitarianism of the Dinka. Ironically, Howell argued that the emphasis on the power of the chief was the outcome of the

---

6. In which nine Southerners, four Northerners, and a Greek merchant were killed.

remoteness of the central government, which necessitated dependency on the local authority of tribal leadership:

> The Ngok have not been subjected to an intensive system of administration. Their country is practically inaccessible during the rains from May to November, the nearest point which can be reached by car during that period being Muglad, 130 miles away. As we have seen, at one time the Ruweng Allor (now in Upper Nile Province) were included in Western Kordofan district, but administration consisted mainly of occasional visits by the District Commissioner rarely totaling more than a few weeks in the year. For this reason, and because of their remoteness from any of the main lines of communication, the lack of a permanently navigable river and the absence of commercial enterprise by merchants from the South, the Ngok have been subjected to less external influences than most Nilotic tribes today. Moreover, administration, essentially in the form of personal visits by the District Commissioner, has for the most part been conducted by men who had relatively little experience of Nilotic peoples and did not speak the language. This has had a definite result in the political organization of the tribe. The principal *Bany de Ring* [Chief of the Flesh] has acquired powers which are undoubtedly greater than would have been the case in the past. An administration must in its initial stages demand some form of indigenous leader through whom order may be transmitted.
>
> There was therefore an attempt to find some institution equivalent to the Baggara "Nazirates," or the "Sultans" or "Meks" of the Nuba and Dagu of the District. One reads early reports which describe the most important *Bany de Ring* as the Nazir," "Sultan" or even "Mek" (King) of the Ngok.
>
> The principles which characterize these institutionalized authorities among the Baggara, Nuba and Dagu in no way even approximate the political functions of the Dinka *Bany de Ring*. Since, however, there has been an attempt to read a preconceived idea of a "Chief" into the existing functionary himself, a Chief with considerable autocratic powers has been in the process of evolution over a number of years and if Kwol Arob was not a Nazir to begin with, he soon became the Dinka equivalent. His son, Deng Majok, has carried the evolution a stage further and has a burning ambition to pattern himself on the Ali Gulla "Nazirate" of the Homr (Baggara) with all the pomp of state visits to Khartoum, tribal gatherings, and in addition the Dinka ideal of wealth, a company of wives. There is no serious danger in this except that former administrative policy has tended to build up an effective autocracy in an essentially democratic society; a system which might prove a stumbling block to the introduction of a democratic system of local Government.[7]

---

7. "The Ngok Dinka," 263–64.

Apparently, as a result of Deng Majok's policy, accepted by the government, that he be the only channel of communication with his people, together with the remoteness factor explained by Paul Howell, and the concomitant emphasis on the system of indirect rule through which the British consolidated their control over the tribes—not to mention the power of his own personality—Deng Majok became virtually the ultimate authority over his people. As Chol Piok put it:

> Deng Majok was the governor. And he was the judge. And he was the chief. All three were his responsibilities in his own tribe. If a major problem should come to his tribe, the government would only come to assist him in assessing the punishment in the case of a major offense. The government would then come to help sentence the wrong-doer and help lay down new orders. All the rest would be left to him. If it were compensation for homicide, he would settle that. If it were an imposition of fines, he would also do that. And his decisions would be backed up wherever the matter might go.

Deng Majok's leadership represented a peak in the evolution of tribal authority from the role of a spiritual and moral functionary to an autocratic government institution backed by the coercive power of the state. The erosion of the egalitarianism and democracy of the traditional society has been counterbalanced by the effectiveness of the new institution in establishing and consolidating a broad-based adherence to the rule of law in the broader framework of the nation-state. Deng Majok and other tribal chiefs in both the North and the South were indispensable to the maintaining of order and security among the masses of the rural population and in a context in which the central governmental machinery was otherwise remote and costly.

Part 3: Family

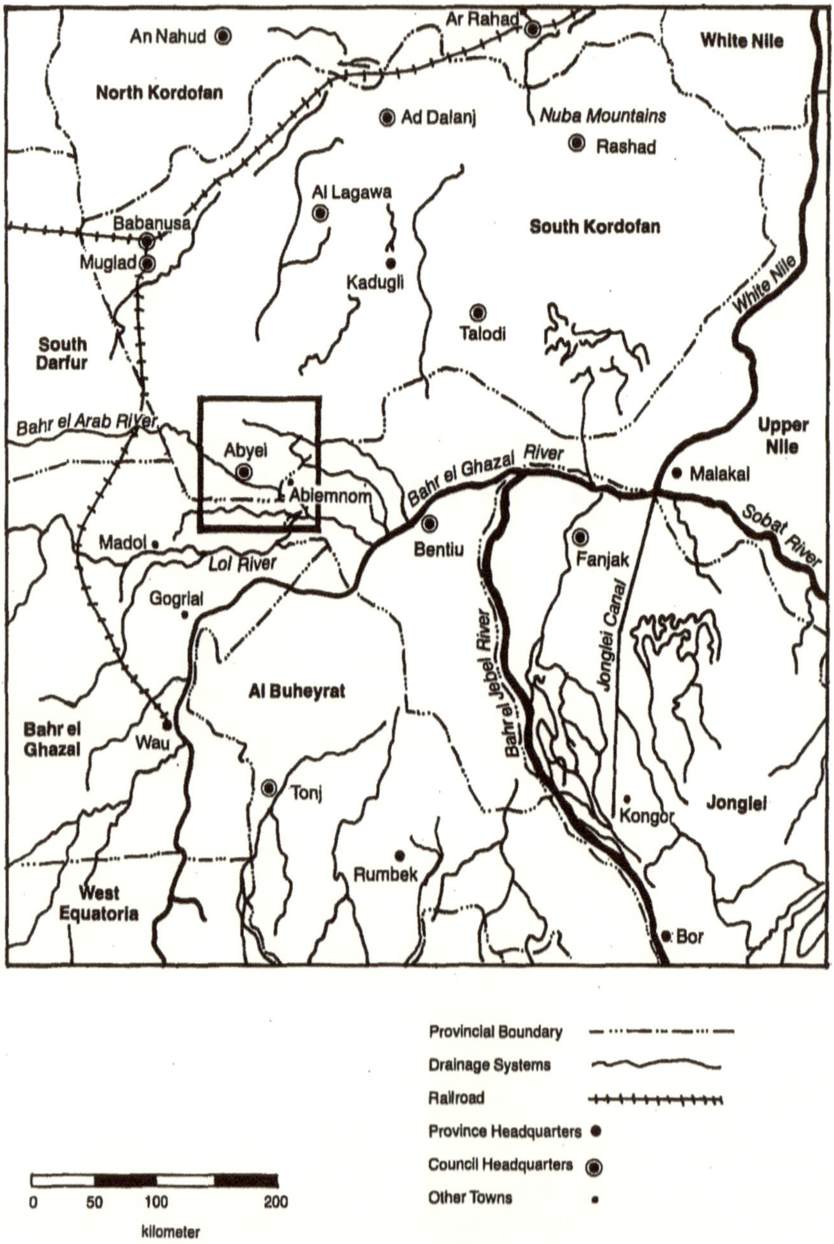

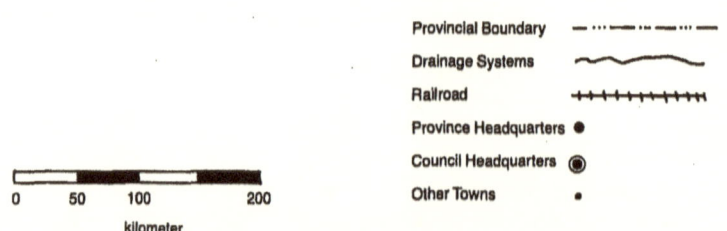

Map 3   Regional Map of the Sudan

9 The Curse to Love

"The only thing for which Deng Majok was criticized was that he married far too many wives," said Chief Lang Juk. "He married a uniquely large number of wives. No Chief has ever married so many wives. His wives were truly numerous. . . . Deng Majok used to travel a great deal, and whenever he found a girl he admired during his tours, he married her. . . . Whenever he returned from a trip, he came back with at least two wives. He married from all corners of Ngokland and neighboring tribes."

There is general agreement that when he died in 1969, Deng Majok had married approximately two hundred wives, and some estimates go as high as four hundred. And these were not loose arrangements; they were proper marriages into a family which, despite its size, was close-knit and tightly controlled.

Matet Ayom said:

> Why Deng Majok was criticized on the issue of marriage was because his marriages were far in excess of what any other chief had ever had. In Dinkaland, a chief, such as your great-grandfather, Arob Biong, was a rich man with a lot of cattle; and Allor Ajing had a lot of cattle, and he was a great chief. Their wives never exceeded ten each. But when it came to Deng Majok, he took marriage beyond the norm. He would marry a wife this season, and the following season he would again marry another girl.
>
> That was what made some of us come into conflict with him. We would say, "Deng, people will dislike you for this excessive marriage. You see a girl betrothed to a poor man without cattle and you go and snatch her away from him." And the chief is the wealthiest man who holds the largest herds. Deng would go and find a girl being com-

peted for by two or more people and he would throw himself into the competition and snatch the girl. He would find a girl paid for in marriage and would throw himself into the situation and snatch her away from the man. The wives he captured from other men were many. In fact, the girls he married who had not already been claimed by other people were few. Most of his wives he captured from other men.

"His first three wives were of the same age," said Achwil Bulabek. "Since then, he never left marriage nor did he ever interrupt the chain of marriages. People tried to persuade him against marriage, but to no avail. As soon as he saw a beautiful girl, he immediately took his cows for her bridewealth. Even during our visits, if he found a beautiful girl, he would negotiate the marriage right there."

"Deng Majok started his liking for women before he married," intimated his half-brother, Deng Abot. "He first did so by flirting with girls who were related to us. He would court the daughters of our relatives, and whenever father heard of that, he would get angry and they would quarrel. Then he seduced a girl who was engaged to our father's relative, Kur Deng Goch; that is when my father quarreled with him very badly."

"He went and impregnated the girl," elaborated Chol Piok.

> She had originally been from Pajok clan. But she had been adopted by someone who seemed to have been related to Deng Majok's maternal relatives. He was from the Dhiendior Clan. That man placed a curse on Deng Majok. He took a billy goat and a small she-goat. And then he would raise the billy goat and place him on top of the small she-goat. He repeated that several times while he spoke, comparing that to what Deng Majok had done.[1] He said, "Deng Majok will only die in the way of women. That is how he will die." He cursed him that way.

Nyanjur told of a conversation between Deng's daughters and their uncle, Biong Mading, on the issue of their father's excessive marriages and the supposed curse behind it:

> We had approached Uncle Biong on the matter. I personally addressed a question to him. I said, "Uncle! What is the matter with our father on this question of marriage; is it that he cannot be persuaded or is it that people think he is right in what he is doing?"
>
> Uncle Biong said, "My child, for a child to reflect on her father's conduct and ask questions about it, such as the issue of your father's marriages, is a good thing; it is not at all bad. Your father's excessive marriage is not good; it is bad. It is this marriage which will one day kill him. But there is a reason for his excessive marriage and it is something that could be corrected. It is only that he has refused to be cured."

---

1. Again, a symbolic act of faith based on the belief that what is justifiably willed will in fact occur.

He then told us about the curse of a man called Deng Goch, the father of the man called Kur Deng Goch.

And truly, Mading, when our father died, we found that what had killed him was the issue of women; nothing else killed him. How? He became involved in many problems over the issue of marriages.

Nyanbol Arob, Deng Majok's first wife, had no doubts at all: "Deng Majok was cursed to marry excessively; he was cursed by Kur Deng Goch. And of course that is why he died so simply in the end."

In other words, the popular belief among the Dinka is that Deng Majok was cursed to love women and to die pursuing them. He loved them and, although he died of cancer, the Dinka claim that it was women who caused his death.

Since he neither believed in nor minded the curse, Deng Majok never asked his uncle to remove it through a cleansing ceremony, which is supposed to follow apologies and an appeasement fee of cattle. When his uncle died, he empowered his heir to cleanse Deng Majok if he should repent and seek atonement. But Deng did not think it necessary to remove the curse even though it began to work very early in his adulthood.

As soon as he started to marry, one marriage followed after another. Nyanbol Arob was the first, followed shortly afterward by Nyanbol Amor. Almost at the same time, he was involved with Kwei. Achok followed at a time when he was already engaged to Aker Tiel. Nyanbol Deng came next. Then he took Nyanawai from an engagement to another man. Others followed in rapid succession.

It soon became apparent to everyone except himself that Deng Majok was indeed suffering from a curse and that he needed to be cleansed of the wrong that had brought about that curse. But all efforts to do so were to no avail.

"Deng Majok refused any reconciliation, saying 'What harm can it do?'" recounted Chol Piok.

> He would marry even if his father opposed the marriage. He would not surrender. Even if his father said, "The man who was engaged to the girl is our relative," he would not concede. And whenever anyone of us tried to persuade him, he would just conclude that the person had turned against him and would stop talking to that person about the matter of marriage. We once took him deep into the woods and said to him: "O Deng Majok, a Big Chief like you should not behave this way. Stop marrying more wives and give full attention to the affairs of your tribe." He said, "Anyone who says such words should stop coming to me." He frightened people that way, so we all dispersed.

"We once tried to reconcile father with Kur Deng Goch," said Achai-Chol:

> We talked to our father in front of Uncle Biong Mading. We said, "Uncle, we have come from the cattle-camp to talk to our father in front of you because we are disturbed by father's excessive marriage. We have come to realize that this is the result of the curse which his maternal uncle cast upon him." The three of us, Adau, Abul, and myself, had contributed a cow each. We said to our father and Uncle Biong that we wanted to give them to the family of Kur Deng Goch to appease them and request them to remove the curse.
>
> When Father heard that, he got angry and told us to stop that nonsense. He said that there was nothing wrong with his marriages and that even if he had been cursed to do so, that was no reason to dislike his marrying. He completely refused to let us appease the family of Kur Deng Goch.

According to Nyanluak, Deng Majok used to say: "My purpose is to enhance myself with people. And even if I were cursed to do so, there is nothing bad in a man cursing me this way. That man has done me a great deal of good. Anyone who will dare take a cow to appease the family of Deng Goch to seek the removal of the so-called curse will provoke me into a serious conflict with him."

The curse to love was to be a source of more problems than his excessive marriages or the initial wrong that brought it about. Deng Majok was soon to come into conflict with another relative over the love of a woman. The cause of the conflict, as narrated by Chol Piok, indicates that the circumstances of his mother's marriage were sometimes a subject of gossip about which Deng Majok was most sensitive. "Deng had contested a girl with Allor, the son of Miyan Biong," said Chol Piok.

> He contested a girl with him, a girl from Anyiel tribe, the daughter of Marayin. Allor went and insulted Deng Majok to the girl. He said to the girl, "You should not go with Deng Majok." Then he spoke vilely of Deng Majok's mother. How Deng Majok came to know what he had said to the girl is the one thing that has escaped my knowledge.
>
> One day the drums were taken out for a public dance at Kolom. Then Allor came. You know in our Dinka dance gentlemen all line up in a warlike display. Right there, he threw a spear at Allor. Allor dodged it. Deng took out another spear and was about to throw it again when the spear-shaft was caught.
>
> The clan of Miyan and the clan of Arob then pulled apart. They drew up their front lines for a fight. Those of Anyiel who were there and Abyor were then pulled apart and prevented from clashing.

Kwol Arob's reaction, as reported by Deng Abot, could not have sat well with Deng Majok: "My father's reaction was, 'Even if they insult one another, they are children of the same family of one woman. This is not an issue for our clan to involve themselves in.' Your father's mother's side is of course related to the family of Biong Miyan's mother."

Chol Piok's account reveals some political aspects to the conflict of which Kwol Arob could not have been unaware:

> The following winter, the Abyor made a plan. They said, "This is the man whom the tribes want to be the chief! Have you not seen now what he has done?" He was still only a deputy to his father; he had not yet been chosen as the chief.
>
> They sent a letter of complaint to the government. And the people waited until the dry season. Then the government came. The District Commissioner asked for the case against Deng Majok and why he had speared a person. The Commissioner said, "Deng, why did you spear the person?"
>
> Deng Majok said, "I speared him because he had insulted me." He said, "How did he insult you?"
>
> Deng said, "He said that my mother was a soiled woman: that she rejected Kwol Arob and was eventually given to him after she had been soiled. He also said that my maternal relatives were lepers. That is why I speared him. And had he not been rescued, I would have killed him."
>
> The Commissioner then said, "What about you, Allor, did you say those things or did you not?" Allor said, "I said them."
>
> Then he said, "Very well. Now, you, Dinka, what is your word?"
>
> The court members then gave their views, the senior court members of those days, including people like Kat Chol and Deng Nyach. It was then said, "It is true, in our Dinka ways, that if a man insults another man in front of a girl, it is a matter which causes people to kill one another. And this Deng is a man we want to be our chief. If he has speared a person, we shall impose a punishment on him, but we will not depose him."
>
> Kwol Arob spoke and said, "So, while you were here with me all this time, was it in your hearts that Deng Majok would be the chief?"
>
> Katdit spoke and said, "Do you mean that this other silent Deng of yours who does not respond to people is the one to be chief? We have imposed a fine of five cows on Deng Majok. But he is to remain in his position."
>
> The Commissioner then said, "Very well! You, Deng Majok, your people like you very much. But never repeat such a mistake again; never commit another wrong. Let this be your last mistake."

"When the matter was later discussed," noted Pagwot Deng, "Kwol Arob said, 'And that is the man you say should be the chief?' People said: 'He is truly the chief. We did not say that someone who would spear people should be a chief. But a person can be provoked by something that could make him behave that way. What provoked him to behave that way is separate from the reasons we wanted him to be chief. We still think of him as the best suited to be chief.'"

But the curse seemed to have already set in motion a series of problems for Deng Majok, as Chol Piok recounts:

Then Deng did something else; a second wrong. The District Commissioner had said, "Once a man is betrothed to a girl, anyone who goes after that girl, whether he be a chief or a commoner, and goes to change the mind of that other man's wife, that man will be sentenced to years of imprisonment. And if that man be a chief, he will be dismissed from his position."

Deng Majok went with Agorot Anhiany, the daughter of a man called Anhiany at Mareng. The girl had run away and come to him after she had been married with a great deal of cattle. The man called Angui had married her. She went with Deng Majok and became pregnant. Deng Majok and the girl were the only two who knew the facts.

Deng Majok one day convened a meeting of all the court members and said to them, "This is the wrong I have committed, you court members. The prohibition of the law knows no chief. I have committed a wrong. It is now for you, court members, to decide. You may choose to sentence me before the government comes; it is up to you. If you prefer to leave my case until the government comes, that is also up to you; you can refer my case to the government.[2]

The court members said, "O Deng, that is a simple matter. Even if you had killed a person, we could manage it. What we will do is collect cattle." Each one of us provided a cow and we gathered the same number of cattle as the man had paid in marriage. Sixty cows were collected. And then all the court members rose with elders of the tribe. They drove the cattle to the father of the girl at Mareng. Our offer of marriage was very much debated. The father of the girl refused. Everyone spoke, but he did not agree. He said the girl belonged to the man to whom she had already been betrothed.

The matter was discussed for three days. Then he eventually agreed. The cattle of Angui were then paid back. That case never even reached the government. It ended there. The woman remained for a while and then suddenly ran away from Deng Majok. She was a terribly brave woman.

Although the curse to love initially involved sexual offenses outside marriage, it was eventually manifested in Deng Majok's excessive marriages. Matet Ayom offered this account of Deng's first three marriages:

His father arranged his first marriages in the conventional way. It was his father who saw Nyanbol Arob, Deng's first wife; it was not Deng who went and found Nyanbol Arob. In those days, a man did not marry a girl he had met at a dance. Instead, your father would send you, "Go to the descendants of So-and-So and see whether one of them has begotten a girl." So, Kwol sent his son Deng, saying: "Go to

---

2. Deng Majok's obvious preference was for his people to take action before the British District Commissioner got involved. He expected the former to be lenient and the latter to adhere to the strict letter of the law.

the family of Arob Kwot. I understand that there is a small girl there. Go and visit your maternal relatives in that area and see the girl. If you like her, come and let me know. I shall marry her to you." That is how Deng left and saw the girl. Then he returned and said, "Father, I like the girl. So it will be according to your words. Even if I had not liked her and it is your will that I should marry her, I would have told you to proceed with the marriage." That is how Kwol married Nyanbol Arob to Deng.

Then he competed with another man for his second wife, Nyanbol Amor, now the mother of Abul. He competed with a man called Dan Deng Piok. Dan Deng Piok had paid betrothal cattle for her. Deng went and told his father, "Father, I have found a girl, the daughter of Amor Mioriik."

Kwol said: "But Deng, did you not marry only recently? I thought you should return to the cattle-camp and spend some time enjoying camp life. But if you are in love with the daughter of Amor Mioriik, then go ahead and marry her." So Deng went and released cows from his own herd. He released seven cows. But Dan Deng Piok did not surrender. They competed for the girl. In the past, no one could successfully compete for a wife against the son of a chief. The chief would not allow his son to be defeated by wealth because that would embarrass the chief. So Kwol got involved in the marriage.

The Mother of Arob, Kwei, his third wife, was the first girl he procured on his own.

According to Deng Abot, his father wanted him to be the first to marry as the senior son of the first wife, but Deng Abot preferred to give priority to Deng Majok because he was older and without a mother.

> When it was time to marry, my father said, "This issue of marriage [if not handled according to the seniority of the mothers] can cause spiritual affliction leading to illness. Deng Majok, here is Deng Makuei insisting that you marry first. You had better provide a cow-calf to symbolize his betrothal as the senior son. He is arguing that you cannot both marry at the same time because you need to substitute for your mother's hut first, since his mother is still alive." My father wanted some cows to be paid for my engagement to prevent what the Dinka regard as the curse of the senior son. But I refused, saying that I did not want to marry.
>
> Deng Majok took out a white cow-calf with black spots and she was consecrated to become part of my bridewealth when I later married.[3] And I proceeded to release cattle for Nyanbol's marriage. Of even a cow which pulled a peg out of the ground, I would say, "Let that cow go into marriage; it has volunteered itself."

As Allor-Jok explained, "Deng Majok, being older, was the first to marry,

---

3. The allocation of a cow symbolized that Deng Abot married first as the senior son, even though in fact that was not the case.

even though Deng Abot's engagement was first arranged by the payment of a betrothal cow. This meant that Deng Abot was regarded as the senior son even though Deng Majok was older, just as Deng Abot's mother was senior even though she was younger."

"Then I engaged Nyandeng Adija as my second wife," resumed Deng Abot.

> Your father turned on Nyanbol Amor. When [Deng Majok] eloped with her, my father said, "You have committed a wrong. The girl is the wife of my maternal aunt's son." But when my father was prevailed upon to consent on the grounds that things had gone too far, my father released an atonement cow and persuaded the other side to withdraw their claim. Then we released our cattle into the marriage of Nyanbol Amor.
>
> As for Kwei, he did not initially marry her; he only made her pregnant. When he made her pregnant, she was engaged to Deng Monytoc, who had paid cattle for her. But then my father said, "Since she has borne a son, she should no longer be allowed to go to someone else. So you, Deng Majok, release your cows and marry her." So, Deng married his third wife, Kwei, paying with his own cattle.

The story of Deng Majok's first three marriages is told by the wives themselves, beginning with Nyanbol Arob:

> In the beginning, all I had heard of the Deng brothers was their reputation as the two Deng-sons of Kwol Arob. The Deng brothers were well known throughout this tribe of nine divisions. Deng Majok's father said, "Deng's mother is dead. I should let him marry so that he may assist me in producing children for the family."
>
> Our cattle-camp was in the *toc*. Kwol Mariew went from here with Deng Awak. Kwol Mariew's mother, Nyanagon, was my father's sister. I was told, "Nyanbol, please prepare the food for the guests." So we prepared and served the food. And when we went to fetch the dishes, Deng Awak said, "Whose daughter is that small girl?"
>
> They said, "She is the daughter of Arob, son of Kwot, son of Juac."
>
> He said, "The daughter of Ateng of Manhiany [Nyanbol's mother]?"
>
> "Yes!" they answered.
>
> He said, "Her mother was nearly married to Miyan Biong; it was just that her grandfather refused."
>
> Deng Awak returned and said, "Kwol, since you are intent on marrying for your son, I have found a little girl in Diil; would you please have her seen? If you are agreeable I think she should be married to your son."
>
> When Kwol Arob heard that, he sent his brother Mahdi Arob [to see the girl]. Mahdi went. My father said, "Nyanbol, a man from the family of Nyanagon has come; prepare food for him!"

I prepared food for him. He ate and proceeded to Ruweng. Then he returned. And when he returned, he told Kwol Arob that he had found the appropriate girl. Kwol Arob sent word to Deng Majok's maternal uncle, Deng Kir, who lived in the same area, saying, "Let it be known to Deng Kir that his sister's son will marry that little girl."

Deng Kir said, "Yes! My sister's son has truly found a wife."

That was how I was seen and chosen, if that is what you want to know.

Then Kwol said, "Deng, you go and see the girl!"

Deng went accompanied by those of Ajing Ater. And when they went, they stayed in the cattle-byre of those of Akur Deng Kir, his maternal cousin. Their home was some distance away, but we used to share our meals together. I passed by. They were in the cattle-byre. As I passed by, they all looked through the door of the cattle-byre. Someone said, "The girl has come!" They all looked through the door! I continued to walk by. We went and ate. And then I returned, walking the same way.

When I thought of it, I said, "Akur Deng Kir, who are all those men who were peeping through the door?"

She said, "They are guests of the family!"

"I see," I said.

We spent the day. Then, in the evening, it was first rumored that there were guests who had come. The girls of the village were asked to gather to entertain them. The girls began to gather. I was asked to join; but I said I would not go. For two days, I totally rebuffed the people. In the end, the guests left; but they came back again. He himself decided to remain at home; he did not return to see me. But they proceeded with the marriage. That was the beginning of your father's story with me. I first resisted everybody's pressure to bring us together.

The men who had first approached me were two; there was Agorow from Mareng. I told him, "You have overstayed in the cattle-camp unmarried; I cannot welcome you." There was Deng Akolith. I told him, "I do not know your word." That was where those relationships ended. Deng liked the idea that I had rejected those men; that I would not go with just any man. When I initially turned him down, it was not that I rejected him as a person. It was that I despised men in general. Even if a man was handsome and he appealed to me, I would not give in.

Nyanbol Amor's account of her marriage to Deng Majok was equally candid:

What I had heard was that there were Deng Majok and Deng Makuei, the senior sons of Kwol Arob. They were very much praised. If a man did something people thought arrogant, they would say, "Who do you think you are, Deng, the son of Kwol?" And if the person was a girl, people would say, "Who do you think you are, Agorot, the daughter of Kwol?"

> We were still blooming teenagers. And their names sounded quite exciting. I wished I could see them. We wondered whether their bodies were created in the same way as those of all the men we saw were or whether there was something quite different about them. People said, "They are created as all men are." Time passed. Eventually, we met for the first time. None of us had seen the other before. Then we looked at one another very closely. By the time he approached me and we actually met, we had already had a good look at one another. That meeting then developed into a relationship which eventually took me to his house as a wife.

Because of the importance the Dinka attach to a father's consent, Nyanbol presents Kwol as not only agreeable but as the initiator:

> His father had said to him, "I would like you to marry the daughter of Amor Mioriik. They are a family stock which are well-known and highly praised."
> The cattle for the marriage were brought to our family while I was away in the cattle-camp. I heard it and objected. I eloped with another man, Dan Deng Piok.
> My family were very much angered by my conduct. They came and brought me back. And they insisted on giving me to Deng.
> Your father himself continued to pursue me with vigor. He would get onto his horse and attack the family of Deng Piok. It was a bad situation.
> In the end, all the friends of Deng Majok, men like Biong Achol and Akoc Ajith and many others, all gathered and dressed up very glamorously and called on me at home. They spoke to me so much that I eventually gave in. I said: "If you people have taken the trouble to gather and call on me, there is no more I can say. My objection is ended. What I was rejecting was the idea of a man releasing his cattle to marry me when we had never exchanged words to create a relationship. But since you have come all the way to convince me, I will honor your words." That was how I surrendered. It was because a whole age-set had assembled and implored me to consent.
> The other man and I had grown up together and he was also a very handsome man. He and I were very close. But what could I do? Isn't chieftainship a great power? Your chieftainship is a power that cannot be beaten. After I was given to Deng Majok, the other man was appeased with payment. My father-in-law, Kwol Arob, appeased him and I was then sprinkled with the sacred ashes for blessing.

Nyanbol evidently manipulated Deng Majok on an issue closest to his heart, and that was the comparison with the case of his own mother, including resentment of the subordinate status of a second wife:

> My story with Deng was similar to that of his own mother and father. First, Nyanaghar resisted marriage to Kwol Arob until she eloped with another man. Then Kwol Arob took her back from the

other man. It was similar to our situation. Deng would say to me, "How could you reject me to the point of eloping with another man? In what way is he better than me?"

I would say, "What is so strange about a girl preferring a young man from her section of the tribe? Even if you are a very handsome man, you come from another section of the tribe and he is from my own section."

One of the reasons I rejected Deng Majok was that I did not want to be a second wife. I wanted to be a first wife. Later, whenever I had a claim, I would tell him that I had opposed him because I did not want to fall in the middle, subordinated to another wife.

The story of Deng Majok's third wife, Kwei, goes back a long way into their childhood and seems to have been a romantic tale of mutual love from the start:

Deng and I started to dance together when we were still children. We were both from Abyor section. Our home was in Nyinchuor and their home was in Abyei. We grew up together until we matured and began the courtship that ended in marriage.

The family of Monytoc were the first to betroth me. I was betrothed to his son, Deng Monytoc. They paid forty-five cows. It was said that he would pay five more cows and then be given his bride. The Pajok all gathered and said, "We should not let Kwei be married to someone else. Kwei is the daughter of a woman with a strong character. And Deng Monytoc has no mother." I rejected Deng Monytoc. Other people were also interested in me, but I rejected them. It was Deng whom I wanted.

Eventually my engagement to Deng Monytoc was broken. After that, Deng and I eloped and he brought me to his home. Only our father Kwol Arob opposed the marriage on the ground that we were blood relatives. But even that did not prevent our marriage. Our blood-tie was ritually severed to permit our marriage. And we were made to drink the medicine of Deng Jokngol, Deng Mathii.

After marrying Kwei, Deng betrothed Aker Tiel from the family of Juk, a leading family in Twichland. But before completing Aker's marriage, he married Achok Mijok and brought her home. The story of Achok's marriage as told by several informants is long, not only because of the complications involved, but obviously because of the special interest the speakers associated with my status as Achok's son. Although I was at first tempted to omit this material in the interest of objectivity, I decided to keep it, though in a highly abbreviated form, for the same reason.

Achok's lineage, Dhienagou, a branch of the preeminent Dhiendior clan, had been the divine chiefs of the Biar section of Bongo tribe. As a result of a blood feud, Mijok's grandfather, Maluk, had migrated from Bongo to Abyor at the time of Kwol's father, Chief Arob Biong. Maluk's father, Dau, and Arob's father, Biong, had maintained cordial ties as leaders of preeminent lineages. Maluk was well received and honored by Arob Biong and the whole of Abyor. He and his descendants became close associates and advisers to the line of Pajok chiefs. Achok's father, Mijok, who was a member of Kwol Arob's age-set, Koryom, was the latest in the association.

Pagwot Deng, the chief of Bongo, confirmed, "Your maternal relatives were the leaders of Biar. The section called Biar was theirs. In those days, there was no government, but chieftainship was determined by divine authority. So, they were the divine chiefs of Biar."

"They were the center of the very ancient Bongo," added Achwil Bulabek, chief of Abyor.

> Maluk Atokbek, son of Dau, was the man who immigrated into Abyor tribe. That is why you hear of the war song of Abyor: "Milk the Cow, Ayan, of Maluk, the son of Dau; Milk Ayan of Maluk, the Buffalo."
>
> When Arob was the chief, he called your grandfather and said, "Mijok, here is my son [Kwol]; take good care of him." Mijok and Kwol were members of the same age-set, Koryom. They were also very close friends.

Achok had already been betrothed before puberty to a man called Kweng, son of Kwol Arob's sister Achai, when Deng Majok came and proposed to her. Kweng had paid twenty cows and two bulls for the engagement and was expected to pay a large bridewealth when Achok reached puberty and was ready for the completion of the marriage. According to Achok's brother Ngor, Deng Majok saw Achok at a dance and went and told his father:

> "I want to marry the daughter of Mijok Duor." Chief Kwol said, "She is already engaged to Kweng, the son of Achai."
>
> Deng said, "No, I will not leave her to Kweng; I want to marry her."
>
> Kwol said, "Deng, you will not marry into the family of Mijok Duor. You will bring conflict into my relationship with Mijok. This chieftainship of mine is protected by the family of Maluk. Abyor has prospered because of the family of Maluk. You will not marry Mijok's daughter. You will only drag our relationship into problems. If you were not already married, I would encourage you to take your wealth to marry the daughter of Mijok as your first wife. But you have married several wives. Your wealth has already been spent. You cannot afford the daughter of Mijok."
>
> Deng said to his father, "I will not accept your word."
>
> Kwol then said, "In that case, consider me out of this matter."
>
> They discussed the matter a great deal, but could not agree. Kwol remained opposed while Deng persisted.
>
> Their age-set, Koryom, which was the age-set of both your grandfather, Kwol Arob, and my father, came to our home at Nok-Jur. They came on horses. They all gathered there and tethered their horses. Father slaughtered in their honor, and after entertaining them he

said, "Gentlemen, my dear age-mates, what brings you? Is anything the matter?"

They then introduced the subject. They talked a great deal to persuade my father to give his daughter to Deng Majok.

Mijok said, "Gentlemen, is the man for whom you are speaking without a father's voice behind him?" Where is the voice of Kwol?"

"Kwol has excused himself to us," they said. "He said, 'Gentlemen, my age-mates, I am out of this. Deng is placing Mijok Duor and me in potential conflict. Should Mijok accept, Deng will not be able to match the aspirations of Mijok. So, I better keep out of it.'"

According to Matet Ayom:

Mijok Duor had reacted rather negatively, saying, "Deng Majok, if yours is a marriage of a son without the involvement of his father, then I shall not accept. Kwol is my age-mate and my associate. If he has not shown interest in the marriage of my daughter to his son and it is only the desire of the son, I cannot accept."

When Kwol heard this, he sent a message to Mijok Duor saying, "Please tell Mijok Duor that he is not a man I can reject. It is just that my respect for him inhibits me. I have already married for Deng Majok with a lot of cows. I am afraid of his getting involved with Mijok's daughter at a time when he does not have the same number of cows at his disposal as he had for his first wives. I fear that Deng may not be able to afford a bridewealth appropriate for the status of Mijok Duor, a great man in whom I find support, for it is with the words of Mijok Duor that I am running this tribe."

Kwol was attending the engagement of Aker Tiel in Twichland and had not yet come home when Deng Majok wanted to marry Mijok's daughter.

The marriage of Biong Mading, your father's brother, came immediately after that. The cattle Deng had were not sufficient. He would take some cows and send them to Biong's marriage. And then Arob, his younger brother, got a girl pregnant and wanted to marry her. So his own marriage was also added to these other marriages. All four marriages were performed by your father at about the same time.

But your maternal grandfather was a cool-headed man. He said, "Tell Deng Majok, if his father says that it is permissible for his son to perform his marriage with me, then let him not concern himself with paying me the bridewealth. Let him occupy himself with other urgent matters. I have cattle for my food; I am not in need. I shall also not reject his marriage on account of cattle. Let him perform the marriages of his younger brothers."

That attitude from your grandfather was very pleasing to your father.

Deng Abot gave the friendship between his father and Mijok Duor as the reason for Kwol Arob's opposition to the proposed marriage:

Mijok was a very dear person to my father, a friend with whom he shared one bed.... When your father wanted your mother, my father said, "Mijok, Deng is going to create problems between you and me.... It is better to let him find a wife wherever else he can and you and I remain in the close relationship our families have enjoyed for long. You and I have been very close; your father and my father were also very close; your grandfather Maluk was also very close to my grandfather; and your great-grandfather Dau was also close to my great-grandfather. Let us not allow this marriage to cause conflicts between you and my children."

That was how my father refused. He was concerned about a close relationship that might be affected by the marriage. Both families had important roles to play for the welfare of the tribe. Your maternal relatives were also people of divine authority. If disease appeared in the tribe, my father would call upon Mijok to perform curative rituals.

Chol Piok saw a different motive for Kwol Arob's opposition to Deng Majok's proposed marriage to Achok:

Why your grandfather Kwol Arob refused at first was the fact that Deng Majok was already marrying more women than Deng Makuei. That he did not like. That disturbed him deep inside. He did not want Deng Majok to be an equal of Deng Makuei.

You see, if Deng Majok had not stood firm, he would have been left far on the periphery of things because of that grandfather of yours.

After Achok and Aker came Nyanbol Deng. And then came the very controversial case of Nyanawai Monyjok. Patal gave this account of the contest for Nyanawai.

Deng had designated Nyanawai from the time she was a little girl. Then Minyiel Deng Kur said he wanted to marry her. Deng Majok sent for Agal, Minyiel's older brother, and said, "Son of my maternal aunt" (Agal was the son of Deng Makuei's maternal aunt, so Deng Majok also referred to him as the son of his maternal aunt), Deng said, "Son of my maternal aunt, please do not let your brother marry my wife. I chose her while she was still a small girl. Do not marry her."

Agal said, "But Deng, son of my maternal aunt, now that your younger cousin Minyiel has fallen in love with the girl, should you not leave her to him?"

Deng said, "That cannot be. I chose the girl when she was small."

They discussed the matter all day inside the cattle-byre at Noong. Agal eventually came out of the byre without giving in. He left and went to Kwol Arob and said, "Uncle, I am disputing about the girl with Deng Majok and I begged him to leave her for his cousin Minyiel, but he is refusing. I want to release my cattle for the bride-price."

Kwol Arob said, "Deng will be advised to give in."

Deng Majok heard of this and went to his father. Kwol said, "Deng, my son, if Agal wants the girl for Minyiel, why don't you let her go?"

Deng said, "Father, how can I leave a girl that I chose when she was still small? That cannot be. You better advise Agal to leave my wife alone!"

Kwol said, "Since Minyiel wants to marry her, I ask you to leave her to him. Let him marry her."

Deng said, "That cannot be."

Deng Majok then went to the family of Monyjok and said: "Give the cattle of Minyiel's marriage back to their owners. The girl is my wife. We cannot compete over the girl."

The family of Monyjok then rejected the cattle. But when the cattle were rejected, Minyiel eloped with Nyanawai. Deng Majok then went to Kwol Arob and said, "Father, has what we talked about become the truth? Have you abandoned me and made Minyiel your son? Have you truly abandoned me?"

That was what made them quarrel. That quarrel continued until the case went to the government.

Matet Ayom elaborated:

> It was that case that made Deng Majok realize how much he was out of his father's favor. When the case was tried at Muglad by the District Commissioner, Kwol sat next to Minyiel on one side while Deng Majok sat alone on the other side. When Kwol proceeded to state the case for Minyiel, Deng Majok began to weep. He wept openly and said: "Has my father truly become the father of Minyiel Deng Kur? Has my own father turned into someone else's father against me?"
>
> An elder called Kur Anyar remarked: "O people of our land, you used to speak of feuds, you have now witnessed the bitterness of a true feud; that is why a man is crying with his back turned to his father. That is the feud that never ends; there it is, you have witnessed it." The man turned to Kwol Arob and said: "Father of Agorot, if this child who is crying with his back turned to you should turn to face you one day, you will be in trouble. There he is, crying and saying, 'Is my father truly taken over by another man? I will not face my father defending the son of another man against me.'"
>
> That incident made Deng Majok put his heart into taking over the chieftainship from his father, Kwol Arob. What embittered Deng even more was the fact that Minyiel was Deng Makuei's maternal cousin. Deng Makuei's mother was Abiong Malek and Minyiel's mother was Nyanriang Malek. Their mothers were sisters. And Kwol stood with Minyiel while Deng stood alone. That is the feud Deng never forgot.

One of the most controversial cases in Deng Majok's marriages was that of Nyananyuat (Anyuat) Nyok. The story is told by Monyluak Row:

> Nyananyuat Nyok was borne by a girl called Achwei, who was the daughter of a girl called Akwol from the Jur-chol tribe. Akwol was captured and adopted by Arob Biong as his daughter. It was during the upheavals of the slave raids. Arob Biong adopted her and allocated her to the section of the mother of Allor Mabil. She became a daughter of the house of Man-Abul.
>
> When she matured, Deng Majok said, "I want to marry this girl." The family of Man-Abul rose up in protest and said, "How can you marry her when she is your sister?"
>
> Deng said, "This is not true; she is not a blood sister; she was adopted."
>
> That was how your father came into conflict with his cousin, Michar Allor.

Michar had been educated by Deng Majok and was very close to him, but his objection to the marriage developed into a political opposition which provided a rallying point for Deng Majok's enemies. Michar not only took the case to the government but also accused Deng of corruption in his marriages. This naturally threatened Deng Majok politically.

"That autumn," continued Monyluak, "the British District Commissioner came and said, 'Deng, if your relatives are against your marrying the girl, you would be well advised to abandon the idea. On the other hand, you relatives of the girl, if your daughter wants to marry Deng Majok, then you better let them get married. If Deng is trying to impose his will on the girl, that will not be allowed. But if the girl has consented to marry Deng, then you should permit them to get married according to their mutual desire.'"

The British Commissioner apparently gave his "if" opinion and left, intending to have formal hearings later on, should the parties concerned fail to resolve the dispute by themselves. Monyluak went on with his account of the case:

> Later on, your father came to our area in the middle of the night and asked for me to be awakened. I was sleeping inside the cattle-byre. He sent a man called Ngor Deng Agany to wake me. I got up.
>
> Your father had come on horseback. It had rained that night. I went and we greeted one another.
>
> Deng said, "Monyluak, I understand that the girl has gone to the cattle-camp at Bil-Tong. I would like you to guide me to her camp."
>
> I said, "I am afraid I will not go with you."
>
> He said, "Why not?"
>
> I said, "You, Deng, this is not the only girl you can marry. Do you want this girl to be the cause of destruction to your chieftainship? What if your chieftainship should be destroyed, who do you think is going to lead us and take care of this tribe? And are you risking all this because of a single girl, a girl who is not carrying your child so that you feel attached to her because of the child? I will not go along with you."

The case was later tried by Abyei court and decided in Deng's favor. Suspicious that the court might have been biased for their paramount chief, the British District Commissioner took the case to a special court of prominent chiefs from other Dinka tribes; and, although it was to prove difficult and divisive, the majority decided that the relationship involved, being one of adoption through slavery, did not constitute a marriage bar according to the rules of exogamy.

After winning the case and marrying Nyananyuat, Deng spoke to Monyluak Row and gave him a full account of his struggle for his rights within his clan and, in particular, against his father's negative attitude toward him as he was growing up and as an adult. He recalled his conflict with Deng Abot over the move of the cattle-camp, concluding: "It is the challenge with which I was confronted over that issue of herding and camping that has continued to this day. This is what I have once again faced in this case of the girl. And it was the same challenge which put me and my lineage in confrontation over the issue of chieftainship. That was what made me contest chieftainship with Deng Makuei."

The case of Nyanthon, one of the relatively junior wives of Deng Majok, is part of a pattern that had already become familiar and was to continue to the end of Deng's life. The story is told by Nyanthon herself.

> Your father saw me and simply proposed to my family and paid his cattle. Then it was said that the girl should be surrendered to her husband! When I heard that, I escaped from home. I ran away. But he persisted. My people searched for me. They found me and brought me to his home. I was initially opposed to the marriage. I rejected Deng Majok and said that I did not love him. I said that he was not my age. He was the age of my father. And there were men of my age who were interested in me. And those were men whom I knew well. With Deng Majok, we were total strangers to one another. We got to know one another only after marriage. We got to know one another at home.
>
> Deng Majok's wives could be said to fall into two main groups. There were those who were his own age or close to his age. And then there were those, beginning with us, who were far younger than he. He was virtually our father. But because of his power as chief he was able to get any girl however much younger than he she might be. As you know, among our people the Dinka, even if a girl hates a man but her people like him, she must go with him in honor of her people's word. So I was seized and brought to him. I came and fulfilled my marital obligations.

"As for the many girls Deng Majok took away from other men, he did not take them by force," concluded Chol Piok. "Deng paid well for his wives, and the relatives of the girls accepted him in preference to other men. And the girl would come and fall in love with Deng Majok at once."

10 The Empire at Home

Although there were of course exceptions, the more general pattern seems to have been that however Deng Majok acquired his wives, and even when they had been opposed to marrying him at first, he won them over by living up to certain objective standards of what was expected of Dinka married life. The wives also lived up to their marital obligations according to tradition. And their children followed the principles laid down by their parents and society. Much of the credit for this goes to what everyone agrees was a unique system of administration headed and controlled by a unique personality.

The family was divided into three main groups called "houses," headed by the top three wives: Nyanboldit (Nyanbol Arob), Nyanbol Amor, and Kwei. Aker Tiel assisted Nyanboldit while Achok assisted Nyanbol Amor. Kwei was punished for insubordination, and that, among other things, entailed leaving her without junior wives until much later, when Amou was married and made her deputy. That was when Deng Majok decided to have a branch of the family at Abyei to which he transferred most of his junior wives, leaving Noong as the traditional home where his senior wives continued to live. At Abyei he appointed three middle wives to represent the seniors in the leadership of the groups. Amel represented Nyanboldit, Nyanawai represented Nyanbol Amor, and Amou represented Kwei. When Deng Majok later established another village at Nainai, more junior wives were appointed to head the groups there. The segmentation process continued with the expansion of the family and the increase in the number of villages or settlements.[1]

---

1. In all those villages, beginning with Noong to the latest establishments, junior wives of all levels were associated with senior wives to render services.

Deng Majok handled much of the control through the leading wives. Many conflicts between the wives were investigated and settled by them. They wielded much authority and commanded great respect. Junior wives addressed them as "Mother," but gave them greater rituals of respect than Dinka children show their mothers.[2] Each wife could go directly to Deng Majok; but in most cases their demands were chaneled through their leaders, who also represented their husband to them. Any form of insubordination, divisiveness, or jealousy was met with stringent measures, ranging from severe reprimand and physical punishment to the husband's abstention from the wife's food and bed.

"When Deng married," said Nyanbol Arob, his first wife, "he gave his junior wives to the senior wives, saying, 'This is your wife, and this is your wife.' That was the way he distributed his wives among us, his senior wives. He did not have to say much more than that."

His second wife, Nyanbol Amor, spoke in the same vein: "He married wives and allotted them to us, and he saw to it that his wives lived together in harmony. What he used to do was to praise his mother's conduct and urge his wives to follow the way his mother had managed her home. He said, 'Follow my mother's ways. I shall withdraw myself and I want you to live well together.'"

Deng Majok was particularly intolerant of any manifestations of jealousy in his family. To him, as Nyanbol Amor observed:

> Jealousy was a disease which he loathed. . . . He wanted the family to live as one big family. He said, "This woman belongs to the house of so and so; this one belongs to so and so; and this one belongs to so and so. But you, the senior wives, should continue your relationship together as one family. And your attitude toward the junior wives must not be divisive. They are all your wives together. Treat every one of them as though she were from your own group, whatever the group to which she has in fact been assigned. Anyone who discriminates against a woman because she is assigned to another group will offend me severely. I will show her my anger."

"The unity of the family was the main goal," stressed Kwei, Deng's third wife. "We used to receive great respect from the junior wives. Our three houses were full of women, and of all those women, no one would call us by our names. We were addressed as 'Mother' by the junior wives."

"Each wife came next to another wife," explained Amel, "and the system proceeded up and down along those lines. If anything went wrong in the order of decision making, it was because someone did not know who came after whom. The seniority system, which ranked each person next to another person, was the way of life in our family."

---

2. Dinka children, small ones excepted, generally refer to their mothers by their first names rather than "Mother," a restriction that did not apply to the courtesy which junior wives showed their seniors. Indeed, the reverse was the case.

Senior wives not only welcomed but encouraged their husband's continuing marriages, as they gave them power and status over larger numbers of junior wives. "The fact that he kept marrying was not bad," remarked Nyanawai, "it increased our numbers so that if anything happened and found us together, we would manage our own situation."

Amel was even more positive:

> People tended to believe that cowives must hate one another. They thought we would say, "Why is the chief still marrying when so many of us are already here as his wives?" But they were wrong; we never spoke or even thought that way. Quite the contrary, we liked his marriages. Whenever he brought a wife and allocated her to a house, it was no longer his marriage alone; we used to be happy. We wanted to increase our numbers; yes, we wanted to increase our numbers.

"In fact," explained Ali, "our father's wives were in part responsible for his excessive marriage. If a woman during her travels came across a girl whose appearance or manner or working energies impressed her, and she also thought highly of her family, she would come and approach our father, saying, 'I want you to marry the daughter of so and so for me.' Father would go ahead and marry that girl. She would then be assigned to the wife who had recommended her for marriage."

Married life for the Dinka carries two main sets of obligations for the husband and the wife. The main purpose of marriage being procreation, the husband is obliged to give the wife the opportunity to realize her childbearing potential. As a corollary to this, he must provide her with sufficient means for maintaining herself and her children. For her part, the wife is expected to render domestic services and show due deference to her husband, a right often attributed to his having paid cattle for her. Her status also depends to a considerable extent on the moral and material support she and her husband continue to receive from her relatives. In particular, it depends on the extent to which they live up to their obligations in paying the reverse bridewealth and giving her husband the share to which they are entitled in the distribution of the cattle that accrue through the marriages of her female relatives. Discharging these mutual obligations is the Dinka yardstick for measuring the success or failure of a marriage.

Asked how she found the house when she eventually accepted her husband, Nyanbol Arob remarked: "How else could I find it? It was a home well provided with the good things of life. There were people in the family and children being born. What else does a woman want from marriage?" Thus, to Nyanbol Arob, echoing tradition, procreation, maintenance, and togetherness were the essentials of a happy family life.

"I came with a reluctant heart," said Nyanbol Amor. "But when I came, Deng Majok gave me a great deal of attention and established me well. He did everything for me, including all the things a woman needs to be happy in her home." And indeed, it was common knowledge that on all grounds—

childbearing, support, and harmonious relations—Nyanbol Amor fared well.

"I did not find anything bad in the home of Deng Majok," said Kwei, ironically the only one of the senior wives who had reason to complain. "When I came, he gave me a share in the cattle of the marriage of Ayan, the daughter of the mother of Allor." It is noteworthy that Kwei mentions only the material side of things and makes no reference to procreation, for that was where her main grievance lay.

"Deng did indeed establish Achok's house with children," said Ngor Mijok. "The only thing is that they turned out to be girls, except for yourself. But as we reflected, we realized that this was part of our ancestral blood. In the family of Duor, the pattern is generally one single son among daughters."

"Once I came home, there was nothing I disliked," said Nyanawai. "We were well provided with all the things we needed: there was food to eat, clothes to wear, and a good word whenever anything had to be discussed." Nyanawai's avoidance of mentioning procreation may be purely incidental or a reflection of her tragedy, as she lost a succession of children, even though several have survived.

"When I came, I never found anything to disappoint me in the house of my husband," said Amel, "whether with him personally or with his other wives or with his children. Nothing ever caused any conflict between me and my husband. Only God separated us in the end." Not having had any children, but undoubtedly one of the most favored wives, Amel appropriately placed her emphasis on relationships.

Even Nyanthon, who initially rejected Deng Majok as old enough to be her father, settled down to a happy married life with him: "Of course, you no longer felt that he was like your father; that thought vanished. I did not find anything that displeased me in the family; nothing that would compel me to leave my home. I lived with him until he died. To this day, I have not left my home."

Undoubtedly there is an element of reverence for the dead husband in all these positive accounts, but the criteria by which Deng Majok is appraised are clear, and the extent to which he lived up to the required standards is also quite evident.

Commenting on Deng Majok's relations with his earlier wives, Chol Piok observed: "Of his first four wives, your mothers, it is only the mother of Arob who used to quarrel with Deng Majok. As for the first two wives and your mother, they were very much loved by Deng Majok."

Kwei herself commented on her quarrel with her husband: "We quarreled while Deng was claiming reverse bridewealth from my relatives. I was pregnant with Achai-Chol and I had already given birth to Arob." While Kwei does not give any reason for the quarrel, it was generally known to have been caused by her defiant violation of the prohibition against tobacco. Chol Piok sees it as insubordination: "When Deng Majok quarreled with Kwei, the mother of Arob, that was because she was obstinately disobedient. She thought that she herself was the daughter of a spiritually powerful clan, Pajing, and therefore did not want to obey the words of Deng Majok. That was what put them into conflict and affected their marriage."

According to Monyluak Row: "The quarrel was the result of exchanging insults. As you know, a man may insult his wife in our Dinka ways. One might utter a bad insult against his wife and the wife might cry, but she would never insult her husband back. An unruly wife, on the other hand, might retaliate with an insult. That kind of retaliating insult is strongly resented by a man who has paid his cattle for a wife."

From the next class of wives, falling into virtually the same generation, Chol Piok singled out the case of Nyanbol Deng: "Nyanbol Deng turned out to be a really unruly person. She was so bad that your father used to wish that Atem were not her brother. He would say, 'Atem is so good: a man without a bad word.' Whatever Deng wanted, Atem would give him. Atem would even offer him what he had not asked for. Whenever Deng Majok had important guests from outside, Atem would be there to contribute."

"Father was the kind of person who wanted everyone to follow the line of behavior he had prescribed," said Ali, explaining the cause of Deng Majok's quarrels with Nyanbol Deng.

> He detested anyone who behaved in accordance with his or her own will. Among the wives we found to have problems with our father and with whom he frequently fought was Nyanbol Deng. And father's fights with women approximated death. He would beat a woman fiercely, tie her to a pole in the hut, and torture her in a dreadful way. Some women might remain chained for three days. And no one would dare intervene to resolve the conflict. His fights with Nyanbol Deng were frequent and intense.

"Father's discipline over his wives was extremely strict," commented Nyanjur.

> If you turned into a bad person who was prone to quarreling, you would be subjected to disciplinary measures not any less than those to which soldiers are subjected. He would first talk to you in words that would be hard to forget. If you forgot and committed another wrong, you would be subjected to so much beating that you would probably never commit that wrong again. If despite that you committed another wrong, then yours was a completely hopeless case that nobody on earth could control. But it was extremely rare to find any one of his wives reputed as foul-mouthed and quarrelsome. That was extremely rare, and largely because they did not dare to be that way.

Ali elaborated on his father's reaction to wrongdoing on the part of his wives:

> His reaction to wrongs was the greatest deterrent among his

wives. Even a woman who was prone to wrongdoing, once she saw how others were punished, would be deterred by Deng Majok's manner of punishment.

Father's abusive language was extremely foul. If he subjected a woman to verbal abuse, all the woman did was cry. If she was a woman who was not affected by insults or by admonitory speech, then he would resort to beating.

He would chain a woman to a tree or a pole for a period of time until the woman underwent immense suffering; sometimes, when he punished a woman by chaining her, he would insist that she not be provided with food or water. The woman would suffer and suffer and no one would dare to ignore his order and relieve her pain.

Sometimes, after he was gone, someone might sneak some water or food to her in secret. But in doing so she must avoid being seen by another woman who might report back to Deng Majok.

"The law by which Deng Majok controlled his family was unique," remarked Nyanthon.

> In this entire tribe known as Ngok, the tribe of Kwol Arob, no one had anywhere near the kind of discipline that Deng applied to control his family. The law by which he controlled his wives was that he forbade them to quarrel. If one woman offended another, the woman in charge of them would report to Deng Majok in the evening: "So-and-so quarreled with so-and-so today." Deng would have the two women summoned. He would ask, "So-and-so, why did you quarrel with so-and-so?" The woman would explain, "The reason I quarreled with so-and-so is this-and-that." He would investigate the case until he uncovered the wrong. He would take the guilty person, have her lie down, and flog her. The next day, other women would hear of what had happened to the guilty woman and learn their lesson from that. No woman would dare to think of offending another woman and be punished as the guilty person had been. That was how he controlled us.

"In his relations with his wives," said Nyanbol Arob, "if two wives fought or quarreled, he would call all his wives to a meeting with him. He would investigate the situation. When he identified the person responsible for the fight or the quarrel, he would dismiss the rest of the wives and keep the wrongdoer in his room. He would beat her."

According to Kwei, after punishing those he found to be responsible, Deng would call another meeting of all his wives: "The room would be completely filled with women and he would talk to them, with a piece of advice for every ear. Then he would make the women take an oath of good conduct."

Deng Majok's wives also praised him for his soothing tongue. In Nyanthon's words:

> Deng was very thoughtful. Even when he quarreled with a wife, he would not do what many men do. Many men would quarrel with their wives, beat them badly, and leave them alone. They never reflect, "What about the woman I have beaten, how is she feeling now?" Deng Majok would beat you and beat you, and leave you only for a while. Then he would send someone to you saying, "Let so-and-so come to me!" He would receive you and seat you very nicely. Then he would talk to you in sweet words, explaining everything in such a gentle and considerate way that when you left him your mind would never think of anything bad. Even the quarrel would disappear from your mind. You would forget it all.

Another sanction Deng Majok used against his wives, and one not uncommon among the Dinka, was abstention from a wife's food, whether brought from her relatives, acquired by her own efforts, or prepared by her from what he himself provided. This also implied avoidance of sexual relations, and therefore deprived her of the fundamental objective of a Dinka marriage—children. The Dinka consider this the severest punishment against a woman; it therefore calls for speedy settlement. The procedure of the settlement is usually for the woman to inform her relatives. As the man is generally assumed to be in the right, her relatives apologize to him, offer him a cow or more, according to the gravity of the conflict, as a token of appeasement; and, assuming that he is reconciled, a ritual is performed with a feast to end the abstention.

Nyanjur told of an incident involving a violation of the prohibition against drinking. As said earlier, Deng Majok never smoked or drank. But he was not very moralistic about his position on either, and while he strongly objected to his junior wives drinking or smoking, probably on the aesthetic grounds of decency and dignity, he showed a certain degree of tolerance toward the conduct of the senior wives and children in drinking the native brew, which was not considered to be particularly intoxicating and is indeed generally acknowledged to be nutritious. Nor did he strongly oppose their smoking, although his early quarrels with Kwei indicate that he must have been stricter about this prohibition at that early stage.

The rule against drinking was particularly stringent with respect to the more dangerous modern distilled liquor, *aregi*, now available in towns. As Nyanjur recounts, such was the wrong committed by Amel and Amou, two of his favorite wives:

> My mother was very close to Amel. They were very close friends. Amel used to drink. My mother learned from her. First they drank the white native brew. And then they began to obtain distilled alcohol from Amel's mother. Amel said that one day fate made them take a bottle into father's hut and place it under his bed. Then they sat and drank. Suddenly Father surprised them by turning up unexpectedly. They tried to hide it, but it was too late. He appeared suddenly and entered the hut. So the women sat with their heads bent down.

He said, "Amel!"
Amel said, "Yes."
He said, "Amou!"
Amou said, "Yes."
"What are you doing?" he asked.
Amou said, "Nothing."
"It is not possible that you are doing nothing," he said.

As soon as he bent his head down, he saw the bottle under his bed. He took it, sniffed it, and found that it was *aregi*—alcohol. Then he said, "Were you drinking *aregi*?"

Amel said, "No, we were not drinking *aregi*."

He said: "And what brought this bottle in here? If that is how far you have gone, then you have reached a point where you could poison me to death. For you to drink distilled alcohol means you have totally rebelled against me. You are no longer to be counted among my wives."

Amel said, "He went on reprimanding us while we sat unable to say a word. Then we left him. From that time on, he would not eat any food we prepared. If one tried to bring him even water, he would react furiously."

For days he maintained that attitude toward them. Eventually, my mother went to her maternal relatives. She was given a cow with which he was then appeased. My mother said to me that until Father died, she never again tasted any form of alcohol. She said that my father's behavior on that occasion completely shattered her.

Deng Majok's main power of control was the force of his personality. As Ali explained:

He had certain chanting utterances of abuse, what the Dinka call *mioch*, which when he said them, made us shrink and shrivel with fear. When he uttered his *mioch*, he made you feel as though you had committed a dreadful wrong. One such intimidating *mioch* was, "My Bull Marial has mounted his mother!" Once he uttered that, we would disintegrate in fear, run away, and forget all that we had gone to talk about.

"There are some people who are blessed with radiating awe, people with exceptional charisma," said Nyanjur.

Our father had exceptional charisma. His was a powerful personality which not only evoked great fear in the people under his authority, but also awe in anybody. If you heard his voice calling your name and telling you this or that, you suddenly felt your body shrinking and shriveling. He truly frightened his wives. He was a man of rare administrative abilities.

It was impossible for women to eat in his presence. Even senior women like my mother, until our father's death would never eat in his presence. The only persons who could eat in his presence were senior mothers from the generation of Achok upward who had become sisters to him. Those were the ones who would dare to eat in front of him.

"The sense of respect that prevailed in our family was extraordinary," corroborated Ali. "Although the wives were so many, they all had exceeding respect for Father. Even after they sat down to eat, as soon as Father came within sight of the wives, they would jump up and run away from the scene of the food. None of them would want to be seen eating by him."

"There is something called respect," elaborated Nyanjur.

> Respect for the husband was a very important principle in our family. It is respect which strengthens a relationship between a husband and a wife. When a husband says something while he is angry, a wise woman will refrain from retaliating. But some temperamental women would quickly respond to a bad word with a bad word. Replying to the word of a husband is what soils relations between a man and his wife. It is the woman who keeps quiet in the face of the husband's angry words who is regarded as a good wife.

According to Ajuong, Deng's administration of the family, particularly scrutinizing the conduct of the wives, was effected through a complex intelligence network among the wives.

> He would call a wife and say, "I would like you to be my eye. Whatever happens, whether it be a lack of something, or a wife who provokes others, or a wife whose manner is disgraceful or reckless, observe all that and let me know."
>
> So there were two sources of information, responsible wives who would inform him through the normal channels, and any other wives whom he trusted and asked to be his secret agents among other women. That's the way he controlled the situation.
>
> Deng never handled his family problems in front of other people. He always handled them privately at home so that, should there be something disgraceful involved, it ended there within his family confines.
>
> Deng never liked a woman whose conduct was in any way notorious. But he would not divorce her and return his cattle from the marriage. He would say: "If I divorce her, I might be giving her what she wants. Perhaps she behaves this way because she has something hidden. Perhaps there is a man secretly behind the way she is behaving."
>
> What he would do was gradually to take any privileges away from her and deprive her of her marital rights. He would abstain from her bed and have nothing to do with her. But he would not let her go free by divorcing her. Should she then go further astray and commit a wrong in that direction, he would say, "That's it; I have known the whole truth."
>
> Should any man talk and defend her against the way Deng was

treating her, he would say, "Now I see!" and accuse such person as being involved with his wife.

It is generally recognized that the only person who could intervene and take the side of the wife with any hope of success was Deng Majok's brother, Biong Mading. In the words of Nyanbol Amor: "Our brother Biong was a man of great virtue. If Deng quarreled with a wife, Biong would come and intervene with his brother in support of the wife. Were it not for him, even some of the children who were born might not have been begotten. He would intervene and quarrel with Deng in support of the wives. Our brother Biong was not an ordinary man."

The same principles that governed Deng Majok's relations with his wives more or less applied to his children. And, indeed, he often saw the mother's influence in the behavior of the children, be they girls or boys.

"Father's control over the girls was tough," said Ali.

> His language of verbal abuse against the girls was terrible. He would first look into anything objectionable in the girl's mother's ways and give her detailed accounts of her mother's misconduct. Then he would build on her mother's wrongs to attack her conduct as something inherited from her mother. When you saw the intensity of abuse and the indignity you were subjected to as a girl, you worked harder to avoid the recurrence of any wrongdoing.
>
> The same was true of the boys. If he had a cause to dislike your mother, he would dislike you on account of your mother. If he had a quarrel with your mother, he would come and involve you in his feud with your mother. He would attack you with that grievance in mind, and even if he later changed his mind and forgave you, he would already have associated you with your mother's wrong.
>
> I believe that was why he always pointed a critical finger at [Nyanbol Deng's son] Miyar; it was because of his mother's wrongs. But by doing that he motivated us to do our best to avoid being viewed as Miyar was viewed by him. You told yourself, "I do not ever want my father to feel toward me the way he does toward Miyar."
>
> If one did anything which he disapproved of, he would send for you and speak to you in words that invoked many emotions in you. In the end, you would break down and cry.

Charles Biong articulated what is generally true of most, if not all, of Deng Majok's children.

> Frankly, I grew up with a very high opinion of Father. Even inside the house, the women, our mothers and stepmothers, were always talking about him and referring to him as the chief whose word was final. Whenever his name was mentioned, there would be panic. You would see women eating, but the moment they heard that Father was entering their side of the enclosure, all would be paralyzed into dead silence. Everything they were doing would be pushed aside and the

women would sit with heads down. The talk would be repressed. That gave me a kind of feeling of some special character in Father.

The same was true outside the circles of the family. Wherever one went, one found people talking about Father. Wherever he went, one saw crowds running after him and gathering around him whenever he stood or sat.

I grew up with the feeling that there were some special characteristics or qualities in Father. And that gave me the feeling that he was more than a father. I did not feel free to talk to him as someone who was his son and could therefore talk to my father whenever I chose. I was always reserved in my talk with him. Mostly I would just see him in the company of people all of whom looked upon him with a special deference for his status.

Strangely enough, until the end, I never really freed myself from these feelings about Father, although at a later age I became close to him. He would ask me to write his letters or to accompany him on his journeys. I came to understand him more. But I was still haunted by the belief that he possessed very special qualities.

Some of the awe and distance his children felt for Deng Majok resulted from the burdens of his responsibilities in running two great institutions—a large tribe precariously poised between difficult borders, and a family of unprecedented size. Ali's earlier account of his father's daily activities links up with the domestic scene:

When he returned from court in the afternoon and went to his bedroom to rest, we never took him to be literally resting. Why? Because he had so many wives and the problems of women were many and complex. He would resolve those problems during his brief period of rest. So, while people might say that Deng Majok was resting in bed, in reality he would be involved in discussions of affairs that were just as formidable as the affairs of the tribe and the court. If some things had gone wrong at home, he would call the women and talk to them in earnest, directing them to live together in unity and solidarity, and without any manifestations of the conventional cowife rivalries and jealousies.

His abilities still confound us to this day. We have since married and some of us have two wives. When we see how formidable the problems of cowives are and you think of so many wives, numbering in the hundreds, and how Deng Majok managed to control them all to the point where one hardly heard any bad words, and then you think of the kinds of problems that only two wives can generate, you really wonder and marvel at Deng Majok.

He ran his family in much the same way as he ran the tribe. He solved the problems of his tribe and his family in the same way and worked toward the same goals of eliminating hostilities, establishing peace and unity, and encouraging people to live amicably without quarrels or jealousies. These were totally lacking in our father's family.

Nyanjur provides a daughter's insight into Deng Majok's daily program of activities:

> It was impossible to find him at any given time accompanied by just three or four or even five persons. Even as he emerged from his bedroom where he slept, he would be immediately joined and followed by ten or fifteen persons. As he proceeded away from home, to see the crowd following him it always seemed as though there was a public demonstration about to boom with war songs.
>
> He would go to work followed by this huge crowd and would remain in the company of increasing crowds until his return in the afternoon. Even as he returned home after the day's work, the same sized crowd would follow him, unless the police took measures to stop the crowd from following him back home.
>
> The police would then let him enter his family courtroom and close the door so that no one could enter. But unless the door was locked, and as long as he was in his sitting room, it would be impossible to stop the crowds. One by one, they would infiltrate the room. One would say, "Chief, I have just a small word to say"; "Chief, I too have this"; "Chief, just a little word"; and so on and so forth.
>
> The women at home, too, got their word through. From the time he left in the morning, messages would reach him in court from the wives at home. One of the servants would be sent; or a child would be asked to go: "Tell the chief, this or that is needed at home."
>
> After returning from the big court and sitting for a while in his family court, where he would have lunch with the people, he would then proceed to his bedroom, supposedly for a rest, only to be confronted by a long queue of wives waiting to see him, each one with her own issue to raise.
>
> Then he would emerge again toward evening to sit outside, in front of his courtroom at home, and again be confronted with public issues until bedtime, when he would once more face another queue of wives. The same situation over and over again.

One day, according to Matet Ayom, an English District Commissioner asked him, "Deng, how do you know the words of all your wives?"

Deng said, "I know their words."

The English Commissioner said, "When you go to sleep at night, how many wives do you listen to each night?"

He said, "I listen to the words of about ten women."

The English Commissioner said, "And then don't you become irritated and disposed to fight with them?"

Deng said, "Why should I fight? If any of them has quarreled, I stay up late at night looking into their cases. I have my own family law in my mind, and on the basis of that law I try their cases."

The English Commissioner said, "We shall give you seven days' leave in order to look into your family cases, both at night and during the day."

Deng said, "It is not necessary; that night which I have every day is sufficient for my domestic purposes."

The English Commissioner said, "What about sleep?"

He said, "I can also sleep."

But according to Nyanjur:

> Father knew no rest at all. We would fall asleep hearing a crowd of wives all lined up to see him. You would wake up in the night to find them still waiting. And then you would fall asleep again. Until we became grownup children, we did not fully realize what was happening, but one saw that something was happening.

Nyanjur also laid great stress on her father's physical strength and virility, citing the large number of children he begot as evidence.

> The strength of our father was astonishing; he was truly a very strong man. Just see all the children he himself begot! And it is quite obvious that they are his biological children. If you were to count the children begotten by other men among his wives, they would not exceed ten or at most fifteen. And most of these would be children who came with their mothers, children whose mothers he married knowing that they were pregnant with other men's children, or children who were born before marriage and were adopted along with their mothers. Some children did return to their natural fathers. As for children conceived through adulterous relations, believe me, Brother Mading, they never lived; they all died. Only one child is now alive, and it is a case of unique luck.

Using strength in a broader administrative sense, Matet Ayom remarked:

> The strength of your father, Deng Majok, over women is extraordinary. Deng's grip on his wives does not leave even a small portion of the rope loose on the women. And yet he treated them all very well. Even in maintaining women to appear beautiful and well looked after—Deng knew how to maintain women extremely well. Every one of his wives who had not committed a serious moral wrong was very happy with her marriage to Deng.

Nyanjur saw her father's administrative success in his even-handedness with his wives.

> Father's administration over his family was probably unmatched by any living man. Why? Because of the unique way he related to his wives. He was even nicknamed "Deng Awendol," meaning "Deng, the Reshuffler of Smiles." This means that he would smile or laugh with a woman today and people might believe her to be especially close to him. But tomorrow he would smile or laugh with another wife and cease to smile with the earlier one. That was the policy through which he managed his family. I do not believe you could find

among Father's wives a woman who was so favored that she excelled over all the wives all the time. No one was in such a privileged position.

Even in terms of childbearing, the women who remained without children were those who were simply unlucky. Besides, he was not a husband of a few wives who could be available every time a woman wanted him. The older women, such as our mothers, had to safeguard the interests of the junior wives. If one of the women with you was in her period of fertility, it was your responsibility to go to him and say, "Chief, this woman is due." That is when a woman had cleansed herself after menstruation and was in a fertile stage. They would work to arrange for her to be with him. It was all a matter of an intermediary because it was impossible for him to know which wife was in that condition. Each wife would pass the message on to the wife senior to her, on and on up the ladder, until it reached the husband.

Resuming the theme of her father's physical ability and virility, Nyanjur went on to say:

But Father was a truly strong man. This fact has to be emphasized. Indeed, we used to wonder how he could possibly have children with so many wives. We feared that there might be some witchcraft behind all that virility, for it could not have been natural. Our hearts were truly frightened that the strength of our father might one day reveal some dreadful things in our midst, for, as you know, if there was some witchcraft behind it, that is the kind of thing which the Dinka believe eventually results in some evil or disaster, such as illness and death. And what led us into thinking that way was the extraordinary strength of this man. God may create a man with great strength and virility, but our father was unique; and it was puzzling to people that his strength could have been his own, unaided by other supernatural forces.

Addressing himself to the way bed relations were regulated, Deng's cousin Ajuong Deng observed: "The way Deng did it, he gave his word to his wives, saying, 'Any woman who has cleansed herself of menstruation, wherever she might be, she should come to me the very day she cleanses herself.' That was his arrangement. Word would then be passed on to him, 'So and so has cleansed herself and she has come.' Senior wives would be the ones to transmit the message."

"If one saw a wife neglected and not called," observed Nyanbol Amor, "a senior wife like ourselves would go to him and say, 'This is wrong; why do you neglect this woman?' That was the same role which people like Amel played."

"Of course, all the wives realized that the husband was for everybody," elaborated Amel.

It was the senior wife of each division who knew the wives in her division best. And it was she who would speak on their behalf. If the husband said, "Call so-and-so,' and the senior wife did not agree with his preference, she would state her objection and say why she would recommend someone else. She might say that the other wife had cleansed herself and was in her fertile period or she might say that she had been unfairly neglected and was looking unhappy.

According to Charles Biong,

> A head wife would normally consult with the heads of the other divisions and make adjustments in the schedule of Father's bedtime contacts to ensure that opportunities were not lost for the deserving women. Sometimes it happened that four or five women would be in a similar period of fertility at the same time. Since that would be their only chance, Father was very keen to offer them opportunities. Father was with women day and night.

Although Deng Majok granted equal opportunities for procreation, "the question of whether a woman had a child or not was also God's will," to quote Kwei's words. "Achwil Miyan remained without a child even though she was one of the more senior and favored wives. She never had cause for complaint against her husband."

Amel was one of those who were not blessed with children even though she was unquestionably favored by Deng. As she put it: "If a wife did not conceive, that was the will of God. Even if a husband did not favor a woman but fulfilled his duty and slept with her when her time was due, even if he slept with her only once, she might conceive. But even if he were to love a woman very much and wanted to be with her often, if God did not will that she should have a child, then she would not conceive."

Procreation was considered as the only legitimate ground for a wife to take the initiative in seeking her husband's company. As Nyanjur intimates: "If a woman wanted to be with him just for the sake of being with her husband rather than because of the legitimate desire for children, then she had to struggle on her own. If she could manage on her own to be with him, that would be her own achievement. But such a daring approach was not promoted or facilitated by the senior wives."

But as Biong observed, "Of course, he also had his own personal desires and would call in any woman he felt like having at any given time. His expressed wish would then prevail. But there was always the normal organization, the standard procedure that was not prejudiced by his personal preferences."

Amel also concedes that there was a measure of discretion for the husband and that a degree of favoritism, even in bed relations, was natural:

> Wives were not, of course, exactly equal in his heart. There might be a wife for whom he had a very special liking and another whom he might not desire as much. That I cannot tell. It is the function of a

man's heart. Even you [addressing a young interviewing son of Deng Majok], in the future if you marry two, three, or four wives, they will not all be the same in your heart. One or two may turn out to be very dear to your heart.

"Was the issue sometimes a cause of conflict between the wives?" Nyanthon was asked. Her response was: "How could it cause conflicts when it was the husband himself making his own choice? Any woman who felt jealous would have to nurse her jealousy silently. How would she dare voice her feelings? To whom would she say anything? Even if a woman was daring enough to go and complain to him and he did not feel it in his own mind or heart, he would simply send her away."

"No wife would go to a man just because she felt like it," said Nyanbol Arob. "But Deng never left any wife out. He knew them all. And none of them lived far from him. They all lived together in nearby settlements. But, of course, some wives resented the large numbers of wives who had to share one man."

As Kwei observed: "Later on, with the younger wives, some would become disenchanted and would escape and run away. When these young wives began to see so many complications among wives, if one did not have a child, she would escape and return home. But it was only the weak-hearted who left. The good-hearted woman realized that Deng was her husband and that she would sooner or later have a child with him."

11 Turmoil beneath the Calm

The picture that emerges from the empire at home is that of an intricate and complex social web in which conformity to the ideals of unity, harmony, and solidarity was paradoxically highlighted by strong undercurrents of jealousy, tension, and potential conflict. Just as these undercurrents were suppressed through rigid measures, so they were subjectively repressed and concealed with remarkable success.

Given the obvious competition over one man, the extent to which the wives of Deng Majok are said to have lived in relative unity and harmony was astonishing. This was particularly true of vertical relations, but less so in the horizontal relations of those with parallel, and therefore more competitive, positions in the family hierarchy. "We all lived together quite amicably," observed Nyanbol Amor. "Never did a quarrel arise between us and the junior wives that provoked even an insulting gesture from a junior wife. Never!"

To Achai-Jur, the example which the senior wives offered their juniors and equity in Father's treatment of his wives were the keys to family unity and harmony:

> The good thing our father did was to place a senior wife in charge of a group to supervise the junior wives and guide their behavior. Junior wives came and followed the example offered by the senior wives. He also brought his wives together and gave them things on equal bases. One day, he would bring things and distribute them among a number of wives. Next time, those who felt dissatisfied with the way things had been distributed before would receive things; it would be the turn of those who had received before to remain without. That way, he compensated those who were dissatisfied and comforted them.

Any inequities based on seniority or preference were balanced by social consciousness and a sense of moral obligation toward the less privileged. According to Nyanbol Amor, "If any one of us saw a wife in need, even if she were from the section of the other senior wife, she would assist her without any jealousy. You would take a cow and give it to the mother of any child in need of a milch-cow."

Nyanjur elaborated:

> The relations of Deng Majok's wives among themselves, if you found them sitting together, all gathered together, you could not believe they were cowives. The thing called respect[1] was very important to them. If a woman was married this year, and the other was married next year,[2] the junior wife would refer to the wife who was senior to her by only one year as "Mother." She would never call her by name.
>
> The cordial and polite way they behaved toward one another was unknown among wives of the same man in Dinka society. Even quarrels, where a person might come into conflict with this person or another with that or yet another with that other, was extremely rare. What was the norm were laughter and joking and playing.

Ironically, Nyanjur sees in the very size of the family a positive reinforcement of unity and harmony:

> You see, our father's family is so large, involving so many people, that you cease to carry a grudge against any person. Against which of the very many wives would any wife direct her jealousy or rivalry? Where jealousies come in is when a man has two, or three wives, or four wives, each of whom feels her position threatened by one or more of the others. But where the number of wives is virtually a tribe, such personal rivalries cannot exist.[3]

With respect to the children, Nyanbol Amor observed:

> We never saw any bad relationships among our children. During the days of Deng Majok, beginning with Arob Deng, who was the eldest son, to the next generation of Bol and Kwol and Mading, they all lived very closely together without any jealousies whatsoever until they all dispersed into their various professions.
>
> They would own a cow together to provide them with milk. And they lived together as brothers. They would put up in the house of Achok and place their things in Achok's hands. And whenever their

---

1. The Dinka word translated here is *athek*, the meaning of which corresponds precisely to the English word "respect."
2. The logic of the English might have required the sequence of marriages actually having taken place "last year and this year," but the text says "this year and next year," an illustration of the fluidity of the concept of time among the Dinka.
3. The idea is that, not only do they all find themselves in the same boat, but that it becomes difficult to single out one person as responsible for one's misfortune in the family.

cow from which they obtained milk for their tea ran dry, Kwol would say, "This cow should remain with our mother Achok for her little daughters!"[4] That became somewhat disturbing to some women from the other section. Some of the wives would say: "What a problem! This issue of Nyanbol's house! How can one boy outwit people? Bol, why are you behaving that way? How can you allow yourself to be outwitted? Whenever tea is brought, it is placed in that house; whenever any groceries are brought from the market, they are placed in that house!"

Bol said, "What nonsense! She is our mother together. And in any case, these are our collective cattle, they all belong to our father. Wherever they are placed, we share them together. Yours is sheer jealousy; our ways are different from yours." Bol would ridicule them that way. There was no problem between them whatsoever.

With respect to the girls, until our senior daughters all married and went to their homes, there was never any tension or jealousy in their relations; not at all.

According to Nyanbol Amor, Deng Majok's success lay in his fairness and equal treatment of his children: "What Deng Majok did was that he showed no preference or discrimination among his older children, boys and girls. He brought them all to him and treated them equally. And even with our middle children who remained with us, nothing went wrong with their relations among themselves. He left them united and in full harmony."

"How did Father unite us to the point where there was no divisiveness or hostility among us?" reflected Ali.

Among the Dinka traditionally, when one has two or three wives, one divides the family property among them. Even the cattle dedicated to the spirits were classified so that when a girl was married these cattle would be divided accordingly. Color patterns would also be distributed. Each faction would have its own herd and cattle-hearth.

At the beginning, Father followed that practice. He divided the cattle among the groups. But there was a difference in his way of dividing them. He did not follow the Dinka custom of keeping the herds of the respective wives in separate camps. The cattle were all kept together, and he would take cattle from one group and use them to marry a wife who was affiliated with the other group. That helped diffuse any potential jealousies. Besides, he did not permit the wives to act freely over their allotted cattle. Among the Dinka, if a woman has been allotted cattle, it is her own children or the children of her group who may dispose of the cattle. But in our family, Father used the cattle freely for any cause. If children needed school fees or pocket money, he would take cows from all the groups without discrimination and sell them for the boys, irrespective of group identity.

---

4. In addition to myself as the firstborn, Achok had four daughters. A second son, fifth in line, died in infancy.

Achai-Jur also applied her thesis of equality to Father's treatment of his children: "Father made all his children eat the same kind of food so that nobody felt discriminated against or ill-treated. If children of one family are treated equally and they eat the same kind of food, and they are happy, nothing can bring conflict between them."

Achai-Chol held the same view:

> If a man brings things and divides them unfairly, giving some people a larger share than others and other people none at all, that is what causes jealousies and conflicts. But with Father, even if only one asked for something, he gave that thing to all his children, including those who had not asked. He used to divide things equally between his wives, his daughters, and his sons. No one was favored. What else would people dislike each other for?

"I don't think you could find any family where the children of one man were as close and affectionate as were Father's children," Nyanjur commented. Continuing to explain her theory about numbers, she observed:

> Even the small fights that are usually frequent between children did not exist among our father's children. Why? If you sat at a meal, the number of persons who would share a dish would not be only four or five or six. Never! If your number was really limited, you might be ten. For people who are so close that they share their meals not to be close and friendly is rare. This was true of both boys and girls.

Nyanjur goes on to give a complex analysis of the dynamics involved in promoting the spirit of unity and solidarity in the family.

> Now, Mading, when a father has begotten children from only two or three wives, and the wives are all classified according to seniority and things are divided unequally between them, that is when competition over family resources creates jealousies among the wives and their children. In our family such a situation did not arise. For one thing, none of the boys was in the cattle-camp to claim the bulls of his respective color pattern according to his position in the family. This meant that there was no question of Father causing problems either by denying a son his rightful claims or by giving some sons the bulls to which others were entitled. There was no such a situation in our family.
>
> All the boys had gone away to school and later found their own means of livelihood away from the family wealth. They would only converge on the family during their vacation period. They would then live at home together as a group. Some women would be designated to take care of them and to prepare their meals. It would not be the mothers who would care for their own children.
>
> Under those circumstances, children would not think of their own mothers, nor would they feel that others had more or less than themselves and therefore feel a sense of rivalry and disharmony.

Besides, if you quarreled with your brother or sister and Father found that you were in the wrong, he would not leave you alone; he would punish you severely. He would also talk to you: "Why did you do that? Don't you realize that he (or she) is your brother (or sister)? Is he (or she) not your backing? Where will you find your backing if you alienate your own brothers and sisters?"

All that tended to deter the children from any quarrels. And as I said before, he was a man who evoked considerable awe in people. No one would want to get into any conflict with him. And that applied to everyone, including his children. So, the small children watched the way the senior children behaved and imitated them. For instance, when the younger children saw how close you and Bol were, that provided them with a model to follow. All the succeeding age-groups would follow the same path established by the older boys. No one would branch out in his own way.

As for us, the girls, our way was clearly marked by the manner in which our father directed us, since we were always at home and under his observation. The things he did for us also fostered solidarity among us.

If we wanted clothes, either one person or all of us would go to him and say, "Father, we need clothes." He would buy clothes for all of us, including those who might be absent. We would all be mentioned by name: So and So and So. That way, it was not possible for anyone to hold a grudge against anyone else. You all lived like the children of one man and one woman.

In fact, we never used to refer to ourselves as half-brothers and half-sisters, as the Dinka do. No, we never did. We would refer to one another as full-blooded brothers and sisters.

And if I, for instance, went to the house of Mother Achok, or Mother Aker, or any other of our senior mothers, I would not be treated as the child of another woman. And I would not behave as though I were in the house of a stepmother. I would behave very freely as though I were with my own mother. I would behave just as her own daughter would. And all that contributed to family solidarity.

And where does a good family relationship come from? It comes from the head of the family himself, the father of the children. Everything requires direction and advice, when a man talks to his children saying, "My children, behave toward one another this way or that way." If what a father says penetrates the minds and hearts of his children, then what he says guides their conduct. It is when a person is not respected that words are ineffective. But when a man is feared as was our father, no one can afford to disregard his words. There are always bad people prone to misbehaving, but the crucial factor was whether they dared to expose themselves to our father. Considering the large size of our family, such exposure was more easily avoided.

In the words of Charles Biong:

The organization of the family setup was such that women who belonged to a given division considered themselves as members of one line of approach, one line of thinking, and one way of doing things. And this to a great extent developed the links between the children of women in a given division. Even the problem of some women not having had children in a way developed some kind of love between those women who did not have children and the children of other women within their division. This, together with the traditional attitude of the Dinka that children, especially boys, should not identify themselves clearly with their own mothers, helped to develop affection and close contacts between the children and their stepmothers within the group. I remember so many women and so many children in the family being identified as mothers and sons even though the truth of the situation was different. The children seemed to take this association very positively. The women also found pleasure in the practice.

While Biong concedes that Deng Majok was not close to his children, he also explains some of the methods their father adopted to ensure their proper behavior:

To be frank, Father was not really very particular about guiding his own children. I would say in a word that he was really overconfident. He felt that his character or his name was quite enough to inspire a child to pick up from there and continue. This is why he gave very, very little time to his children. Maybe he gave more attention to the older brothers. But as for the brothers of our generation, we never had that kind of attention or the devoted care of a father toward his children, which gives them a clear sense of direction to follow.

But whenever problems came up, it would happen that Father would call together all the children, boys and girls, and would talk to them, warning them that such attitudes of jealousy and tension, which encourage people to go their separate ways, were not to be tolerated. He would say that he was sure nobody among us wanted a bad reputation for the family. The best way of silencing outsiders was for the family to demonstrate good and harmonious relations, to be an example to others, and to invalidate any allegations that they were fighting over scarce resources.

"Father never gave us a chance to be influenced by our mothers," added Ali:

Usually, a child learns first from his mother even about his father. But we, the sons of Deng Majok, never gave much attention to our mothers.

I, for one, had no close relations with my mother. I suppose her only time with me was when I was a baby and she raised me from childhood. But after that we were constantly in Abyei while our own mothers were back at Noong. So one did not really feel a special relationship with one's own mother. The person we came to look upon as our mother was Nyanawai; she was the one we, the children of the section of Nyanbol Amor, looked to as our mother.

So our relations with our father's wives were not bad; every wife of our father, when she saw any son of our father, would receive him well; and even if she had other instincts toward divisiveness, she would conceal all that negative sentiment and display the sentiment of solidarity. And particularly after we had grown up, they showed us a great deal of respect, a respect almost approximating their respect for our father.

Our relations with one another were also influenced by the example provided us by our senior brothers. When we grew up, we found our older brothers going together in unity and harmony without any divisiveness on the ground of groupings. Chan and Arob [Ahmed] were the oldest brothers. Arob had gone ahead with his education. Chan had been forced back home by illness. Had he also proceeded with his education and been close to Ahmed, they would probably have lived together in unity and solidarity. The next group comprised you, Mading, and Bol and Kwoldit. You used to be together. Every group that emerged maintained a unified front. It was the same with our group, comprising myself, Monyyak, and Miyar. Nothing would come between us. We shared our meals. That was one of the ways in which we reinforced our bonds and eradicated jealousies. Today, all the children of Deng Majok are one. You never know them as children of that house or that group. That is because we all grew up together, living together and eating together.

Although some wives had the tendency to foster divisiveness and group sentiment, we did not give them the opportunity to do so among us. We remained together, conversing and speaking our minds to one another. If a person allowed himself to be tempted by the divisiveness of the women, he was so rebuked by his age-mates that he would immediately discard the divisive words from his mind.

The generally positive appraisals of the interrelationships between Deng Majok and the dependent members of his family, as well as the relationships among these members, have to be seen as a matter of degree. Polygynous families in Dinka society are recognized as being fraught with tensions and conflicts that emanate from jealousies. Since it is generally assumed that these tensions and conflicts would increase in direct proportion to the size of the family, Deng Majok's ability to contain them to the point where they were less manifest than in ordinary families was most impressive. But this should not conceal the fact that considerable turbulence and potential explosiveness still existed beneath the veneer of repressed jealousy and hostility presented by those wives who suffered from the inequities of the system; and despite the praise of their situation spoken in retrospect, quite a few, perhaps the majority, fell into this category.

Charles Biong points out that organization of the family into groups was in itself a factor both for unity within the group and divisiveness between groups.

> The relations between the wives were really mixed. You would find some with such a friendly attitude that you would not believe they were cowives. Their relations with one another were so good that you would never think of them as rivals. This was especially true of women who belonged to the same unit of the family administration. You would find them behaving like sisters and seeing things in the same way and from the same perspective. And mostly, should there be a problem, it would always be between a woman from a given division and one from another division. And, as such, it would be taken as a challenge to the whole division. The whole group would move against the other group.

Although virtually all the members of the family who furnished me with information underestimated its existence, jealousy was an unavoidable consequence of polygyny; it could only be controlled and constrained but never totally eradicated. Nyanawai expressed the point this way:

> Women are like children. They may all cluster together in one seemingly harmonious group, but suddenly they will quarrel and fight for no obvious reason. Then each person will find something to say against the other as a reason for the fight. When they are over the fight and feel better again, they will get back together and settle down as members of a harmonious group. Then a fight will flare up again. Women's jealousies do not rot; they keep flaring up and falling on relationships like rain.

Not only was jealousy inevitable in such a setup but, worse, the unscrupulous use of witchcraft was to be expected and repressed in advance. "Of course there were jealousies," admitted Nyanbol Amor.

> It is just that Deng was a very strong personality who was able to contain these jealousies. Even in our generation, as we had our children, there were jealousies. But he would stand up and silence any voices raised in jealousy. If he saw a woman displaying jealousy, he would call her and say, "Why do you behave this way?" He would talk to her. The following day he would call another wife and talk to her. And then he would call us all and talk to us.

Here, Nyanbol indicates the way Deng Majok intimidated potential witches or evil-doers by hinting that he was aware of them and what harm they could do:

> He would say, "You must remember that I know you very well. Before I married you, I first discovered everything about you. I know whatever there is in your background. I even know those of you who have some hidden things about them, such as witchcraft, with which

they might do harm to others. I know all that. And yet, I chose to bring you together to live together. And there are my children among you. I do not want anyone to be afflicted with any harm. That is what I want you to know."

On this issue of witchcraft, Kwei also observed that "Deng had brought together all sorts of people, including women with the evil eye and those without witchcraft. He would put them together. Some would wish others ill because of envy in their hearts."

This was both a potential source of danger and an additional reason for living up to the ideals of unity and harmony to avoid giving anyone any grounds for harmful evil practices. Nyanjur goes so far as to argue that the tensions and hostilities inherent in such a large polygynous family as Deng Majok's were in themselves a deterrent to any misconduct or behavior that might disrupt the desired unity and harmony:

> Our father once summoned us, the girls, and said, "My daughters, let me tell you something. The number of wives I have married is virtually a tribe. You are girls who will one day be married. All the young men you see walking outside there have some relationship to someone inside this family. If you should behave toward these women here on the assumption that they are your mothers with whom you can feel free to talk as you please, I am afraid you may become old maids. No men will marry you. So let me warn you: be careful in your manner of behavior. Always behave with the realization that you are amidst strangers who will act as the eyes and the ears of many potential husbands outside there. They are watching you and listening to you and reporting on you. Be careful. Do not view them as your mothers."
>
> And it is true, Mading, that among the ordinary Dinka, where a child has only one stepmother, you can feel free to quarrel with her or show your grievances against her and it is unlikely that she will go about besmirching your name to strangers because she identifies you with her interests within the family. Should she come across a man who is interested in marrying you, she cannot speak against you because she knows that the cattle that will come from the marriage will go to her. But in our family, a stepmother can spy and report on a stepdaughter. And indeed, it did happen. . . .
>
> So you see, we and our father's wives lived together, but we realized that we were among strangers. You did not assume that you were with relatives. Even in the way we treated them, we were quite reserved. It was difficult to have even a small quarrel or a disagreement with our father's wives. In such an atmosphere, even jealousies could hardly be said to exist. At least they were not visible to us.

And there was the main deterrent of Deng Majok's suppression of any conflict or divisiveness in the family. As Nyanjur expressed it:

> Of course, there were sometimes minor quarrels that ended

quickly without anyone really noticing anything significant. But if a quarrel was grave enough to involve a fight, then the persons involved were summoned and lashed, both of them. And the punishment was so severe and indiscriminate that everyone worked hard to avoid a fight. And this was true of both wives and children.

Father's punishments were truly dreadful. When he got angry and punished a person by beating, he was merciless. Of course, he rarely found wrongs on the part of his wives or children, but when he did, his reaction was absolutely dreadful.

He once spoke to us about the case of Nyantibiu. Nyantibiu had fought with one of the wives under the seniority of her mother, a woman by the name of Nyanchar Miyan. Father at first wanted to beat Nyantibiu, but she was rescued from him. It was one of the very rare cases where he allowed a person to be rescued from his beating.

Then he called us and the women together in a meeting. He said, "Let me tell you women, take very good care of your daughters' conduct. And you children, if any of you wants to become like Nyangei [Nyanbol Deng's daughter], then please let me know right now so that I may decide what to do with you before you grow up. I do not want to have another child get out of my control as Nyangei did."

While Nyanjur focused on the negative factors that paradoxically promoted positive conformity to the ideals of family unity and solidarity, Charles Biong qualified the extent to which relations among the children were really positive, given the inherent disposition of the mothers toward rivalry, jealousy, and conflict.

Generally, I would say they were good, but in the younger age group I would say children were more influenced or affected by the attitudes of their mothers. When a woman quarreled with another woman, even though it was between them as individuals, the conflict might extend to the respective divisions. Likewise, the children of those women might be implicated. Sometimes conflicts between the sections might result from members of the groups defending their respective children. This used to affect their relations. You could find children fighting for no good reason of their own but reasons spilling over from the mothers. Also, the arrangements over children's meals could be another source of quarrels that might provoke a conflict between women. Some women encouraged their children to have meals by themselves, while others observed the ideal way, which was to encourage children to take their meals with their half-brothers, or half-sisters, as the case might be. Children who ate alone might be rebuked by the group. One of the boys who shared with the group might begin to call a solitary eater ugly names, and even touch on the mother for encouraging that behavior. The insulted child might convey this back to his mother. And it all might in the end result in a quarrel between the mothers.

But I would say that this was only true among children of younger ages; I don't recall it to have been true among the older ones, even though I could be skeptical to some extent about the girls. There was some kind of factionalism among the divisions of the family, and among the children those who reacted positively to this kind of divisive attitude were the girls.

The viewpoint of the girls as represented by Nyanjur was radically different: "The relations among father's daughters were more cordial than the relations among the sons. Let me tell you the truth today, we the girls were far closer than you the boys. Father once said, 'If I had begotten my sons with the qualities of my daughters, I would feel satisfied that I have procreated well. But my sons are not as close as my daughters.'"

To reinforce the solidarity of the children across maternal lines, siding with one's own child against the child of another wife was seen as an act of jealous discrimination that was strongly disapproved of. Nyanjur tells of a case involving the suppression of such behavior:

My young brother, Biong, once fought with Miokol, Nyanawai's son. Biong and Miokol are not the same age. Miokol is a little older than I. When they fought, word came that they had. I said, "Miokol, why is it that you fight with Biong when you are not the same age? That is not right."

Miokol said, "Are you defending your brother?"

I said, "It is not that I am defending my brother. It is just that people should be fair. This child is not your age."

As I was talking to Miokol, Nyapath [Miokol's older sister] came in. And Nyantibiu, their sister, also joined in. We took sides. We were about to fight when we were caught. My mother [Amou] and Nyanawai took over. They quarreled. They quarreled until they exchanged insults. Father was outside, sitting in front of his home courtroom. All this was happening inside the enclosure. Suddenly, he emerged. As soon as I saw him, I shut up. I did not talk any more. Nyapath also shut up. But Nyanawai and my mother continued their quarrel.

Father said, "I want the people involved in the fight to come immediately."

So Nyanawai and Amou went. He asked what the issue was. They told him that the children had been the first to quarrel—Miokol and Biong.

Then he said, "Let Miokol come!"

Miokol was called. Amou and Nyanawai were still there. Since we had already withdrawn, no one knew that we had been involved in the fight.

Then Father said, "Amou, do you regard yourself as the one to defend your son? The boys who are fighting are both my sons. Even if they should kill one another, even if the older boy should kill the younger boy, they are both my sons. None of you has the right to feel responsible for her own child. They are both my children. So why did you get involved? Tell me what I should do to you; should I punish you by beating you or by doing to you again what I once did—abandon you, not have anything to do with you, not eat your food, not ask anything of you at all?"

Amou said, "It is better that you beat me."

So he took a hurricane lamp and went to the trees along the river to get a whip-branch. It was nighttime, around about seven o'clock. He went and brought long branches. He said, "Nyanawai, leave the room!"

So Nyanawai left. Then he said to Miokol, "You lie down first." Miokol lay down. He beat Miokol. And then he told Amou to lie down. He beat Amou. Then Nyanawai came and said, "How could you beat the child so hard whereas you were easy on Amou?"

He said, "Do I understand you to be complaining about what I have done?"

She said, "Yes!"

He said, "So you do not approve of my having beaten Miokol?"

She said, "You cannot treat a child like an adult and beat him so hard!"

Father became so infuriated that Nyanawai herself received a beating. He said to her, "Lie down yourself."

Nyanawai lay down. She was beaten. All three of them were beaten.

Ali gave a comprehensive account of the tensions and conflicts inherent in what was an inevitable disparity in the sharing of husband, father, and available resources:

Our father did not discriminate among wives, but he was very much under the influence of Amel. And that was because Amel was quite clever. Of course, she was married after she had been brought up in a northern town where she had learned Arab ways. In particular, she was very hospitable and knew how to cook delicious food. Whatever she cooked left no room for improvement. Father's visitors, whether Dinkas or Arabs, would leave fully satisfied with the quality of Amel's food. She always prepared very high-quality food that won her great admiration. So Father saw Amel as a very valuable wife.

Then there was Amou. Father loved Amou very much. Amou was supposed to head a separate group, the group of Kwei. But when Father saw that he valued Amel because of the quality of her domestic work and loved Amou, he decided to group them together so that they would live together and work together in tandem.

Nyanawai, on the other hand, was a very quiet person who rarely spoke up for her rights. She was rather neglected, not so much because Father did not love her, but because it was in his character to neglect anyone who did not speak out, however much he or she might suffer in need.

One of the reasons we used to quarrel with our father was because of Nyanawai. Her section was not always well provided for by our father in comparison to those of Amel and Amou, who received all the special commodities for delicious food. And you could tell from the very character of the food that was contributed by these groups to Father's court. The food coming from Amel and Amou was always more desirable to our father than that coming from Nyanawai.

As I recall it, Nyanawai never complained; we were the ones who defended her cause. As soon as we noticed that Amel and Amou had received something that Nyanawai had not received, we would immediately jump on our father. We would say, "And why did you leave Nyanawai out?" Nyanawai was such a quiet person.

Just as Father had Amou and Amel together in Abyei, so he put Awut and Alang together in Nainai, with their huts facing one another in the fashion of Amel's and Amou's huts in Abyei. He followed exactly the same system as that of Abyei. Whenever we visited Nainai, we felt offended. Anyuat, the head of our section, had her hut there on the lower plain away from the higher grounds where the huts of the other, more favored wives were located.

Ali's brother, Osman, after confirming some of the themes in his brother's account, went on to tell what he did about the inequities of their father's treatment:

I spoke to my father and said: "Why do you do that? All the things you bring, you place in one house and you overlook the others. Even the junior wives you marry are mostly allotted to that house. You overlook the other houses, Kwei's section and my mother's section. What is that?"

He said, "I have not overlooked them. It is just that there is a small thing I am pursuing here. One day you will realize what it is."

I said, "What shall we find one day? Father, such disparity is not good. You should treat the women equally. You should distribute the new wives equally. Now you take cattle from women to marry wives they believe will be allotted to them. Then you bring these wives and give them to another woman who did not contribute to the bridewealth. Such treatment can provoke quarrels between the wives. That is not good."

As years passed and the numbers of Deng Majok's family continued to increase, problems of sharing the husband and father and the resources available to the multitudes became increasingly aggravated, and the empire at home began to disintegrate from within.

"Indeed, there were always problems for Father to solve in the family," said Nyanluak.

Some women were happy with him and some were dissatisfied. Of course, in such a large family people could never be absolutely equal. Only the first generation of his wives, each of whom was allocated her share of the family means, felt equal; and even though what was allocated to one might be depleted by circumstances, she at least felt well treated by their husband. With the increasing numbers of young wives, grievances increased. Some would try to see him to voice their complaints. They might get close to his door. But as they reached the door, he would emerge and leave. They had to stand and watch him go, for they had taken a vow not to chase him and force him to listen to them.

Another woman might send a boy or a retainer to convey her request to Father. But he might never transmit the message, or Father might choose to be silent and not respond. He might even rebuke the messenger. Word would come back to the wife. And what could she do? If she were a light-hearted woman, she might be heart-broken and choose to leave, saying: "I am never going to be able to reach this man. I'd better leave! What am I doing in a house like this?"

Some of those who left had been very well treated by Father. But just because God did not bless a woman with a child, she often thought that her misfortune was due to the number of wives in the family. She would say to herself, "What should I do in a family where I cannot have a child?" And she would leave.

It is said that the memory of a dead man should not be stained with unnecessary complaints. It would not be right to do so. But there are wives whose hearts feel profound grievances against Father. Some wives would be in need of clothing and would keep waiting for it until in the end they would despair and leave; they would leave without any clear indication as to why they were leaving.

"They left because they felt that things were not enough for them," commented Kwei. "And this was not because Deng Majok did not provide enough; it was because distribution in their own group was inequitable. It was the division between the wives of any given house which caused grievances. As for Deng Majok, he provided adequately for his wives."

Kwei also added the procreational dimension as a reason for wives' leaving: "A small grievance would just make one get up and leave. But it was mainly because those women had no children. All the women who ran away were without children. None of them left pregnant."

"No family has ever been perfect in terms of the relationships between its members to the point where no one could see any problems," concluded Nyanluak. "Given its exceptionally large size, this was particularly true of our family. After all, Father's family was so large and so widespread that one would be lying to say that one knows the number of his wives, far less the number of his children. However modestly we might talk about the number of his children, one could not be presumptuous enough to count them one by one. Their numbers cannot be determined. And so they go their own way, unnumbered."

12 The Economics of Polygyny

Deng Majok's excessive number of marriages continued to be a matter of intense controversy, not only in his family but throughout the tribe. Many people talked to him about it, but to no avail. It was widely believed to be a disease resulting from his uncle's curse, but one that could be remedied only if he would repent, apologize, and consent to be cleansed by his cousin, the heir of his uncle, now dead. But Deng Majok was totally uninterested in that superstition.

While Deng Majok's marriages were clearly unprecedented and most would agree excessive, it was not so much the mere fact of numbers as the social, economic, and political implications that made them so controversial and such a source of tension and conflict. All would agree that there was nothing legally wrong with the number, according to Dinka custom. As Chief Chier Rian explained:

> Among the Dinka, there is no limit to the number of wives a man can marry. The Dinka marry as many wives as they can afford. It is one's wealth and age that determine when to stop. One stops when one has become old, poor, or has begotten many children. When one has many children, one stops marrying more wives in order to give one's children the chance to marry and increase the population of the clan. They marry with the cattle that the family has.

"The idea of marrying many wives did not begin with Deng Majok," said Allor-Jok.

> Our grandfather, Arob Biong, had many wives. He did not have a number that would match Deng's because there were upheavals in our land. As a result, Arob limited the number of his wives to nine. Our father, Kwol Arob, had more wives. Deng Majok was, in a way,

following the example of our father. It all depends on one's wealth and one's status. If one has wealth and one is a leader, one marries. That was what Deng Majok observed and followed. Deng Majok also carried his generation with him by his example. When they saw him marrying many wives, they all followed him and married as many wives as they could.

Each one of them would reach a point where their means forced them to stop, but Deng Majok continued to the end of his life.

"According to the Arabs, so many marriages are not considered good," began Ibrahim El Hussein. "Arabs marry up to four wives only. But according to Dinka custom, there is no limit to the number of wives a man can marry. A man may marry up to one hundred wives and more. That is the Dinka way. The Arabs were not critical of Deng Majok. They realized that he was acting according to a different tradition."

"Why Father was criticized," said Nyanjur, "was the effect his marriages had on others."

Many of the women he married had been engaged to younger men before he came on the scene. But he would come and say, "So-and-So, I have come to like this girl. Please leave her to me." The man would be afraid and say to himself, "He is the chief; it is not possible for me to argue with him." So he would say, "I have surrendered my claim." In some cases, he would marry a girl and then she would be courted by a younger man with whom she would elope. That, too, became a problem. Father would never relinquish a girl who eloped with another man after being betrothed to him. He would insist on bringing her back home. He would take it as a challenge. As a result, people's hearts turned against him.

Accusations of corruption and misuse or misappropriation of public funds against Deng Majok were frequent because they seemed to be logical, in view of his extensive marriages and the uniquely large size of the family he was supporting.

Atem Barach was categorical in his statement of these accusations: "This was the only negative in Deng Majok. Whenever he went on a visit and found a good girl, or heard people saying that the daughter of so-and-so had blossomed into a beautiful girl, cows were collected from the people there so that he could marry that girl. When he came back, he returned with a wife. Cows were collected from the Ngok, the Ruweng, and the Abiem for him to marry with."

Babo Nimir, who was at first a close friend of Deng Majok but later became his political adversary, drew a distinction between the legal issue of numbers which he ascribed to custom and therefore not subject to scrutiny by outsiders, and the social and economic implications of such excessive marriage, which he thought prompted understandable suspicions and accusations of corruption.

The issue of marriage was, of course, a matter of tradition; and according to Dinka tradition, there is no limit on the number of wives a man can marry. A man marries according to his ability, his material means, and his physical strength. But we felt that Deng had exceeded the reasonable limit. Of course, I did not count his wives. But it was rumored that he had more than two hundred. People used to say: "What is this excessive marriage of Deng Majok? And how can he afford to maintain such a large family?"

The Dinka poll tax was not customarily paid in full to the treasury of the Council. So people used to say that Deng must be maintaining his family with Dinka taxes. His wives were dressed in clothes like the best worn among the Arabs, not merely ordinary Arab dress. Where did all that come from? These were the accusations being bruited about by gossipers.

"The Arabs felt that such immoderate marriage was very costly," commented Tigani Mohammed Zein. "It was the practical aspects that the Arabs were concerned with. Some even thought, and here I should say that we must tell the truth, that part of the poll tax he collected from the Dinka probably went into his marriages or similar expenditures, and that was why the Dinka often had arrears in tax payments. But despite that, he was loved by the Arabs."

Matet Ayom, who was in alternating positions as a close friend and a political enemy, was ambivalent on this point, implying corruption but justifying it on account of Deng's generosity with the public:

> An old man called Deng Akolith, the son of Allor, once said something. It was rumored that Deng Majok had misappropriated tax money. When this old man came to Abyei, he saw a large gathering of people in Deng Majok's house. More than ten large trays, each laden with several dishes and *kisira* (native bread), were placed in front of the crowd. There were also numerous platters and gourds full of food. He later recalled the rumors about the tax money and said, "You people of our land, do you not see now that this man is supporting you, the people of this tribe? Why did you not ask Deng where he found all those platters and dishes of food that were presented to the crowds? All that food could only be secured by spending sixty pounds or eighty pounds per meal. And you know he has no shop. If you people do not want your tax money to be spent by the chief, then you had better avoid going to Deng's house. Stay in your own houses. I have now come to believe that Deng has spent the tax money. But I have also come to know that it is the people who have consumed the tax money. So, if the tax money is to be refunded by Deng, I would say that we, the tribe, should also pay our share. Deng will pay the portion his wives have consumed. And the public should pay for what they have consumed.

Some people, though not accusing Deng Majok of blatant corruption, argue that he acquired his means through transactions involving a complex network of social and political relationships: "The Dinka in the past used to respect and entertain a chief," said Chief Lang Juuk. "Whatever a chief wanted from any person was given to him. When Deng traveled throughout his area, he visited friends and relatives. Wherever he found a girl during the tour, he married her with the cows contributed by the people he visited. He did not take the cows by force. People volunteered to help him. Each person decided of his own free will to help the chief."

Mithiang Aguek was quite elaborate in his allegations of how Deng solicited the means to marry:

> After an official visit by a government representative, Deng Majok would gather the people and pass word around that the government had authorized him to make a number of appointments to certain positions and that he would be considering nominations for suitable candidates during his forthcoming visit around the tribe. He would also send a message to a particular area saying that he would be coming to marry the daughter of a particular person in the area. Then he would get onto his horse and ride to that area shortly after the visit of the government representative.
>
> When the marriage talks were conducted, he would usually have only a few cows available for the marriage. But then those attending the talks would have heard the earlier talk about nominations for the new positions and would try to influence Deng Majok by offering him gifts of cows, normally a cow and a calf, as a free contribution to his marriage. These gifts would add up until the marriage was finally settled. This would be repeated wherever he expressed his desire to marry. That way, the bridewealth was easily collected.
>
> Another method of getting cows was when an individual would approach Deng Majok and express his desire to contribute to Deng's marriage were it not for the fact that a particular person who owed him some cows was evading the settlement of his debt. Deng Majok would have that person summoned and would settle the case. The police would execute the judgment against the debtor. Thus the creditor would have been accorded the means by which to fulfill his promise to contribute one or more cows to the marriage of Deng Majok.

Mithiang Aguek then proceeded to give a specific example from his own experience:

> While Chol Jifur was in prison, Malei committed adultery with Chol's wife, Nyanajith. When Chol got out of prison, Malei was made to pay him damages. Among the cattle he paid was an ox, Mayen. Chol Jifur later sold the ox. It was bought by Meride, the Arab trader. Then my cousin, Kwol Chol, came from Arabland with some money. I liked Mayen when I saw it with Meride. So we went and bought it.

In the long run Mayen grew to become a very beautiful ox. He had beautifully shaped horns. Because of that, Madit Kat, Malei's brother, went to Deng Majok. He claimed that their ox, Mayen, had been unjustly taken from them and was now with me. They claimed that Malei had never committed adultery with Chol Jifur's wife. They pledged that if Deng Majok retrieved the ox, it would be his.

Deng Majok sent three policemen to get the ox from me. That ox we went and stole one night, I and my cousin. We took it to Ngol. Deng sent the police after us. Because of that ox I was flogged. He said, "Mithiang Aguek fought with Juac Dau some time back. He is a criminal."

That was the reason why he jailed me. They took Mayen from us. Deng Akonon led the way in the role of judge, but Deng Majok was behind him. They said that the ox should not be given to Mithiang.

I was taken to Arabland to serve my prison sentence. There I opened a case before the district judge. The judge took me back to Abyei. When Deng realized this, he called my cousin Kwol and gave him a pregnant heifer that he could claim to have been given in exchange for the bull. He knew I had come with the judge. He asked my cousin to leave with the heifer. That is how he took Mayen.

Such cases were many, but what you must note about them and the excessive number of marriages of Deng Majok is that individuals, out of what they saw as a means to advantage or gain or as an expression of gratitude, willingly offered something to Deng Majok. In most cases, it was something under dispute which people promised to pass over to Deng once they had obtained their rights.

According to Allor-Jok, though people proferred such conditional gifts, Deng Majok did not succumb to temptation:

> We were members of his court. It is true, a person would come and say, "Chief, I have a claim against So-and-So. If you get it from him, I will share it with you or give it all to you as a contribution to your marriage." Is that not a form of bribery? It is bribery, but Deng would never give in to such practice. What he would do was settle the case justly and give the person what was due him. Later on, when he was about to marry, that same person would come forward with a cow and offer it to Deng Majok as a contribution to his marriage in appreciation for the favor he had done in giving him his rights. It was someone who was grateful for what Deng Majok had done for him on an earlier occasion who would come and say, "Chief, here is a cow; it is a contribution from me." Deng Majok never took anything from anybody by coercion. People volunteered gifts to him because they were happy with him.

Allei Chol, a Twich elder, concedes that accepting a favor as a consideration for adjudicating a case was not good,

> but it was willingly given by the owner; Deng Majok did not go and

solicit the favor. What is bad is when a chief solicits favors from his people. But if someone voluntarily gives him something, there is nothing wrong with his accepting it. Today if someone came and said, "Chief Kwol, have this!" would Kwol not take it? He would take it. And that is not what people hold against their chief.

Deng did not rob anybody of his property. If he took from the government, then that is something we know nothing about. It is not our problem. If he took from the taxes, then that was an issue between him and the government and none of our business. As for the cattle he used to marry with, some of them came from his age-mates, who willingly offered to help him. Many of his age-mates took pride in offering him material help. But he never took anyone's property by force. For instance, he once asked me for a cow and I refused. Did he force me? He did not!

And as for the relatives of the girls involved and their consent or opposition to Deng's proposal of marriage, the family would often be divided. The father might refuse to give his consent, but he might have sons who approved of Deng, and he would be outnumbered.

"One thing about Father which people did not realize," said Nyanjur,

> was that he paid well for his marriages. People slandered his name unfairly, accusing him of taking people's daughters for nothing. Of all the girls he married, not a single one came to him without his paying the bridewealth. If a girl came without his paying, she must have been someone whose father had decided to offer her to our father for nothing with the understanding that he could pay her bridewealth later on. But a man who valued his daughter and required payment would challenge Father to pay as many as fifty, sixty, seventy, even a hundred or more cows.

According to Chol Piok, "When Deng later compounded his marriages, after your mothers were established, he had by then accumulated a great deal of wealth."

"Deng Majok had his father's daughters, the daughters of Kwol Arob," said Allor-Jok. "He also had his own daughters. A man marries with cattle received from the marriages of girls or from help given him by relatives and friends or age-mates. When Deng Majok's sisters were married, each one of them was married with a hundred cows."

"Deng's cattle came from many sources," observed Nyanbol Amor:

> He obtained cattle from his maternal relatives—from the marriages of their daughters; he obtained cattle from the marriages of his father's daughters; and there were the daughters of his uncles, such as Arob, Kwol Mariew, and Kwoldit—all that was his. He would share in the marriages of their daughters and would also reciprocate with his own sources. Whenever he asked for help, people would release cattle to him without ill feeling. Should any of these persons need

help, he would be there to render help. That was what the Dinka misunderstood. They began to say that Deng was misappropriating other people's wealth, that Deng was corrupt. But he was not.

"Father had great wealth," said Osman (Mijak).

He would take his cattle into marriage and receive cattle of reverse bridewealth. The cattle he would receive in reverse payment were often not brought home; he put them under the custody of people in that area to use for other marriages to come. And when he saw a girl he wanted to marry, he would send word to his relatives, paternal cousins, maternal cousins, and many other kinsmen. He would also send to people upon whom he had legitimate claims. Suddenly his wealth of cattle would flow from all directions. People would not know how all that wealth was collected. They simply assumed that he had extorted it from others. You see, one of the reasons why Father was always suspected is precisely because he did not bring his wealth home to be kept in one place. He kept the cattle away from him to use when opportunities arose.

"If we are to tell the truth, then we must tell the truth," declared Ali.

People used to say, "Where does Deng Majok find all these cattle which he uses for marriage?" But those of us who observed him closely know that Father used to marry so as to benefit materially as well. And the way he benefited was in part due to the reverse payments he received as part of the customary practice. He also received shares from the marriages of his female relatives-in-law.

The only area where one could say there was some corruption was that every relative-in-law of Deng Majok who had a legitimate claim against someone else always obtained his rights very speedily. The case of a stranger might take months, but the case of a relative-in-law or a case where Deng stood to benefit in some way was settled very quickly. For instance, if his brother-in-law had a claim for a cow which he promised to pay to Deng Majok as part of a reverse bridewealth or as part of his share from the marriage of a female relative-in-law or had been offered to him by his brother-in-law as a contribution to his bridewealth, he would see to it that that case was settled quickly. But he would not prejudice the case of the other party, he would only accelerate the cause of a relative-in-law whom he would have established to be clearly in the right.

Once he was convinced of the legitimacy of his relative's cause, he would oil the machinery of justice in his favor no matter what the difficulties. Once he got the cow, he would take it for himself either as part of the reverse payment or as a share in a relative's bridewealth or as a contribution to his marriage. His brother-in-law himself would have initiated the idea, or he would willingly concede.

Some people would come to him and say, "Deng Majok, you have a claim for reverse bridewealth of our sister who was married and we have no cattle, but I have a claim for a cow against this man. That cow is yours. If you can obtain it for me, I will give it to you."

As for tax money, one cannot say that Deng Majok was completely clean on tax money. When tax money used to be collected, brought and counted in front of our father, we were still children. We would see heaps of money piled up in front of our father in pounds of the old silver coins. As the money was being counted, we would be given some to go to the market with. I believe in those days the government did not pay the chiefs decent salaries. And I do not think there was a system such as now prevails whereby money is paid against a receipt and other protective measures. The chief was the custodian of the government money from the poll tax. However honest a person might be, considering that he received all that money without any controls, whenever something urgent came up that required money, he would be forced to spend money to offer hospitality.[1]

And in those days, Deng Majok used to do a great deal to defend and protect the interests of his people, the whole tribe of Ngok. In particular, when the country was undergoing the destruction of civil war, our father sheltered the tribe from many threats. And how did he protect his people or his tribe? Whatever he might have obtained from public sources in a way that may seem illegitimate would not be used for his selfish ends; it would go back to public guests or some other interest of the tribe.

Even though hostilities had prevailed in the South since 1955, they remained far from our territory because of our father's handling of the situation. The Arabs hardly ever regarded us as having a conflict with them. Everyone who went to Abyei, whether he was from the army or from the police, would leave Abyei feeling quite pleased with Deng Majok.

So our father's generosity and hospitality toward guests from outside, as well as toward his own people, were remarkable. No poor man in Ngokland ever suffered once he reached Deng Majok. A poor man would come all the way from Diil, and Father would give him relief either in the form of a cow or, if he was a person without kindred, he would offer him a home in our own family where he would receive food.

One looks at all that and comes to the realization that Deng Majok obtained his wealth because he also gave lavishly. The Dinka marriage system was such that spending for marriage was a form of investment from which one derived a great deal of advantage. In the end, you might find that what you received from the network of marriage ties might turn out to be more than what you spent for marriage.

"It is true, Mading, that we are considerably younger than you people," said Nyanjur,

---

1. According to Nyanjur, Deng Majok might help himself to government money in situations of urgent need but would always pay it back and straighten out the accounts.

but we grew up, and by the time our father died he left us as adults. We were no longer children. We of course heard the accusations against our father as corrupt or as a man who misappropriated other people's property. It may be that a person becomes so biased in favor of a father that he or she cannot see any wrongdoing on the part of his or her own father. That I do not know.

But to tell the truth as I believe I know it, our father was a man of considerable wealth, Mading. Among the Dinka, wherever you marry, you receive a share in the marriage of every girl relative of your wife. This is called *riek*. Then there is the reverse payment which the relatives of a girl make to her husband when he pays a brideswealth. This is called *arweth*. And perhaps because of Father's position, it was not possible for his rights to be lost. If he was entitled to a share in the marriage of a sister or any relative of his wife, his share would immediately be offered to him. Consider the number of wives he had and the fact that the family of every one of them gave the reverse bridewealth. They also gave him a share in the marriages of all their other daughters. There was also another source called *pel*, whereby if any cow that once belonged to you or to a close relative is received as bridewealth or reverse payment by another relative, you are entitled to reclaim it. He also had claims to the share in the marriages of all the girls related to him by blood, whether on his paternal side or on his maternal side, including his maternal grandfather's side and his maternal grandmother's side; then there were his own daughters' marriages; and moreover, if he married in a section where his daughters were married, they would contribute to his marriages. And there were many other sources built into the kinship system.

Father's sources of wealth were truly numerous because he was a man of a large circle of relationships, a circle large in the true meaning of the word. Had he stopped somewhere in the middle—say, even with as many as fifty or seventy wives—and decided to accumulate and keep his cattle, the size of his wealth would have been impossible to manage.[2]

You see, when we talk about it, it may sound like a lie, but cattle flowed into Father's ownership at the rate of as many as fifteen per day. These cattle would be tethered and kept for three or four days, and on the fifth day they would have moved into yet another marriage. Many cattle would go straight into his marriages even before they reached our home. I am only counting those that reached home and we saw with our own eyes.

Frankly, Mading, all those accusations against our father that we used to hear cannot be acceptable to any child of Deng Majok who observed what was going on. Because, even in theory, if you recog-

---

2. Of course, there is an inherent contradiction here, for if marriage is an investment and his many marriages themselves a source of wealth, Deng Majok could not have amassed that wealth had he decided to stop marrying earlier. This is therefore a clear exaggeration of numbers.

nize the large size of the family, and the Dinka customs that entitle all those people to share in the wealth of their respective families, and the fact that bridewealth for his marriage was also contributed through kinship ties according to custom, then you can easily see that he would not need to support his family through corruption, as some claimed.

Some claimed that Father maintained his family by misappropriating tax money. We heard all that. The year when all the arrears in taxes were being collected, our father paid a number of cattle to help bridge the gap. And those cattle were sold to make up for any government money that might have been lost. Father was very afraid of the government. He was extremely careful with government property.

Charles Biong illustrated his defense of his father with a specific experience:

> I remember we went on a trip with Father that lasted for about seventeen days. And when we came back there were two new wives with us, and another two had cows paid for their betrothal to Father.
>
> I will begin with Mijak, where we had the first stopover. I remember one evening about seven or eight cows came in. I would hear people talking to him saying, "This is my contribution." And they would be talking the language of members of one family. They would explain, "My mother is So-and-So; she received this or that favor from you, and if it were not that my situation at present is bad, I would not have come to you with this one cow (or two cows), there would have been many more than this."
>
> And the next stop was Wun-Yai, which is very close to Mijak. There, I remember there was the case of somebody who came to pay back cattle which Father had paid to marry their daughter. But the girl had eloped with another man and Father's cattle had never been returned. That evening the man came to pay Father back. I remember there were also about eight or nine. And I remember them also talking of something like a payment of appeasement, another two or three cows. Well, those cows we dropped along the way and went to Agany.
>
> At Agany, the only person who came was, I remember, our late uncle Arob-Col. I remember him talking of bringing some three cows as his contribution. People argued, "It should not be you, Arob, who pays three cows when people who are much more distant from Deng have contributed as many as that; you should pay more than that." Well, in the end, he came with four cows.
>
> All this happened in only three days. As a result, there were over thirty cows in Father's possession. The same thing continued to repeat itself. We stopped at Rumamer, where Kwol Kon was. A lot of talk took place among Father's maternal kin, Pabuk-jaak. They said, "The brides are from Diil (actually there were two girls from Diil) and the person who is marrying is the son of our daughter."

In fact, I witnessed two marriages. For one marriage, I saw the cows given in front of me at the place called Taramat. I counted the cows myself—there were about forty. Forty cows and six bulls were paid in my presence. And they were cows collected in the same manner as I have told you.

We proceeded to Abiemnom in the land of the Ruweng, where we were met by Makwac Deng, who was the chief. We were traveling on horseback; I was riding a brown horse. It was quite a good horse. As we entered the village, I let it loose to give it a run. The chief came to like it. Once we sat down, he expressed his wish: "You are fortunate that you are so close to the Arabs and have access to such beautiful horses. We here, unfortunately, cannot get them. It is my wish to acquire such a horse. And had it not been your son riding this horse, I would have expressed my desire to have him."

Father later talked to me and said, "What do you say? There is somebody here who says he would have expressed his wish to have the horse if you were not using it. Now his wish is not addressed to me; it is addressed to you."

I told him, "Father, if it is a question of me using the horse, I don't have a problem. We have so many stopovers, all short distances, I would not suffer much by walking back home."

Then he casually said to the man, "The boy is giving you the horse; the horse is yours." The man was very happy. He said, "Anyway, I am happy your son said that, but I will let him use it to take him back home and one of my retainers will accompany you to bring the horse back."

The following morning, they brought about nine cows and a bull. They brought them to me. Chief Makwac said, "I will not say that this is the price of the horse. If I said that, I would spoil the good spirit in which you gave it to me. You and your father did me that favor. Consider this also as a gift." Father came and said to me, "You have been given a present. I have marriages, some of which, as you have seen, I have left hanging. What will people say? That I just wanted the girl but don't have the means?"

I told him, "Father, since you are the person who provides for all my needs, the cows are yours."

We were talking while Chief Makwac was present. He said, "Although you are doing it that way, your father had not talked about the marriage, even though it is indeed very close to our place. I would be ashamed if a person like Deng Majok came and married so near to me, and I did not contribute a share to his marriage."

He went and contributed six cows in addition to the nine and the bull he had offered me. And some people in his court also volunteered help. Actually, many of them knew the girl who was being married, and they came up with cows to contribute. Frankly speaking, Mading, when we left Abiemnom, we had over fifty cows with us. This is precisely one way Father acquired cows for his marriages.

Biong's account is substantially corroborated by Deng Majok's halfbrother, Allor-Jok, who concluded, "The cattle Deng Majok obtained through such contributions were more numerous than the grass you see in the thatching on that cattle-byre."

"A person who has many wives can not easily become poor," said Chief Chier Rian.

> Marriage is also considered as wealth. If one bears many daughters, they are married with cows. Cows given as bridewealth among the Dinka are the equivalent of money saved in a bank. That is how we save our wealth. We save it by marrying many wives. The number of wives married by a man reflects that man's wealth among the Dinka.
>
> Some people say that Deng Kwol was cheating people. Deng did not cheat. Whatever he took from his friends or other people, he reciprocated. Among the Dinka, there is a bond of friendship that ties people together. The fact that Dinka marry with up to a hundred cows does not mean that this number of cows comes from one person alone. All the relatives of the groom join hands and provide a number of cows each to make up the required number. If a person kills somebody, all the relatives contribute toward the blood compensation. People help one another. That is the Dinka way.

"Whenever the number of your wives increases, your sources also increase," commented Achwil Bulabek. "I do not know of anything your father misappropriated from anyone! Otherwise, he could never have escaped all the accusations that he was subject to. His cattle were freed on the basis of the evidence I gave with my tongue."

The case Achwil alluded to was a complaint made by Chol Jipur, Deng Majok's deputy from the rival lineage, Dhiendior of Mannyuar. Allor-Jok, citing the case, remarked:

> Until Deng died, the government never found him in possession of any property he had wrongfully acquired from anyone. The only case that ever went to court against him was the case of the cattle he collected to pay the arrears in poll taxes, and they were found to have been collected and receipts given to those from whom they were taken. Chol Jipur went and raised a case of misappropriation against him. The cattle were taken into government possession, pending the trial. When the case was tried, Deng was found to have paid for them and given the people receipts. The money he paid was found to have been deposited in the government chest. No case was proved against him.

Although Deng Majok was exonerated, his son Ahmed, who was then the executive officer of the Council, was arrested, tried, and condemned to imprisonment, naturally losing his position in the process. Mithiang Aguek was one of the witnesses for the prosecution. He later furnished this information:

We had collected the tax money and passed it over to Ahmed Deng, who had us issued receipts but did not remit the money into the government chest. I believe Deng Majok knew it. When the audit took place, the misappropriation was discovered, but it was first reported that the clan-heads and sectional chiefs were responsible for the loss of the tax money. We had to defend ourselves and put the blame on Arob [Ahmed] and his father. That was the point of the conflict. Deng Majok had decided that the tribes had to contribute cows to make up the difference. We objected and preferred to be imprisoned. We were in fact imprisoned and sent to Fulah. There, we showed the authorities copies of the pay list and receipts. Omda Abiem had also been arrested and imprisoned with us. The authorities came to realize that we were in the right. Arob was arrested, and Abiem, who had been threatened with dismissal, was released and reinstated. But Deng Majok was excluded from responsibility.

Ibrahim El Hussein observed on the alleged corruption of Deng Majok:

On this issue, if people complained and the government saw cause for their complaint, would the District Commissioner not have revealed the justice of their cause? Would the government not have asked him to divorce his wives or to explain how he maintained such a large number of wives and children? Nothing of this sort was ever revealed. It was never obvious to me. But Deng was a man whom God decreed to be able to provide for people. He not only supported his wives and children, he was also the source of maintenance for the whole Dinka tribe. And his means of income were multiple and varied. He had his government salary. He had cattle from the marriages of his daughters and female relatives. And he had gifts from relatives, friends, and followers. I never heard that he ever misappropriated anything from anybody.

Gawain Bell, who first met Deng Majok in 1947 as a newly appointed District Commissioner, observed of Deng Majok's marriages: "I don't think if he had had twenty wives—I don't know how many he had, I am sure—that it would have worried me in the least. Different people have different customs in this respect. And I can't remember that it interfered at all with his official work and responsibilities as leader of the Ngok." To the question of whether there were any allegations of corruption against Deng Majok, Bell replied, "When I was there, none. I never remember any at all."

Paul Howell, who was also British District Commissioner in the area, observed of Deng Majok: "I knew he had many wives—that merely suggested to me that his special position among the Dinka brought him wealth in cattle. To me, there were no moral issues involved. I would have investigated charges of injustice, not social norms." However, he received no complaints "officially" against Deng Majok. In his assessment, "the answer given above might suggest that his official as well as ritual position enabled him to acquire cattle in return for favors. That would be corruption in European official circles, but is it so in Dinka mores?"

Despite the overwhelming support Deng Majok received from his family, the public, and official circles on the issue of his alleged corruption, there was general criticism of his marriages. Some of this was based on the mere fact that the number of them went far beyond normal limits. On that premise, there were also the arguments of injustice to the wives and the inevitable limitation of resources—if not for the support of the family, certainly for facilitating better conditions for modern living. And then there was the constant fear that accusations of corruption by political opponents might be credited by the authorities merely because of the size of his family. For all these and other reasons, relatives, friends, and others tried to persuade Deng Majok to stop marrying, and it was generally in that context that he articulated his reasons for marrying.

In defending his marriages, Deng Majok gave different reasons to different people. To some, especially his family, he might talk of marriage as an investment and a source of economic and social security. To others he might mention the need to broaden the circle of relatives and relationships by affinity as a strategy of extending political influence. But the reason he stressed most often and which cut across all others was procreation. And, in a curious way, all those who discussed the matter with him now report his arguments with considerable sympathy and nearly always end up agreeing with his point of view, if only in retrospect.

"When his marriages began to be excessive," said Nyanbol Amor, "we went and said to him: 'Deng, what is this? Cattle should be allowed to remain for some time to increase in number. You now seize a cow a woman uses for making butter and you send it off to marriage; why is that? Aren't we enough? We do not want you to continue with your marriages!'

"He replied, 'Are you people fools? Have you no sense of judgment? I am marrying these wives for your own good. These women will have children. And it is these children who will remain with you!'"

Kwei, the third wife, also recalled: "He became angry. He insulted us, uttering his famous chant: 'My big bull Marial has mounted his mother! Is that why you came to talk to me? Get out of here! Get out! If that was why you came, then get out! The wives I am marrying are your children. They will give you the protection of numbers. They will remain and reproduce.'"

Our generation of brothers, Bol, Kwol, and myself, spoke to him formally on two occasions, once when we were barely teenagers and again when we were in our late teens. On both occasions we spoke of the depletion of family wealth through marriage, the negative implications for the living standard of the family, and the political danger of allegations of corruption being believable because of sheer numbers. We emphasized the future of the children, the need for their education, and the advisability of investment in areas that promised greater returns in keeping with the requirements of modern conditions.

The first time, Father appreciated our point of view and even intimated that he had been told by successive administrators that, according to reports in the files, his performance as a chief by far exceeded that of any other tribal chief and that the only reservation people had about him was the issue of marriage. He enumerated several girls to whom he was then already engaged and told us that he could not break those engagements, but that he would end his marriages with those wives.

The second talk was more elaborate, as we organized a seated, formal tea party to which we invited key personalities, including Uncle Biong Mading, Omda Achwil, and I believe Sheikh Biong Mijak. We made a presentation, stating our well-known views but adding, not only the political hazards of possible dismissal or premature retirement, but the long-term view of things in terms of old age or even death. What did he think would become of such a large family and so many dependents without his strong guiding hand? We urged him to stop marrying and invest in projects that would guarantee a decent future for the family.

Father appeared genuinely offended, quite in contrast to his reaction to our childhood talk. He spoke of marriage primarily as an investment in our future, whether because of the security in numbers or the economic returns from the marriages of the girls. But the thrust of his remarks was that the subject was not appropriate for children to discuss with their father. What we were entitled to do was make requests for the things we wanted him to acquire for us; should he fail to procure them, then we would be justified in complaining. As for the time beyond his life, his contribution was that he would leave us sons and daughters behind. How we managed would be our affair, not his. The subject was closed, never to be raised again by us.

But younger brothers, among them Ali, later made another attempt and ended up as we had, only apparently worse, as Ali recalled:

> Once we sat and talked among ourselves, myself, Monyyak, and Miyar. We said, "Why is Father marrying so much? Should he not stop now to allow us to collect our cattle and accumulate a herd?" Our main concern was to accumulate cattle wealth. I believe we were then at Noong. Finally we went to him and said, "Father, why don't you stop this excessive marriage?"
>
> At first, he seemed receptive to what we were saying, and of course he realized that we were right. But later he grew impatient and made that famous utterance that made us shrink and shrivel with fear: "My bull Marial has mounted his mother." He used that on us and we dissolved in fear and left.
>
> What I later understood from him was that he was marrying so many wives in order to increase his backing in the tribe. There is not a single tribal section into which he did not marry. And according to

Dinka customs, when a man marries into a group, he is affiliated with that group and treated as though he were a blood relative. He also receives a great deal of respect from the group into which he marries. And when their daughter begets children, they add to the ties between the two groups because they also establish very close relationships with their maternal kin. From a political point of view, if his adversaries should incite people in a tribal section, for instance the Bongo tribe, saying that they do not want Deng Majok, if he has married three or four wives, his relations-in-law will back him against the opposition. That, too, was a reason for marriage. He wanted to have a large circle of relatives so that wherever people conspired against him, he would have a relative among the conspirators.

Achai-Jur tells of a rather unusual discussion Deng Majok had with his first generation of daughters on the subject of marriage and his own initiative:

> One of his junior wives had gone and looked for another man. She later died. Father was most distressed by that. We were in the cattle-camp. He sent for us. We went to him at home. Of course, we were the eldest; there was no son at home who was older than we.
> He called us into his hut and said, "Why I have asked you to come, my children, is because I have found the behavior of wives to be bad and want to consult with you on an idea I have about what to do with them. I have decided to distribute my junior wives among my relatives. So I want you to help me with their distribution. I have decided to give up women."
> All the girls agreed with him. Those of Adau and Abul, our senior sisters, agreed with him. They said that they, too, were very unhappy about the problems of his wives and that they were pleased he had made up his mind to get rid of them.
> That was when I decided to speak. I said, "I am of course younger than our sisters who have agreed with your decision. But I have one word to say in response to their words." I said, "If you give your young wives away to other men, none of them will bear a child with your qualities. If they remain with you, then however bad they may be, you might have with some of them children who will inherit your qualities. If it were up to me, I would say that there is nothing wrong with your marrying many wives because it will increase your family and reinforce your strength with your children. In the future, those children will be of value to you."
> Father reacted by clapping his hands. He said, "I am going to ignore what you, the older girls, have said and I am going to follow the advice of your younger sister."
> That was how he gave up the idea of distributing his junior wives and continued to marry as many wives as he married.

Deng Majok's arguments to the members of his family were broadly reflected in the tribe. According to Pagwot Deng, the reason he gave in defense of his marriages was procreation: "When people began to say, 'Why is he marrying so many wives?' his answer was: 'Some of these wives will miss and bear children who do not know how to speak; others might bear only girls; another woman might bear a son who can speak well. That is why I am marrying so many wives. Among them will one day emerge a leader that will sustain my people.' That was why he married so many wives as he did."

It would seem that Deng Majok wanted a large number of children that could one day become a clan and perhaps a tribal section. In a way, it was as though he intended to take over the Abyor through the power of sheer numbers in order to conquer their opposition to his leadership. "Deng Majok used to say," according to Malith Mawien, "that he wanted to have a whole tribal section known by his name. He said that through his marriages, he would increase the size of Abyor tribe: he might have four children with one wife, five with another, three with another, and four with yet another."

Ajuong gave a variety of motivations for Deng Majok's marriages:

> He said, "Why I do it that way is because, first, if one's heart likes something and one has the ability, one should not leave his heart to ache with want. If you see a girl, someone's daughter, and you like her, and you have the ability to have her, you should not just watch her and keep away from her when you can have her. Second, if she bears children, that is another value. If a woman bears three or four or five children, among these women will be a woman who might bear girls, another woman who might bear a useless child, yet another woman who might bear a child to compensate all you put into her marriage. And with respect to the children of a chief, if they are few, there is always the chance that they might all turn out to be useless. But if they are many, then the chances of their all not turning out to be useless are much better. Third, marriage is like an investment in a shop. How? When you marry, you pay the bridewealth, but your wealth comes back to you eventually. Your wife may have a sister, in which case you will be entitled to a share of her bridewealth. You will also receive *arweth*, the reverse bridewealth. Your things continue to multiply and return to you."

Matet Ayom told of a conversation he heard between Deng Majok and an Arab elder:

> I was once approached by an Arab, an elder called Mussaad, from the Fadhiliya section. He called me and said, "Come with me, I have something to ask the chief."
> I said, "What is it?"
> He said, "I shall say it when we are with the chief."
> So we went. It was at Abyei. Then he said, "Chief, we are all very happy with your leadership. Whenever you see one Arab visitor in your house, you slaughter a sheep and when you see three Arab

visitors, you slaughter a bull. This shows us what a noble leader you are.

"But there is a story about an Arab chief called Haron. He was a very wealthy man. He had many wives and a large herd of cattle. His money wealth was carried on camels.

"One day, a gazelle came running through the forest. One of its horns was made of gold, and one of its legs was made of gold, and the tail was also made of gold.

"The children came and said, 'There is a gazelle standing there with a horn of gold and a leg of gold and it waits until we get close and then runs away.'

"When people started to run, this great chief said, 'Do not go; no one is to go. I myself shall run after that gazelle with my horse. Let everyone else come back.'

"So people came back. He was a chief who, like yourself, frightened people.

"So he ran after the gazelle with his dogs. He ran and ran and ran. The gazelle would wait and then run and outrun the dogs. They ran that way until they entered a waterless area of thirst. Thirst eventually killed the chief. And during the night an old man in the camp said, 'O people, because the chief has not returned this late, I am afraid he may not be alive. Greed makes a man leave behind a hundred pieces of gold for the sake of one piece of gold. The greed of Haron might have led him to death. Can the gold or the gazelle he wants be as much as the gold which is now carried on camels? Go after him.'

"So the camp stampeded after him. The dogs that had gone with him were met coming back. First one dog met the people and then two dogs. And people continued to trace his footsteps. Eventually, he was found dead of thirst. So his body was carried back.

"That old man spoke to the dead chief: 'Chief, let me preach to you in your death. Because of greed, one piece of gold lost a hundred pieces of gold. It is because of greed that you allowed one piece of gold to take you away from a hundred pieces of gold. And you have no one to blame.'

"So let me ask you, Chief Deng Majok, what are you hoping for? What do you see lying ahead that you hope to achieve through all these many marriages? Because of greed, you will find that one wife may one day make you leave behind all your many wives.

"Every generation comes and goes leaving beautiful girls behind; every generation comes and goes leaving beautiful horses behind; every generation comes and goes leaving beautiful clothes behind; every generation comes and goes leaving beautiful food behind. Beautiful things never end; they have never ended. Why, then, do you want to come to the end of all beautiful things in this world? Where did you get that idea from? Please tell me so that I know. I am older than you, but you are the chief and it is the chief who knows what will become pleasing to the people in the future."

Chief Deng laughed and said, "Is it only this question which brought you?"

The old man said, "This is what brought me to come and see you. I have been hearing that Deng Majok has married and married and married, that his wives are numerous. So my question is, what do you see in the future that will come out of these numerous marriages?"

Chief Deng then said, "It will not bring much that I can say I know. But I will tell you what I hope it will bring. There is a snake called the python; it is said that this snake begets all the different kinds of snakes. It begets the brown snake called *biar*, and it begets the snake called *akelek*, and it begets the black snake called *pien*, and it begets the snake called *kuryath* (the puff-adder), and it begets the snake called *gor*, and it begets the snake called *bok*. It begets snakes that can inflict instant death and it begets benign snakes that will not harm.

"So what I am doing is not because of the beauty of sleeping with women; it is the desire to beget children. In the future, there will be a child among these children who will live up to my character and there will be a child who will deviate from my image. It is like the case of the snake; there is a snake which kills instantly and there is a snake which does no harm and both are from the same parent-snake called the python."

Then the old man said, "That is sufficient for me; I accept your argument. Among the children of one man there will be a rogue, a coward, a man of noble character, and a man of vile manners. Your answer has convinced me. The heart which enabled you to shoulder this leadership is a great one; if you have five or six children who can assume your role, there will be a better chance of their filling your position in the distant future." Those were the words of an Arab elder. And Arabs loved Deng Majok very much.

Tigani Mohamed Zein saw Deng Majok's ambitions for his children as an extension of himself: "Deng Majok was talking to our father and he learned from him that our father had children being educated in schools. I remember he said to my father, 'God willing, my children will be educated not only to be leaders in Dinkaland, but also in the Sudan as a whole. I would like every area in the Sudan to have my son among its rulers, or at least in a position of influence.'"

Indeed, the preponderance of defenses of Deng's marriages is retrospective and largely based on the ground of the children he has left behind. Nyanbol Amor ended her account of the discussion the senior wives had with their husband on the subject of marriage with these remarks: "And truly, that is why you are here taking the pictures of the family. That was what Deng Majok meant when he said, 'It is the children these wives will bear who will look after you and your children. Do not resent my marriage; it is in your own interest.'"

The position of the sons, as represented by Ali, was also supportive in retrospect:

> After Father died, one was able to see that there was much to what he had said. Sure, we have suffered because of his death. But when one looks at the situation, one also sees that our numbers are not altogether a negative fact; they can also be a source of strength. Even in the case of the suffering I referred to, when one sees the children Deng Majok begot and how they are faring, there is no longer much suffering to be endured for long. Even if there is still some suffering, one is optimistic that it will not last for long.

"It is because of his marriages that he has children like you," said Atem Moter to the sons of Deng Majok who conducted the interview.

> That made him the man he was. I like it. He was a man who died a good death. His father's name today is not as widespread through children as is his own name. His name will continue to spread through his children. I like his marriages.
>
> Today, if I were sterile, I would leave Dinkaland and go to the land of the Arabs. I could never live in this country eating and paying taxes and call that living. It would be better to leave and go to Arabland.
>
> No one knows whether a man will die at night or survive the night. And if one has wealth, why should one not marry? Why is it that some shopkeepers stock their shops with goods and acquire as many as ten lorries? Why should a wealthy man not marry many wives into his home?

"If Deng had not married this and that wife, there would have been nobody interviewing me now," remarked Juac Dau to the young sons of Deng who conducted the interview. "Maybe the children of Deng Majok would have been few. But what do you call responsibility? To be in charge of a large area and have only two or three children? How could you administer the area? It is better to marry many wives so that when one wife bears a bad child another wife may bear a good one. That is what a wise man does and that is what our people want."

Allei Chol, indeed, sees what Deng Majok achieved as a dream-world fantasy: "Deng Majok's marriages were out of the ordinary. He exceeded by far the extent to which any chief has ever married. He reached the point which everyone wishes for but cannot attain."

"Some people now say, 'I wish I were like Deng Majok and married as many wives as he did,'" concluded Malith Mawien.

13 Invasion from Within

The previous chapters in Part 3 have dealt with Deng Majok's marriages and the relationships within the family. This chapter concludes the part with a discussion of the sexual relationships with and the problems of unfaithfulness on the part of wives which posed a major threat to the cohesiveness and tranquility of the family, especially during the later years of Deng Majok's life. Although the main fabric of the family remained intact, the "empire at home" began to suffer an aspect of disintegration.

Whether Deng Majok was prompted by biological drives or by the desire to widen his circle of social, political, and economic influence as a base for increased power, or by the wish to immortalize himself in a grand manner, he remained relentless in his pursuit of women and marriage. And so some two hundred, perhaps more, wives lived together, bound to one man in a close-knit, highly controlled family in which opportunities for secret, undetected self-indulgence were virtually nonexistent. But the invasion from within was only to be a matter of time.

Osman, who of all Deng Majok's children was perhaps the most favored by his father and had the closest proximity to the wives, gave this account of the situation:

> Our father's system was that he only had a special appetite for his new brides, whose companionship he clearly favored. Otherwise, he told the women that any woman who was in her period of fertility should be made to come to him. He would be with her that night. If God blessed her with a child, that was that. Otherwise, she missed and the turn went on to another wife.
>
> There were junior wives who had genuine grievances. Some of the senior wives manipulated the situation by saying, "Wait! Wait!

The other woman is still there!" Sometimes, when I saw such a situation developing, I would go and tell Father quite candidly that some women were being deliberately kept away from him by other women. Then he would take my advice and call the women who were being kept away from him.

"It is true that there was an obvious system of preferences among the wives," remarked Biong. "A new bride always enjoyed a degree of attention which you could call a kind of honeymoon. Each wife was granted that right during the first days of her marriage. After that, the relationship would depend on her merits."[1]

Ali elaborated:

Personality counted a great deal. When Father would enter his bedroom, unless a woman was daring and outspoken about her conjugal rights, to tell you the truth, she would never get close to our father.[2]

Sometimes, women would encourage a woman to try to force her way to him by saying to her, "You go ahead, enter the hut without anybody's permission, and remain there! Do not listen to anybody who tells you to leave." But even if a woman became daring enough to attempt that, the more senior wives, whose words were heeded by Deng Majok and who were charged with the responsibility of introducing the wives to him, would never allow access to a wife they did not want. It was as though they played the role of his bodyguards, who would not allow entry except to those they liked and favored. So there was considerable rivalry, tension, and jealousy over that issue. And there was a great deal of injustice in our father's treatment of his wives. There were women he never cared to bring close. He would go and marry a woman, perhaps give her a child or two while she was still a young girl, and then abandon her, never to ask for her again. That was why many women complained of his treatment.

In the face of this competitiveness and relative deprivation, Deng Majok's wives, at least once, tried to be creative in meeting their pressing needs. Nyanjur tells this story:

Father's wives once invented a game which later caused conflict with Father, eventually entailing the payment of cattle to appease him. The women used to play as though they were children. First, they sang and danced. And when the dance was over, they played the game of *alalepoke*, a children's game where boys are supposed to line up on one side and girls on the other. A number of boys or girls move, dancing flirtingly, to the other side, select the partners of their

---

1. By which it is meant her appeal and winning personality.
2. But female aggressiveness in these matters was frowned upon as morally depraved, and although rare cases of such behavior were notorious, it was by no means an expected way of solving the problem.

choice, and then dance back with the persons they select. Those, in turn, select their own partners and dance back.

After this game, they continued to play other games that you may remember from your childhood. Eventually, they began to play a game in which some pretended to be male youths. Some women acted the role of men while others played the role of girls. They played the courtship game in which Dinka male youths run after girls to escort them for courtship after the end of a dance. Acting the role of a man, a woman would snap her fingers at another woman who was playing the role of a girl, and say, "Girl, would you wait for me?" They acted in that way, pretending to be boys and girls. This was in the village at Nainai.

Those who did not play went and reported to Father the following day. He was not there when this happened, but he was given all the details of who had done what. Father had them summoned immediately. He was then in Abyei.

After they were brought to him, he asked them, "Why did you do that?"

They said, "We were just playing."

"And did you really play a courtship game as boys and girls or did you not?"

They said, "Chief, we were only playing and pretending in our game."

Then he chanted his famous insult, "My bull, Marial, has mounted his mother. What do you mean pretending when you did it? So, you are about to bring shame on me? How could you do something that has never been heard of anywhere?[3] Right now, every one of you who was involved in this should leave my home and go back to her relatives. You have ceased to be my wives. Go away!"

So, the women left and went home to their relatives. Each one of them informed her family of what they had done. The responsible elders of those families then came to him one by one to apologize for what their daughters had done and to pay him cows of atonement.

Deng Majok kept a jealous guard over his wives, and even his sons were not above suspicion, especially as some of the girls were their age-mates and younger girls whom the sons could have encountered in the open fields of Dinka flirtation and courtship. The attitude of the older sons in keeping a distance from their father's junior wives established a tradition that was maintained down the line, as Ali reveals:

> The way we related with our stepmothers when we began to mature was that we were rather careful not to get too close to the women. And that was because we had already observed that our

---

3. Lesbianism, like homosexuality, is unknown to the Dinka, despite abusive language with sexual overtones directed by men against men, which implies threats of physical power without serious sexual associations.

father did not like it when he saw his sons mingling with the women. So we kept our distance. Whenever something forced one to get close to the women, one behaved as though one was a guest. You would leave the male section of the enclosure and enter the female section with the carefulness and distance of a guest. One guarded one's self very carefully.

One of the elders, Matet Ayom, who knew Deng Majok very well, commented:

> The way Deng managed his house, no man could come in his absence and be accommodated in the hut of any of his wives. That he completely forbade. He ruled that whenever he was away, four wives had to share a hut; five wives would share a hut. Deng's rope for tying women was an extremely tight and sturdy one.[4] The only rope that could approximate his rope for women might be that of the Arabs and their harems. The rein of a wife never slipped his hand. Deng never loosened his grip on women.

But, as he advanced in age, with ever-increasing numbers of wives young enough to be his grandchildren, Deng Majok's grip on his wives began to weaken until it eventually gave rise to a chain of scandals in the family. While most of his sons never had any problems with him on account of his wives, perhaps because of their own cautious attitude or their distance from home, several were to fall victims of what was obviously a difficult situation for both sons and wives, and of course for Deng Majok, who suffered severe emotional strain on account of the invasion from within.

"Unfaithfulness was something our father really hated," said Osman.

> For anyone to commit adultery with his wife was extremely hateful to him. This was especially the case with his sons. In the beginning, his sons went freely to the women's section. But later he stopped his sons from mixing with his wives. I was the only one permitted in the women's section. The problem was that his sons were becoming adults while he was still marrying very young girls. Many of the wives were the same age as his sons, and many far younger. When he later married literate girls who were known to educated youths, Father became very suspicious. He felt that unfaithfulness was on the increase.

The first and most dramatic case involved Deng Majok's oldest son, Ahmed (Arob), who was occupying the then powerful and prestigious position of local government officer. Ahmed's status as representative of the central government placed him in a position of rivalry and struggle for power which some people sought to exploit for their own purposes. Litigants who felt unjustly treated by Deng Majok complained to Ahmed, who some-

---

4. A metaphor for control.

times unwittingly meddled in tribal affairs that were not directly within his jurisdiction. While some of his critical attitude might have been justified, it soon became a subject of gossip, identified as a form of vengeance against his father for the manner in which the latter had treated his mother, Kwei. Tensions and conflicts continued to brew until they reached a climax in Ahmed's committing adultery with one of his father's younger wives. By that time, Chol Jipur and others had brought charges of corruption against Deng Majok and Ahmed, and although Deng Majok had been exonerated, Ahmed had been suspended pending trial. Ahmed moved out of Abyei and settled on the Bahr el Arab (Kir) River where he rapidly drifted back into traditional ways, smoking the Dinka pipe and tobacco, drinking the local brew of beer, flirting with girls in the company of his traditional age-mates, and composing songs against the Arabs, with whom he associated the government.

It was then that we came on vacation from Khor Taggat Secondary School and, in the company of Father, escorted some visiting dignitaries to the river, where we met Ahmed. We greeted him warmly with an embrace in front of our father. When we returned to Abyei that afternoon, Father called a meeting of his senior sons, in the presence of his sister Awor, his daughters, and his wives, and spoke to us in the most solemn manner we had ever seen. He recalled the themes of our family morals on the issue of married women: the advice of his great-uncle that to have an affair with a married woman, or even to smile at her desiringly, was accursed; his own attitude toward his father's wives, how he had never seen the inside of any of the huts of his father's wives, except for Deng Abot's mother, Abiong; and the conduct he expected of his sons. He commented on Ahmed's wrong, his feelings on the matter, and how he had contemplated shooting Ahmed and forgetting all about chieftainship or even his own life. Then he spoke of how painful it had been for him to see us embrace Ahmed with such obvious love, as though he had done no wrong. He said that he had decided to convene an all-family meeting at Noong, where he was going to administer the traditional ritual of disaffiliating Ahmed from the family, never again to be considered his son. Each one of us would then have to decide either to join Ahmed and sever ties with his father, or to remain with the family and cut all ties with Ahmed.

So hurt was Father and so intimidating were his words that we could not do much more than reassure him of our moral support. But as soon as we parted, we were approached by Aunt Awor and Uncle Biong Mading, who argued that it was our duty as sons to stop our father from carrying out the ritual of disaffiliating Ahmed from the family. Whatever Ahmed had done, he was his son and there was no way he could escape the tie. They said that although Father was not now in a mood to listen to the advice of anyone else, the challenge of making him listen was certainly ours, his sons.

Bol, Kwol and myself asked for an appointment and talked to him in earnest, not only stressing the inescapable blood bond, but also alerting him to the fact that Ahmed, having worked so closely with his father and having full knowledge of all his secrets, could be pushed into becoming a very dangerous enemy. People would believe that he obviously knew the facts and, whatever his motivation, was a reliable witness. Father reacted with rage, stating that he had always thought that when he looked at us he had procreated well, but he had never realized he had a bunch of cowards for sons. So what if Ahmed became a political enemy? He was going to proceed with his plans and it would be for each one of us to make up his mind as to where he stood.

Shortly after this confrontation, Ahmed wrote a letter to our father, which he sent me to read to him. I caught up with Father early in the morning as he was going from his bedroom to his home courtroom. Reluctantly and with obvious impatience, he listened to me as I hurried through my translation of the letter with sincerity and candor. Ahmed said that he had heard that in addition to Father's own dismissal of him as a son, he now intended to deprive him of all his brothers and sisters and the rest of the family. He did not feel he deserved such treatment, and all he could say was that God would ultimately be the judge. At that point, Father's tolerance ran out: "So be it; God will be our judge," and he signaled an end to reading or translation.

Although Father would never admit it, our advice must have had some impact on him, for he never called the intended family meeting. On the other hand, his bitterness toward Ahmed persisted for a long time, if indeed it ever left him totally. Ahmed's eventual conviction and dismissal from the service was widely believed to be, at least in part, due to his having lost his father's favor and perhaps drawn down a curse. According to Ali:

> In a way, it is very much in line with what the Dinka say that if a father is unhappy with his son, he can inflict great harm on him through the will of God. Even though it is fashionable these days to say that this is a Dinka superstition, one feels that if your father's heart is offended with you, God can inflict harm on you. Arob's end came from the time he committed adultery with Father's wife. Since then and until his recent death, we never saw anything good on the part of Arob.

Many years later, Ibrahim Mohamed Zein, then the headmaster of Abyei School, was to recall a conversation he had with Deng Majok at the crucial time of Ahmed's arrest:

> I recall one incident. His son Ahmed was then the executive officer of the Council. Some problem occurred between Ahmed and Mukhtar El Tayeb, who is now a Commissioner of a province and was then the District Commissioner. Mukhtar El Tayeb gave instructions to the police to have Ahmed arrested. Ahmed was not only an executive officer, he was also the son of the chief. On his way back from court, Deng Majok passed by my house and told me all that had happened with Mukhtar El Tayeb, adding, "I left because I could not tolerate watching what was happening and I was afraid also that any

one of the Dinka might be provoked into committing an offense, seeing my son who is also their officer treated that way. It would be difficult to tolerate."

Then he proceeded to tell me, "But to tell you the truth, there is something deep inside me between me and my son. First of all, I educated him until he completed his schooling. I then said to the authorities that I was the man controlling this very difficult area between the North and the South: Here was my son educated, knowing both English and Arabic, knowledgeable in every aspect of modern government, 'I would like you to help me by appointing my son an executive officer and bringing him here to be with me.' Thanks to them, they appointed him executive officer and brought him here. I said to him that he should not view himself as simply an executive officer, but also as the chief of the tribe and my righthand man. I gave him my full authority and responsibility.

"I am a man of many responsibilities, both public and family, and I have many children in various schools. Ever since Ahmed became an officer, he has never given me a helping hand with the education of any of his brothers. Second, he left our girls here and went to the South to marry a girl who cost me considerable wealth. I paid all that, brought the girl, built her a home close to me, and made her settle as a member of my family.

"I began to see one of my most beautiful wives whom I loved dearly go frequently to my son's house. I called the woman and told her to stop going there because that was the house of my son's wife who was an outsider, and in any case that I did not want people to get the impression that my wife might be interested in the things available in my son's house, which might be better because he was educated and an officer. I asked her to stay at home and be content with my own way of life. Yet I noticed that she continued to go to him. I had a feeling that the situation was not normal.

"One day, I sat the woman down and questioned her very closely. Then I found out that Ahmed had been sleeping with her. I became extremely angry. I called his maternal uncles and explained to them what the son of their sister had done. His mother, I said, was one of the most senior wives. 'But from today,' I said to them, 'her position is relinquished; she no longer occupies that status and I bear no further responsibility for her.' That conduct from my son affected me very deeply. But God Almighty has acted on my behalf. I am his father and a father is the second God to a person. He has offended God and God has punished him for raising his head above me and against me. But, despite all that, he is my son and I cannot feel good to see him treated that way in front of me."

As it was, Ahmed went to jail in far-off Nahud, suffered a greater emotional ordeal on account of his father's disregard for his fate, lost a dedicated wife who died in Nahud while trying to provide him with some care and consolation, and ultimately served his full term and survived to the extent he did only because of the resilience and strength of character that was—ironically—a heritage from his father.

Ahmed's case was apparently far more significant than anyone seemed to realize at the time. It was the tip of the iceberg, and other scandals soon followed in rapid succession, involving relatives both within and beyond the immediate family. Although loyalty and faithfulness remained the norm, and violation of them a most resented exception, the unfaithful were not without sympathy in the family. Monyyak (Abdalla) and, ironically, the wife concerned in the second case of adultery with a son, both confided their secret to Charles Biong—and won his sympathy:

> Monyyak discussed the situation with me even before he committed adultery with Father's wife. At first, he started by posing the general question of what would be the position of a son if he did such a thing. I told him that no one among us could possibly think of doing such a thing. Then he presented an argument assuming that the deed was done not on the initiative of the son but the woman. We discussed the issue along these general lines and agreed that the son should resist such a temptation. And then, later on, he told me that there were women after him. He said that one woman kept talking to him, but that he was against it. I still encouraged him to resist.
>
> But then he began to come to me and say that he could not resist any longer because the woman was so persistent. Later on, I was forced to talk to the woman. At first she did not want to talk to me. But I talked to her very frankly, trying to warn her and to discourage her from doing any such thing. That was when she came to explain to me her point of view. She confronted me with a situation about which I could not blame her or Monyyak. She told me that she thought it would be wiser to go with the son of Deng Majok and have a child within the family. "But if you people say that you cannot do that, if you reject me, I will be forced to go and pick any man regardless of who or where he is. The child I would beget would also be called the son of Deng Majok. I am ready to take anything. The child will carry your name anyway. Whether your father accepts it or not, he or she would be my child. It is because I respect your family that I want a child by Deng's son."

Biong's account of the case goes on to show that, as expected, Father "reacted furiously! For a period of at least two months, he did not talk to Monyyak. Then he called Monyyak's mother—I recall—and rebuked her. The only person who tried to help the situation was Uncle Biong Mading. In the end, he managed to reconcile Father and Monyyak. Father had taken an oath not to regard Monyyak as his son anymore, something similar to what he had done with the late Ahmed, Arob Deng. But even after they were reconciled, his opinion about Monyyak was never what it had been before the incident."

Ali elaborated: "Father's reaction to a person who had committed adultery with his wife was to hate him bitterly, however much he might have loved him before. He used to love Monyyak very much. When Monyyak committed that wrong, it hurt Father a great deal."

Ali gave another case of a young uncle whose mother had been inherited by Deng Majok from his father through the levirate, but who was himself begotten by Kwol Arob:

> When another wrong occurred in the family, it was our uncle, Alfonse Arob Kwol. Father had given Arob's mother, Amir, a number of wives. Those women lived with Arob's mother at Nyongreng. And Arob, too, lived there. I believe he assumed that since the women were living there with them and they were under his mother and had no way of meeting their husband, Deng Majok, it was appropriate for him to have relations with them. That caused bitter hostility between our father and Arob. Before that incident, Father had been very fond of Arob's mother, Amir. He used to listen to her words and take her advice.

Nyanjur witnessed the punishment suffered by and the curse inflicted upon the offspring of the women who committed adultery with Alfonse Arob:

> Both women were taken from Nyongreng and brought to Abyei. Father beat them very hard and chained them both. Their feet were bound together by iron chains. They were placed in the hut of Nyanawai. When he came back from work, he would summon them to his hut. They would walk together, each holding one end of the iron chain. They would be escorted to his hut; he would again beat them and then have them returned to Nyanawai's hut.
>
> They went through their pregnancies with those babies until they were born. The children were both given the same name, Mijok. One was about six years old when he fell very ill indeed. He lay in the sun shelter of my mother where we used to spend the day. His condition worsened as Father was about to sacrifice a Pied Bull (Mijok) for the spirit of his father, Kwol Arob. The bull was tethered under the shrine, waiting to be sacrificed. You know, our father was sometimes capable of doing terrible things. He obviously desired the death of the boy. As he was saying the invocation, the prayers which accompanied the sacrifice of the bull, he said: "Father Kwol, Mijok [the bull] and Mijok [the boy], I have given them both to you. Take them." As soon as the bull was slaughtered, the boy passed away. When his mother cried, Father reacted with rage against her. He not only insisted that she should not cry, he said that the joyful dancing that was part of the sacrifice to his father must continue. He insisted that the women should continue their singing and dancing and the cries of joy. Some of the senior wives went to him and said, "Deng, a child has just passed away!" He reacted by saying, "If any woman stops playing, I will take that as a serious issue between her and me."

Nyanjur gave a graphic description of another instance of beating which was so extreme in its horror that it brought tears to her eyes:

> One woman was suspected of having an affair with someone from the Twich, a man called Atem Madut. She claimed that he was a cousin to her. But what was really happening was that he was courting her. Atem Madut was caught and beaten by the Anyanya. He had become a spy for the security forces. When he was admitted to the dispensary, this woman would go and nurse him, claiming that he was her cousin. No one knew that something else was going on.
> One night, she left her hut to go to Atem. She had a child who was quite a big girl, but she would still cry at night and her mother would sing lullabies to her to the tune of a rattling gourd. This was despite her being so grown up that she not only spoke but was very articulate. That night, after her mother had left, the child began to cry. Father came out of his hut and said, "Why is the child crying so much? Where is her mother?"
> The child immediately responded by saying, "I do not know where she has gone. She left a long time ago and has not returned. She left me alone."
> Dead silence followed. Suddenly the woman appeared. "Where were you?" Father asked.
> "Nowhere!" she said. "I only went outside."
> "What outside?" he asked.
> "I went to the forest," she replied, implying that she had gone to the toilet in the woods.
> "What would take you into the woods for that long in the middle of the night to stay? Do you have diarrhea? Even a person with diarrhea would have returned sooner. I want you to tell me tomorrow exactly where you went."
> He went back to bed. The following morning, he began to investigate the situation until it was revealed that she had gone to Atem Madut. He began to beat her. And then called to Mijak to beat her more.
> Mading, brother, the woman was beaten while she was menstruating. It was a dreadful sight. If this had been in the modern world, it would have been condemned as a crime. In the condition she was in, it would have been more appropriate for her husband to be the only one to punish her. It was not appropriate for another man to get involved. It was such an ugly scene you cannot imagine how revolting it was. But Father did not care at all how embarrassing and repulsive the situation appeared.
> Mijak fell on her with a long whip of leather and beat the woman. She could not even run away because she was bleeding, and the more she was beaten the more the blood flowed. So she would fold herself up and try to be modest about her condition while Mijak mercilessly beat her exposed body. I could not help it; I broke down and cried.
> When it was over, Mading, you cannot believe the sight. The

woman's back was totally invisible except as a whole sheet of streaming blood. The wound exposed her flesh glowing and shimmering with blood. Not a single part of her body looked free of blood.

When Mijak stopped beating her, she got up and said she had to go and report to the police station. And frankly, had she reported to the police station, people would have been arrested and charged with a criminal offense. But, of course, she was immediately stopped. Everyone said to her, "How could you possibly think of taking a family affair to the police?"

I was of a different opinion. I was so outraged that I said: "Let her go to the police. Don't you see that she is dead? Why cover up what happened? What will we do when she dies?"

But everyone urged her not to go. Her back was then covered with ashes, the traditional way of treating such a condition. Her body was all covered with wounds so that she had no place left to lie on; not a single spot. Nor did anyone give her proper nursing or feeding. Of course, when you had committed such a wrong or had a quarrel with Father, you suddenly turned into an animal in the eyes of the rest of the family members—a real animal shunned and avoided by everyone.

From time to time, I would take pity on her. I would go and bring her and her little daughter food. That was why she became so fond of me, even though she later became notorious for being a loner. She turned into an isolated person amid the crowds in the family. She no longer felt responsible for anybody, nor anybody for her. She created for herself a small insulated world within the family. How she managed to live that way is known only to her.

Shocking as it is, the incident should be judged in its social and cultural context, as an extreme example of what was otherwise a not uncommon practice in the family and the society at large. And it must not be forgotten that Deng Majok was not only an exceptionally jealous man but one who never doubted the supremacy of his power over others, especially women. As Nyanbol Amor testifies, his reaction to infidelity was an effective deterrent to the wives: "the overwhelming majority of his wives, some of whom died before him and most of whom survived him, all remained faithful to him and never betrayed him in any way." Indeed, given the numbers of the wives sharing one man, their loyalty to Deng Majok and to the integrity and the dignity of his family was astonishing.

Part 4: Diplomacy

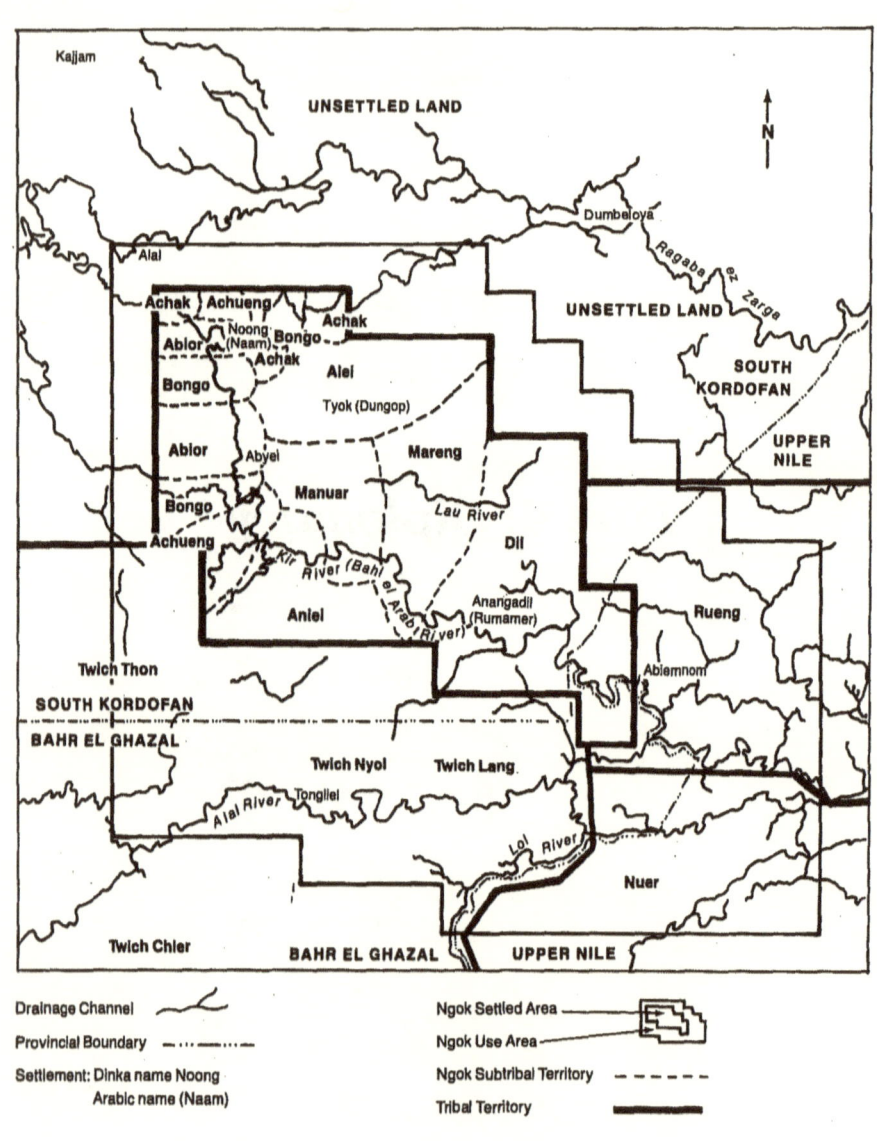

Map 4   Approximate Tribal Territories

14 Bridging North and South

In 1951, the British once more gave the Ngok the option of joining the South, a choice they had offered them under Chief Kwol Arob, Deng Majok's father. Deng Majok, like his father, opted to remain in the North. There is every reason to believe that he saw in his selective adoption and adaptation of certain aspects of Arab-Islamic civilization an opportunity for self-enhancement. But the accounts of all those who were interviewed—whether members of the family or strangers, Dinka or Arab, southerners or northerners—indicate that Deng Majok kept a delicate balance between the African South and the Arab North. His success in maintaining peace on the very difficult South-North borders was due largely to his evenhandedness in his relations with both sides. That he was a Dinka and therefore ethnically and culturally southern but chose to remain in the northern administrative context was the best evidence of this evenhandedness. But it was by no means an easy balance to maintain, and the general consensus seems to be that it was only the unique personal qualities of Deng Majok that enabled him to succeed so remarkably well.

In their attempt to persuade Deng Majok to join the South, the British used the good offices of the southern chiefs. Chief Giirdit, who had discussed the same issue with Deng's father, was among them. He was later to recall the circumstances:

> More recently, after you were born, we spoke with Deng Majok. We went and talked to him.... The British told him, "You are wanted by your people of the South." We were all gathered—the Chief of Ajuong [Yor Maker], Boldit, the family of Rian, and others. We talked a great deal. I said to your father, "You, Deng Majok... we discussed the matter with your father a long time ago. And your

father told me the truth then. But what my uncle told me no longer holds. We must now leave it and unite. We will make you our shield. And you cannot take our shield and turn it to the Arabs. That cannot be. You should come and be our shield!" We talked a great deal. Then we left the matter, hoping we would meet again to discuss it further.

The Arab elder Ibrahim El Hussein, a descendant of Azoza with whom Arob Biong had entered into a pact of friendship, gave this account of Deng Majok's consultation with them on the issue:

Deng consulted with us. He got on his horse. And with him were all the omdas and a number of sheikhs. Deng Thokloi [Deng Rahma, otherwise known as Ali Rahma] was in Muglad. He came with them. We were on the farm in the area called Ajbar. The crops were ripening. We poured in from the villages on the surrounding highland. We were told: "Deng Majok has come. Your brother, Ali Rahma, has brought him. They are camping on your farm on the pond."

When we heard that, we left early in the morning and went to them. We found them settled on the farm. I brought a bull with me, a fat young bull. I told the young men to slaughter it. It was slaughtered. The chiefs were seated. We went and brought grain from the farm for their horses.

As we left them to rest, Deng said to us, "I would like you all to come back this evening. I would like to talk to you." We came back, as he requested, with our fathers. He said to us, "I went to see the governor, the Englishman. And he said to me, 'The English are about to leave. Their period of rule in the Sudan is coming to an end.' And he said to me, 'Join the South.' I said to him, 'Why should I join the South?' And he said, 'Listen to my advice; join the South.' And he said to me, 'You see, you have a brother on the White Nile; he is going to be a member of the Senate.' I told him I was going to consult with my people. So I have come to seek your views. What is your opinion?"

Our fathers, who were elderly people, did not even understand what he was saying. "Son Deng," they said, "what sort of a thing are you saying?" I said, "Listen Deng, go and tell that Englishman who asked you to join the South that he found you a northerner. The English found us as brothers from a long way back. We were brothers when the Turkish government came. The Mahdiya also found us brothers. And when the English came, they found us sitting together on one rug. The South is not suited for you; it is not for you." We said a great deal to him.

In front of all the people assembled he said, "That is precisely my word." Malei, son of Kat, also spoke and said, "That is our word!" Omda Achwil spoke after him and said, "That is our word." And Abyiem, the father of this young man here [Tiglei] also said, "That is our word." All the eight chiefs of sections said the same thing. They said, "We are not going to the South." Deng then said, "Very well!

That was what I wanted. We are not going to the South. That is my opinion."

Matet Ayom also witnessed the developments:

> Before the English left, an administrator by the name of Mr. Owen called us and Deng Majok and Rahma, the interpreter. He said to Rahma, "Please, Rahma, tell Deng Majok that the English are going to leave. In the distant future, after we are gone, the Arabs will ill-treat you. So I suggest you join the administration of your people in the South. It is we the British who have brought the Arab and the Dinka together and made them become relatives. But when we leave, Babo will ill-treat you."
>
> Deng Majok answered: "Your honor, the words you have said are true. But that Babo will ill-treat me, even if it proves true, I cannot say now that it is true because I have not yet witnessed it. When you the British leave, it is not Babo who will assume responsibility for this country; it will be the leaders in Khartoum who will assume the responsibility. This land of mine I cannot abandon. This is the land of my ancestors. We do not know where the Arabs came from. But we can say when they came to this land. As for when we came to this land, the Arabs cannot know. It is the man who is found settled in a place who knows when the newly arrived came and where he came from."
>
> The British administrator said, "Well, I will let you travel through the South and acquaint yourself with that part of the country. I will let you visit Wau and visit Aweil and visit Gogrial. You go and travel around and meet your brothers there. If you find nothing that appeals to you, then come back and let me know."
>
> That is when Deng Majok called Chan Dau and called me, Matet, and called Achwil, three of us, and called Deng Angok, our police chief, and Malual Wol, a policeman, and Arol, another policeman. We left. The British Commissioner left before us and went to Wau. Then he sent us a car and spoke to the chiefs of the South saying, "If these people come, treat them well. Let their hearts turn toward you. They have been led astray by the Arabs. And they say they do not want to leave the North. I have turned their faces to you. Treat them well so that they will be happy with you.

On their way to the South, the delegation met with some Arabs from Kordofan. Among them was Tigani Mohamed Zein:

> I recall that in 1952, after my first visit to Wau [Bahr el Ghazal], I returned by car. When I reached the mission at Mayen, I met your father traveling by government car, and with him were tribal chiefs and elders. I met them there. Then he pulled me aside and asked me, "Are you coming from Wau?" I said "Yes." Then he said, "I have been asked by the District Commissioner to travel with my chiefs and elders to Wau to see our southern people." He said: "The English

want to take us to the South. What is your opinion on this issue? You have just been to the South yourself, what do you think?"

I said to him: "When a person seeks your opinion, you should give him your opinion. I have not studied the whole South, but I have traveled as far as Wau and have spent about a week there and have seen the conditions of the tribal chiefs. I believe that your position in the North is far better than their position in the South. And this is considering many things. If you joined them today, you would be a newcomer and they would not give you a role comparable to theirs. And yet your present level is far superior to theirs. And I believe that your future here is much brighter than their future. You have children being educated in the North and the whole country is clearly open to you. This is my personal opinion."

He said to me, "Thank you! What you have just said agrees entirely with what is deep inside me." This was exactly in 1952.

Matet Ayom recounted:

When we went to Aweil we were met from a long distance away, each person with his car. And when we got there, three bulls were slaughtered for us by the chiefs of Aweil. We spent six days at Aweil. Then we were sent and taken to Wau. We spent seven days at Wau and three bulls were slaughtered for us. Then we were taken to Nyinakok [Tonj]. After some time, Deng Majok said: "My area has remained alone for too long. And mine is an area lying on the borders of tribes. The Rek have now gone into my area to graze. And the Arabs have also gone to my area to graze. The Twich have also gone there. And Nuer and Ruweng are also there in my area. And it is I who am in charge. I must return." So we returned. Then your father posed the issue to his people. He said, "You people of my tribe, if you say you want to join the South, then a chief is only one man, you can pull me along and I shall go with you. If you do not want to go to the South, then tell me so that even if something formidable should confront you in the future, you will not blame me." Abyor said, "We want to join the South." Anyiel said, "We want to join the South." Diil said, "We want to join the South." Mannyuar said, "We want to join the South."

Then he asked us [Alei]. And what I am now saying is the truth, a truth witnessed by people who were there and are still here. People like Achwil witnessed it. We refused. We said to him: "Deng Majok, if you should join the South, we shall not go with you. We do not have a share of the river Kir; we do not have a share of the river Lol. Our share of the water is Ngol and Gok. We cannot join the South. The South is not our area."

He said to us: "You go to sleep. I shall raise the matter again tomorrow and we shall see then." That same night, Deng Majok came and woke us up, me, Aywel Mawan, Akuei Deng, Chol Akuei, Milang Deng Aguer, and Adhung Juet. He told us, "Hold to that position of yours. I like your word. I have seen the South. Should we join the South now, the black people will be harassed and reduced to a small entity. It is our path which stretches the height of the black people. And it is our path which guides the black people.

"And one day, should tragedy befall this country, the survival of the black people will start here at Abyei. The black people will not find their survival anywhere else. Should we abandon this land with all its blessings, our descendants will one day blame us."

That is how Deng Majok refused to join the South. He later declared to the people, "I will not go to the South. And if you should choose to go to the South, I shall not be your chief; you will have to find yourselves a chief to lead you there. Should some people remain here, however few, I shall remain to lead them. But I shall not keep you here by force."

Matet Ayom's words would seem to indicate that, at least to some Dinka, joining the South was viewed as synonymous with abandoning Ngokland and moving southward rather than as a mere shift in the channels of administration. On that understanding, Chol Adija recounted: "Deng said: 'I am not a man to tether my cattle on the fringes of a camp. I am now in the center of the camp. I shall not go to the fringes. What you [the English] want is to keep me on the periphery, to go and settle on the edge of the camp? That cannot be; I am remaining here.'"

To some people, by choosing to play a bridging role between North and South Deng Majok was simply continuing the tradition of his forefathers. His grandfather Arob had established the link; his father, Kwol, had taken a determining position; and, as Chol Piok put it, "Deng Majok decided to follow the word of his father."

"Deng told the southerners that he was already used to being with the northerners," said Mithiang Aguek. "He said that since his grandfather and father had managed to live with the Arabs, he too would continue to live with them. Although the southerners were his kith and kin, he had an obligation inherited from his father and grandfather to continue in the North."

"No one abandons the word of his father," concluded Chol Adija.

Chief Babo defended the unity of the Missiriya Arabs and the Ngok Dinka on the same grounds. "The relationship between the Ngok Dinka and the Missiriya, in particular the Homr, is one that predates me and Deng. It predates even our fathers and our grandfathers. It is a relationship that goes back a long way. Our fathers came and found this relationship prevailing. And we came and found the relationship prevailing." Babo went on to give an account of how the British unsuccessfully urged Deng Majok to join the South:

> They [Deng and his chiefs] came back [from the South] convinced that the situation they had here in the North did not exist there. Their situation here was far better. As soon as they returned, they met

my brother Ali on the way. "O Ali! Congratulations! Congratulations!" They were congratulating Ali. That was their way of saying: "We are now convinced that it is in our interest to remain here with you; it is in our interest. We do not want to join the South, not at all."

So Deng was with us one hundred percent. He had no problem at all.

We are certain that the bond between us was in large measure due to Deng Majok. The strong cordial ties which prevailed between the Arabs and the Dinka Ngok during the last phase were very much due to the brotherhood between me and Deng Majok.

Ibrahim Mohamed Zein recalled an incident during Deng Majok's visit to the Arab town of Muglad in 1952 or 1953; while in Muglad, Deng Majok called on the school and made generous financial gifts to the students. But more came of the visit, as Ibrahim recollects:

> Before the end of his visit to Muglad, some people came to the school with a bull and a lamb. They said the animals were from Deng Majok; the bull was for the pupils and the lamb was for the teachers. We, the teachers, met and decided to pay a courtesy call to the chief in his house to thank him for what he had done. So, I went to him accompanied by a number of teachers, Abdalla Abdel Karim, and Fawzy Mohmoud. We went to Dafaa where the chief was sitting under the tree, and next to him sat the man now talking to us, Dr. Francis Deng, and his brother Dr. Zachariah Deng. They were all seated there. Three bulls had been slaughtered for the public and were being skinned. A public dance was in progress. He received and greeted us very warmly. And we thanked him for his generosity to the school. I recall his precise words to us: "The English have tied my neck with a turban and they are pulling me while they chant, 'South, South.' I, on my part, I am pulling myself the opposite direction chanting, 'North, North.'" He said, "I am doing all that in order to find people like you and schools like yours for our children; so that they can learn. So I have done nothing that calls for your thanks." We spent a very pleasant time with him.

Ibrahim El Hussein believes that Deng Majok chose to remain in the North because of the recognition and respect he enjoyed there:

> Here in the North, Deng was highly respected by the government of the English and highly regarded by the Arabs as a leader. I do not know what the situation was in the South, but in the North he was highly regarded. When an Arab woman saw him pass by, she would take pleasure in greeting him, "Chief Deng, peace be upon you." They knew him very well—all the Arabs, the Ajaiyra and the Felaita. They regarded him highly.

According to Chief Lang Juuk, so did the central government in the North under the British:

> Deng Kwol was under the same jurisdiction as the Arab chiefs,

and the British used to respect the Arab chiefs. When a Britisher visited an Arab chief, the chief did not go where the Britisher was putting up to greet him. The Britisher went to the chief in his house to greet and converse with him. When they returned to the sleeping place, the chief in turn went to their place and conversed with them. This was not the same way the British stayed here in the South. Southern chiefs were not respected much.

The British liked Chief Deng Kwol and he also liked them. He understood things very quickly. Whatever the British wanted to convey to the people, he understood it quickly. In discussions he contributed ideas that helped to clarify the issues. That is why the British liked him.

Monyluak Row stressed other practical considerations behind Deng Majok's decision. "Deng Majok used to say that he could not join the South because the standard of living of the people of the South was not as good as that of the people of the North. The reason why your father liked the people of the North was because of the things we wear, these clothes. There was nothing else. Where people told us to go had little to offer."

Nyanjur elaborated on the attraction of the North for her father in this way: "You see, Mading, it was Father's own efforts that made Abyei what it is today as a town. And how did he do that? It was not because of his relations with the South; it was because of his relations with the North. That was how Abyei came to build shops, a dispensary, schools, and other services. Father left Abyei in a 'Thank God!' situation. All that was the result of his relationship with the Arabs."

But according to Nyanbol Amor, Deng's preference for the North was only a matter of degree, for he felt a sense of belonging to both areas:

> He was able to combine them both, the South and the North, though the North was a little more favored by him. Most of his activities outside his tribe were toward the North, but he also maintained friendship with southern chiefs, with whom he met periodically. And those among the southerners who knew him well were not disturbed by his close relations with the Arabs because they realized that he benefited the Dinka through those relations.

In fact, perhaps the most central element in Deng Majok's position was the importance of the bridging role he saw himself playing between the South and the North. This was stressed by Chol Adija: "Deng said, 'I am now the thread of the Arabs and the South. I am a thread like the thread with which clothes are mended. If I pull away, the country will break apart. And if that robber [the Arab] jumps across the River, it would not be good.'" As Chol Adija indicates, Deng Majok felt that by remaining in the North and playing a bridging role, he would be in a better position to provide protection for his own people, the Ngok, and his fellow southerners, as indeed both his father Kwol and grandfather Arob had done. As Chol Piok put it:

Whenever anything wrong was done to us and our chief got up to ask, he was given a remedy. Whenever our people were captured, they were collected by the Arab chiefs and given back to our chief. And even if the people captured were from the Twich, the Rek, the Ruweng, the Nuer, or any other people from the South, Kwol Arob would come to the North and collect them. He would say, "They are all my people, the people of my father Arob."

"Deng Kwol was like a guard at a gate between the Arabs and the Dinka," said Chief Chier Rian of the Adiang Twich Dinka. "He was the Dinka voice among the Arabs. He felt that if he moved from the Arabs, the Dinka would have nobody looking out for them among the Arabs. That is why Deng Kwol remained in the North. It was not because of his love for the Arabs. No! His interest was for the Dinka."

"You see, Mading," explained Pagwot, "when your father refused to join the South, he was being clever, he was calculating. It was a clever way of doing things. He would say one thing to the northerners and say another thing to the southerners. Whenever the Arabs came and spoke about the laws of marriage, he would say, 'I am just on the border and since I am on the border, I will pay my taxes to you, but as to the question of marriage and our customs, we belong to the South."

Malith Mawien agrees that Deng Majok's refusal to join the South was a ploy in favor of the South. "Deng Majok said that if he came to the South, the Arabs would be frightened by our unity and would treat us as strangers. If anything that belonged to us were plundered, nobody could reclaim it. The Arabs would say that we are aliens. 'But now that I am on the border, they fear me. If I went to reclaim something that belonged to the Twij, the Nuer, or the Malual, they would say that Deng was the person responsible on the border." "At this point," observed Malith Mawien, "I cannot comment on whether the Ngok should come here to the South or not. What I can say is that the descendants of Arob Biong are well known as the people who guarded our borders with the Arabs. It was they who guided the ship in that area."

Shortly after Deng Majok's decision to remain in the North, the Missiriya Rural Council was established, with its headquarters at Rigl El Fulah, to include the Missiriya Homr (The Brown Missiriya), the Missiriya Zurug (The Dark Missiriya), and the Ngok Dinka, a third category humorously termed Missiriya El Tawil (The Tall Missiriya). As Ibrahim Mohamed Zein recalled, Deng Majok soon distinguished himself in the council through his unity line:

> I used to hear a great deal about his personality, and among the most prominent things I heard about him was when they came to form the Missiriya Rural Council after it had been disaffiliated from Nahud. Some of the things that had been said in the meetings were being repeated on the streets. And among the things that were said to have been said by Deng Majok to Nazir Babo Nimir was: "Here I am;

I do not want wealth; and I do not need people. But I consider my being in Abyei for the Sudan as a whole to be like a needle and a thread which binds the two parts of the *toub*[1] into one piece."

These words were said in a meeting, but they circulated outside and had considerable effect on people. It made people look to Chief Deng Majok as a great leader and thinker.

"As the paramount chief of the whole District of Missiriya," observed Ali,

Babo [Nimir] was supposed to be senior to all the chiefs, including Father, Serrer, Ali Nimir, and Izzeldin Hemeda. These were the chiefs of the respective tribes, and Babo was their paramount chief. Babo was the appellate authority for all the appeals from Arab chiefs. His jurisdiction was also supposed to include appeals from Father's court. But Father completely refused to have appeals from his court heard by Babo. He wanted his appeals to go directly to the central authorities. In the end, things went Father's way. Appeals from his court never went before Babo; they went directly to the District Commissioner, who was then also the judge, totally rejecting any notion of Babo being senior to him.

Pagwot, the chief of Bongo and one of the senior members of Deng Majok's administration, confirmed this: "We said, 'We are a separate tribe. Izzeldin and Serrer are the people whose appeals Babo can hear, but our appeals he will never hear.' We argued about that. That decided our situation. Deng Majok's appeals never went to Babo."

Not only did Deng Majok object to Dinka appeals being heard by Babo Nimir, he "would never accept being placed in a subordinate status," to use Ali's words. In the view of some people, Deng Majok much preferred remaining in the North because being a Dinka chief among Arabs would give him a unique status that was superior to being classified as either a northerner or a southerner.

Charles Biong elaborated on his father's sense of pride as a Dinka in the northern context:

I would say that Father paid great attention to his position as a Dinka in an area where the bulk of the inhabitants were Arabs. He was always stressing, in every move he made, that he had a special status. And he really used that to the best of his ability. Every single time he found difficulty breaking through, he would draw the attention of the authorities to the fact that he was not racially or culturally part of Kordofan's administration. This was especially the case whenever there was an issue which required the approval of the majority in the district. If he felt that something would prejudice Dinka interests, especially in matters of tradition and custom, he would always draw the attention of the administration to the fact,

---

1. The sari-like Arab dress.

arguing that he should not be regarded as a member of the same cultural group as the other tribes or be required to adhere to the cultural ways of the other members of the district. But he would never lag behind in matters that required the full representation of his tribe as a separate entity. He was very firm on those matters. He never gave up the fundamental cultural identity and values of the Dinka.

And yet, according to Biong, Deng Majok was fully integrated into the Arab context: "To confirm that he was fully accepted into the northern community or the district, he was elected president of the Council by the Arabs in the district. And this indicates that his maneuvering was as good as any other person's in the district."

That incident, in which the Arab chiefs rebelled against their paramount chief by supporting, indeed engineering, Deng Majok's election as president, was the climax in the political rivalry between Babo Nimir and Deng Majok. It was a blow that won Babo some sympathy from the leadership in the province headquarters and the national capital, Khartoum, so that he was appointed to the Province Council despite his defeat. And yet Deng Majok's election by the Arab majority was, and has remained, a symbol of his stature as a hero of national unity between the South and the North. It is also one of the rare examples of magnanimity shown by a majority toward a minority leader, a gesture badly needed to foster unity.

Through his unflinching defense of his people, his self-assertiveness as a Dinka among Arabs, and his acceptance by the Arabs not only as an equal but even as a leader of their combined Dinka-Arab council, Deng Majok gave the Ngok much to be proud of, even though they were a minority in the northern Arab context. Mithiang Agwek, somewhat sarcastically, contrasted what he viewed as the oppressive domestic policy of Deng Majok with his protective policies in his relations with leaders of other tribes or officials of the central government:

> Deng Majok was good. What was particularly good about him was that he protected his area against any outsiders. But he did it like a hen that fights fiercely to protect her eggs against invaders. Then, once the outside danger is gone, the same hen breaks the shells and drinks the eggs. The same thing happened with Deng Majok. He could not tolerate any offense against his people or his land. But he always felt free to choose whatever he wanted; not everything, but some things and sometimes.

Deng Majok was not only a defender of his people against outsiders; he also protected all the peoples of the neighboring tribes who came into his territory, whether by granting permission to graze or letting them benefit from the Ngok market, which offered more opportunities for buying or selling. In the words of the Arab elder Ibrahim El Hussein: "Deng kept the Arabs in one hand and the Dinka in the other hand. He protected the Dinka and he protected the Arabs. He guided the Arabs with words of wisdom as he guided the Dinka. And the Arabs fully accepted his word. The Arabs looked to Babo's chieftainship only when they were back in Arabland. But when they were in Dinkaland, their chief was Deng Majok."

According to another Arab elder, Abdalla Hamadein, it was indeed Babo Nimir who initially directed his people to look to Deng as their chief:

When Deng Majok became the nazir, Babo said to the Arabs, "You people, go over there; you have a nazir over there in addition to your nazir here." Thereafter Babo stopped coming here to look after his people. He would only come on official occasions. Otherwise, he left the Arabs under the authority of Deng Majok. Deng Majok had influence even within Babo's inner circles. This was particularly the case in the Council, which was a form of parliament similar to the Assembly which you now have in this country. In that parliament, Deng Majok won over Babo among the Arabs. People left Babo and voted for Deng Majok to be the president. Did you not know that? And it was all because of Deng's qualities as a leader.

Even though he and Deng Majok became rivals, Babo Nimir himself confirmed Deng's popularity among the Arabs:

When Deng became chief, we found what we had hoped for in him. By God, we in our area had not the slightest doubt that no man who went before Deng Majok would ever leave feeling that he had been treated unjustly. Deng would give him full justice. With Deng Majok, we felt assured of the protection our people would get whenever they went there.

There, on the river, whenever there were problems among my own Arab tribes, I would send for him and he and I would get together to solve the problems. And the Arabs would accept his word. He was very highly respected by the Arabs.

Under Deng Majok, as Malith Mawien observed:

Neighboring tribes would go to Ngok area with their cattle and return without any incident. The Nuer went and were not robbed; the Twich of Lang Juk were not robbed; the Twich of Awic Ayuel were not robbed; the Rek of Yor Maker were not robbed; the Rek of Makuac Kuol were not robbed; the Rek of Aguer Geng were not robbed. They all returned in good condition. The cows, too, returned in good condition. Not a single cow remained behind—no cow was said to have been taken by the Ngok. If a cow remained behind, it was a cow eaten by a lion. If a cow remained behind, it was a cow killed by disease.

In the past, Arabs did not used to come here to the Lol River with their cattle. But Deng Majok said that the land was one. The Twich could go with their cattle to the Ngol River, and the Arabs could go with their cattle to Warliet on the Lol.

"Deng Majok was a great leader," remarked Atem Moter.

It was he who held the country together. He subdued the Arabs. He tightened his grip on the situation. We, the Twich, were no longer subjected to the kind of treatment that used to be imposed on us by the Ngok.

With Deng Kwol, we were all his people, the people of Rian, the people of Bol Chol, and the people of Ayuel Longar. We were all his people. We were part of the Ngok. If we were attacked, the Ngok came to our defense. The way Deng watched over all of us endeared him to the Twich, to the Abiem, and to the Nuer. If a man wanted to take his cattle for sale in the market, it was to the land of Deng Kwol that he would go. If there should be a shortage of food, grain would come from the land of Deng Kwol. And whenever the Twich went to Abyei to buy things from the market, if an Arab tried to cheat the people by inflating prices, Deng Majok would immediately close down his shop. So, while the Arab shopkeepers were cheating people here in the South, Deng Majok never allowed them to do so in Abyei. It was because of Deng Majok that our people had food aplenty.

Deng Majok also cultivated close personal relations with the leaders of the neighboring tribes. After the death of Deng Majok and shortly before his own death, Babo was to say: "As for my relationship with Deng Majok, by God, no other relationship can exceed it except perhaps that with my own brother, Ali. We were absolutely together. This brought the Arabs and the Dinka close together. Our relationship with Deng Majok made the Dinka and the Arabs become closely tied with one another."

Chol Piok elaborated on the theme of Deng Majok's relations with his neighbors:

From the time he became chief, Deng Majok never quarreled with other chiefs; no chief could file a complaint against him. It was he who would mediate between other chiefs. Cases used to be brought all the way from Gogrial to be settled here in Abyei. Cases would be brought by people of Mading Aweil to be settled in Abyei. Cases would be brought even from Nuerland; Nuer chiefs used to come here to Abyei.

And all those chiefs would find cattle waiting. Every court member and every clan head would be asked to bring an animal. Food would be plentiful. Our plans were never made on the spur of the moment. People would be told about them two months in advance. And people would begin to gather things. And then the Assembly would meet. Deng Majok would be found to have prepared everything. Nothing at all would be lacking. The huge baskets of the Dinka would be found filled with fermented flour for beer. They would all be lined up and lined up and lined up.

And when the Assembly met, beer would be brewed by the women all over the land. Those who knew how to cook Arab food would also be hard at work, preparing special Arab food. Of course, special delicacies and Arab food were no longer sought after in the home of any other person. They would come out of Deng Majok's house. The wives of Deng Majok had all learned from Amel. Not a single woman would cook embarrassing food. The food produced would be enough for days without end. Also, bulls would have been slaughtered for meat. These are some of the things the southern tribes liked about Deng Majok.

And when the Assembly sat for people to talk and cases were considered, he would be made the judge in those major cases of war from the Twich. And the war cases from the Rek he would also settle. And the cases between the Rek or the Twich with the Arabs he would also settle. And then he would reconcile them and make peace between them.

When the chiefs came to leave, each of them would receive a bag, and each a bag, and each a bag—bags of money. He would distribute all that money to the chiefs of the Rek, the Twich, the Nuer, and the others. He would then take them into the market. Each one would buy the things of his heart and each one the things of his heart and each one the things of his heart. Tea would be bought by those chiefs to be loaded onto the heads of the carriers. There would be no room in the shops for our Ngok Dinka on the day the Assembly ended.

After the southern Chiefs had left, the Arabs would not leave the same day. They would usually stay so that we could hold our own separate meetings afterward to understand our words alone with them. We would then rediscuss all the significant matters, including those that had been discussed with the southern chiefs. Any chief of the South who had told the truth, we would then consider our view of what he had said; and the person who had said something wrong, we would then consider our own view of what he had said. The Arab chiefs would again be given their gifts before they left.

Those were the things that held us together.

And indeed, it is generally agreed that hospitality and generosity were among the instruments of Deng's policy in his relations with leaders of other tribes and government officials. As Nyanjur observed:

What was really the nature of his relationship with the Arabs? It was due to the warm way he received them and the lavish hospitality he showed them. Whenever any representative of the government came, he was taken very good care of; he would have to acknowledge that he was visiting a significant area. And what is more, Father's mind was such that if he had any shortcoming at all, it was only not knowing how to read and write. But even then, you would hardly ever see anything lacking in him because of his lack of education.

Nyanjur proceeded to illustrate by describing the visit of Saadig El Mahdi when he was prime minister:

When he arrived at home in Abyei, he visited our family. When he came, really Mading, the shelters that had been built were carpeted and furnished in a manner not that different from this house of yours. The carpeting and the furnishings were so impressive that your house surpasses it only because it contains things that cannot be obtained here in the Sudan. The shelters were thatched with grass. Then mats were placed over the grass. And the whole thing was curtained inside and outside. The ground was fully covered with beautiful carpets; several layers were placed on the floor. First there were the *mushamaa* [waterproof] sheets. Then there were layers of heavy materials to cushion the floors. And last, soft carpets were placed on top. On the walls were curtains of transparent, weblike material of very fine fabric. The only thing lacking to make it comparable to any place in Khartoum was electricity.

That was the way Saadig El Mahdi was received. And that was the only occasion when Father permitted his wives to come out and see. He said, "I want you to come and see what I have done for my guests." All those materials were cut up after his death. We turned them into skirts and bed sheets. Some of the fabrics even went back to the shops. Saadig was first met and received in the public square. And then in the evening he was brought to our house. It was at home that the moving picture was displayed.

It was things like that which Father did for the leaders of the Sudan that won him great admiration, so if he wanted anything from the government it would immediately be granted. Besides, they recognized a great deal of wisdom in his words. They realized that there was something in what he offered them and from which they could learn. And this happened in every meeting Father attended. There was not a single meeting in which Father's name did not figure very prominently. And that was because of the great words of wisdom he would utter in the meeting.

The Ngok Dinka, particularly, miss Deng Majok's role in their negotiations with the leaders of other tribes. Ajuong gave some insight into the way Deng Majok prepared his people for confrontations at intertribal discussions of problems:

Whenever a problem came from outside, such as the problems we now have with the Arabs, the conflict would end with your father's words. He would see the truth in the words of his people: this man and that man and that man and yet that man. He would privately talk to all those whose words he saw as reflecting the truth. All those words would be communicated to him and he would eventually reproduce them as his own words. Then he would add to all that his unique qualities, which everybody recognized.

In the words of Chol Adija:

When Deng Majok was alive, no one except him would speak on

foreign matters. It was he alone who spoke. He would be told everything: That this happened here; that this incident occurred there; that this or that had happened. But when we met with leaders from other tribes, he would be the only one to speak. And no leader from any other tribe could defeat him! His words always revealed the truth. Deng Majok was never judged to be in the wrong. Until his death, he never lost a case. His word was always the word on which any case ended.

"The government accepted him fully as the chief," commented Achwil Bulabek.

Deng Majok made a classic statement. Chier Rian and Lang were complaining: "Why is it that Deng Majok's word is always taken to be the truth? All governments that come always see truth in the words of Deng Majok, whether in Wau or anywhere else." Deng then said: "Gentlemen, how can you complain when it is you who can write and read? Did I not tell you that words can be exchanged on paper but they will eventually be pronounced by the tongue? Now that you who can write and read complain about my words being accepted as reflecting the truth, you have brought peace to my heart."

Atem Moter, after giving the leadership genealogy of the Pajok and their role on the South-North border, went on to say: "When it came to your father, it was he who said to the chiefs of the Twich who had broken away from the authority of his father, Kwol, and established themselves as independent powerful chiefs, that a gentleman who once threw your father down [in a wrestling contest] can no longer throw you down—you, the son of the man he had thrown down. Deng Majok said to them, 'Do not compare me with my father.'"

As Chief Madut Ring indicates, Deng Majok's ambition was to restore the Twich tribes which his father had lost to the South:

> He used to say that the area called Kuach and Lang's area belonged to his father. He said he wanted to regain his father's territories before he could join the South. He did not say it halfheartedly. He said it with complete resolve. When Deng Majok died, Lang and I took a bull each to sacrifice on his grave because we regarded him as our own chief. When a chief of another tribe dies, would people from another area take bulls to his funeral if they did not have a very special liking for him? No! They would not. We took bulls and sacrificed them on his grave because he was our chief.

In the words of Atem Moter: "He indeed protected our land from there until he fell. And when he died, that was when I said to Malual Giernyang that with the death of Deng Kwol, true destruction by the Arabs had now emerged. The like of Deng Majok will never be found again. There are men whose voices are well-oiled to charm others into obedience. Deng was such a man."

It was perhaps during the South-North civil war of 1955–72 that Deng Majok's identity as a southerner and his hostility toward his northern neighbors became conspicuously manifest. For a considerable part of the war, Ngok area remained sheltered from its effects, and to a large extent was the only secure area in the southern cultural-ethnic-geographic complex. However, as the war continued to intensify, the Ngok began to sympathize and identify more and more with the South, and some of their young men began to join the military wing of the southern movement—the Anyanya—and even assumed leading positions in the struggle. During the mid-sixties, rumors began to reach Abyei that the Anyanya might attack. This naturally heightened the anxiety of the Arabs. One incident after another continued to fan the fire of hostility, but the Dinka-Homr war of 1965 was triggered by what the Ngok saw as a brutal insult of their fellow Dinka when the Arabs killed a Rek man, amputated his arms, and used them to beat their drums. The Ngok could not control themselves in the face of that gross violation of the dignity of a fellow Dinka. They attacked the Homr Arabs, thereby starting a conflict that soon assumed the form of a South-North battlefront. Several hundred people, and many estimate a lot more, lost their lives. As it was during the dry season, when the Arabs were on their seasonal migration southward, the war was fought on Ngok soil and the Arabs suffered defeat. In retaliation, Dinkas in the North suffered death under more brutal and inhuman conditions, first being locked up in prisons for protection, which then, at least in two places, were set on fire, killing all inside—men, women, and children. Chief Pagwot addresses himself to this bitter aspect of Ngok-Arab conflict:

> Now that we are here, if we fight with these people in Khartoum, will they take people to be burned inside government prisons to which they were taken for protection, including children who were three months old, who had said nothing wrong? Is this the behavior of people who are related? No! These are brothers only by order of the government—now that the government has come. A person burning a child of three months in a hut, can you be happy with him? But the country is the country of the government; nobody can say anything.

Deng Majok, loyal to law and order, cooperated with the authorities to restore peace. Eventually a reconciliation was reached between him and the Arab chiefs. The then minister of justice went to the area and ruled that the Dinka should move southward across the river Kir (Bahr el Arab), to minimize the chances of further clashes between the tribes. Deng Majok is reported by Biong as having responded to the minister in a fury with his famous chant, "My bull Marial has mounted his mother!" and having ordered his interpreter, Achier, to translate his words literally. Achier, not used to translating such expressions, aggravated the situation by saying, "Chief Deng says his bull Marial has mounted your mother," using a four-letter word in the place of *mounted*. Deng Majok then proceeded to pose a question to the minister: "If a conflict should arise between the owner of a house and his guest, which one should leave the place, the owner or his guest?"

Deng Majok's rhetorical question and his obvious anger ended the issue: the Ngok were unquestionably the owners of the land, and the Missiriya nomads were herding there by permission of the Ngok.

Ibrahim Mohamed Zein recalled that Deng Majok worked very hard to restore law and order.

> A delegation went from here [Khartoum] comprising Rasheed El Tahir and Ahmed Jubara El Awad. They went and held a very large meeting among the tribal leaders in order to reach a peace settlement. There was, of course, bitterness in the speeches, but the end result was commitment to the unity of the country and a reaffirmation of his leaning toward the North. His attitude had a considerable effect on the restoration of peace and stability. The result was a recognition of strong bonds between the Dinka and the Arabs.

The peace conference that was to reconcile the two parties was convened later. Pending the conference, Tigani Mohamed Zein bore witness to the depressed mood Deng Majok was in then:

> We came to Abyei at that time. My brother Ibrahim was the headmaster then. The situation was extremely difficult. The deterioration was immense. Muhktar El Tayeb happened to be on a trip to see the elections there. So we joined him. Then we left on our way back. I believe the time was about five thirty in the morning. I was with Muhktar El Tayeb in the car. He said, "Let us pass by Deng Majok's house! Let us see whether he is up or not." We went and found him awake and sitting in his courthouse, and with him were his tribal elders and with them was Abdullai Dugal from the Arabs. Only Abdullai was with them from the Arabs. Muhktar El Tayeb greeted him and said, "Chief Deng, I am now leaving. I came to see the situation and must now go to report to the governor. I thought I should stop to bid you farewell."
>
> He said, "I would like you to take a message to the governor. Please tell him that I say: 'Here we are afflicted with a problem that has burned down a large number of villages. Many people have left for the northern towns. There is no grain and there are no homes to live in. We want him to let us know whether we should build on our old spots or in new areas. And tell him that whether we build our homes to the south or the north of the river Kir, we will still remain in Kordofan; whatever the number of deaths or the burning of villages, we are in Kordofan and nobody is going to force us out of Kordofan.' Just tell the governor that."

Apparently, at the peace conference the Arabs claimed that the fertile northeast area of Ngokland known as Ngol was theirs, and that point gravely offended the Dinka. Matet later recaptured the mood of the tense discussions that ensued at the conference:

> When Deng and Babo were disputing the place called Ngol, Deng said, "You, Babo, this land is not yours. Your ancestors in this area do not reach ten, while my ancestors go at least that far. Which of us therefore found the other on this land?" That was the case which was seen at Alagawa. The president of the court was Moneim Mansour.[2] Those present included El Tayeb Haroun and Abdel Gabar and Mohamed Timsah; they were the chiefs the District Commissioner had convened. Ngol became established as ours. But Deng's contention was that he should swear with Babo over Denga [Muglad] itself.

Matet was even more ambitious in his territorial claims for the Dinka:

> This man called the Arab is unknown to us. This man called the Baggara came from the French territories to the west. In fact, to this day, nomads still come from those French territories. Why we are now required to produce nationality certificates is not because of us, the Dinka; it is because of the Arabs who keep coming from the west. That is why the government requires nationality certificates. We the Dinka do not come from anywhere; the country is ours; we are the owners of this country.[3]

The evidence of Ibrahim Mohamed Zein reveals the extent to which the northerners were convinced that only Deng Majok among the Dinka could represent the interests of both sides even during times of racial animosity:

> I was in the car with Mukhtar El Tayeb on the trip when, as I told you before, we met Deng Majok early in the morning. After leaving Deng Majok, we found Arabs on the way. Mubhtar El Tayeb said to them, "Here I am leaving, what I want to tell you and ask you to tell every Arab who might not understand the situation well, is that Deng Majok is the only person who binds the South and the North together. If we lose Deng Majok, it means that we will have lost this vital link and God only knows what things will happen."[4]

Ironically, because Deng Majok continued to identify himself with the

---

2. Chief of the Hamar of Western Kordofan, headquarters at Nahud.
3. The Dinka are among the few ethnic groups without branches in any of the neighboring countries.
4. In his book *Baggara Arabs* (Oxford: Clarendon Press, 1966), viii, Ian Cunnison wrote of the hostilities: "The trouble dates back to the rains of 1964, and is said to be connected with the activities of the Southern Sudanese rebels. They are particularly tragic because the Dar Missiriya Rural Council had been a sphere of apparently friendly and fruitful cooperation between the North and South of the country." K. D. D. Henderson, commenting on the widespread South-North hostilities of 1964–65, noted: "Even the prototypes of North-South Cooperation, the Ngok and the Missiriya Homr, had come to blows" (*The Sudan Republic*, 218).

North for calculated strategic reasons despite his bitterness against the Arabs, Ibrahim Mohamed Zein contends that this in itself was evidence of his love for the North and his dedication to national unity: "I can truly testify to the fact that Deng Majok was a man whose sense of national unity and love for the North remained strong even in the most critical moments of relations between the Dinka and the Arabs."

After the 1965 Ngok-Missiriya hostilities, Deng Majok, in order to guarantee peace, called in security forces, but he still saw to it that they did not usurp tribal power and turn their existence into a military occupation, as had been the case in the South since the civil war began. In due course, he had to play the high-risk game of maintaining cordial relations with both the security forces and the rebel army without compromising his integrity to either party. All this left him politically anxious but unscathed; indeed, it enhanced his already monumental image and made him a heroic leader even to his opponents within the Ngok and to the tribes further south.

Atem Moter gives some insight into the kind of protection Deng guaranteed the South on his borders, even during this most critical period:

> When the civil war was rampant here, and Chier was in the North, and the Anyanya were dispersing the chiefs here and Monywiir was pursuing them, Monyror went and settled in the home of Deng Kwol with his cattle. Those were the cattle that survived the Anyanya. And in those days, one could never count on surviving. But Monyror survived with his herd because of Deng Kwol. Eventually, when he returned, Deng Kwol gathered all those Arab soldiers and had him escorted by horses. They brought him through the forest where the Anyanya had been rampant. They came right through, and the Anyanya dispersed away as they approached. They brought him and placed him safely in his home. What other goodness would you want from a chief? Here was a chief who protected another chief in hard times and had him returned with glory! Great celebrations were held here for Monyror when he returned. What more would people want?
>
> All the chiefs had lost heart in the South. People like Arob Malith who are now still alive owe their lives to Deng Kwol. And Madut Tor is still alive because of Deng Kwol.

According to Babo Nimir, with the intensification of the civil war things got to be extremely difficult for Deng Majok: "Toward the end, when the children entered into rebellion, it became a question of conflict between competing loyalties. As the expression goes: 'O my back; O my stomach!' He could not admit that the children were rebels and out of his control; nor could he crack down on them. The situation became very difficult for him; it was extremely difficult."

Mijak (Osman) intimates that his father's relations with the South were so good that "even during the period of the civil war he was not uncooperative with the Anyanya." And according to Mithiang Agwek:

> When Deng was alive, and the Anyanya used to be around, at any time he heard that the Anyanya were planning something, he would secretly send some cows to the Anyanya with a message asking them to retreat farther away from the area, so that people would not be killed on the ground that they had collaborated with the Anyanya. He used to caution the Anyanya to keep away from the people to avoid implicating them and say that he was ready to meet their demands short of personal contact with them. But once Deng Majok was dead, all those who used to fear him rose up and started reporting individuals as Anyanyas and had them arrested by the Arabs. Such practices disrupted the peace of the area, and many people died. I assure you, if Deng Majok had been alive, the killing of innocent people would never have taken place.

Nyanjur gave this account of the delicate and precarious balance her father had to keep between the security forces and the southern rebel army, the Anyanya:

> When the Anyanya began to be active in our area, if our father had not had relations with the Anyanya, he would have been killed. Whenever he heard that the Anyanya had come, he would send a secret messenger to the Anyanya and would send them food quite secretly. No one would know what he was doing. That was one of the reasons why our father never came into conflict with the Anyanya. Because he was in contact with them, whatever else he might say or do, they realized that he recognized them and was mindful of them. Publicly, whenever he heard that the Anyanya had come, he would go looking for them with the security forces.

But as the South-North war intensified and extended into his area, Deng Majok became increasingly vexed about the fate of his border area. According to Achai-Chol, "That was what made him become ill; it was the heart talking that gave him the disease which eventually killed him." Ironically, he was one of the mediators in a peace conference between the Dinka of the South and the Rezeigat Arabs of Darfur when he began to feel the symptoms of his terminal liver cancer, which had spread into his lungs. And even then, he obviously expected to be the star and experienced hurt pride when outside comments focused on the contribution of a southern chief. Nyanjur recalled:

> When people went for the peace conference between the Arabs and the Malual Dinka, a southern chief called Yol Madeng came to the meeting. After the meeting, everybody was commenting on Yol Madeng's words. Yol was reported to have said in the meeting: "I would like to know the meaning of the Arabic word *Malesh* ["Never mind," or "Forget it"]; why do the Arabs always commit a wrong and then say *Malesh*, even when they have committed the wrong intentionally? What exactly is the significance of the word *Malesh*? I would really like to know."

The Dinka were very pleased with Yol Madeng for those words. Everybody kept mentioning the name of Yol Madeng. Father had not spoken much. The fame that Yol Madeng derived from the meeting vexed him a great deal. That was the year before he died. He said, "My people, I must be afflicted with something that will soon surface. In my entire life, since I became chief, no meeting has ever been held, whether in the South or in the North, that ended without my words being the talk of everyone. In this meeting, it is Yol Madeng whose words drew everyone's attention. I do not believe I am going to live much longer."

Deng Majok was right; he did not have long to live.

Part 5: Tragedy

15 The End to Glory

Deng Majok's death in August 1969 was a tragedy not only for the Ngok Dinka but also for their neighbors to the south and north.

Ali, who was a policeman at the time, heard the news of his father's death while under detention for having extended his leave to be with him when he was in the hospital in El Obeid. His thoughts on hearing the news reflected concerns that were shared by many:

> When I heard the message, my mind began to wander. I thought back to the tribe and wondered how the Ngok could survive without Father. And who could take his place? And would anyone be able to show the same abilities and wisdom as our father had on matters pertaining to the tribe and its borders? Then I would reflect on our numbers in the family and how our father had maintained such a large family: he was the only one who knew all the family sources of wealth. He knew where his cattle came from; it was he who knew how to manage the affairs of the family; it was he who knew how to talk to his wives and children to resolve conflicts and keep them united. Who could replace him? The more I thought, the more I realized the magnitude of the problems and the difficulties that would confront us.
>
> I also thought of the differences that could flare up again. For instance, would the family of Abiong [Deng Abot's faction] come up to claim the chieftainship again or would the Sacred Spears be contested once more? Those were the thoughts that ran through my mind. And as I reflected I realized that Father's death had left us with a monumental set of problems.

And indeed, during Deng Majok's absence on account of his illness, the situation in Abyei had already taken a turn for the worse. Awor Kwol, Deng

Majok's sister, had been tortured and crippled by the security forces because her son was a local rebel leader. Anyiel Kwol, Deng Majok's half-brother, had just been killed after having been badly tortured. The family had gathered in Abyei for the mourning. Nyanjur recalled:

> We were told that there would be a security inspection the following day. Our mother [Father's wife], Amel, said to us, "You girls know how to write and read, would you please look into your father's papers. Your father used to receive letters from the South and from other sources. If anything is found which is suspicious, it might incriminate your brothers."
>
> So we got up in the morning. All of us were sleeping in our father's big bed. We got up. We were about to wash our faces and to have our morning tea before going to Anyiel's house to visit the people there. Suddenly a car came. It was filled with police. We were about to rush out of the hut. There was a religious man at work, performing protective rituals. It had been rumored that the boys would be killed, people like Monyyak [Abdalla] and Arob Minyang and all those who were at home in Abyei. As soon as the car arrived, the religious man who was working to provide protection was told to leave the house. Everybody thought that the police were there for the security inspection. But as soon as we got dressed, we heard some wailing. We wondered who was crying. They said that it was our cousin, Allor Biong. Immediately, we assumed that he was crying because our brothers had been killed. So we all joined the wailing.
>
> Then Deng Abot came in and saw my mother crying. He said, "Amou, is that you?"
>
> Amou said, "Yes."
>
> He said, "What are you crying about! Deng Majok is dead."
>
> Suddenly, each person stopped crying and listened to what had just been said and then began to cry again. It was a terrible way of delivering the news. If it were not for the strength of their hearts, people might have died of shock. It was not a well-handled situation at all. Some people were crying, thinking that some of the boys had been killed. And then in the middle of the crying, people would say, "It is Deng Majok; he is dead." People nearly killed themselves with the shock.
>
> Then you arrived with the body at 4:00 P.M. That was when you brought his body by airplane.

Deng Majok's first wife, Nyanbol Arob, had a prophetic view of the events:

> When I heard the news of Anyiel, I said, "Oh! Now that Anyiel has been killed, Deng Majok cannot be alive!" People said, "Nyanbol, why do you talk that way?" I said, "You will prove me right by tomorrow afternoon." Then we slept. The following day, as the sun was moving from the center, people came to Noong, running from

Abyei and wailing. I said, "What is the matter? Have our children in Abyei been killed?" They said, "Deng Majok is dead."

We were caught as we struggled, wailing, and were tied down. Then I asked, "Now that he is said to be dead, will he be buried where he died or will he be brought here?"

They said, "He will be brought by his sons."

Then I said, "In that case, release me." We ran to Abyei. Then you brought him.

Charles Biong began to reflect on the implications of his father's death when he learned of his terminal cancer and the fact that the end could come any time:

> The situation was too big to weep over, though one could not help tears from time to time, simply because one found oneself confronted by a situation that was really impossible to manage. But the first problem that presented a real difficulty for me was who would succeed him. I had in mind only two at that time: they were Monyyak and Kwol [Adam]. And Father used to talk about the two in very conflicting ways, which made it so difficult for one to know exactly where he cast his choice. And in making my own judgment I found it really impossible to decide exactly where my choice would go either, though I never hesitated in preferring Kwol as the most appropriate successor. The only problem I saw was that Kwol used to drink too much. I thought that if that were his only problem, people could talk him into stopping. Unfortunately, he had had sufficient opportunity to reform when he was being prepared by Father, but he had shown no signs of improvement. Indeed, Father had confronted him openly about it. And yet Kwol had failed to give up the habit. That made me fear that he might continue drinking even if he were to succeed Father. On the other hand, Monyyak used to drink too, but when he heard that Kwol was being prepared for succession, he decided to give up drinking. This made me believe that he could adjust himself to the public affairs of the tribe. But one main defect of Monyyak was that, to me, he was rather reckless. And watching Father continually walking around with people, up and down, day and night, always composed and in control, I thought that characteristic in Monyyak would be a major defect. So, that was the real problem for me. I found great difficulty deciding which of the two would be the suitable successor.

The choice of a successor was no longer a matter for theoretical reflection once the chief was dead. The discussions about succession had to accompany the burial, so that the new chief could be installed as the body was being lowered into the grave, thereby leaving no gap in leadership. Deng Abot voiced his old claim to the chieftainship, arguing that it had been wrongly usurped by Deng Majok. But he was jeered into silence. As expected, the two brothers directly involved in the conflict over succession were Abdalla (Monyyak), third son of the first wife, Nyanbol Arob, and Adam (Kwol), first son of the second wife, Nyanbol Amor.

When we arrived in Abyei with Father's body, Adam was away, but there was a large measure of consensus over Abdalla's succession. When Adam arrived, he refused to acknowledge Abdalla's succession except as a temporary measure pending resolution by the central government. As Abdalla had been at home trying to play the protective role his father had provided for his people but without his father's power over the security forces, he had already developed tensions with the security authorities and was suspected of sympathizing with the local rebels. Adam was more favored by the security people and felt hopeful that, in a decision involving the government, he would probably secure the succession.

We struggled very hard for a month to try to restore cooperation between the legitimate tribal authority, now headed by Abdalla, and the security forces under the command of a young officer by the name of Ali Sid Ahmed. We even tried to reach some understanding with the local Anyanya leaders, who were our cousins, to ensure the security of our people, situated as they were in a sensitive, exposed, and vulnerable border area. But although we were able to achieve a measure of peace and security, we were left with a most precarious situation, in which the people remained under constant apprehension of arrest, torture, and death.

We met with the central authorities in the district, the province, and the national capital to explain the situation, present our findings, and suggest measures for alleviating the crisis. The reaction of the central authorities was positive. In accordance with our recommendations, administrative and judicial powers were conferred on Abdalla; the officer and his men were transferred from Abyei, an older and more experienced—although less educated—officer was sent to Abyei with a new regiment; and a commission of inquiry was set up to investigate the situation, in particular the circumstances of Anyiel's death. Bol and I then returned to our own occupations abroad.

Soon our family was to be afflicted with another tragedy. Abdalla and two other of our brothers, along with three uncles, were assassinated under circumstances that pointed the finger at the security forces and their opportunistic informants.

The circumstances of their deaths were later described by Michael Wolfers in an article entitled "How Six Sudanese Died: Family Massacre Threatens Peace Effort," in the *London Times* of October 19, 1970:

> Mr. Joseph Garang, the Minister in the Sudanese revolutionary government responsible for Southern Sudan, has just announced a year's extension of the amnesty for southerners who have been engaged in secessionist activity but wish to return to their own country. Tension and sometimes open warfare between northerners, of partly Arabic stock, and southerners, of African origin, have been the most

disturbing factor in Sudan's development for years, and it requires a considerable act of confidence and faith for a southerner to return to territory still garrisoned and administered by northern troops and officials.

The growth of their confidence may be seriously damaged by some new information on the recent killing of six members of one of the leading Dinka families (one of the main tribes in Sudan), including the paramount chief of the Ngok Dinka. The critical point about these events is that they take place in a family which has traditionally favoured cooperation between north and south, and at Abyei in Kordofan Province, not on the southern borders of the country, but in the borderland between northerners and southerners. Kordofan is geographically in the north, but the Ngok Dinka are a part of the complex of southern tribes.

The paramount chief, Abdalla Deng, was elected only a year ago on the death of his father. It is alleged that last month he was killed, with two brothers and three uncles, by seven Sudanese Government soldiers. He was then 27. His grandfather, Chief Kuol Arop, had sought cooperation with the Anglo-Egyptian Government in Sudan, and his father, Chief Deng Kuol Arop, had cooperated with the Sudanese Government.

The following report of the circumstances of Chief Abdalla's death has been prepared by his relatives:

"In all, six were killed and these are Abdalla Deng, Bulabek Deng Kuol, Lino Chan Deng Kuol, Arop Mahdi Arop, Thuc Col Gueny, and Kiir Jal, as they were just having a walk on the evening of September 17, 1970. Eyewitnesses say that they were shot by a group of about seven soldiers which included the local commanding officer, Mohammed El Basha.

"The immediate cause which resulted in the killing in cold blood of these people was that during August or early September, Mohammed El Basha, with a number of his followers, following a false report of an Anyanya (southern rebel army) cattle camp at Dokura, went to Dokura where they found a camp and killed four persons from Tuic. As usual, they took away the cattle of those killed, in all amounting to about 150 cows. Mohammed El Basha wanted to sell these cows as is the normal practice, but he could not do so without the local (chief's) court approval.

"Thus he came to the court and Abdalla told him that those who had been killed were not rebels but law-abiding citizens, and consequently he saw that there was no reason why those cattle should be sold and told him that he was referring the case to the resident magistrate. As a result of this, Mohammed El Basha became serious and threatened Abdalla to the effect that this was his last time to come to his court and if anything at all happened, the first bullet that he would fire would be for Abdalla.

"With this threat, Abdalla wrote to the Provincial Commissioner at El Obeid reporting the incident and actually asked for the Province

Security Committee to visit Abyei to see for themselves what was going on. However, a few days after the quarrel, specifically on September 17, Mohammed El Basha and six other soldiers ambushed Abdalla and those killed with him and opened fire on them. All six died on the spot."

The family point out that the Tuic Dinka, four of whose men were killed in the cattle raid, by tradition come from the South to graze their cattle at Abyei. The Ngok Dinka, believing in the good faith of the Sudanese central government, look to the northern administrators in the provincial capital for protection of law and order. Documentary evidence supports this. Two of Chief Abdalla's brothers living abroad have once before had to rely on provincial administrators after an alleged murder by Sudanese soldiers. They are Dr. Francis Deng, with law degrees from Khartoum and Yale Universities, who is now a senior official of the Human Rights Division of the United Nations in New York, and Dr. Zakaria Bol Deng, with medical degrees from Padua and Bologna Universities, who is a senior house physician at Waddon Hospital, Croydon, Surrey. . . .

Chief Abdalla's family are now seeking public enquiry into the killings this September. Dr. Bol Deng said that . . . he and his brother still believe in the intentions of the central government, but argue that the test is whether the government will control the army on the ground. Their initial hopes for the new government which took power nearly 18 months ago are now tinged with scepticism.

The appointment of Adam by the security forces to succeed as chief, along with his known ambition for the position, raised suspicion of some involvement on his part in the conspiracy to assassinate his brothers. This suspicion was later reinforced by the attitude Adam displayed to the committee which the government established to investigate the assassinations, for although the evidence was presented in secret, it was commonly believed that he testified in favor of the security forces. Since the evidence was given under oath sworn upon the Sacred Spears, those who swore to opposing positions were ritually considered to be engaged in a blood feud and had to sever all ties, not eat or drink in each other's homes, and to all intents and purposes, regard each other as enemies. Adam was thus severed from the family and isolated. His mother, one of his sisters, his wives, and some of his father's junior wives whom he had inherited according to the custom of levirate sided with him. Otherwise, his own brothers, Ali (Monylam) and Osman (Mijak), stood with the family against their brother, and so did all the wives and children from their mother's section of the family. It was a truly tragic break, far worse than the one following the death of our grandfather. Our attempts to reunify the family proved futile and had to be shelved until a more opportune time.

Nyanluak was later to recall the impact on the family of these two tragedies, their father's death and the assassination of the brothers and uncles:

When word of Father's death reached us, we felt sure that our own death was the easiest way out of the tragedy that had befallen us. We tried various means of ending our lives. We sat on his grave all day in the burning sun and we drank large quantities of filthy water from the stinking stream in the trees where people disposed of their waste. We drank it knowing what was in it and hoping that it would give us diarrhea and kill us all. We did not care about life any more.

When you came with Father's body, we did not even feel the pleasure of your return. It was only when you asked, "Let the girls come," that we raised our eyes to look at you.

Then God added to our tragedy by having Monyyak, who had succeeded our father, and our other brothers murdered by political opportunists conspiring with the security forces. On the day of their death, we went through the marketplace of Abyei in our underwear though we had never gone through it even fully clothed. But on the occasion of their death, we went through the marketplace in our underwear, carrying their bodies to the hospital. The following morning we went back to the hospital and carried the bodies back to our house. The Ngok were all frightened. As for us, we resigned ourselves to fate and decided to let death take us all, the family of Deng Majok. We completely surrendered our lives.

When we first carried the bodies to the hospital, Monyyak's was missing. His body was lying hidden in the stream between the trees. When he was eventually found, Father's wives began to wail all over again. When we heard their voices, we objected violently; we felt that they had died as heroes in war and should therefore not be mourned in the ordinary way. What was required was the courage to face the challenge of the feud.

Whenever the women raised their voices in wailing, we felt as though they were responsible for the death of our brothers. We would seize whatever was around and beat them into silence. We said to them: "It is better you leave. In any case, this is no longer a family with men. Anyone wanting to cry should go and leave us alone."

And truly, we turned ourselves into men. We refused to allow a tear to fall from our eyes. Our hearts were filled with courage. That was how our brothers went.

Kwol was nearly killed afterward. To this day, when I think of the accusation that was later leveled against him—that he was one of the people who had conspired in the death of his brothers—I personally feel revolted by the thought; and even as I am sitting here, I find it impossible to believe that the thought ever crossed people's minds. It is just that Kwol had strayed into the company of our enemies and he did not stop to think what people might read into his being in such company.

The tragedy of the Deng family following his death is more than political; it is also social and psychological. Nyanthon, one of Deng Majok's middle wives, consented to be interviewed about her husband only with considerable reluctance, because she could not see any value in speaking words about him. She expressed sentiments widely shared by Deng's widows, who, according to Dinka tradition, remain his wives:

> Mading, the heart is a small and feeble organ. Our hearts have broken with the death of Deng Majok. However much we may speak, there is nothing that can be said to please the heart of a person like myself sitting here. There can never be anything in this entire world that is as good as Deng himself. Our hearts ache with his death. And with the aching of our hearts, words have been shattered from our memories. You can no longer hold words in your mind. I, Nyanthon in particular, my head has disintegrated so much that I no longer find anything stored in my head. I am only wandering in the wilderness. We are only waiting for death to come and take us.

"Father's death is something we still ponder to this day," said Achai-Chol.

> And it is the message of the heart which is destroying people in our family. For a family that was once so great to fall so low; for a man whom everyone looked to as a person who could solve all their problems and make people relate to one another very well, for such a person to die suddenly without a single child who can fill his place! In the past, wherever we walked, no one could cross our path. But now our family is viewed as bad. This is what one thinks about day and night. When one thinks of the way women and children used to be and what has now happened to them all, it makes one lose weight in one day. One does not lose weight because of lack of food; one has something to eat; but it is what has befallen our family that one thinks about and makes one lose weight.

Osman (Mijak), undoubtedly the most favored son of Deng Majok, had this to say about the implications of his father's death for him personally, and for the family.

> By God, Mading, the implications of my father's death for me, I believe I am the most affected. I have lamented his death beyond description. Why? As you know, I never completed my education. I always leaned on my father and was totally dependent on him. It never crossed my mind that my father would die. I could not imagine it. I was so comfortable with him that I was incapable of conceiving of his death. But nothing can be done about it. One only nurses the pain in one's heart and otherwise remains silent. Father cannot return. If only one could live twice, die and return to life! But one does not! Father is forever gone.

16 In the Shadow of a Giant

A pervasive theme in the story of Deng Majok is the extent to which comparisons favored him against all others. In the case of comparisons with his own father, Chief Kwol Arob, there is a degree of qualification to this general principle, for the Dinka, despite the negative view of him held by the British in his last days of leadership, think of Kwol as a great leader in the traditional sense of the word: "There was no equal to Kwol Arob," remarked Deng's first wife, Nyanbol Arob.

> Kwol Arob was taken up to the sky. There was nothing he and his father, Arob Biong, did not do to redeem their people from foreign domination. Arob even drank human waste to free his people who had been enslaved by the Arabs. He was told by the government: "If they are truly your people, then you eat this," and he was given human waste. He ate it.
> When Kwol Arob took over, he was called and told: "If the land is truly yours, then you come and pass this way." He went and climbed the iron ladder up toward the sky. Nothing ever subdued Kwol Arob. Deng did not go as far as Kwol Arob went. Deng became a leader of strong words, sitting on his own ground. He was not subjected to the kind of things that Kwol Arob and his father had been subjected to. But each of them had his own strength of leadership.

Achwil Bulabek agreed that each had his own distinctive merits and went on to show the main difference between Kwol Arob's era and that of his son, Deng Majok.

> The most important side of Deng was that he established the government in the tribe so that law and order according to the policy

of the government became deeply entrenched. Before him, relations with the government were still marginal. People were still suspicious of the government and there was no mutual trust between them and the government. It is true that Deng Majok inherited his father's power, but it is really with Deng Majok that government power enlarged itself in the tribe. It became really big.

"In the days of Kwol Arob," said Mithiang Agwek, "it was believed that any person who disobeyed Kwol Arob or Allor Ajing or did anything which they disapproved of would die." Deng Abot saw this spiritual fear of death as "respect" and contrasted it to the fear of government, which he saw as the power behind Deng Majok's authority.

> If your father appeared between warring groups, they would clash and fight, nevertheless; but if the warriors even as much as heard my father's voice, they would say, "Kwol Arob has arrived!" I tell you, son of my brother, the war would stop!
> With your father, Deng Majok, his was only the power of the government. Listen to my words! My brother Deng is dead, but we will meet again in the next world. It was the power of the government and not his charisma. One must say a truth which will be heard by God there above and by the powers here on earth.

Ironically, this was perhaps the difference that enhanced Deng Majok's image in the eyes of the government, for since he depended on government power, he knew how to use it efficiently and effectively to establish government control and to consolidate a system of law and order.

Ibrahim El Hussein comments on the shift between the spiritual powers of leadership to the secular power of modern government as the dividing line between Kwol and his son Deng.

> The government of Kwol was a calm government. But it was what these young people describe as defunct. Kwol's government was loose and defunct. Deng Majok's rule was strict and effective. It was truly a government.
> During Kwol's rule, if a man did wrong, he was brought and treated according to the customary ways of the Dinka. But during the time of Deng Majok, people were governed according to strict principles of modern government. Deng Majok was a strict ruler.
> Deng Majok was strict as a person, but he was also a man of ideas. He would sit and discuss with the District Commissioner and with the rulers of the country who would come to visit the tribes, and when he spoke, they would agree with his words. He was a man of brains. Your father, Deng, ruled with the power of the brain. As for our father, Kwol, there were no councils at his time. He would meet with the District Commissioner and would be told to do this or that and would leave.

The bottom line in the comparison between Kwol Arob and his son Deng

Majok would seem to be that one was in many ways a good leader in the traditional mold while the other was an efficient leader in the modern fashion. Nyanjur explained the situation this way:

> If we tell the real truth, nothing but the truth, those elders who knew grandfather, Kwol Arob, and our father, say that our grandfather Kwol Arob was a man whose word carried great weight. He was an extremely good person. But he did not match our father. Why he did not match our father is because . . . Father's responsibilities were truly enormous. They were so many that only a man with almost unique qualities could discharge them as successfully as he did. If he had been a man of lesser qualities, you would have noticed gaps in his ability to discharge his responsibilities. But with Father, you would never see any shortcomings or failure to live up to any challenge. You never felt he left something undone which someone else could have done better.

After presenting a balance sheet in which the two appeared virtually equal, Monyluak Row concluded in favor of Deng Majok: "If they were to stand for election in the way people do nowadays, Kwol would not be elected in preference over Deng Majok. It is Deng who would be elected. And this would be so even if they had been born twins on the same day."

Comparisons between Deng Majok and other leaders to the south or north make him at least equal to the best of them, and often far ahead. According to Ibrahim El Hussein:

> Deng Majok, Babo, Ibrahim Musa [Madibo] and the chiefs of our neighboring tribes, if anyone excelled over Deng, it was only in writing, because Deng did not learn to read and write. Ibrahim Musa could not write either. But Moneim Monsour could write and Babo could write. And the chief of Missiriya El Zurug, the son of Daffalla, could also write. If the comparison was through writing, then I cannot tell; but if the comparison was by performance in meetings and the power of words, no one could surpass Deng Majok. Whether the talks were with Sudanese leaders or with the English rulers, no one could ever surpass Deng Majok.

"Let me tell you," said Abdalla Hamadein, "and I challenge anyone who will dispute what I am saying: from Wau up to El Obeid, during times of peace or crisis, Deng Majok was the unshaken chief. Deng managed to contain both the Arabs and the Anyanya during the civil war. Abyei was never attacked by the Anyanya. My son, nobody will ever fill the position of Deng Majok."

Atem Moter was even more biting in his comparison with southern chiefs: "Don't tell me that there is any Southern Chief who could match Deng Majok. Deng was truly the unrivalled leader of the Dinka. When the country was destroyed by war and no one knew what would become of it, Chier Rian said to me under this tree, 'Atem Moter, I wish Deng Kwol was alive in these dark times. He was the strong man who could have saved the situation.'"

To the question as to how he compared Deng Majok with the chiefs of the South, Babo remarked:

> Deng Majok, compared to chiefs in the South: chiefs of the Nuer, or the Ruweng or the Twich or the Rek? All those, compared to Deng Majok—there was a very, very great difference, truly a great difference. Deng Majok was a real leader; he was a real leader; he had no equal among the others. To us, Deng Majok, by God, even among the Arab leaders, he was one of the best; not like most of the Arab chiefs.

In a private letter to the author, Douglas Dodds-Parker, who had met Deng Majok in 1934 while he was the Inspector in the Dar Hamar district, ranked Deng Majok among the most prominent chiefs of Kordofan. "Few countries," he wrote, "can have had such leaders as Ibrahim Moneim Mansur, Babo Nimir, Ahmed Omar, and your father."

"And indeed, from everything one heard and witnessed through experience," remarked Ibrahim Mohamed Zein, "Deng Majok was one of the extremely rare personalities who have emerged and entered history. He was certainly not an ordinary person who came and went as many do."

To what extent did Deng Majok find what he wanted from marriage? The answers given focused on the sons as the principals in the continuity of the male-oriented lineage and the ones who received modern education, the daughters having been left largely illiterate and relegated to traditional roles. "He found what he was looking for in his children," said Ajuong.

> He had children about whom he made some confidential remarks to people like myself whom he liked as his special relatives from the maternal line. When he was alone with such people, he would say, "Don't you see? What I used to say has come true! Don't you see that son of mine is already showing a great deal of usefulness." He began to speak of how right he had been about the question of children when he was still going strong. He would say, "There is always that one child who will promote the name of his father. There is always that one woman who will bear the child that will reflect the good name of his father. Now I have already seen the children who will bring value to my people." And the people have come to recognize what he was talking about. They came to accept his words.

"He knew you, his sons, well," commented Achwil Bulabek.

> After you were grown up, he knew where you were heading. For instance, he knew that you had become too well educated to remain in the tribe and that your education would take you farther away into the national government. And that is what has happened today.

As for the leadership at home, he had his two sons Abdalla and Kwol under him to assist him. But according to the word of his own heart, which I knew, he wanted Kwol to be the chief. Then we would ask, "Why?" The matter dragged until Abdalla committed adultery with his father's wives. He went with two wives. That was Deng's main grievance against Abdalla. He then argued that Kwol should inherit his leadership. He said, "The household of Nyanbol Amor has not impurified my bed!" That was an issue which he and I used to debate. I would say, "This is wrong! Abdalla will be the chief!" And Abdalla became the chief. But your father was against that. He even wrote a letter on the matter. This was not an issue he simply talked about; he had it written down on paper. He said, "I will place Abdalla in El Obeid, the Province Headquarters, to be my representative there and Adam will be the chief at home." That was what he used to say.

As for you and Bol he left you up there! You had distinguished yourselves in education and your names had become associated with success in education very early. That was your father's word; he wanted chieftainship to go to Kwol.

Ajuong believes Deng later changed his mind about Kwol:

At first, he said, "Kwol is the person to assume chieftainship." Why? When we looked into the matter, we found that it was what his heart had considered, but in his explanation to the people, he would put it discreetly by saying: "Kwol was born first; Kwol also learned the law from his services in the police. So that is why I say that Kwol is the one who should be chief."

But later he began to reconsider the situation. Kwol had started to drink heavily while Deng was still alive. Deng would be pleased with Kwol when he saw his appearance walking, but when he heard him speak, in situations involving Kwol and his brothers or strangers, he would look at Kwol's behavior with disfavor. That is how he began to withdraw from his earlier position about Kwol.

Ajuong goes on to explain Deng Majok's reluctance to groom one of his sons as the eventual heir to his throne. It was as though Deng feared that the history of the power struggle between him and his father might repeat itself.

He knew that youth have their own way of behaving. Did you not see yesterday [in the 1978 peace talks with the Arabs] the way in which these young people were speaking, the reckless and aggressive way in which youth speak compared with the cool-hearted way in which elders speak about painful matters? Your father felt that if he were to share power with a young man, a young man who might jump here and jump there and jump here, such a young man might introduce his own view of things into the leadership. He might come with his own words and change things. Or he might do things that might undermine his father.

Even more was the threat of education against an illiterate chief. The policies of an educated man are not the same as those of an illiterate man. The words of a literate person are secretly passed on through writing, and you fall victim to the written word without knowing. But the words of an illiterate person are easily exposed and remain stagnant in one place.

That was why your father was reluctant to appoint one of his sons as his deputy. Your father's heart was afraid. You see, your father handled his leadership with great care.

And so, when Deng Majok died, no one had been earmarked and prepared as a successor for a number of reasons: some of the senior sons had left to pursue education or employment opportunities outside the tribe; and among those at home, he could either not make up his mind as to which of them was best qualified for the position, or he feared that whoever he placed under him as his assistant might be carried away by ambition, and since his sons were educated and he illiterate, there was always the possibility that they would be even better equipped to do to their father what Deng Majok himself had done to his father. In any case, for the most part, those who remained close to him at home soon came into conflict with him over the issues of power or women and were otherwise destroyed or overshadowed.

The consensus today is that Deng Majok did not leave behind sons qualified to fill his shoes. "Although death limited the number of children Father could ultimately have had," said Nyanluak, "he also left behind a good number of children. It is only that the education of his children has not really been enhanced by heredity; Father did not pass his qualities on to his children. Had they inherited his qualities, and combined them with their education, they could have remedied what they disapproved of in him, such as his excessive marriages, and accumulated their wealth in a prosperous, united, and harmonious family. The situation would have been ideal."

Some people explain the problem in terms of the absence of the senior sons of Deng Majok from the tribe. In the words of Juac Dau: "Now as we are talking here today, we, the Ngok, say that the children of Deng Majok will not run the area as well as their father did. And, indeed, you cannot administer the area as well as Deng Majok did: You are educated and you live in your own areas of work away from the tribe. Wherever you find a job is where you live. But Deng Majok's education was the kind that allowed him to live among us and solve our problems."

Chol Piok spoke in the same vein:

> Today, as we speak, we the elders, we do not believe that you people will be able to do the same kinds of things Deng used to do. Your ways have become the ways of the modern world. There is no one among you today who comes and stays for even one year before he travels again. If you were present, you would watch and see what goes on. People like you, who are ministers, of course, no one can go

and settle in his own area any more; you cannot go and settle among your people, to talk with them, and to provide them with food. That can no longer be. So you only visit. And that is the most that can be expected.

The leadership position of Deng Majok's sons within the tribe has thus been undermined by a number of factors. One of these, paradoxically, is Deng Majok's success in having educated his children to assume roles outside the tribal context. Those who assumed leadership within the tribe were also handicapped by the fact that they were unduly young, inexperienced, and torn apart by rivalries and conflicts over power. Worse, in their attempts to defend their people from the atrocities committed by the security forces in the South-North civil war even prior to their father's death, they clashed with the authorities in a way that eroded the age-long cooperation between Ngok leadership and the central government. Their political adversaries within the tribe immediately took advantage of the rift to discredit the leadership of the family and to consolidate their own position. But despite these difficulties, the dedication of the sons of Deng Majok to serving their people has never diminished, whatever their level of education or wherever their occupation has taken them. Since their father's death, they have been unrelenting in their efforts to secure for their people political authority over their local affairs and an effective role in provincial, regional, and national power processes.

David Cole and Richard Huntington have observed of the sons of Deng Majok that: "all of them, for whatever comfort and prestige their education has granted, remain passionately committed to the welfare of the Ngok people although they often disagree fundamentally among themselves about the best political course for the tribe. Additionally, they are competitive among themselves since there are always more qualified sons of Deng Majok than there are opportunities for scholarships, offices, or notoriety."[1]

Even when divisiveness and rivalry were eventually overcome and family unity and solidarity restored, with Kwol Adol as the accepted leader and Ali as his senior advisor, the family continued to suffer crippling blows from the political problems of Abyei as an area poised between the South and the North. Although the family remained united on fundamentals, the strategic or tactical question of whether it was in the interest of the area for the family to lead the political movement to join the South or to maintain the delicate balance which the forefathers had kept became a divisive issue.

A year and a half after the family massacre, to be precise on 27 February 1972, Nimeri's government ended the civil war that had raged in the South for seventeen years. The Addis Ababa Accord, which brought peace to the country, granted the South regional autonomy within the framework of

---

1. *African Rural Development*, chap. 5, p. 18.

national unity. The status of Abyei between the North and the South was discussed but left unresolved, except by a clause which stated, without mentioning Abyei by name, that the South includes, in addition to the southern provinces, "such other areas as may be decided by a referendum to be culturally and geographically a part of the Southern complex."

It soon became obvious that the issue of the referendum was far more complex than the Addis Ababa Accord had envisaged. Certainly, the North did not want the Ngok to exercise that right and the South was not prepared to rock the boat of their newly acquired peace and unity over the Abyei issue.

That was when some of us came to the conclusion that instead of suffering the strains of a disputed territory, it would be more advantageous for the area to build on its positive history of linking North and South and the prevailing postwar climate of peace, unity, and reconciliation. We felt sure that if the grievances of the people of Abyei were addressed by granting them control over their local affairs within Kordofan, and if, in addition, they were provided with basic services and a development program that would recognize and build on their distinctive features, their aspirations would be satisfied and they might become reconciled to the positive aspects of their bridging situation. Their area could again become a peaceful border in which the neighboring tribes could meet and interact in a harmonious atmosphere, reinforcing national unity and integration.

The idea was well received in the relevant decision-making circles on the national level. President Nimeri visited Abyei in the winter of 1972 to announce the policy, but as we could not be there to explain to our people our own thinking behind the policy, the president was met with a strong demand for joining the South and an angry reaction to the government's reluctance to implement the relevant provision in the Addis Ababa Agreement. People also called for the dismissal of Adam, using his drinking as the reason but obviously really because of his political alliance with the North. Infuriated by this hostile reception, Nimeri made an impromptu decision to abolish the institution of chieftainship among the Ngok Dinka and left without delivering some of the benefits he had intended to offer toward the implementation of the new policy. Tribal power was vested in a council of elders and lay magistrates dominated by the political opponents of Deng Majok and his family. This supposedly offered the revolution an opportunity to experiment with the erosion of traditional authority and the substitution of new "revolutionary" forces for tribal leadership. But it soon became evident that vengeance and vindictiveness were the guiding principles behind the behavior of the new wielders of power.

Cole and Huntington observed the way in which old grievances against Deng Majok have continued to provoke political rivalries and hostilities that external interests have manipulated against the best interest of the Ngok Dinka.

There are those who will use almost any opportunity to oppose the *Pajok* lineage and favor the *Dhiendior* chiefly line whose powers were so reduced during the colonial era. And always there are those who favor the line of Deng Abot over the line of Deng Majok. These events intensified the structural complementaries and oppositions of Ngok political society. And always this increased schism relates to external alliance with the Arabs and the state, an alliance which strengthened the *Pajok* at the expense of the *Dhiendior*, and favored Deng Majok at the expense of his father and brother.

Deng Majok has been dead for a dozen years and during that time the Sudanese civil war intensified and then ended, President Nimeri came to power, and much has changed throughout the country. Yet in Abyei one still feels the presence of the man.[2]

In yet another context, Cole and Huntington go on to explain the structural principles that underlie this harmful divisiveness.

A segmentary social structure facilitates an ever narrower and shorter-term perception of self-interest allowing an adversary to pursue a policy of divide and rule. The Ngok know painfully that it is the very essence of their society that provides for such extremes of unity and division. In their experience, the negative divisive element appears to predominate. This divisiveness depresses them in the face of their ideological awareness of their potential familial unity. Often during these difficult times, Dinka lament, "We are a terrible people; we bring destruction upon ourselves through constant disunity and betrayal." . . . The divisiveness of recent years making Ngok society vulnerable to external advances is directly attributable to the jealousies among the members of the chiefly lineages. Furthermore, among those with chiefly credentials, there is a further hierarchy at the apex of which stand the direct descendents of the recent paramount chiefs. Always there are chiefs who stand to gain by the diminution of the status of those closer to the center than they. . . . As the Ngok polity has become increasingly stratified, the negative and divisive aspect of the segmentary social structure has come to predominate.[3]

Despite this divisiveness and the way it has been exploited by outside interests, those who were favored by the new system were viewed by the bulk of the Dinka as opportunistic stooges of Arab oppression and as wanting in the fundamental moral principles of leadership. Although some of them were descendants of chiefly families with some claim to leadership, they were viewed as lacking any legitimacy as representative leaders. The sons of Deng Majok continued to be popularly viewed as the legitimate leaders, on whom the moral obligation of serving their people under the most difficult

2. Pp. 10–11.
3. Pp. 36–37.

circumstances inevitably rested. The result was that, far from being effective, those who had been placed in repressive positions of power proved to be a source of instability.

After intensive efforts on our part, the government eventually agreed in 1974 to appoint one of the sons of Deng Majok to head the judicial and administrative hierarchy of the tribe, provided we unified the family, which we were able to do, though with considerable difficulty. Kwol Adol, intelligent and dynamic though very young—barely in his twenties—was agreed upon as the chief. Kwol not only succeeded in finally uniting the family behind him, but was to emerge as a fighter for his people and a very popular leader.

The central governmental authorities also agreed to proceed with the implementation of the policy of giving Abyei special administrative status and a development program. President Nimeri reiterated in Kadugli, the provincial capital, in his Independence Day speech in January 1977, the government policy for the area, solemnly pledging his personal responsibility for its development. Placing it in the context of the overall development of the province, President Nimeri stated:

> I would like development in this rich province to be an overall and integrated development. . . . If this is what we want for your province, I want the area of Abyei—where the great Dinka and Missiriya tribes meet and coexist—to be an example of the interaction of cultures. Abyei is to the Sudan exactly what the Sudan is to Africa. This project will be implemented under my personal supervision in cooperation with all the institutions of the state, universities, and international organizations.

The administrative status of Abyei was raised to a subprovisional level. On our recommendation, Justin Deng was appointed Assistant Commissioner to head the administration of the area. Although he happened to be the son of Deng Majok's sister, Awor, Justin was well qualified in his own right, having studied law and economics in France after years of government service as an accountant. Back in the Sudan, he was absorbed into the Regional Ministry of Public Administration, from which he was seconded to Abyei. A number of Ngok policemen were transferred to Abyei, and Dominic Kwol Arob, a Ngok officer in the South, was sent to head the police force in Abyei. Others from the area were also expected to be appointed, trained in local administration, and sent to join Justin Deng. With funding from the United States Agency for International Development, we invited the Harvard Institute for International Development to undertake the designing and implementation of an integrated rural development project that would take into consideration the distinctive political, social, cultural, and economic features of the area. With considerable effort, we succeeded in bringing to the project a number of government officials from Abyei.

The project, however, met with serious obstacles. Vocal elements of the educated Ngok youth, who were politically militant, saw the project as a way of neutralizing the pro-South nationalist movement in the area. Some of these differences reflected long-standing rivalries between factions of the tribe. Beyond the Dinka, the Arab tribes and Kordofan authorities saw it as favoritism to the people of Abyei and a circumvention of provincial authority. They also saw any autonomy for Abyei, and in particular the appointment of Justin Deng, as a step toward ultimately severing Abyei from Kordofan and annexing it to the South. Through their political pressures and intimidation, often involving armed incursions, the Arabs forced the provincial authorities to transfer Ngok officials from Abyei, and some even from Kordofan. Abyei autonomy was progressively diminished. As for the project, so entangled in political conflicts did it become that absurd allegations were made to the effect that the Dinka were receiving arms from abroad through the institute.

The outcome of the project turned out to be the exact opposite of its intended results. Political problems over Abyei and the project itself continued to mount, erupting into a series of violent conflicts between the Arabs and the Dinka and among the Dinka themselves. With the compounding of all these problems USAID eventually decided to terminate its funding and withdrew from the project. Harvard, too, left. The project was declared a failure.

All this aggravated the situation and turned Abyei from a bridge of peace between the North and the South into a point of confrontation. Quite apart from Abyei being a contested area, the relations between the Ngok Dinka and the Missiriya Arabs became characterized by frequent clashes involving the use of modern weapons, with considerable destruction to human lives and property. The security forces and the authorities of Kordofan inevitably became involved. And because the family stood up in defense of their people and became increasingly identified with what the authorities of Kordofan and the Missiriya Arabs viewed as a separatist leaning toward the South, their influence within Kordofan began to wane, as the authorities preferred to deal with those who advocated Abyei remaining in the North, whether out of conviction or for personal gain. As long as some members were active on the national level, they maintained a certain amount of control and balance over the situation on the provincial and local levels. But once the checks and balances of that moderating influence at the national level disappeared with the departure of the individuals involved, the scale was inevitably tipped against the interests of the family and the tribe at large.

As the security situation drastically deteriorated and the family continued to be devastated by the manipulations of both the local authorities and political adversaries, it became necessary for some of the leading sons to intervene and make policy adjustments to restore a workable balance in the family stand between South and North. While this move in itself was controversial within the family and in southern and northern circles, it improved the security situation in the area and brought the family back to a position of at least a working relationship with the authorities in Kordofan and the neighboring Arabs. But the situation remained precarious, with ripples spreading southward—certainly a long way from what it had been for generations of family leadership at the South-North crossroads.

In April 1983, as a result of the increased tension and unrest over the problem of Abyei, provoking armed resistance in the area that threatened to spread farther South with one of the senior sons of Deng Majok leading the movement, most of the educated elite of Abyei and a number of tribal elders were arrested and detained by the security authorities, which threatened to charge them with treasonable offenses. Among these were leading sons and relatives of Deng Majok. Some of us took a peace initiative which, after several months of intensive efforts involving security authorities, the presidency, and provincial authorities in Kordofan, was blessed with success. This resulted in the release of all the detainees. The plan of action, which was agreed upon with the authorities of Kordofan and sanctioned by the central government, promised special administrative status for Abyei in Kordofan, with increased autonomy, services, and development facilities. It was in essence an agreement to reactivate the implementation of the initial policy on Abyei without touching on the sensitive issue of the referendum provided for by the Addis Ababa Accord of 1972.

The government and the media gave the agreement intensive coverage, echoed in the Middle East and other parts of the world, in which the name of Deng Majok figured prominently as an inspiration. On that occasion, other members of the Ngok Dinka and the sons of Deng Majok issued two statements. The statement of Deng Majok's sons follows:

> We, the undersigned sons of Deng Majok, hereby reaffirm our commitment to the noble principles which our late father and our forefathers before him pursued for centuries within the framework of Kordofan to advance the cause of peace and unity as a link between the southern and the northern parts of the country.
>
> Some of us have recently felt themselves driven to the call of separating the area of Abyei from Kordofan and joining it to the Southern Region in the hope of ensuring participation in the government of the country on equal footing with fellow countrymen in that region. We have now learned that one of us has even taken up arms in pursuance of this objective and with most regrettable consequences to the peace and security of our people.
>
> While we recognize the frustrations which have led to this sad development, we remain unequivocally opposed to this destructive means of attempting a solution to the problem of Abyei.
>
> We also declare that our objective in the area has always been to secure for our people the dignity of equal partnership in the government of their country. To promote this objective in line with the ideals which our forebears have always spearheaded in the area, we have

resolved to work within the framework of Kordofan and in full cooperation with our brothers and sisters in that region for the common good of all our people in the region.

The declaration of the sons of Abyei was similar in essence, although it did not, naturally, attribute the bridging role of Ngok history to any individual or family.

We, the assembled sons of Abyei, have been watching with profound sorrow and anguish the recent developments in our area and the general threat to the security of innocent people in the area. We are also deeply concerned that these developments have had the effect of reversing the historical image of our area as a vital link between the southern and northern parts of our country. Rather than the symbol of national unity and integration which it has been for centuries, our area is now seen as a point of confrontation and animosity and a threat to peace and unity, the most precious achievements of the May Revolution.

We have always considered it absolutely essential that the call for joining the South be conducted peacefully and in accordance with the constitution and the laws of the country. While we therefore recognize the frustrations of the political tensions and conflicts which have recently prompted some people in the area to resort to violent means, we totally oppose the use of violence as a means of solving the problem of Abyei.

We would also want to emphasize that we have always regarded the call for joining the South as a means and not an end in itself. The main objective has always been to secure for the people of Abyei the enjoyment of full rights of citizenship as free and equal partners in the government of their country. We therefore declare ourselves willing and ready to work within the framework of Kordofan as long as opportunities for the enjoyment of full rights of citizenship are offered to our people on equal footing with the rest of the people in the region.

We have also concluded that the policies and principles declared by His Excellency the President of the Republic for the administration and development of Abyei area as a symbol of national unity and integration constitute a sound basis for the realization of the common interests in the area. We hope to achieve this in accordance with such programmes as may be agreed upon with the authorities of Kordofan in a spirit of cooperation and mutual understanding.

In a way, then, the policies which had been successfully pursued by traditional leaders for centuries, but which had become endangered, both by the political realities of our times and by lack of historical perspective or knowledge of ancestral legacy, were revived at a high level of political consciousness and sophistication. Although the chain of ancestral contribution in this respect is long, Deng Majok certainly remains a central figure in this development. Indeed, what he was able to achieve remains only an aspiration for this generation.

The understanding that was reached in April 1983 between the authorities of Kordofan and elements from the Ngok Dinka brought back only a small patch of calm in what had become a sea of turbulence that would soon swell and engulf the whole South, virtually plunging the country back into renewed civil war.

The outcome of all this is that the peace, unity, and harmony which the Ngok enjoyed during the life of Deng Majok is in sharp contrast to the devastations of local and national conflicts that have since invaded their area. To the Dinka, the central explanation for the calamity the Ngok Dinka have suffered is the death of their protector, Deng Majok, and the failure of his sons to fill his shoes.

Atem Moter expressed the sentiments of most Dinka in the comparison between father and sons:

> You children do not know the truth, even though you are educated. I feel that this thing [Arab aggression] is going to finish off our people. The Arabs have now sharpened their claws and you will just sit and watch them mutilate our people. Unless Deng Majok rises from his grave, no good will come out of you, even those who have emerged as leaders.
>
> Whenever I go to Wau and I see an Arab driving a lorry, I refuse to get into that lorry. If it is the Arabs, they could have him fill the lorry with people and then turn it over to kill them. It is we, the Dinka, who would be concerned about human life. But none of you has the ideas with which to confront the Arab. Only Deng did.

"The qualities of Deng Majok, you children will never achieve," said Chol Piok. "His many great qualities, Mading, you people will never match. As you saw your father, a chief does not get so loved by all, including members of other tribes, for a simple reason; he cannot be loved so much for nothing. Deng Majok was not loved for nothing. He was loved because of his exceptionally good work."

During the discussions of a tragic conflict between the Dinka and the Arabs in which hundreds died, Monyluak Row recalled the significance of the loss resulting from Deng Majok's death. After enumerating Deng Majok's attributes, stressing his diplomatic talents, Monyluak went on to say: "We have reflected a great deal on this. A man lies at night thinking to himself, 'This great man we have lost, has he truly gone with his charisma and wisdom or has he left them to anyone?' You, Mading, your father's charisma was comprised of many aspects and they have all gone away with him. We believe it will never be found again. Indeed, we say it will never be born again." A few years later, things worsened in the area and Monyluak became even more pessimistic: "The truth has to be said. If Deng returned from the grave today, he would be asked to come back because his children have failed. What his death has shown is that we are dying. What it has shown is that we, the Ngok, now belong nowhere, neither to the South nor to the North."

Another elder, Matet Ayom, a man who was as much an enemy as he was a friend to Deng Majok and who was to emerge as the leading personality in the wave against the Deng family and as a protégé of Arab oppression, ironically also missed the protective role of Deng Majok. As he put it, "When Deng died, I also said that I hoped God would help us to have no war with any other tribe, whether Arab or southern. There is no chief who knows how to fight a case against a foreign adversary as Deng did. His ability to argue his case and his ingenuity in formulating strategies, no one will ever match."

When news of Deng Majok's death reached Twichland, according to Atem Moter:

> One felt that the world was destroyed. And that is what it is: the world is not only spoiled; it will continue to be spoiled. Nobody seems to be able to bring it back under control. If Deng Kwol were alive, he would have checked the Baggara Arabs. He would have asked Nimiri, "Why do these people go and kill people and you do not punish them? Why?" Deng would tear the Arabs apart with his teeth. And indeed, we and the Arabs have always been cannibalistic with one another. People run away from a person when he is brave and strong or when he has some supernatural powers. The power of Deng Kwol was unique.
>
> My sons, your coming to talk about Deng Kwol reminds us of him again and strains our hearts! No one can compete with Deng Majok for the quality of leadership in all the nations of the world I hear of.

In language that uses the word *King* metaphorically, since there are no kings in the Sudan, Chief Ayeny Aleu of Bahr el Ghazal Province said after the end of the seventeen-year civil war: "You see, your father, Deng Kwol, now that we have assumed control over our country—the South—if he were alive today, he would be our king here in the South. He managed to contain the Arabs well. But unfortunately, God took him away. That is what makes us sad. We all wish that these things had taken place while your father, Deng Majok, was alive to see."

Babo, a man who had turned from being a very close friend into a political adversary, also saw disaster in the death of Deng Majok:

> "O God!" we thought. "What a loss!" It was as though the link binding the Missiriya and the Dinka had been broken. Once Deng was dead, the door was open to the young men who had gone and studied in missionary schools in the South, men who did not have the spirit of Deng Majok. We thought, "Now that Deng is dead, these men will find the freedom to unleash their aspirations. The area will certainly be in trouble."

And, "Truly, after the death of Deng Majok," commented Tigani Mohamed Zein:

> many problems occurred which people believe are due to his death. The present generation is different from the older generation. Today leaders, whether they are sons of Deng Majok or others, are educated and their view of things is different from that of their older generation. This is also true of the North. Of course, the traditional society in both the North and the South has remained the same because education has not affected the predominant position of the population. But there was special wisdom in the manner with which Deng Majok was managing the affairs of the area. The tribe has not found anyone who can fill the position of Deng Majok. So Deng Majok has left a vacuum; his death has created a big gap. This is my opinion.

"Of course, God always gives a leader something special and unique to him," observed Ibrahim Mohamed Zein.

> For instance, the Prophet Mohamed, who was very dear to God Almighty, was from Ghoreish Tribe, and during the days of ignorance, all the Arabs, with the exception of Ghoreish Tribe, used to go naked. The Ghoreish were dressed and their women used to be veiled. This was a special blessing from God to the Ghoreish because it was from them that He would select his Prophet.
>
> And so it was with Deng Majok. God gave him special qualities so that he could fill his unique position. Among his greatest assets for leadership was that he was a man of unusual intellect and wide comprehension of issues. In politics, for instance, one felt that he always achieved whatever objective he had set for himself. No situation ever confronted him that he was not in full command of. His broad outlook and unique capability placed him in a natural leadership position. He was always able to make delicate and precise calculations in any decision-making situation in time of peace or of war. He always gave great attention to showing hospitality to visitors; gifts must go to visiting dignitaries. These are qualities which are not possessed by everyone; they are the qualities of leadership. He treated problems with wisdom, with full understanding, and he went after whatever he wanted to achieve, clarifying his objective quite clearly and pursuing it with diligence. These are rare leadership qualities.

"Deng had the qualities of a true leader," said Babo Nimir. "He was just, generous, and hospitable. He never feared the truth. If one was bad, he would tell him so."

A former governor of Kordofan Province, Mohamed Abbas, a northern Sudanese, concluded about Deng Majok:

> I knew many of the tribal chiefs of the South. With some exceptions, they tended to be instrumental, waiting to carry out instructions, rather than being suggestive. Deng Majok was a man of ideas.

He was so paramount that you could hardly apply to him the North-South distinction of measurement.

Chief Deng Majok could compete favorably, both in performance as a chief and in strength of character and dignity with the best chief in Kordofan or elsewhere in the Sudan. In his clean white Jibba and turban, he looked like a pyramid.

But perhaps what made Deng Majok so unique was his ability to run efficiently and effectively two formidable institutions, a large tribe sensitively poised between the major racial and cultural divisions of the Sudan, South and North, and an unprecedentedly large family, where jealousies, tensions, and conflict were surprisingly outweighed by the values of unity and harmony, with the husband-father as the focal point of love and affection and the symbol of family solidarity.

"Whatever took Deng Majok away from us and before we ended our days with him is something we cannot understand," declared Deng's second wife, Nyanbol Amor.

Our hearts have gone away from here. It is just that one feels it necessary to continue with his family. Otherwise, we would have left and gone anywhere, including the forest. Whenever one hears the name of Deng Majok mentioned, as we have now spoken about him, one does not sleep; one remains awake with a tormented heart until sunrise in the morning. Your heart would speak alone all night. To this day, he comes back in our dreams. The way you see us today, so emaciated, it is not because we have nothing to eat. What is missing are those precious words which your husband would say to you and those very special things he would acquire for you. It is true, we have aged, but if Deng were with us, we would not look this old; we would not be this old.

Greet his spirit! If this machine of yours records well and keeps a good record of what one says, it should transmit our greetings to him. His spirit is still alive; it follows you, his children, wherever you go. So, greet him; tell him that we miss him very much.

17 Deng Majok in Perspective

Deng Majok can be appraised in three capacities and following the sequence in which this account of his life has been presented: as a tribal leader, as a family man, and as a national figure.

As a tribal leader, Deng Majok lived up to what the Dinka regarded as the ideals of leadership: he was generous, hospitable, just, kind, and persuasive; but he was also tough and firm. In addition, he successfully met the standards which the central government under the British had introduced as criteria for evaluating administrative competence, especially with regard to public order, respect for the law, and fear of authority. And he extended the moral responsibilities of leadership beyond the narrow confines of his tribe to encompass all those who fell within his jurisdiction or sphere of influence. These were the standards, combined with the traditional yardsticks, which he effectively utilized to maneuver his father, Kwol Arob, and his half-brother, Deng Abot, out of the chieftainship.

Deng Majok not only succeeded in ensuring peace, security, and civic order among a people whose life had been dominated by the power of arms, but he went beyond that to start a process of development which, however modest by today's standards, was revolutionary in the context of his time. He introduced modern education, cash economy, medical facilities, and veterinary services at a period when they were still unknown to the Dinka. Indeed, education, trade, and modern medicine were initially rejected by them as repugnant to Dinka moral principles and displeasing to the ancestral spirits. But in due course the Dinka saw the merits of Deng Majok's innovations and now look back to his achievements with appreciation and gratitude.

It was largely to enhance his image in the eyes of the British administrators and his Arab neighbors as a progressive leader, and therefore the one best qualified for chieftainship, that Deng Majok embraced various elements of modernity. In the clothes he wore, the food he ate, the homes he built, the way he traveled (using mules, horses, and later cars instead of walking), and in his general receptivity to foreign ways that he viewed as desirable, Deng Majok set himself up before his people as a model of what they could be. Over and above this symbolic personal demonstration, or education by example, he introduced modern services and a market with consumer goods previously unavailable to the Dinka. Furthermore, he worked hard to help his people appreciate and utilize these modern facilities. So many of the services and commodities that the Dinka take for granted today are the result of Deng Majok's efforts, backed and supported by the central governmental authorities, who favored and encouraged his program of modernization. Deng Majok in effect turned a hitherto isolated area into one of the best-known spots in the Sudan, with a high political and administrative profile and a population strongly motivated toward economic, social, and cultural development. The influx into the urban areas of the North for which the Ngok Dinka are so well known today is the direct consequence of the momentum for change which Deng Majok generated and which raised his people's expectations and demands for modernization far beyond what is available or sustainable in their local context.

The question can, of course, be posed as to whether Deng Majok's achievements were due to his personality and abilities as an individual or were products of the historical context and, in particular, to the authority of the modern state behind him. It is difficult to discern the relative weight of these factors, but it would be safe to assume that they all contributed to reinforcing his image and effectiveness. Deng Majok was not the only tribal chief who benefited from the historical context or the central government's backing. Nevertheless, he was head and shoulders above all other Dinka chiefs; he also fares well in national comparisons with Arab chiefs.

And yet, despite all the unqualified praise heaped upon Deng Majok, one critical question persists: given the fact that he was such an exceptional, perhaps unique, leader who towered far above his forebears and descendants, was he a blessing to the Ngok Dinka, or would they have been better off with a leader more reflective of the level of his people? Was Chief Kwol Arob purely prejudiced against his son or did he see something in Deng Majok that made him prefer Deng Abot as leader of his people? And what did Kwol have in mind when he counseled Deng Abot not to claim the leadership in a court of law, predicting that the Sacred Spears and the authority that went with them would eventually fall by themselves? Was he forecasting Deng Majok's downfall or a loss to the clan and the tribe? Knowing that the latter would mean tragedy for the tribe, it would seem a most unlikely thought for Chief Kwol Arob to have. After all, he had objected to Deng Majok's succession as a violation of tradition that could result in the destruction of the tribe. Whatever Kwol's motives or initial justification, given the fact that his attitude was a contributing factor in if not the raison d'être of the feeling of competition that drove Deng Majok to excel beyond expectation in everything he did, might it indeed not be argued that Kwol's objection to his son's leadership was a self-fulfilling prophecy?

Deng Majok was the product of his own society—inspired by its ideals, challenged by its inequities, and reinforced by the material and cultural resources made available to him by his surroundings, both local and national. He was a blessing in that he lifted his people up to a level commensurate with his own dreams, ambitions, and achievements. But he was also a curse in that he outstripped everyone else in his tribal world, leaving no one to sustain the momentum he had generated. Once his unique powers began to weaken and diminish, his people inevitably fell from the great heights to which he had raised them, and not even his posterity has been able to compensate them adequately for the death of their great leader and protector.

The issues for Deng Majok's family are virtually the same. He was motivated, perhaps by his relations with his father, perhaps by something deeply ingrained in him, to marry more wives than any man ever has in the history of the Dinka. As long as he lived, he kept them united and harmonious, whatever tensions, jealousies, even occasional conflicts, existed beneath the surface calm. He also provided for them at the economic level, which, by tribal standards, was well-to-do. Even more important, he sent all his sons to school and encouraged them to build their future around education.

Many people wonder how he could possibly have afforded such a large family, and some are quick to see corruption and abuse of public funds as the explanation. But there is ample evidence that in the Dinka context marriage is a form of investment which not only broadens one's circle of influence and political support but also generates wealth.

And yet there is little doubt that polygyny as Deng Majok practiced it not only subordinated his dependents, wives, and children to an authoritarian patriarch but was founded on a system that entailed considerable indignity for women. His wives obviously realized this, even though they resigned themselves to it as an integral part of being a woman and a Dinka. Once they had accepted that cultural premise, most of them loved their status and even viewed themselves as members of a privileged group. Nevertheless, objectively speaking, it was a situation of inequity and unhealthy competition for the wives, who had to share with hundreds of other women a man who ran a tight ship and was so jealous that he could not tolerate a flirtatious smile passing between his wife and another man. The scenes of his reaction to a wife's unfaithfulness were dreadful and could arouse tears of sympathy; indeed, tears came to the eyes of his daughter Nyanjur as she watched a young stepmother beaten for adultery.

Deng Majok left behind a multitude of dependents, wives and children whose welfare has been severely jeopardized by the loss of the one person capable of the seemingly impossible task of providing a decent living for a family of such unprecedented size. What is more, since his death the size of his immediate family has continued to increase, as his widows, many of whom were very young, have continued to have children by Deng Majok's senior sons and other relatives, according to the custom of widow inheritance. These children are known as Deng Majok's own, not as the offspring of their biological fathers. And what is even worse, some wives have strayed from Deng Majok's sons and relatives to cohabit and beget children with strangers; these offspring, to the disgust of Deng Majok's children, are also being referred to as his sons and daughters. So not only did he have a large family to begin with, the circles of his family continue to enlarge ad infinitum, with all the hardships that such a situation entails in the modern context.

But, while there is no doubt about the hardships and miserable conditions under which his widows and children now live, compounded by the political difficulties confronting them in their drastically reduced status, they do find security in their numbers, as indeed Deng Majok had intended. Even more significantly, his towering image and the ideals that guided his life and propelled his achievements, despite ambivalences on the South-North issue, still provide members of his family with a deep-rooted sense of purpose, dignity, and inner strength that defies the trials of their otherwise reduced circumstances. Indeed, the blanket assessment of Deng Majok's sons as failures should be viewed more as emphasizing the high standards he set for his descendents rather than as a lack of effort on their part to serve the interests of their people under extremely adverse political circumstances. Relative to the obstacles they have had to overcome, and considering that their father never actively prepared them for the eventual assumption of leadership except through education, Deng Majok's sons can objectively be judged as having done their best and achieved a reasonable degree of success in maintaining something of the high profile their father projected for himself and his family. Given their numbers, their extensive age-span, their high-achievement motivation, and their competitiveness both among themselves and with others, the potentials of their capabilities and accomplishments are far from exhausted, ascertained, or even ascertainable.

To evaluate the life of Deng Majok from a national standpoint, there is no question that his rise to power generated ripples of authority and influence on the borders of his many neighbors, southerners and northerners, which, once they settled down, brought peace, harmony, and cooperation to peoples who had previously been torn apart by tension and conflict. As his father before him had done, Deng Majok turned down the offer extended to him by the British to join the South, preferring instead to remain on the borders as a "needle and thread" binding the two parts together in national unity. He projected the image of being pro-Arab, adopted those Arab cultural elements that he found desirable, and safeguarded the interests of Arab neighbors in his area. Sometimes he even appeared to favor the Arabs over his own people. But in doing so, he won their full confidence and was able to confront them and fight for the rights of his people whenever they were threatened by the Arabs. In due course, he became known to the southerners, not as a traitor who had opted for the enemy camp, but as a leader who had wisely taken the other side to protect his own people. And while the Arabs of course understood his protection of his people, they also looked to him as the only Dinka leader in whom they had full faith to do justice and defend Arab interests in Dinkaland. Even Babo Nimir, for whom he turned out to be a politically dangerous protégé, as he would not accept second place, could not find a substitute for Deng Majok in the cause of Arab-Dinka unity.

As tension mounts and the security situation in Abyei deteriorates, the Ngok Dinka recall the memory of Deng Majok with ambivalence. Some argue that he gave too much for too little in his relations with the North. But that is undoubtedly a hindsight that involves expectations raised by Deng Majok's achievements, which not only brought benefits to his people but left them at a point far more advanced than where they were when he assumed leadership. And yet, perhaps for the same reason, Deng Majok also left his people in a precarious spotlight that a more modest leader might have avoided. Certainly, Deng Abot would have chosen to join his own kith and kin in the South rather than opted for the glamour and strategically important national position of being the link between the Arab North and the African South. Under Deng Abot's leadership, it is conceivable that the Ngok (Abyei) problem might have been discreetly solved without national, far less international, attention being focused on the area.

But the issue cannot be side-stepped with such easy assumptions. Other questions must be asked: Would the Ngok have been better off by avoiding crises through setting modest goals? Is greatness not measured by critical choices made at heightened levels of risk? And does not progress imply an increasing level of responsibility with more at stake? It is true that Deng Majok left his people facing problems of heightened intensity in the modern Sudanese context, but it is because he brought them further into the modern world and to a much higher level of awareness.

What is more, through his performance, Deng Majok proved that by recognizing and safeguarding the vital interests of people who might otherwise be driven into becoming enemies, it is possible to win their confidence, trust, and cooperation. Once that is done and the parties have freed themselves of their defensiveness, it is possible to work together for goals that unite. Furthermore, while the dominant group is usually assumed to hold the controlling cards, Deng Majok proved that a minority does not have to be a passive recipient of majority favors or else rebel; far from it, he demonstrated that there is room for initiative without defeat to allay the deep-rooted insecurities that lie behind the unscrupulous repression and denial of minority rights. Although himself a minority leader in the North, Deng Majok made the Arabs feel secure enough about him to elect him president of the interracial council of which they were the overwhelming majority. And in that position he was able to ensure an even greater level of protection for his own people.

I should not give the impression that Deng Majok made all this possible through his initiatives alone, and that the supportive role of his Arab neighbors and the central governmental authorities was merely a response to those initiatives. Quite the contrary, the relationship between his own wisdom and abilities and the support and reinforcement he received from his friends and administrative superiors was dynamic and mutually productive. Deng Majok was a very proud man who would not tolerate insults or disrespect from anyone, including his seniors. As Babo Nimir later discovered, recognition, respect, autonomy, and equal treatment that favored him to the point of elevating him above the majority leaders were crucial to his strong identification with the North. Whenever those bases of unity were threatened, Deng Majok would retaliate with a rage that was in itself a deterrent, especially as he had sufficiently cultivated his northern connections to be able to count on the support of the powers that mattered and knew how to divide the Arabs to his advantage. And so whenever the wisdom of Deng Majok is cited, it should also be remembered that it came as a result of mutual recognition, accommodation, and respect.

Deng Majok regarded himself as a favored son of God who was better off than those favored merely by their worldly fathers. Because of this, it may not be easy to evaluate him by the normal standards of his fellow mortals. Perhaps the words of his younger brother Arob, who claimed that God had created him (Arob) perfect but had made the mistake of placing him in the context of Dinka society, might have been more appropriately spoken by Deng Majok about himself. And yet, ironically, it was Dinka society which produced him, reared him, and made him grow to excel and outdistance his people, not only on the tribal level, but indeed in his vision for the nation.

A final question that poses itself is whether the story of Deng Majok has anything to teach us beyond the tribal and the national spheres. Apart from its inherent interest as a story and its significance to the Dinka and the Sudan, does the life of Deng Majok offer us any lessons that might be useful in addressing the challenges of leadership in the wider human sense and in the changing world of today? The answer is unequivocally yes, and in several respects.

First, it is often said that a child needs maximum love from both parents in order to grow up with confidence and inner strength. While this is of course indisputable, Deng Majok's case would suggest that doubts about the love of a father may also have the effect of challenging one to prove oneself in a constructive way, provided one has alternative sources of affection and support. Deng Majok clearly enjoyed the affection, admiration, and support of a wide circle of relatives, especially his maternal kin, so that his father's ambivalence toward him was an exception. But the ambivalences in his relations with his father were, in a way, an aggravated form of the general Dinka attitude toward their children, in which the outward demonstration of love and affection is constrained, allegedly to deflect the evil eye of the envious or to avoid spoiling the child. Interestingly enough, while Dinka parents are expected to be discreet in expressing love to and for their own children, others in the family, especially grandparents, are not so constrained and may indeed be quite lavish in their demonstrations of love and affection. Something inherent in these checks and balances characterizes the upbringing of virtually every Dinka child. The degree involved in Deng Majok's case was less common, though by no means exceptional.

Second, the life story identifies quite clearly the qualities considered important to leadership, and while these do reflect Dinka values, it would seem that they are universal. Viewed in local terms, these qualities are often associated with "the tongue" and "the belly." By the tongue is meant the ability to speak soothing and conciliatory words that bring harmony and mutual cooperation to human relations. The belly connotes not only showing hospitality to visitors but also generosity to the needy. This raises the question of the means necessary to discharge the obligations of leadership. If one is not independently wealthy, which is desirable, but is nevertheless wanted as a leader, which may be justified, it then becomes necessary to find a way of equipping oneself adequately to discharge this obligation—if not in a personal way, which is expected, at least in an institutional one, a practical substitute. Indeed, some of the alleged tendencies toward corruption and abuse of public funds in Third World countries might have their roots in the pressures exerted on leaders who do not have the means to fulfill the material obligations of their leadership. And by leadership I do not mean prominent public positions only. An individual from a modest background, whom education and employment opportunities have given access to more means than his peers in the village or neighborhood, may, in the eyes of those people, be a leader and potential benefactor. The temptation to take advantage of any opportunities for self-enrichment in order to be better able to meet the obligations of a leadership role may be irresistible to some.

Third, social theories about traditional societies often exaggerate the dominance of the group and minimize the importance of the individual and the dynamics of individual motivation, initiative, and resourcefulness. The story of Deng Majok demonstrates the fallacy of this oversimplification and underscores the potentials of the individual as a vital spark in the social fabric, whose energies can effectively generate and sustain a self-enhancing process of change beyond the confines of tradition.

Fourth, to the extent that the individual is a leader, this can mean engineering a significant degree of change that can affect the society as a whole.

The story of leadership among the Ngok shows that the leader is indeed in a unique position to be a prototype for beneficial change. He is usually the first person to whom foreign visitors go or are directed; he is therefore more exposed to external sources of influence. At least among the Dinka, the home of the leader is the central meeting point for the tribe, and, as a corollary to that, he is the person to whom all information, whether internally based or externally generated, tends to flow. For these reasons, not to mention his qualifications for leadership and the confidence of the people in choosing or accepting him as their leader, he is generally the best equipped to decide on the best course for his people to follow in order to maximize their benefits and minimize the risks involved.

This does not mean that a leader should impose his will on the people. Quite the contrary, as the embodiment of the social ideals of his people, he should be sensitive and responsive to their aspirations and expectations, listen to all the voices that ask to be heard, and reflect seriously on what they have to say. Only after exhaustive consultations and consideration of the situation should he decide on the course to follow. But in doing so, his overriding guide must be the welfare of his people rather than the popularity of his decision or action. The challenge, however, includes an endeavor to explain to his people why he has done what he has, to persuade them to his point of view, and eventually to demonstrate that his course of action was indeed in the best interests of his people. Where he is unable to persuade them to support his position or give his course of action a chance to prove its worth, the alternative for the leader is to abdicate, as Deng Majok threatened to do if his preference for remaining under the administration of the North rather than joining his fellow Dinkas in the South was not accepted by his tribe.

Fifth, implicit in this process of change is the interplay between the motivating and supporting values and institutions of tradition and those of change—development or modernization. There is a common belief that the Dinka, and indeed all the Nilotics of the Sudan, are a proud and conservative people, impervious to foreign ideas and resistant to change. Recent trends, of course, have exploded that myth. But the story of Deng Majok would tend to suggest that those same values of pride can indeed make people more receptive to change, provided it enhances rather than violates their sense of dignity. Tradition can thus become not a constraint that must be overcome in order to permit change, but a potential catalyst to development or modernization.

Sixth, the story of Deng Majok illustrates some of the bases for mutual accommodation and cooperation among racial, cultural, or religious groups, and, in particular, between a dominant majority and a minority. It also shows that the application of the principles involved can be the result of efforts on both sides. While magnanimity in the attitude of the dominant group is often the most critical factor, there are certain initiatives which the minority can take to break the vicious cycle of mutual mistrust, fear, and animosity.

Seventh, in a paradoxically unifying yet fragmented world marked by racial, ethnic, religious, and cultural diversities, and in which the influence of leaders often extends beyond the limits of their own subnational or national boundaries, leadership is called upon to broaden the vision of moral responsibility to benefit all those affected by their widened sphere of influence. Admittedly, in the case of Deng Majok, the extension of the moral responsibility of leadership was sanctioned, encouraged, and rewarded by the British colonial government. In the global or international arena, there is no comparable authority to sanction and foster effectively this broadening of moral responsibility beyond national confines. This is perhaps all the more reason to stress the moral dimension of the challenge. On the other hand, the world has become so interactive and interdependent that the influence of world public opinion on the image of any leader with an international scope of influence, although understandably discreet and constrained, cannot be underestimated.

Eighth, and finally, another aspect of Deng Majok's story has transcendent implications in that it places in perspective an area which, though remote and little known, has long been acknowledged as the microcosm of a country that is in itself the microcosm of the continent and a link between Africa and the Middle East. When the Sudan attained independence in January 1956, the then foreign minister described the role of his country on the international scene as essentially Afro-Arab:

> The Sudan is, in the main, a cognate part of the Arab world and this is why we hastened to join the Arab League immediately on the declaration of our independence. . . . Our relations with the Arab countries will not make us lose sight of our African ties of affinity. We will always look south to Africa, strengthening our relations with the different African peoples and trying to help them in their progress and evolution towards freedom and a better life.[1]

These aspirations of intermediacy were applauded on the international scene. The United States evaluated the position of the Sudan as follows: "As a new African nation, the Sudan . . . will be deeply involved in [the] future cause of Africa. But as a Middle East nation, too, the Sudan will also be a bridge to Africa, imparting to it ideas, philosophies, and forces which may have great influence on Africa's decisions and on its future."[2]

A major consideration in the challenges now facing the country is the recognition and respect that will or will not be accorded the identity of the South, a people who, in the context of the Sudan, and in particular the history

---

1. The United States, Department of State, Background (1957), 20.
2. Ibid., 1.

of the South-North division, cannot adequately be described as a minority. The second consideration will be the level of sincerity in working toward narrowing and eventually eliminating the economic, social, cultural, and political disparities that give rise to grievances and a sense of hostility among the southern peoples. On the part of the South, the factor likely to make the difference will be the level of national involvement, a sense of direction and purpose in this involvement, a higher level of self-confidence in contributing to the shaping of national destiny, and, above all, exploring and building on the common grounds that foster mutual confidence and diminish deep-rooted fears and prejudices.

The view is widely shared among Sudanese today that "Abyei is to the Sudan what the Sudan is to Africa," to quote words that have been used. As Deng Majok's rival brother, Deng Abot, put it in a discussion of Dinka-Arab relations, "Abyei is like an eye, so small and yet it sees so much."

In its own way and within the limited context of his role and responsibilities, the story of Deng Majok has something to tell us about what is required from the North and the South in order to build an equitably united Sudan. It demonstrates the way in which the identities and the interests of minorities and dominant groups can be balanced to foster a working community or mutuality of interests. Indeed, long after his death Deng Majok continues to shine before his people and the nation as an example of what has been done and is therefore possible: unity in diversity, mutual respect, and equitable cooperation toward common goals.

Appendix on Sources and Method

I. LIST OF INFORMANTS

All the participants are listed alphabetically within the defined group. Unless otherwise indicated, the age estimates are as of 1984.

Family Members

Wives
The interviews with the wives, except for Nyanthon, were conducted by Luka Biong (Magwang), a younger brother, in 1979 at home in Abyei. Nyanthon was interviewed by the author in Khartoum in 1978.

1. Amel Yual, a middle wife, probably in her late fifties or sixties
2. Kwei Deng, third wife, now deceased, recorded in her late seventies
3. Nyanbol Arob, the first wife, in her eighties
4. Nyanbol Amor, the second wife, also in her eighties
5. Nyanawai, a middle wife, in her late fifties
6. Nyanthon, a lower middle wife, in her forties

Sons
As will be noticed, the sons bear both Dinka and Christian or Muslim names. This is one of the indications of Deng Majok's flexible approach to the two religions on the South-North border. Those who went to Christian missionary schools became Christians, while those who attended Muslim schools became Muslims. Some moved from the one faith to the other for various reasons. All the sons were interviewed by the author, most in Khartoum in 1979, and one, Charles (Hassan) Biong, in Ottawa in 1981. They include:

1. Ali (a Muslim with the Dinka name Monylam), in his thirties, the second son (fourth child) of the second wife, Nyanbol Amor;

2. Biong (Hassan or Charles), in his mid-thirties, firstborn of a middle wife, Adit; and
3. Mijak, whose Muslim name is Osman, in his mid-thirties, third son (fifth child) of the second wife, Nyanbol Amor.

Daughters

As will be noticed, the daughters bear no non-Dinka names because, unlike the sons, they were not sent to school, and even when some of the younger ones were later sent to a Muslim school and given Muslim names, they were subsequently withdrawn and went back to their traditional context, so their Muslim names died from disuse. Along with the persons conducting the interviews, dates and places the interviews were conducted, the daughters interviewed include:

1. Achai-Chol (the Black Achai, sometimes known as Achai-Manyjang—the Dinka Achai, because of the degree of her blackness by Dinka standards), in her fifties, the eldest daughter (second child) of Kwei, the third wife, interviewed by Luka Biong (Magwang);
2. Achai-Jur (the Arab Achai because of the lighter color of skin, because her color was light by Dinka standards, especially in contrast to Achai-Chol), in her fifties, the second daughter and second child of Nyanbol Amor, the second wife, interviewed by Luka in Abyei in 1979;
3. Ayan (who was interviewed on a different but related subject by the author), in her mid-thirties, the second daughter (third child) of the fourth wife, Achok Mijok, the author's mother, interviewed by the author in Khartoum in 1977;
4. Nyanjur, in her early thirties, firstborn of Amou Bol, a middle wife, interviewed by the author in Khartoum in 1979;
5. Nyanluak, also in her early thirties, second daughter (fourth child) of Achok Mijok, the author's mother, interviewed by the author in Khartoum in 1979.

Ngok Tribal Elders

Unless otherwise indicated, the elders were interviewed by the author during the Arab-Dinka peace conference at Kadugli, Kordofan Province, in August 1977.

1. Achwil Bulabek, in his seventies, the chief of Abyor subtribe, a close paternal relative, friend, and ally of Deng Majok;
2. Ajuong Deng, in his fifties, the chief of Anyal subtribe, a maternal relative of Deng Majok;
3. Allor-Jok, a half-brother interviewed by cousin Deng Arob in Abyei in 1979;
4. Allei Chol, presumably in his eighties, interviewed by Luka in 1979;
5. Awel Bol, a relative in her seventies, interviewed by Luka in 1979;
6. Chol Adija, in his seventies, interviewed jointly with Dau Agok and Patal Biliw;
7. Chol Piok, in his eighties;
8. Deng Abot (Deng Makuei), the rival half-brother of Deng Majok, in his late seventies when interviewed;
9. Dau Agok, in his sixties, interviewed jointly with Chol Adija and Patal Biliw;
10. Juac Dau, in his sixties, interviewed by Luka in 1979;

APPENDIX ON SOURCES AND METHOD   285

11. Matet Ayom, assassinated in 1982, in his late sixties when interviewed in 1977;
12. Mithiang Agwek, in his sixties, interviewed by Tiglei Abiem in 1980;
13. Monyluak Row, in his seventies;
14. Ngor Mijok (interviewed by the author on a different but related subject), in his sixties, the brother of the fourth wife, Achok Mijok, the author's mother;
15. Pagwot Deng, chief of Bongo subtribe (now deceased), in his eighties when interviewed; and
16. Patal Biliw, in his seventies, interviewed jointly with Chol Adija and Dau Agok.

Southern Dinka Neighbors

The interviews with southern chiefs were conducted in Twichland in 1979 by a group of brothers that included Arob, Monydhang, Kwol, Monychok, and Pieng. While some of these are prominent names whose ages could be estimated, others are unknown to me; but all are probably elderly men, some of whom are only a little younger than the generation of Deng Majok. They include:

1. Chief Atem Barach;
2. Atem Moter;
3. Chief Chier Rian (since deceased);
4. Chief Benjamin Lang Juk (since deceased);
5. Malek Mayar;
6. Malith Mawien;
7. Chief Madut Ring; and
8. Chief Maroor Rian.

Northern Arab Neighbors

Except for Abdalla, who was interviewed by Cousin Deng Arob Kwol in 1979, interviews with Arab elders were conducted by the author in Khartoum in 1981. Those interviewed include:

1. Abdalla Hamadein (now deceased), in his eighties when interviewed;
2. Chief Babo Nimir (now deceased), in his eighties when interviewed; and
3. Ibrahim El Hussein, also in his eighties when interviewed.

Sudanese Government Officials

While former Governor Mohamed Abbas El Faghiri was interviewed by a younger brother, William Biong, in Khartoum in 1980, the two educators were interviewed by the author in Khartoum in 1979. They include:

1. Mohamed Abbas El Faghiri, former governor of Kordofan, now retired, presumably in his sixties;
2. Ibrahim Mohamed Zein, a retired educator in his late fifties, interviewed jointly with his brother, Tijani;

3. Tijani Mohamed Zein, in his early sixties, interviewed jointly with his brother Ibrahim.

British Colonial Officers

British respondents replied in writing, or on tape in the case of Bell, to questions sent them by Charles Biong Deng. Because of the remoteness of the District Commissioners and the language barriers that exist between them and the Dinka, British accounts of the story of Deng Majok tend to be very brief.

1. Gawain Bell, born 21 January 1909, served as District Commissioner in the area from 1947 to the end of 1949 and occupied a variety of other positions in the country, ending as Permanent Under-Secretary, Ministry of the Interior, at Independence in 1955.
2. Paul Howell, born 13 February 1917, was District Commissioner in the area from 1946 to 1948 and also served in a variety of capacities during the British rule in the Sudan, ending as Chairman, Southern Development Investigation Team, in the rank and status of Deputy Governor, at Independence in 1955.
3. Kenneth David Druitt Henderson, born 11 September 1903, served as District Commissioner in the area from 1930 to 1936 and also served in various capacities, retiring as Governor, Dar Fur Province, in 1953.
4. In addition to the above sources, there is a quotation from a private letter to the author by Douglas Dodds-Parker, born 5 July 1909, who at the beginning of his long career in the Sudan, served in Kordofan in 1931–34 as Inspector, Hamar.
5. There is also a quotation from a private letter to the author by Michael Tibbs, born 21 November 1921, who served in the area first from 1949–50 and then as the last British District Commissioner from 1951 to his retirement in 1955.

II. THE QUESTIONNAIRES

Questions for the Wives

1. Introductory remarks about the project
2. Personal identification: name, section, with the family and family background
3. Before you met Deng Majok, how much had you heard about him and what was your view of him?
4. Under what circumstances did he first see you and how did your relationship develop into marriage?
5. Was the marriage simply arranged or did you have a courtship entailing a personal relationship?
6. Was any other man courting you when Deng Majok proposed to marry you and how did you compare the relationships?
7. How much bridewealth did Deng Majok pay for you?
8. Did your attitude toward marrying Deng Majok change after you came to his home as a wife?
9. What was your first impression of the family when you arrived as a bride?
10. Did Deng Majok tell you anything about his paternal and maternal background, his mother's marriage, his early childhood and his relations with his

father, Kwol Arob, his relations with his brother, Deng Abot, and how he rose to chieftainship?
11. Deng Majok was mostly criticized for what people saw as excessive marriage. Did he ever discuss his reasons with his wives, and how did you view the whole issue of marriage?
12. What observations would you make about the relationship of Deng Majok with his wives? Did you observe any discrimination among the wives? If so, how was it expressed and how did his wives react to it?
13. Considering the large number of wives and the fact that most of them had children in varying numbers, Deng Majok must have been reasonably fair in his sexual relations with his wives, and yet there must have been some disparities. How were these relations organized and to what extent were jealousies and rivalries manifest in them?
14. What was the extent of unfaithfulness among Deng Majok's wives and what were its consequences?
15. What observations would you make on the relations among the wives?
16. What methods did Deng Majok use to maintain family unity, harmony, and solidarity among his wives?
17. What observations do you have on the relations among the children?
18. What methods did Deng Majok use to maintain family unity, harmony, and solidarity among his children?
19. What observations would you make about the relationships between the children and their stepmothers as compared with their real mothers?
20. To what extent were jealousies among the cowives reflected in the relationships between the children and their stepmothers and between half-brothers and half-sisters?
21. Deng Majok's numerous marriages and the large size of his family were often used as grounds for accusing him of corruption and financial misconduct. To what extent was this justified and what do you believe to have been the sources of family wealth?
22. What were the activities of Deng Majok's daily life, both as a family man and a public figure, and which features of his daily life were most striking to you?
23. What observations would you make about Deng Majok's relations with, and view of, the southerners and the extent to which he identified with the South?
24. What observations would you make about Deng Majok's relations with, and view of, the northerners and the extent to which he identified with the North?
25. In the context of the above, and considering that some of his wives were somewhat Arabized, were there any differences in Deng Majok's treatment of his Arabized wives as compared to those of Dinka origin?
26. How would you evaluate Deng Majok as a person, a family man, and a chief?
27. How would you compare Kwol Arob with Deng Majok as persons, as family men, and as chiefs?
28. How did you receive the news of Deng Majok's death and what did it mean to you personally, to the family, and to the tribe?
29. What has his death come to mean to your life personally and to the family and the tribe in general?

Questions for the Sons and Daughters

1. Introductory remarks about the project
2. Personal identification: name, mother's name, and family background
3. What significant early encounters with your father do you recall?
4. What early accounts of your father did you hear from paternal or maternal relatives?
5. What image of your father did you grow up with?
6. At what stage of your growth, if at all, did you confront your father, either asserting your rights or criticizing your father, and on what issue?
7. What circumstances often brought you together with your father and under what circumstances did you observe him most as you grew up?
8. How much did you hear from your father or any other relative about your father's paternal and maternal background, his mother's marriage, his early childhood and his relations with his father Kwol Arob, his relations with his brother Deng Abot, and how he rose to chieftainship?
9. Would you know the number and names of your father's wives and children?
10. Your father was mostly criticized for what people saw as excessive marriage. What were his reasons for his numerous marriages and how did you view the whole issue of his marriages?
11. Did you ever discuss the issue of marriage with your father? If so, under what circumstances and what was said?
12. What observations would you make about the relationship of your father with his wives? Did you observe any discrimination among the wives? If so, how was it expressed?
13. Considering the large number of wives and the fact that most of them had children in varying numbers, Deng Majok must have been reasonably fair in his sexual relations with his wives and yet there must have been some disparities. How were these relations organized and to what extent were jealousies and rivalries manifest in them?
14. What was the extent of unfaithfulness among your father's wives and what were the consequences of unfaithfulness with sons and relatives?
15. What observations would you make on the relations among the wives?
16. What methods did your father use to maintain family unity, harmony, and solidarity among his wives? What about punishment?
17. What observations do you have on the relations among the children?
18. What methods did your father use to maintain family unity, harmony, and solidarity among his children?
19. What observations would you make about the relationships between the children and their stepmothers as compared with their real mothers?
20. To what extent were jealousies and rivalries among the cowives reflected in the relationships between the children and their stepmothers and between half-brothers and half-sisters?
21. Your father's numerous marriages and the large size of his family were often used as grounds for accusing him of corruption and financial misconduct. To what extent was this justified and what do you believe to have been the sources of family wealth?

APPENDIX ON SOURCES AND METHOD   289

22. What observations would you make about your father's relations with, and view of, the southerners and the extent to which he identified with the South?
23. What observations would you make about your father's relations with, and view of, the northerners and the extent to which he identified with the North?
24. How would you evaluate your father as a person, a family man, and a chief?
25. How would you compare your grandfather, Kwol Arob, with your father as a person, a family man, and a chief?
26. To what extent was what you know about the relationship between your grandfather and your father repeated between your father and his children?
27. How did you receive the news of your father's death and what did it mean to you personally, to the family, and to the tribe?
28. What has his death come to mean to your life personally and to the family and the tribe in general?

Questions for the Elders

1. Personal identification: name and background in terms of family, tribe, and occupation
2. When and under what circumstances did you first hear of Deng Majok?
3. As a result of the above, what image of Deng Majok did you have before meeting him?
4. When and under what circumstances did you first meet Deng Majok and what impression did he make on you?
5. Would you describe situations in which you observed Deng Majok or any other situations you have heard about which help to substantiate the kind of person or leader he was.
6. Did you know or hear anything about his early childhood and youth and how he rose to chieftainship?
7. Please give any details you know about the relations between Deng Majok, on the one hand, and his father Kwol Arob and brother Deng Abot, on the other hand, especially with respect to the issue of chieftainship.
8. What factors would you consider in evaluating Deng Majok as a person or as a chief?
9. The issue of marriage was what most people, Dinkas and non-Dinkas alike, criticized Deng Majok for as excessive. How did your people view that?
10. Tied to the question of excessive marriage was the suspicion that Deng Majok was corrupt and that he married and supported his family with public funds. What would you say about that?
11. It is often said that Deng Majok was very close to the Arabs and that the Arabs contributed toward his becoming chief. Could you comment and elaborate on this, giving details where possible of the relationships of Deng Majok with the Arabs?
12. It is said that it is because of Deng Majok that the Ngok are in the North. What do you know about this and about Deng Majok's attitude toward the South?
13. How would you rate Deng Majok as compared to the southern and northern chief and as a national character?
14. How did you receive the news of Deng Majok's death, and what has his death come to mean to the tribe, the Dinka, and Dinka-Arab relations?

APPENDIX ON SOURCES AND METHOD

Questions for the Sudanese Officials and British Colonial Officers

1. Would you tell us how you first met Deng Majok?
2. What impression did you have of Deng Majok before you met him, judging from what you had heard of him?
3. Did the impression you had prior to meeting him change after meeting him?
4. What did you think of Deng Majok as (*a*) a person, and (*b*) a leader?
5. Did Deng Majok's excessive number of marriages suggest to you any impropriety in his handling of public affairs?
6. Were any allegations of corruption brought to your attention? If so, what were the arguments against him?
7. Viewing Deng Majok as a leader in a wider perspective, how would you compare him with the leaders of the South and the North?
8. Did the government view Deng Majok and Babo Nimir of the Missiriya as equals?
9. How did Abyei become identified with the administration of Kordofan in the North, and what factors favored its continuation there rather than its affiliation into the African South?
10. Was Abyei area regarded as a separate entity or as an integral part of the Arab North?

Index

For the benefit of western readers, some people are indexed under the last name as family name, which may be the father's or grandfather's name in the Sudanese system.

Abbas, Mohammed, interviews, 138, 270–71
Abdalla (Monyyak; son), 217–18, 249–52, 259
Abdeen, Abdel Wahad Zein El, 4–5
Abdullahi, Khalifa, 41
Abiong (stepmother), 15, 53, 55–58, 60, 67, 70; and Deng Majok, 69–70
Abuk (grandmother), 55
Abul (full sister), 60
Abyei: described, 5, 7; economic status, 130–31, 229; political status, 262–68, 276
Abyor sub-tribe, 23, 101–06, 147, 206
Achai-Chol (daughter), 284; interviews, 56, 60–61, 66, 145–46, 179, 242, 254
Achai-Jur (daughter), 284; interviews, 66, 70, 75, 100, 102, 135–36, 176, 179, 205
Achier (Beshir), 5, 238
Achok Mijok (fourth wife), 153–56
Achueng sub-tribe, 89, 90
Achwil Bulabek, 101, 284; interviews, 53–54, 67–69, 72, 73–74, 85, 98–100, 100–01, 102, 103–05, 118–19, 144, 153–54, 201, 237, 255–56, 258–59
Adam (Kwol; son), 249–50, 252, 259, 262
Addis Ababa Accord (1972), 42, 261–62, 266
Age-sets, 24–26, 34
Agorot (half-sister), 15, 36, 57–58
Ahmed (Arob; son), 201–02, 213–17
Ahmed, Mohamed (the Mahdi), 41, 46–47
Ajuong Deng, 284; interviews, 12, 59–60, 64–65, 102–03, 105–06, 107, 116, 119, 168–69, 173, 206, 236, 258–60

Alcohol, 121, 166–67
Alfonse Arob (half-brother), 218
Ali (Monylam; son), 261, 283; interviews, 112, 117–18, 162, 164–65, 167–68, 169, 170–71, 178, 181–82, 187–88, 196–97, 204–05, 209, 211, 212–13, 215, 217–18, 231, 247
Allei Chol, 284; interviews, 112, 194–95, 209
Allor-Jok (half-brother), 284; interviews, 57, 61, 69, 76–77, 105, 118, 120, 149–50, 190–91, 194, 195, 201
Amel Yuel (wife), 78–79, 163, 166–67, 174, 187, 283; interviews, 78–79, 161, 162, 163, 173–75
Anglo-Egyptian Condominium, 41–42, 47–48, 86, 94–96, 102, 108–11, 223, 225, 227–29, 237. See also British
Anyanya, 238, 241–42, 250
Anyiel subtribe, 23, 57, 102–03
Anyiel Kwol (half-brother), 248
Arabs: and British government, 82, 85; and Deng Majok, 82–85, 121, 224–36, 238, 240–41; and Ngok Dinka, 46–47, 72, 82, 130, 131, 227–28, 231, 238–41, 265–68. See also Abbas; Babo; Hamadein; Hussein; Missiriya Arabs; Zein
Arob (full brother), 14, 60, 277
Arob (son). See Ahmed
Arob Biong (grandfather), 46–47, 55, 56, 190
Atem Barach, interviews, 191
Atem Moter, interviews, 76, 121, 209, 234, 237, 241, 257–58, 268, 269

291

Awor Kwol (full sister), 60, 247–48
Awut, 54
Ayan (full sister), 60
Azoza, 46

Babo Nimir, 77n, 78, 82–86, 191, 231–33, 240, 276, 277; interviews, 11, 36, 72, 82–86, 113, 191–92, 227–28, 233, 234, 241, 258, 269, 270
Bany. See Chieftainship
Beigo, 54
Bell, Gawain, 83, 137–38, 202
Biok, 25, 62
Biong (Charles; son), 284; interviews, 12, 133, 169–70, 174, 180–81, 183, 185–86, 199–200, 211, 217, 231–32, 249
Biong (great-grandfather), 46
Biong Mading (full brother), 31, 75–76, 101–02, 169
Bona Malual, 5
Bongo subtribe, 89–90, 153
British: and Arabs, 82, 85; and Deng Majok, 77, 137–38, 202–03, 272; and Kwol Arob, 48–49, 88, 93–96, 113. See also Anglo-Egyptian Condominium
Bulabek Biong (great-uncle), 53–54
Bulabek Malith, 9

Cattle: as bridewealth, 30, 192–96, 198–201; importance, 30–33; personality oxen, 30–31, 44n, 58, 73n
Chieftainship, 17–18, 24, 37–39, 53–54; 80, 99–101, 111, 138–40, 193, 262. See also Sacred Spears
Chier Rian, interviews, 190, 201, 230
Child-rearing, Dinka, 17, 59, 181, 278
Chol Adija, 284; interviews, 62, 63, 81, 85–86, 133, 227, 229, 236–37
Chol Piok, 284; interviews, 9–11, 36, 58, 60, 63–64, 67, 69–70, 74, 76, 77–78, 79, 80, 88–92, 93, 94–97, 100, 106–07, 113, 118, 120, 121, 133–34, 136–37, 140, 144, 145, 146–48, 156, 159, 163–64, 195, 227, 229–30, 234–35, 260–61, 268
Christianity, 40, 41–42, 123, 129
Cole, David, 23, 125, 261, 262–63
Collins, Robert, 41
Curses, 27–28, 55–56, 144–46, 215, 218

Dan Agok, 284; interviews, 55–56, 68, 69, 133n
Dance, 33, 37
Deng Abot (half-brother): and Arabs, 85; birth, 15; early relations with Deng Majok, 60–61; feelings of father for, 31, 66–67, 76; hospitality, 69; interviews, 11, 56–57, 59, 61, 67, 107–08, 144, 149–50, 155, 256, 284; marriages, 149–50; personality-

oxen, 58, 66; political career, 73, 76–77, 89–90, 100–01, 107, 112, 276; rivalry with Deng Majok, 15–17, 31, 33, 73–76, 82, 100–03, 107–08
Deng de Mathii, 68
Deng, Francis Mading (son), 3–4, 11–13, 250, 252
Deng, Justin (nephew), 264–65
Deng, Zachariah Bol (son), 3–5, 132, 250, 252
Deng Majok: age-set, 24–25, 62–63; assassination attempt, 136–37; childhood, 59–62; death, 5–6, 247–49, 253–54; education, 17; family history, 45–50, 54–58, 275; funeral, 6–7; illness, 3–5, 242–43, 247; initiation, 61–62; personality-oxen, 58, 60; physical appearance and ability, 14, 36, 172–73; religious practices, 12, 120–21; and women, 19–20, 127, 274
—family relationships: with brothers, 31, 60, 75–76, 101–02, 169, 218, 248; with Deng Abot, 60–61; with father (Kwol Arob), 15–16, 19, 36, 63, 65–67; with maternal relatives, 28, 61; with mother (Nyanaghar), 19, 36, 60, 146, 161; with paternal relations, 28, 76; with stepmother (Abiong), 60, 69–70
—marriages and children: adultery of wives, 210–20; betrothals and marriage agreements, 148–55; bridewealth, 192–96, 198–201; children's relationships, 177–81, 185–87; competition with other men, 19–20, 134, 143–44, 146–48, 149, 154, 156–57, 159; co-wives' relationships, 160–62, 168–69, 173–74, 176, 182–86, 208; daughters, 127–29, 169, 180–81, 184–85, 186, 205, 258 (*see also* Achai-Chol; Achai-Jur; Nyanjur; Nyanluak); desire for children, 26, 203–09, 258; discipline and punishment, 161, 164–68, 184–87, 219–20; education of family, 3, 122–29, 260; family organization, 160–61, 165, 168–69, 170–74, 176, 181–85; feelings for wives, 78–79, 152–53, 163–64, 187–89; jealousy, 161, 175, 178–83, 187–89, 211; marriage curse, 144–46; political consequences, 143, 158, 203; reasons for marriages, 162, 203–09, 258; sexual relations, 144, 173–75, 210–11; relations with sons, 169–70, 179–81, 186, 203–05, 209, 212–18, 254, 258–60 (*see also* Abdalla; Adam; Ahmed; Ali; Biong (Charles); Deng, Zachariah Bol; Deng, Francis Mading; Kwol Adol; Osman); wives' feelings for him, 152–53, 159, 162–63, 174–75, 188–89, 220, 254 (*see also* Amel; Kwei; Nyanawai Monyjok; Nyanbol Amor; Nyanbol Arob; Nyanthon)

—personality: Arab evaluations, 7–8, 65, 79–80, 121–22, 202, 232–33, 240, 256–58, 269–71; bravery, 61–62; British evaluations, 77, 81, 137–38, 202–3, 272; charisma, 167–68; fighter, 25, 62, 136; hospitality, 63–65, 69, 78–81, 85, 132–33, 197, 235–36; jealousy, 20, 213–15, 217–218; justice, 119–20, 256; leadership, 18–19, 68, 87, 114–15, 131–32, 137–40, 255–58, 268–71, 272–73, 276–81; negotiator, 63, 70–72, 135–36; pride, 62–64; self-evaluation, 16; stubbornness, 59–60, 134–35
—political career: and Arabs, 15, 82–86, 121, 224–36, 238, 240–41, 275–76; assumption of power, 96–97, 99–115, 116; and British government, 94–96, 102, 108–11, 223, 225, 227–29, 237; civil war, 238–43; conflicts with Deng Abot, 73–76, 82, 100–03, 159; conflicts with father, 67–68, 73–78, 81–82, 84–85, 88, 94–95, 114, 146–47, 155–59; corruption, 158, 191–99, 201–03, 214; court, 82, 116–18; Dinka views of his succession, 53–54, 99, 111–15; father's deputy, 76–77, 81–82; law and government, 136–40, 255–56; modernization, 122–32, 272–73; and North-South relations, 15, 223–42, 269, 275–77; sons' political activities, 7–8n, 214–16, 249–52, 260–67; successor, 5, 16–17, 249–50, 258–60; tribal wars, 90–97, 118–20; wealth, 76, 81, 192–201
Deng Makuei. See Deng Abot
Dinka: class structure, 17–19; description, 21–23; economics, 30–33; family relations, 18, 26, 28–29, 35–36, 181, 278; law, 33, 38–39; morals, 26–28, 33–35, 37–39; myths, 43–45; religion, 26–28, 45n; tribal structure, 23–24, 29n, 47, 77–78; wars between tribes, 70–72, 88–97; wars with Arabs, 72. See also Ngok Dinka; Rek Dinka; Twich Dinka

Education, 122–29

Garang, Joseph, 6
Giir Thiik, 47, 49–50
Gordon, Charles George (General), 41

Hamadein, Abdalla, interviews, 80, 121, 233, 257
Henderson, K. D. D., 45, 46, 49, 50, 71, 77, 81, 113
Howell, Paul, 38, 45, 46, 108–11, 138–40, 202–03
Hussein, Ibrahim El, interviews, 12, 61, 79–80, 97–98, 113–14, 121, 191, 202, 224–25, 228, 232–33, 256, 257

Islam, 12, 40, 41

Juac Dau, 284; interviews, 11, 119, 131, 209, 260
Julla, Ali, 48

Kir Bar (grandfather), 55
Kwei Deng (third wife), 149, 150, 152–53, 163–64, 283; interviews, 66, 122, 152–53, 161, 163, 165, 174, 175, 184, 189, 203
Kwol (son). See Adam
Kwol Adol (son), 262, 264
Kwol Arob (father): and Abiong, 15, 56–58, 67, 70; and Agorot, 26; and Arabs, 48, 83, 113–14; and British, 48–49, 88, 93–96, 113; and cattle, 74–76; conflicts with Deng Majok, 67–68, 73–74, 81, 84–95, 97–98, 114; death, 100–01; and Deng Abot, 66–67, 69, 76, 94; and Deng Majok's marriages, 146–50, 152, 154–57; feelings for Deng Majok, 15–16, 62, 65–67, 94–95, 273–74; marriages, 15, 53, 190–91; and Nyanaghar, 15–16, 19, 54, 55–59, 66; personality, 49–50, 112–13, 255–57; political career, 47–50, 71, 94–95, 99, 108–09, 112, 255–57; tribal wars, 88–89, 91–94
Kwoldit, 45–46

Lang Juk, interviews, 11, 86, 113, 143, 193, 228
Lesbianism, 211–12
Lienhardt, Godfrey, 26, 27, 29, 33–34, 38, 43
Lino Wor Abyei, 122–23, 125–27

Madut Ring, interviews, 11, 86, 237
Mahdi, 41, 46–47
Malith Mawien, interviews, 62, 80–81, 206, 209, 230, 233
Malual Adol, 55
Marriage, Dinka, 30, 55, 78, 160, 162, 166, 182, 201. See also Denk Majok—marriages
Matet Ayom, 284; interviews, 61, 70–71, 76, 82, 97, 106, 116, 118, 120, 133, 135, 136, 143–44, 148–49, 154–55, 157, 171–72, 192, 206–08, 213, 225, 226–27, 240, 269
Medicine, 129–30, 132
Michar Allor, 157–58
Mijak. See Osman
Missiriya Arabs, 46, 48, 72, 77, 82, 230, 238–40
Missiriya Rural Council, 230–32
Mithiang Aguek, 284; interviews, 65, 67, 76, 82, 101–02, 135, 137, 193, 201–02, 227, 232, 241–42, 256
Monylam. See Ali

Monyluak Row, 284; interviews, 9, 10, 62–63, 70, 73, 74–75, 86–87, 97, 101, 113, 134–35, 157–59, 174, 229, 257, 268
Monyyak. *See* Abdalla
Myths, 43–45

Nebel, Father, 34
Ngok Dinka: and Arabs, 46–47, 72, 82, 130, 131, 227–28, 231, 238–41, 265–68; fights with other Dinka, 70–72; myths, 44–45; political position, 42–43, 46–50; tribal organization, 23–24, 45, 263
Ngor Mijok, 284; interviews, 154, 163
Nimeri, Jaafar Mohamed, 4, 6, 42, 261, 262, 264
Nyanaghar (mother): and co-wives, 70; death, 36, 60, 61, 75; elopement, 19, 55–57; family, 54–55, 61; marriage, 15, 53, 55–59, 146; personality, 16, 58–59
Nyananyuat Nyok (wife), 157–58
Nyanawai Monyjok (wife), 156–57, 283; interviews, 78, 162, 163, 183
Nyanbol Amor (second wife), 78, 149, 150, 151–52, 283; interviews, 65–66, 78, 102, 114, 151–52, 161, 162–63, 169, 173, 176–78, 183, 195, 203, 208, 220, 229, 271
Nyanbol Arob (first wife), 148–49, 150–51, 283; interviews, 102, 145, 150–51, 161, 162, 165, 175, 248–49, 255
Nyanbol Deng (wife), 164
Nyanjur (daughter), 284; interviews, 58–59, 112, 144, 164, 166–68, 171, 172–73, 174, 177, 179–80, 184–87, 191, 195, 197–99, 211–12, 218–20, 229, 235–36, 242–43, 248, 257
Nyanluak (daughter), 284; interviews, 56, 66, 128–29, 132–33, 188–89, 252–53, 260
Nyanthon (wife), 159, 283; interviews, 135, 159, 163, 165–66, 175, 253–54
Nyok (uncle), 107

Oral history, 8–13, 44, 283–90

Osman (Mijak; son), 284; interviews, 188, 196, 210–11, 213, 241, 254
Ottoman Empire, 41

Pajok lineage, 23, 40, 43
Pagwot Deng, 284; interviews, 63, 90, 92–93, 93–94, 114, 116, 153, 230, 231, 238
Patal Biliw, 284; interviews, 54, 57–58, 64, 81, 116

Rek Dinka, 72
Rezeigat Arabs, 46
Robertson, Sir James, 49
Ruweng, 77

Sacred Spears, 24, 43–44, 84, 88, 99, 101, 105–12, 121, 252, 273. *See also* Chieftainship
Seligman, Charles and Brenda, 26
Singing, 21, 37
Slavery, 44, 46,48
Sudan: history, 40–42; South-North civil war, 5, 7–8n, 42, 238–42, 248–52, 265–66; South-North relations, 4, 40, 42–43, 50n, 223–43, 280–81

Tibbs, Michael, 138
Titherington, Major, 26–27, 39, 44
Tobacco, 64
Treatt, Court, 32, 48–49
Twich Dinka, 11, 70–71, 77–78, 86, 237

Witchcraft, 183–84. *See also* Curses
Women in Dinka society, 28–29, 127, 274. *See also* Deng Majok—marriages
Wor Abyei. *See* Lino Wor Abyei

Zein, Ibrahim Mohamed, interviews, 7–8, 121–22, 215–16, 228, 230–31, 239, 240–41, 258, 270
Zein, Tigani Mohamed, interviews, 65, 192, 208, 225–26, 239, 270

Afterword

Revisiting the Man Called Deng Majok

The Man Called Deng Majok: A Biography of Power, Polygyny and Change, was published in 1986, over twenty years ago. Although Deng Majok died in 1969, David Cole and Richard Huntington in *Between a Swamp and a Hard Place: Development Challenges in Remote Rural Africa*, writing on Abyei in 1985 observed that although Deng Majok has been dead for sixteen years, his presence is still very much felt in the area. Over twenty years later (2008), the name of Deng Majok continues to be invoked, not only within his family and tribe, but also at the regional and the national level. Much of what he is remembered for almost idealizes him as having been a uniquely remarkable man, whose wisdom, management skills, and creative innovation made him exceptional as the head of an unprecedently large family and leader of a tribe in a highly sensitive area on the volatile North-South border.

The book, however, substantiated a thesis of glory and tragedy. Deng Majok's accomplishments were the result of a relentless effort to prove himself the son most worthy of succeeding his father to the throne of Paramount Chieftaincy, rather than his half-brother, Deng Abot (Makuei), whom his father, Chief Kwol Arob, favored as his successor. Deng Abot was younger than Deng Majok, but his father's preference for him was based on the fact that his mother, Abiong, though married after Deng Majok's mother, Nyanaghar, had been betrothed, was the first to come home. Nyanaghar initially rejected Chief Kwol and had to be persuaded later, in part because of an illness diagnosed as a curse for having rejected the Chief. In traditional Dinka society Chiefs are believed to possess both temporal and spiritual powers to bless and curse, the curse being inherent in wronging the Chief. Deng Majok's endeavor from childhood and throughout his life was to prove himself first to his father and then to the Dinka public and the Arab and African neighbors to the North and the South that he was beyond any doubt the most qualified to be the leader. Another aspect of the tragedy, apart from the immense stress in the endeavor he imposed on himself, was the fact that he excelled far over his people so much so that none could fit his shoes as a successor, and raised his people to such heights that, without him, they fell to the lowest levels of destruction without protection.

In this Afterword, I update *The Man Called Deng Majok* first by presenting a selection of reviews of the book and then by giving an account of the developments in Ngok Dinka society and the country since the book was published.

Reviews of The Man Called Deng Majok

Without exception, *The Man Called Deng Majok* was very well received by all the reviewers, both internationally and in the Sudan. The reviews inside the Sudan were mostly in Arabic and focused on the role Deng Majok and his Arab counterpart, Babo Nimir, Paramount Chief of the Missiriya Arabs, played at the North-South border to foster peaceful co-existence and cooperation between their respective tribes. The reviews included here were published in scholarly journals in Europe and North America.

In his review article, "Biography by Interview," published in the *Journal of African History* (vol. 28, no. 3, 1987, pp. 454-455), Dr. Douglas Johnson, a renowned historian who has written extensively on the Sudan, wrote:

> This book must be classed among the best books written on any aspect of the Sudan. As a literary achievement in biography it compares well with A.J.A. Symons' classic *The Quest for Corvo*. Like Symons, Dr. Deng has constructed his biography around the impressions his subject left on other persons. Even though Deng Majok was the author's father, he remained something of an enigma, and it was only by approaching him from different angles, through the perspectives of those around him, that the enigma was penetrated and partially explained. To this extent, there are similarities in both Symons' and Dr. Deng's quests, but Dr. Deng is forced to rely on impressions and memories for another reason. Unlike Corvo, Deng Majok left behind no record of his own thoughts in his own words, being illiterate like so many African chiefs. Dr. Deng has therefore made a virtue of necessity by collecting virtually no written reports on his father, and gathering the reminiscences of former British

officials in the same manner as from other informants. It is this aspect of historical methodology which will be of the greatest interest to African historians.

The deliberate exclusion of contemporary documents may seem a perverse decision for a biographer, and it certainly runs contrary to the current trend of Sudanese Condominium historiography. But, quite apart from the inaccessibility of the district files Dr. Deng needed, there are defensible reasons for subordinating the written sources to the oral. As anyone who has read through any series of 'Personality Reports' produced by British officials in the Sudan will recognize, the contemporary record on rural leaders is sparse and impressionistic in the extreme. The reports record very few 'hard facts' about the leaders themselves but reveal a good deal about the mentality and opinions of British administrators. The administrators tend to become the heroes of their own reports. Compare, for instance the different accounts of the dispute surrounding Deng Majok's accession to leadership. In the contemporary report of the British District Commissioner (the only one that Dr. Deng cites), we find such comments as, 'I spent the rest of the day finding out the true state of affairs and making a plan of action...I then stepped in with a short summary of the main facts...As I had clearly guessed, this called their bluff...' Very little is recorded of who said what to whom. In the oral accounts of the participants in the dispute, including Deng Majok's main rival, however, the District Commissioner is clearly a minor figure who is seen either as being manipulated, or as being set right. The arguments put forward by the opposing parties are remembered, and are remembered to have been important. We thus learn far more about the politics of Ngok Dinka society from these thirty-year old memories than we do from the contemporary document.

Dr. Deng gives a full list of his informants and reprints his questionnaires. He has interviewed family members, Ngok Dinka elders, Arab and Dinka neighbours, Sudanese and British administrative officials. It is quite noticeable that all outsiders (whether British, Arab, or other Dinka) are far less critical of Deng Majok than are the members of his family. It is mostly from the latter that we learn of Deng Majok's uncertainty about his father's affection, his ambition which led him to supplant his father before his death, his almost aggressive generosity, the cattle he amassed as 'gifts', his extravagant marriages, the way he beat his wives, his jealousies and rages, the way in which he reconciled opposing parties, his eloquence, and the ambivalent feelings he aroused (and still seems to arouse) among his own children. The portrait his son paints is intimate, frank, and disarming. This would be a remarkable achievement in any biography. It stands out all the more starkly against the background of recent histories of the Sudan where character sketches of notables – British and Sudanese – too frequently descent into caricature.

Since biographies tend to be written about literate persons who leave behind some body of written work, it is a rare treat to have the biography of someone who was illiterate, yet who was a master of words. The problem of how to produce such a biography is one that confronts African historians more and more. Most of us would be reluctant to exclude the contemporary record as rigorously as does Dr. Deng, but then most of us, being total outsiders, would not have access to such intimate family memories as he has been able to elicit (I have collected scores of songs composed by the prophet Ngundeng, but I never thought to ask if he beat his wives or played with his children). This book can serve as a model of research methods and composition, and as such should be of immense value to Africanists who otherwise have little interest in the Sudan.

In another article, published in the *Northwestern African Studies* (vol. 9, no. 3, 1987, pp. 81-84), Dr. Douglas Johnson wrote:

Francis Deng has written a remarkable book. It is remarkable as a specific case study in Dinka ethnography, as an analysis of the complex interweaving of local, regional, and national politics in the Sudan, and as a contribution to biographical literature. For Sudan studies it is a welcome departure from the condominium and nationalist centered studies of administration, politics, and power. It is a biography constructed almost entirely from oral sources; it makes little reference to the personalities, policies, and activities of alien administrators; it focuses almost exclusively on events taking place within or immediately around a remote district situated along an internal frontier. These are the strengths on which the book rests, giving it solidity and authority, enabling the author to illustrate and explain many of the contemporary problems of the modern Sudan far more clearly and subtly than those chroniclers of administrative history who have relied heavily on official records to tell the Sudan's story. Rural Sudanese leaders, especially southerners such as Deng Majok, have been underrated or ignored by historians and political scientists and generalized into abstract principles of leadership by anthropologists. Francis Deng has rescued his father from this fate. In so doing he has given us a vivid example of what can be achieved through the careful reconstruction of such a man's life and what can be learned from studying the impressions he left on those around him.

The anthropological study of leadership and power in Nilotic societies has been exceedingly abstract. We have a far more extensive collection of Nilotic myths of the origin of leadership than we have descriptions of the careers of specific leaders. Among the Dinka and Nuer there is also far more in the ethnographies about those religious leaders excluded from colonial (and post-colonial) administrative posts than there is about those men who sought and were appointed to positions within the administrative hierarchy. The former are referred to as "traditional" leaders, while the latter are seen as created by an alien and intrusive structure. Here, in the biography of Deng Majok, we have a merging of traditional and innovative leadership, the manipulation of both indigenous and external sources of power. We can see not only in Deng Majok's life, but also in his son's writing, elements of Nilotic myth which can be found in the traditions surrounding other great heroes: those who were known to have lived in the recent past, such as the Nuer prophet Ngundeng, and those whose precise historicity might be doubted, such as the Dinka spearmaster Aiwel, or the first Shilluk *reth*, Nyikang. Yet, Deng Majok's opportunity to acquire apparently unprecedented authority and influence came about because of colonial occupation. He recognized and seized those opportunities with great determination and skill. The opportunities ended with independence, and after Deng Majok's death in 1969 none of his successors could fully inherit or build on his position. By contrast with the present, Deng Majok's time has mythopoeic qualities, acutely felt now by many who lived through it.

The Ngok Dinka, Deng Majok's people, dominate the main river system (misnamed the Bahr al-Arab) on the southern fringe of the Kordofan savannah. Controlling as they do vital dry-season pastures and watering places, they have had an ecological advantage over the many Muslim, Arabic-speaking Baggara pastoralists, who are their northern neighbors. There has been a symbiotic relationship between the Ngok and the Baggara, fraught with conflict, as in the nineteenth century, but scarcely unequal. With the encouragement of the Turco-Egyptian regime the Baggara raided the Ngok and other southern Sudanese for slaves. But the centralizing states of Turkiyya and the Mahdiyya also threatened many Baggara, and for them the Ngok became protectors and offered refuge. There was a delicate balance to be maintained, and Deng Majok's grandfather, Arob Biong, and father, Kwol Arob, both maintained it with great skill. In fact, to many Ngok today it is still Kwol Arop, not Deng Majok, who embodies the ideal of the great leader: divinely inspired, spiritually powerful, and materially generous.

It was Kwol Arob who first contacted the new Anglo-Egyptian government early in this century and set the pattern for the role Ngok Dinka leaders were to play in confronting and balancing the demands and interests of the Ngok, the Baggara, and the government. The Ngok, unlike the rest of the Dinka and their Nilotic cousins, were administratively included in Kordofan, an "Arab" province of the northern Sudan, rather than an "African" province of the south. To a certain extent administrative divisions made little difference to Ngok relations with the Baggara, bound together as they were by ecological as well as other ties. But as the policies of the Anglo-Egyptian government evolved, the Ngok leaders were faced with a dilemma over the best strategy to adopt to protect their interests against those of the Baggara. Would they be weakened in their dealings with the Baggara if they were to be represented by a "southern" government, that of Bahr el-Ghazal province, where most of the rest of the Dinka lived? Would they not have a stronger voice if they were able to put their case directly to the administrators of Kordofan province?

The choice of Kwol Arob, but more particularly of Deng Majok, seems to have been right for the time. The Ngok secured their rights by direct participation in the rural administration of Kordofan. A minority group, they were fully incorporated in the Native Administration of the area, and provincial authorities saw it in their interest to support the Ngok from time to time, as a way of keeping the Baggara in line. But their real strength came from the fact that they were on a frontier, remote from the nearest Kordofan district headquarters, and therefore largely independent from the interference of any rarely seen, itinerant British district commissioner. Francis Deng does not spell this out, but there is no doubt the Ngok would have been under firmer and more direct control from a Dinka-speaking district commissioner based in Bahr el-Ghazal had they chosen that option. What is more to the point, the opponents of Kwol Arob's family, and even dissatisfied members of that family, would have had more effective access to district and even provincial authorities in their disputes first with Kwol and then with Deng Majok. No other Nilotic leader in the more closely administered districts of the southern Sudan was able to marry so many wives and accumulate so many cattle as "gifts." Those who tried were dismissed for corruption. None of the district commissioners Dr. Deng interviewed seemed remotely aware at the time of Deng Majok's activities in this direction. One later classified these marriages as a "social norm," but even to Deng Majok's family they were abnormal (there were more than 200 wives by the time he died). Yet, clearly, this was one way he attained such extensive influence and by having such influence was so useful to administration.

One can understand better through reading this book Dr. Deng's obsessions as expressed in many of his other books on the Dinka, and why he has felt, far more strongly and far longer than many of his colleagues, that southern Sudanese leaders have a mediating role to play in the national politics of the Sudan. But I, for one, remain unconvinced by his repeated contention that Abyei is a microcosm of the Sudan, and that Deng Majok's path is nationally possible for other southern leaders. What Dr. Deng appears hesitant to recognize is that Deng Majok's strategy is possible only with a government that keeps faith with its subjects. This the Sudan government after independence clearly did not do; not in Abyei and not in the southern Sudan. By the end of his life, Deng Majok had been elected president of the combined Baggara and Dinka. [Council] and he saw himself as a "shield" between the Arabs and the Dinka. But by the end of his life the "shield" had been outflanked, and civil disturbances encroached on Abyei, not from the north but from the south, where civil war had begun. Deng Majok, who had been so accommodating and diplomatic toward his Arab neighbors, was finally upstaged by a young Dinka chief from a neighboring district who was not afraid to voice popular dissatisfaction and publicly denounce Arab deceit.

Deng Majok seems now more of an anomaly than an archetype. He bought some time for his own people, but none for those behind his "shield." The chaos which overtook his people after his death is in part attributable to the dissension he helped create between his own sons and brothers. He was a great man; his failure was a great failure. This is not quite the conclusion Dr. Deng would like us to reach, but it seems inescapable, especially in the context of what is now happening to the peoples along the border between Kordofan and Bahr el-Ghazal. But in many ways Deng Majok's failure is an inspiring one. The way in which he is remembered reminds me very much of the way in which the Nuer prophet Ngundeng is remembered (if a reviewer can be forgiven one of *his* obsessions). Both were men with a vision of peace, and both strove mightily to achieve it. But both, I feel sure, have become inspirational figures whose efforts are (or will be) emulated by later generations precisely because peace was still beyond their grasp at the time of their deaths. If it is any consolation to Dr. Deng, Deng Majok, like Ngundeng, may well be remembered as much for the man he tried to be as for the man he was.

John W. Burton, an anthropologist who has written extensively on the Nilotics, especially the Atwot, wrote for the *American Anthropologist*, New Series, Vol.90. (Mar., 1988), pp.202, 203: 1987:

In the short space allowed for review, it may be best to consider this monograph with reference to work it follows. The sub-field of "Nilotic Studies" (a phrase coined by the late E.E. Evans-Pritchard in 1950) has undergone a remarkable transformation since its colonial inauguration. Evans-Pritchard wrote of the Nuer in a style that intimated he knew these people better than they could then, or might ever, know themselves, and perhaps, with little consideration of the possibility that subject peoples might ever achieve a western manner of literacy. His now classic ethnographic contributions resulted from a scant tent and one half months residence in Nuer territory, spread over a period of some six years. In the main his monographs and articles on the Nuer are marked by an absence of extended dialogue: the Nuer he wrote of spoke in phrases, at least as far as the published corpus would indicate. Their very existence as a distinctive cultural and social tradition was founded upon an inherently ambiguous, if not artificial, distinction between so-called Nuer and so-called Dinka communities. Indeed, sometimes one wonders who or what was most responsible for creating the Nuer: colonial and administrative policy, or the man engaged for its deliberations, Evans-Pritchard. Throughout his published work, one finds reference to *true* Nuer customs and usage, extracted of course, from related phenomena in neighboring communities. There is the sense that *recent* history rather than longer temporal processes have given rise to an infusion of non-Nuer usages. And Evans-Pritchard also seemed to want to argue the Nuer case: the Nuer consider the Dinka to be thieves, *and rightly so*, he editorializes.

These few remarks are not intended to question the value of the many contributions by a pioneer anthropologist in African studies; they serve only to invite and endorse the welcome of F.M. Deng's masterpiece, *The Man Called Deng Majok*. This is Deng's eighth major monograph on the Dinka-speaking peoples of the Southern Sudan. As a biography of his late father it is naturally more focused on the Ngok than the many other Dinka groups, yet this may well be the most ambitious and successful of Deng's studies since his *Tradition and Modernization* (Yale University Press, 1971). It is ambitious since Deng proposes to tell the story of his father's life, and at the same time, make use of this truly unique narrative as a means to explore and document more fully the dynamic and changing features of the Dinka as a people, who comprise the largest named ethnic group in the modern Sudan. It is a stunning success since the author combines the skills of an historian, the discursive style of an anthropologist and the gift of local knowledge. The reader is led through translations of long interviews, observations and commentaries, offered by former wives, brothers, sons, political allies and foes. (In his lifetime, Deng Majok was married to [over] two hundred women, so the author never ran short of potential sources of information). The more notable feat is that the reader closes the book with the sense that she/he has been told a remarkable story through multiple yet highly individual voices. It is a mark of his insight into the values and traditions of his own people, his experiences as statesman, lawyer and anthropologist, and his admirable literary skill, that Deng achieves this synthesis in the absence of an over-bearing, distant or authoritarian style. These are Dinka telling us *their* story about a man they respected, feared, admired and followed. In many ways, the Ngok Dinka have lived their lives through and as a result of, Deng Majok's insights, reason, ambitions and guidance. The final result is an ethnographic contribution that is as authentic as one could imagine. At the same time, and by reference to an earlier moment in Nilotic studies, Deng's most recent book is among the most empirically based and historically accurate contributions in this field, and it is hard to imagine that such quality could be achieved by a foreign observer.

Deng's finely sculptured text is not limited, however, to the particular world of the Ngok Dinka, who have lived for many years in tense compromise with an Islamic and Arab-oriented people to the north, an experience that is somewhat unique in the broader environment of pastoral Nilotic communities. In his concluding chapter, Deng invites the reader into his view on the implication of this study for the Dinka, other Nilotic peoples, the Sudan, indeed, to a world evermore concerned with and aware of "cultural difference". He suggests (p. 281) that the biography of Deng Majok "... demonstrates the way in which group identities and the interests of minorities and dominant groups can be balanced to foster a working community or mutuality of interests. Indeed, long after his death, Deng Majok continues to shine before his people and the nation as an example of what has been done and is therefore possible: unity in diversity, mutual respect, and equitable cooperation toward common goals".

This book is clearly the most important work resulting from research in Nilotic communities in recent years.

It is also a novel and major contribution to African studies. Historians and anthropologists with more diverse interests might soon recognize this book as a milepost promising new directions and questions for future research. Deng's book marks the passing of one era, and proposes challenges to the next.

Peter Woodward, who has written extensively on the Sudan, wrote for *Africa* (vol. 59, no. 4, 1989, pp. 545-46):

The practice of 'native administration' by British officials in the Sudan has been the subject of a considerable amount of discussion in the past. There have been warm and sentimental reminiscences by ex-officials, more critical comments by anthropologists who saw the manufacture of local elitism, and even occasional rather brief reminiscences by a tribal chief himself.

Hitherto, however, there has never been an attempt at a full-scale biography of a native administrator and, moreover, by one of the sons of the project. Francis Deng is well qualified for the task, not only by family but as the author of a number of earlier works drawing together the themes of modernisation and tradition, and north and south Sudan. Since Deng Majok was so central to both themes it was perhaps natural that in time Francis Deng would finally get to the central figure of his considerable body of past writing: his father. The biography falls broadly into three parts, the rise of Deng Majok and the leadership of the Ngok Dinka, his role as a family man, and finally his involvement in national politics.

From an early age Deng Majok was clearly an ambitious and complex figure. As a young man he stood out among the ... sons of his father, his predecessor as chief, Kwol Arob. He developed the belief that his father was against him, and that Kwol Arob wished to be succeeded by Deng Majok's half-brother, Deng Abot. In consequence the young Deng Majok maneuvered to ensure that he absorbed Kwol Arob's intentions and instead was himself accepted as chief both by the Ngok Dinka and by the British administrators.

In doing so Deng Majok displayed one of the aspects of his flexibility for which he was to become most noted: his good relations with the Arab tribes to the north, especially the Missiriya branch of the Baggara, under its equally well-known leader Babo Nimir. Deng Majok used his friendship with Babo Nimir to advance his cause; once chief he built on it to insist that the Ngok Dinka territory be regarded as part of the northern Sudanese province of Kordofan and not incorporated into the southern province of Bahr al-Ghazal. He led his people in adapting to new influences from the north, including the development of Abyei as an important provincial centre where Arab and African interacted peacefully and productively. None the less, at a personal level Deng Majok and Babo Nimir were eventually to fall out, whilst the last years of Deng Majok's long rule (he died in 1969) saw the opening of civil war which, in spite of his efforts to maintain contacts with both sides, was to destroy much of his earlier bridge-building.

As a family man Deng Majok was extraordinary. He developed an unprecedented habit of marrying and ended life with at least two hundred wives, and many more children. These he organised through senior wives, and appears to have kept them under formidable discipline, which included the beating and chaining of those who erred. His motives appear to have been various. He was a very competitive and jealous man who clearly liked to outdo others in the chase for attractive women. At the same time, though it appeared a costly exercise to marry so many, Deng Majok so organised his cattle transactions that overall his wealth grew rather than diminished. Clearly he saw himself as the best child-giver for his fortunate wives, most of whom appear to have adored him, and he may have hoped to beget so many children that he could start his own clan or tribal section. His children appear to have had a rather mixed reaction to having been sired by such a towering figure and, like Deng Majok himself, they have experienced deep rivalries with their brothers and sisters.

The section in this biography on Deng Majok's involvement in national affairs is much shorter than that of his family life. As a Dinka chief in an overwhelmingly Arab province Deng Majok was a clearly exceptional figure, and he both enjoyed and exploited his position. Things came to a head when he refused to accept the paramountcy of Babo Nimir and instead got himself elected as chairman of the Missiriya Rural Council. But in spite of the consequent enmity he remained a respected figure among the Arabs, and it was the eventual experience of civil war rather than any wrong-footing on Deng Majok's part which led to bloodshed between Ngok Dinka and their Arab neighbours.

Deng Majok's most fearsome oath was 'My bull Marial has mounted his mother' and he frequently resorts to it in this book. He would certainly use it now if he could see the way Abyei has become the centre for relief for his Dinka people in the current much bloodier war between north and south, the gap between which Deng Majok worked so assiduously to bridge. There will need to be more people, north and south, with Deng Majok's vision if Sudan is ever to be peacefully reunited.

Sharon Hutchinson, an anthropologist who has written considerably on the Nilotics, particularly the Nuer, wrote for the *American Ethnologist* vol. 15, No 3 (August 1988) p. 589:

What makes this important contribution to African biography so unique is the profoundly personal relationship between the author and his subject of study. The creative tension Francis Mading Deng developed so eloquently in previous publications between an insider's and outsider's understandings of Dinka "values and institutions" is here especially acute. For in this work, he assesses the historical import of his father, Deng Majok, paramount chief of the Ngok Dinka, from 1942 to 1969, as an innovative tribal leader, family man and, ultimately, prominent national figure. Drawing upon an extensive series of interviews with family members, tribal elders, neighboring chiefs, and past and present government officials, Deng weaves together the individual voices and perspectives of his informants to create a vivid and remarkably balanced account of a highly controversial historical figure.

As an ambitious, innovative, and exceptionally capable leader, Deng Majok is openly admired by the author for having managed to unite not only a large tribe sensitively poised between the major racial and cultural divisions of Sudan, South and North, but also an extraordinary large family consisting of more than 200 wives and their children. Viewing himself as "the needle and thread" that sewed North and South into a national whole, Deng Majok boldly integrated into his Dinka heritage elements of Arab-Islamic culture as well as British codes of conduct. He was thus "most pivotal in consolidating the image of the [Ngok Dinka] area as a microcosm of the Sudan" where the cross-cultural dynamics characteristic of the nation as a whole are most evident and intense (p. xi). Deng Majok is also credited with having "brought the government to the people" through his suppression of warfare and his active promotion of a market economy, government education, health facilities and veterinary services at a time when these innovations were still considered morally offensive by most Dinka (p. 119). Yet, Deng Majok is also portrayed as a "curse" to his people "in that he outstripped everyone else in his tribal world, leaving no one to sustain the momentum he had generated" (p. 274). Following his sudden death in 1969, the Ngok Dinka area swiftly deteriorated from a "symbol of national integration" into a brutal battlefield, "What his death has shown" observed one Deng's more pessimistic informants, "is that we are dying. What it has shown is that we, the Ngok, now belong nowhere, neither to the South nor to the North" (p. 269). In contrast, the author, who consistently downplays the tragic implications of the recent renewal of full-scale civil war in the Ngok region, concludes on a more hopeful note: "as an example of what has been done and is therefore possible," Deng Majok's story offers insight into "what is required from the North and the South in order to build an equitably united Sudan" in the future (p.281).

The powerful microcosm/macrocosm metaphor running throughout this work makes it essential reading for historically oriented Africanists. Anthropologists concerned more generally with colonialism and the evolution of indigenous political systems as well as with issues of gender, marriage, and family organization will also find this book stimulating. Embedded in the story of how Deng Majok maneuvers his father and half brother out of the chieftainship, for example, is a concrete history of the transformation of tribal authority "from the role of spiritual and moral functionary to an autocratic government institution backed up by the coercive power of the state" (p. 140). Moreover, nowhere have I seen the sexual inequities and organizational complexities of polygyny depicted with greater candor and intimacy than in Deng's account of how his father effectively commanded the loyalty and sexuality of 200 wives. We learn how Deng Majok exploited his chiefly powers and wealth in order to build an exceptionally elaborate domestic hierarchy of junior and senior wives. Intolerant of the slightest manifestation of wifely insubordination or rivalry, Deng Majok ruled over his enormous family with a mixture of love and terror. In his household: "Procreation was considered the only legitimate ground for a wife to take the initiative in seeking her husband's company" (p. 174). Eventually, some of Deng Majok's younger wives, frustrated by the increasing inaccessibility of their aging husband, turned to his elder sons in the hopes of realizing their procreative potential. Confronted with this "invasion from within," Deng Majok responded by lashing out all the more viciously at anyone suspected of having betrayed him. Instead of safeguarding the outward harmony of his home through a prudent reassignment of some of his wives, Deng Majok clung tenaciously to his conjugal rights. In the end, he left his family weakened and divided.

Some readers may be disturbed by the author's reticence to condemn openly the shockingly brutal treatment Deng Majok inflicted on some of his wives. Others may find the author's dismissal of corruption charges against his father less than convincing. Yet, when making such evaluations, it is important, I think, to recall the opening passages of the book where it is explained that Deng Majok's dying request was that his sons eventually erect a monument on his grave. Clearly, this book is in part a fulfillment by the author of that sacred request.

Janet J. Ewald, wrote in *African Economic History*, No 16, (1987) pp.157-159:

This is a powerful and sometimes painful book, a work of personal engagement as well as scholarship. Francis Mading Deng, a scholar and former government official, reworks the themes of a previous book: the role of chiefs and the value of historical knowledge for his own people, the Dinka of the Sudan.' Here Deng writes not about many chiefs, but about the Ngok Dinka paramount chief Deng Majok, who was also his father. And as in his earlier work, the author demonstrates the importance of oral narratives. Nearly fifty oral informants – men and women, Dinka as well as Arabs and Britons, family members as well as political allies and rivals – told the author and his brothers their memories of Deng Majok.

Quoting extensively from these oral accounts, Francis Mading Deng relates the biography of his father. This skillfully woven narrative begins with Deng Majok's death and final return to his homeland in the rainy season of 1969. The author then reconstructs the cultural and historical settings of Deng Majok's life; his early years in the first decades of the twentieth century and 1942 succession, after much struggle, to leadership of the Ngok Dinka; his many marriages and organization of a huge family; and his mediation between the Ngok Dinka and outside world. A final section describes events in southern Kordofan after Majok Deng's death.

The author honors Majok Deng as a father, chief, and especially as a diplomat who linked the northern and southern Sudan. But Francis Mading Deng has not written a hagiography. Deng Majok acted not only out of love for his people, but from an impelling sense of deprivation of his father's affection and a need to win – and control – women. We read harrowing accounts of Deng Majok punishing his wives. And the son recognizes that his father chose to remain within an Arab-dominated province and to adopt certain Arab customs at least in part to enhance his own position.

The sections of the book entitled "Power" and "Family" add much to our understanding of the dynamics of African societies under colonial rule. The extremely detailed story of Deng Major's hard won victory over his half-brother for the paramountcy traces how a strong and ambiguous personality came to power by playing on both Dinka values and colonial power relations. The chief who gained his political office in the colonial context then used that office to gain the traditional bride wealth payment, manipulating his judicial role to accumulate cattle. Although contracted through cattle transfers, the many marriages did not win Deng Majok the praise of traditional Dinka. His subjects criticized as excessive his two hundred or more wives, attributing their chief's appetite for women to a curse.

If irony is the abridgement of hope, then the final two sections – "Diplomacy" and "Tragedy" – are deeply ironic. Their irony stems from the abridged hopes of both father and son. Deng Majok regarded himself as the "thread" who tied together the northern and southern Sudan. Yet he saw the Dinka heed the words of another, southern chief as the civil war intensified toward the end of his life. After Deng Majok's death the land of the Ngok Dinka became a cockpit of the north-south conflict, the site of bloody confrontations that killed some of the chief's family members. The very style of Deng Majok's leadership that had protected the Ngok also inhibited the rise of a successor equal in abilities to the paramount. Jealous of his power, Deng Majok had not trained an heir. And the foreign education that he provided for many of his sons made it impossible for them to lead their people as their father had.

Francis Mading Deng, one of these Western-educated sons, also has found his hopes abridged. In an earlier book, the author wrote hopefully of the "peaceful and harmonious, though cautious" relations that at the time characterized north-south relations[11]. The last part of *A Man Called Deng Majok* chronicles the sad disintegration of these relations. But Deng Majok's son continues to place his hopes in the use of historical knowledge, closing his book with the statement that "Deng Majok continues to shine ... as an example of what has been done and is therefore possible: unity in diversity, mutual respect, and equitable cooperation toward common goals." A reader can only respect Deng's hopes, sustained by scholarship in face of tribulation. But *A Man Called Deng Majok* also carries a more equivocal message. Deng Majok was an extraordinary man acting at a particular time. And even he proved unable to build a lasting bridge between north and south. Now that no other similar leader has appeared and the political context has changed, what kind of hope does the memory of Deng Majok nourish?

This book nonetheless affirms the value of historical knowledge. Readers may or may not find an immediately instrumental, policy-oriented use in the memory of Deng Majok. But Francis Mading Deng reveals the cultural, moral, and psychological imperatives of remembering the past during a time of tragedy. After Deng Majok's death, one of his widows lamented that "with the aching of our hearts, words have been shattered from our memories .... I can no longer find anything stored in my head. I am only wandering in the wilderness." Piecing together the shattered words, Francis Mading Deng seeks a way out of the wilderness.

---

1. (Africans of Two Worlds, p.XVI)

And E.E. Beauregard wrote in *Choice* (May 1987, p. 1452):

> The author, a scholar and statesman, splendidly discusses his people, the Dinka of the Nilotic Sudan. This work pinpoints his father, Deng Majok, paramount chief of the Ngok Dinka from 1942 to 1969. Meticulously based on extensive tape-recorded interviews with the Dinka, Arabs, and British colonial administrators, the biography emerges as scrupulously objective. Replacing his deposed, incompetent father, Deng Majok ruled remarkably in a strategically located area between the African South and the Arab North. The Dinka, the Arabs, and the Sudanese government (first British and later indigenous) regarded highly Deng Majok's efficiency, justice, and promotion of peace. Although following tribal traditions, Deng Majok initiated modernization—education, health care, market economy, and veterinary services. He became unique in Dinka history, marrying more than 200 and possibly as many as 400 wives; the author fascinatingly explained the reasons for this, and the resulting relationships and problems. Excellent binding, type (including quotes), and index. Four good maps and 24 fine illustrations. Recommended to anyone interested in cross-cultural and interracial dynamics and in a society in transition.

In his review of two books by the author, the novel *Seed of Redemption* and *The Man Called Deng Majok*, Ahmad Alawad Sikainga wrote in *The International Journal of African Historical Studies*, Vol.21, No.2. (1988), pp 339-340:

> *A Man Called Deng Majok* is a biography of Deng Majok, the author's father, who was the paramount chief of the Ngok Dinka of the Southern Sudan, from 1942 until his death in 1969. Although the book focuses on the life and times of this important tribal leader, also it reveals a great deal about the history and politics of the Ngok's region.
>
> The Ngok Dinka presents somewhat of an anomaly on the border-region between Southern and Northern Sudan. Their land, being suited for agriculture and animal husbandry, is a seasonal meeting place for the pastoral groups of both the North and the South. Although ethnically and culturally a Southern people, the Ngok Dinka have been administered in the Northern Sudanese province of Kurdufan *(sic)* since the days of the colonial administration. For these political and economic reasons, the Ngok area has become an arena of economic, social, and cultural interaction. This

unique position, however, has been fostered by the bridging role played by such traditional leaders as Deng Majok. Nonetheless, the struggle over pasture often turned into violent clashes between the pastoral groups of the Dinka and the Baqqara. Yet the charismatic Deng Majok was able to bring peace, harmony, and cooperation between these groups.

In this book, Deng's familiar themes were revisited. Since his earlier work, *Dynamics of Identification* (1973), the author has projected this area as a microcosm of the Sudan and as a model of national integration. Unfortunately, such a projection is shattered by present-day realities. Today, this area is a scene of an intense and debilitating violence which is aggravated by racial tension, the ongoing civil war, and the devious intervention of the central government.

Deng's work is based on material obtained primarily from oral sources such as family members, tribal leaders, government officials, and British colonial administrators. Despite some editing and factual errors, this is an excellent portrait of a remarkable man and a fascinating study in intercommunal relations.

In its evaluation of *The Man Called Deng Majok: A Biography of Power, Polygyny and Change* for the 1987 prestigious Herskovits Award by the African Studies Association for the best book published the previous year, the Award Committee noted:

> This book is the latest in a series of major contributions to African anthropology made by this exceptionally gifted Sudanese scholar. It is a fine work in itself. The life of the subject of the book, Deng Majok, illustrates the interplay of traditional politics and pressures for modernization with which any effective African leader must contend. Deng Majok contended with aplomb."

Updating the Legacy of Deng Majok

The life of Deng Majok reflects four interrelated levels: familial, tribal, regional and national. At each of these levels, since the book was published in 1986, the legacy of Deng Majok continues to reverberate. It also continues to be a contradiction between glory and tragedy, a blessing and a curse, the main thesis of the biography.

At the level of the family, Deng Majok's dream of founding a tribe or a nation that would carry his individual name appears to be bearing fruit. The number of his progeny is certainly unsurpassed by anyone within Dinka society, in the Sudan, in Africa, and, arguably, in the world. Even with the conservative estimate of four children per wife on average, his over two hundred wives must have born him nearly a thousand sons and daughters. This is compounded by the levirate custom, whereby children continue to be born to the name of the dead husband by his widows living with close relatives as genitors, including the dead man's senior sons, inheriting their childbearing stepmothers. The senior mothers, having adult children, and having presumably reached the age of menopause, are not inheritable. Since Deng Majok left many young widows of child-bearing age, this has increased the size of the children born to his name well beyond any reliable estimates.

There is more to the legacy of Deng Majok at the family level. Beyond the value of numbers, he was keen on educating his children, even though he himself was illiterate. Although daughters were not given equal opportunity for education as sons, and not everyone reached the highest level up the competitive ladder of the educational hierarchy, the numbers and levels of education among the sons of Deng Majok remain unmatched for any one family. All the major professional categories: doctors, lawyers, engineers, and military officers, are represented in impressive numbers. Deng Majok's sons occupy more leadership positions than any other single family in the country, if only because of their numbers. If it were not because of the devastating impact of the North-South war on the South and the Ngok Dinka in particular, the position of Deng Majok's family would have been even more pronounced.

Perhaps for the same reason of the impact of nearly half a century of intermittent warfare, the downside of the Deng Majok's family experience is equally striking. The diminishing value of numbers relative to the means for maintaining and educating the children after his death, not to mention the destruction of the war, has had a profoundly negative impact on the family. The family has been shattered with most of its members dispersed within the country as internally displaced persons, and throughout the world as refugees. Many are now found in a number of African countries and as far away as Australia, Canada, the United Kingdom and the United States.

Although the sentiment of family unity and solidarity persists, with phone calls crisscrossing the world at odd hours due to the time difference of which the callers are often unaware, the stretch has been most strenuous and the bonds have unavoidably weakened, a painful contrast to the fundamental norms of family unity and solidarity that Deng Majok had zealously fostered.

At the tribal level, within the Ngok Dinka, the sons and daughters of Deng Majok continue to exercise the sense of leadership obligation associated with the Pajok lineage and carried to greater heights by the accomplishments of their father in the modern context. This has meant taking a frontline of protection for their people against external aggression and oppression from the Arab-Islamic center. For the most part, this is still expected and appreciated by the overwhelming majority of the Ngok Dinka, to whom tradition and heredity are still the sources of leadership legitimacy. Whether it is a quest for justice or defense against the oppressive forms of the state, it is to the sons of Deng Majok and the Pajok lineage that the Ngok Dinka still look. And their number remains a major factor in their capacity to face the challenges of leadership. As David Cole and Richard Huntington observed of the sons of Deng Majok, "all of them, for whatever comfort and prestige their education has granted, remain passionately committed to the welfare of the Ngok people although they often disagree fundamentally among themselves about the best political course for the tribe. Additionally, they are competitive among themselves since there are always more qualified sons of Deng Majok than opportunities for scholarships, offices, or notoriety."

There is, however, also a downside to the role of the family within the tribe. The authoritarian rule of Deng Majok, reinforced by the Central Government's dependence on him to uphold and enforce law and order within the tribe, runs counter to both the traditional image of the Chief as a revered spiritual leader and the modern trend toward democratization and egalitarianism, especially among the radically minded members of the educated class. This is particularly the case with opposition groups from the lineages that have traditionally competed for leadership or from other reform minded members of the educated class, including individuals from Deng Majok's family. Competitiveness and a deep sense of egalitarianism are Nilotic attributes which are both positive and divisive. And these are reflected both within the Deng family and against them.

As a result of these conflicting trends, the Ngok Dinka, once perhaps among the most cohesive and integrated society in the country, are being torn apart and struggling against strong forms of destruction to maintain a degree of integrity and viability as a people.

These destructive forces find reinforcement at the intertribal level, where competition with neighbors, primarily from the Arab North, but also from some Dinka neighbors to the South, are exerting pressures on the fragile position of the Ngok Dinka on the North-South borders. While Abyei has traditionally been a constructive North-South bridge, under the leadership of the Pajok lineage and especially that of Deng Majok, it is now primarily a victim of the North-South confrontation and the manipulations of political entrepreneurs in the politics of identity.

The situation is complicated by contradictory forces within and between the North and the South. In the North, while the Missiriya, having also suffered from the war, would like to restore their erstwhile peaceful coexistence and cooperation with the Ngok Dinka, individuals connected to the center continue to promote animosity largely for personal gains. In the South, while the Government of Southern Sudan (GOSS), the Sudan People's Liberation Movement (SPLM) and the people of the South in general are steadfast in their support for the Ngok Dinka in their vulnerable position at the North-South borders, there are individuals who see Abyei as an obstacle to the independence of the South from the North and are prepared to sacrifice the area. In some cases, this is a genuinely held opinion, but one that is often influenced by the divisive machinations of Northern authorities through the use of power and material incentives to win individuals and divide the leadership and people of the South.

These tensions are most pronounced with respect to the implementation of the Abyei Protocol which is part of the Comprehensive Peace Agreement (CPA), concluded between the GOS and the Sudan People's Liberation Movement and Army (SPLM/A) on January 9, 2005. The CPA gives the people of the South the right to decide in 2011 whether to remain in a united Sudan or become an independent state. During the six-year interim period, the South is to be governed by a virtually independent Government of Southern Sudan (GOSS), without interference from the Center. The GOSS is to have its own army, the Sudan People's Liberation Army (SPLA), while Joint Integrated Units (JIUs) composed of the Sudan Armed Forces (SAE) and the SPLA in equal numbers form the nucleus of a national army, should the South decide in favor of unity.

During the interim period, the South will have its own branch of the Bank of Sudan, which will apply a normal secular banking system, while the Northern branch will continue to apply the *Shari'a* banking system. The oil produced in the South is shared equally between the North and the South, with the oil producing states receiving a percentage. The SPLM is also to participate in the Government of National Unity (GONU) in which it occupies the position of the second major partner with the National Congress Party (NCP), formerly known as the National Islamic Front (NIF), in proportion to the Southern population of about one third of the country's population. The President of the South occupies the position of First Vice President in a collegial Presidency in which decisions are to be taken by consensus.

The three areas of Southern Kordofan (mostly the Nuba Mountains), Southern Blue Nile (mostly the Ingassana Hills), and Abyei were the subjects of different protocols. The first two areas are to be autonomous and will exercise "popular consultation" to ascertain popular opinion on their administrative status, a form of internal self-determination. It should be borne in mind that these areas were fully involved in the war on the side of the SPLM/A and continue to be an integral part of both the SPLM and the SPLA. This continues to raise questions on what the independence of the South would mean for them.

The case of Abyei is recognized as different from that of the two areas. It will be recalled that Abyei became fully involved in the first North-South war (1955-1972) on the part of the South. That war began the devastation of Abyei area. It will also be recalled that the 1972 Addis Ababa Agreement that ended the first war provided that the people of Abyei would decide by a referendum whether to remain in the North or join the South. That provision was never implemented. All efforts to implement the provision or to find workable alternatives failed. In desperation, the people of Abyei started a local rebellion in 1982 in the name of Anya-nya Two, a follow up on the first Southern liberation army, Anya-nya (One), which eventually grew into the SPLM/A. In the full-scale war that erupted in 1983, young men and women from Abyei joined massively and suffered heavy casualties in the early phase of the infighting between opposing forces of the movement over conflicting visions for the struggle. As a result, Abyei became a primary target for the North, using the Missiriya Arab militia, the *Marahleen*, the forerunner of Darfur's *Janjaweet*. Abyei became devastated and depopulated. About 85% of the population fled to the North, the South and abroad. Its infrastructure was totally destroyed and the area reverted to the wilderness, as the Arabs, who displaced the Dinka, did not occupy the land.

In the negotiations that led to the CPA, Abyei proved to be one of the thorniest issues, in the end resolved, and by the determined intervention of the United States in the person of Senator John Danforth, the Special Envoy of President George W. Bush to the peace talks. The outcome was the Abyei Protocol, which gives the people of Abyei the right to decide by a referendum to be carried out simultaneously with the Southern referendum in 2011 whether to join the South or remain in the special administrative status under the Presidency which the Protocol stipulates for the interim period. During the interim period, the oil produced in Abyei, estimated at 70% of all the oil produced in the North, would be divided in six portions: 50% to the Central Government, 42% to the Government of Southern Sudan, 2% to the Ngok Dinka, 2% to the Missiriya Arabs, 2% to Bahr el-Ghazal (now Warrap state) and 2% to Western (now Southern) Kordofan state.

The Abyei Boundary Commission (ABC) was established to determine where Abyei people lived before their area was severed from the Southern province of Bahr el-Ghazal and annexed to the administration of Kordofan in the North in 1905. Membership of the Commission comprised fifteen members, five from the ruling National Congress Party, five from the Sudan People's Liberation Movement and five international experts. The international experts were from the United States (represented by Donald Petterson, formerly Ambassador to the Sudan, who also acted as the Commission's Chairman), Ethiopia, Kenya, South Africa and United Kingdom. According to the agreed rules of procedure, if the parties could not agree, the determination of the international experts would be "final and binding."

Since there were no clear demarcations of the borders and no maps identifying the respective areas, the Commission carried out an exhaustive, scientific process that utilized historical, geopolitical, anthropological, legal and administrative sources as well as early travelers' accounts to determine where the Ngok Dinka lived in 1905. Their finding was that they lived in the areas they continued to occupy until they were displaced by the North-South war in 1965. They, however, identified areas of permanent settlement for both the Dinka and the Missiriya Arabs and "no man's island" or a seasonally "shared area" which they divided equally between the Dinka and the Missiriya.

When the report was presented to the Presidency, President Omar Hassan Al-Bashir said to his new First Vice President, Dr. John Garang de Mabior, leader of the SPLM/A, that the ABC report had given cause for a rebellion by the Missiriya. Garang's response, as he reported to the author, was "that will be our joint problem to confront." Garang went beyond that to suggest that he would be prepared to meet with the leaders of the Missiriya to assure them that their rights to seasonal grazing and sources of water would be guaranteed. For various reasons, the meeting between him and the Missiriya leaders did not take place. Tragically, Garang died in a helicopter crash, less than two weeks later.

Since then, President al-Bashir and the NCP have rejected the report of the ABC on the grounds that it had exceeded its mandate. According to the President's argument, since they did not find any maps identifying the borders in 1905, they should have gone back and reported that they could not fulfill their mandate, which would have taken the issue back to the parties for further consideration. Obviously, if such maps had existed, there would have been no need for the Commission. What the Commission did, and which they were commissioned to do, was to use alternative methods for determining where the Dinka Ngok lived when they were transferred from Bahr el-Ghazal to Kordofan in 1905. Those were the boundaries they determined and then divided equally, the area they shared with the Missiriya.

Whatever concerns the Central Government, or to be more precise the NCP, has for the interest of the Missiriya, it is now widely recognized that the issue is oil, Abyei being the area with the most oil wealth in the North. Various proposals have been made to resolve this impasse, but with no progress. In the end, it will be necessary to find a formula that reasonably serves the mutual interests of all concerned. For, without a consensus, it will be difficult to achieve peace and stability at this sensitive North-South border area, which I initially called the potential Kashmir of the Sudan, a characterization that has since been repeated by others. As Dr. Douglas Johnson, one of the members of the ABC, observed, "If the NCP continues to obstruct the implementation of the Protocol, what can be said about its commitment to the rest of the CPA? If the military build up in the Abyei area, which is contrary to the security protocol, goes unchecked, will this encourage other violations of the cease-fire? If the displaced Ngok Dinka are denied the right of their return to their homes as Khartoum attempts to change the demographic pattern of Abyei, what hope is there for the larger number of displaced Darfuris to return home in the much greater demographic shift currently taking place in Darfur? If the international actors who were directly involved in drafting the Abyei Protocol and supporting the work of the ABC remain inactive, how reliable will they be in backing up their guarantees for the CPA as a whole, or any Darfur peace agreement? And finally, given the parallels between the conflicts in Abyei and Darfur, can the Darfur groups be confident that Khartoum will faithfully adhere to any future agreement it signs?" (Dr. Douglas H. Johnson, "Why Abyei matters: The Breakup Point of Sudan's Comprehensive Peace Agreement?" *African Affairs*, 107/426, 1-19, December 2007).

To go back to the thrust of this Afterword, the question is what the legacy of Deng Majok means in this tragic situation for his people. On a positive note, the names of Deng Majok and his Arab counterpart, Babo Nimir, are often mentioned as prototypes of what should be, indeed what was: peaceful coexistence and cooperation between neighboring tribes. That an intertribal Council, comprising predominantly Arab and Muslim chiefs, would elect a man who was neither an Arab nor a Muslim as their President, which is what the Dar Missiriya Rural Council did by electing Deng Majok as their President, is an exemplary model the Sudan and indeed others can learn a great deal from.

The trend has, however, been in the opposite direction: racial, ethnic, and religious divide in which the Government has played a tragically partisan role by favoring the Arabs over the Dinka. As Dr. Douglas Johnson wrote, "If, as the legendary Ngok Dinka Chief, Deng Majok, once claimed, the threat that stitches the North and the South of the Sudan together runs through Abyei, then this narrow patch of land now threatens to unravel the Comprehensive Peace Agreement (CPA) and, with it, the rest of the country' (id. p. 18). The questions that linger on are: Considering that the name of Deng Majok is often invoked along with that of Babo Nimir, as champions of peace and unity, could he have made a difference in shaping the developments in favor of the security and development of his people, if he were alive? And while the circumstances of decision, as indeed that of his father, to remain in the North to safeguard Dinka borders and cross-border interests, were understandable in the context of the time, has it now turned into an unmitigated tragedy for his people, or are there still redeeming elements in the position they determined? Does the legacy of Deng Majok's leadership at the North-South border still provide a basis for a constructive management of diversity and equitable nation-building or does it represent a unique idiosyncratic experience that is bound to go into oblivion with the passage of time?

Perhaps the legacy of Deng Majok should be seen in that broader context of the national identity crisis which the Sudan has been experiencing since independence. There are two dimensions to this identity crisis. One is that a people who are essentially Arabized and Islamized Africans, see themselves as Arabs, even though the African element is prominently visible in their skin color and their hybrid culture. The second element in this identity crisis is that this distorted self-perception of what is in fact a minority group is projected as the national identity framework, which inevitably discriminates on the grounds of race, ethnicity, religion, culture and gender.

In reaction to these sets of distortions, the liberation movement spearheaded by the South has gone through two major contrasting phases. The first phase was a war of independence for the South, which ended in a compromise in the form of autonomy, as neither the then Organization of African Unity, nor the international community favored secession. The second phase of the war postulated a vision of a New United Sudan, in which there would be no discrimination on the basis of race, ethnicity, religion, culture or gender. This began to capture the imagination of the marginalized Black African groups in the North, beginning with the Nuba, extending to the Ingassana or Funj, then to the Beja, and lately to Darfur. Even the Nubians, at the Egyptian border in the extreme North, while they have not taken up arms, have also joined the demand for the New Sudan. From the perspective of the South, if all these forces were to join hands and succeed in creating the New Sudan, initially a vision from the South, why would the Southerners want to secede, when they would have achieved their national goal? On the other hand, perhaps because the vision of the New Sudan was primarily that of John Garang, it might have ended with his death and the CPA, which was initially conceived as a tool for democratic transformation, is paradoxically being used by the NCP as a tool for containment. Under those circumstances, there is no way unity can be made attractive to the South, as the CPA envisages. On the other hand, even if the South were to opt for independence in 2011, the marginalized Black African groups and other liberal elements in the North are bound to continue the struggle for the New Sudan, most likely with the support of the independent South.

Deng Majok is reported to have asked William Deng Nhial, one of the leaders of the first Southern Liberation Movement, whether the goal of the struggle was separation or unity. Deng Nhial responded by saying that he favored unity. Deng Majok in turn responded by praising Deng Nhial: "You have spoken like the son of a Chief. What the Arabs have done to us, the Black Africans, cannot be remedied by separation, it can only be remedied through unity." What Deng Majok presumably meant was that the Sudan as a whole belonged to all and should not be left to the minority that had marginalized the majority. Some may interpret this as alluding to vengeance against the Arabs in a Sudan liberated from Arab domination and in turn dominated by the Black Africans. But Deng Majok was deeply committed to justice and equality for all. His formula could not therefore have meant turning the tables and victimizing the Arabs in reprisal. His vision, based on what he actually did, was a united Sudan in which all would share a sense of belonging and enjoy all the rights of citizenship on equal footing.

Deng Majok was not educated in the modern sense, but his vision and leadership qualities are widely recognized in the Sudan as excelling and exemplary by any standards. Since he is no longer there to apply those qualities, we can only hope that he will continue to be an inspiration and a guide to those who have the opportunity to influence developments in nation-building. That is why I am most grateful to the Red Sea/Africa World Press for putting *The Man Called Deng Majok* once again in print.

Francis Mading Deng
New York, N.Y.
March, 2008

www.ingramcontent.com/pod-product-compliance
Lightning Source LLC
Chambersburg PA
CBHW030251010526
44107CB00053B/1659